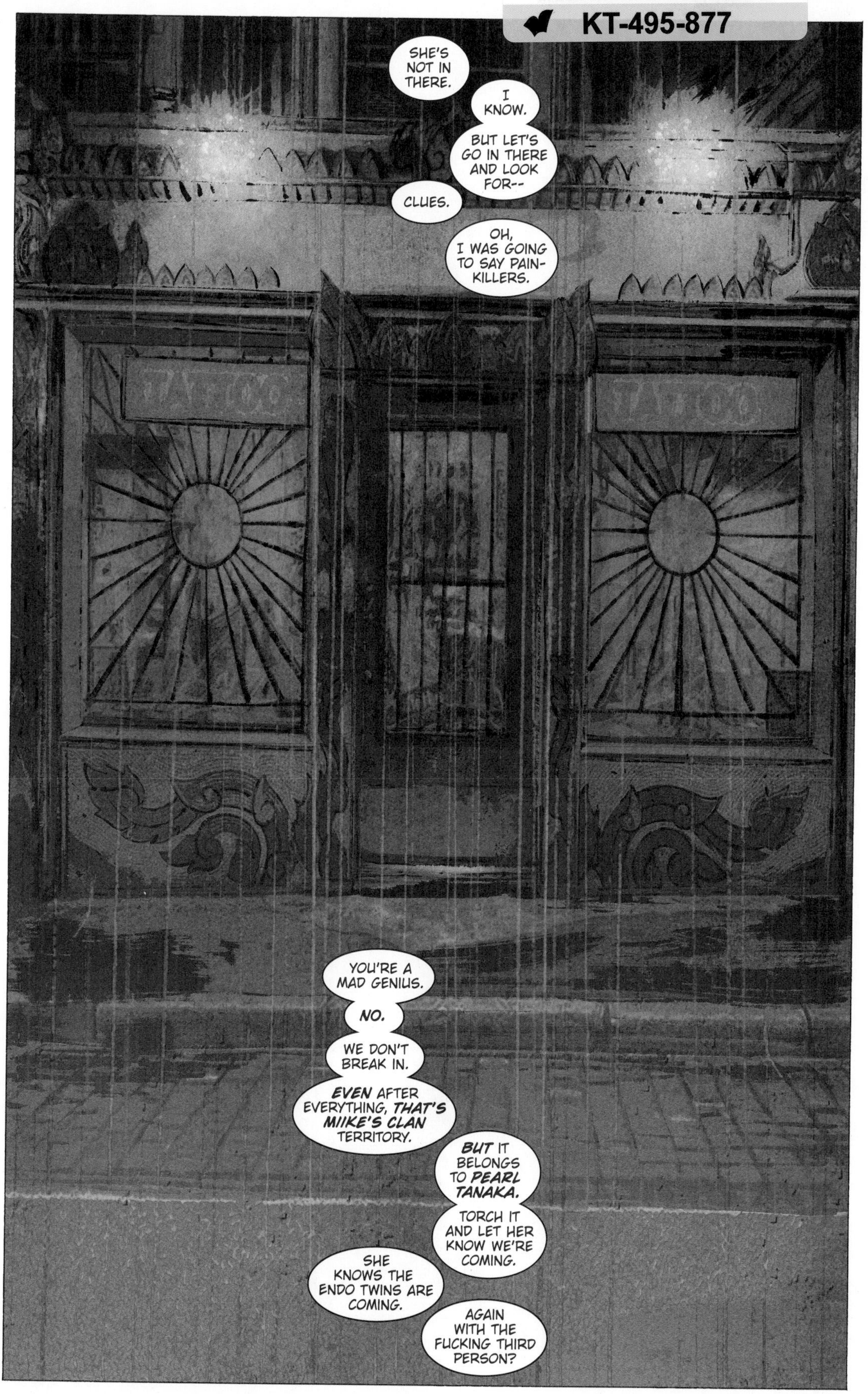
SHE'S NOT IN THERE.
I KNOW.
BUT LET'S GO IN THERE AND LOOK FOR--
CLUES.
OH, I WAS GOING TO SAY PAIN-KILLERS.
YOU'RE A MAD GENIUS.
NO.
WE DON'T BREAK IN.
EVEN AFTER EVERYTHING, THAT'S MIIKE'S CLAN TERRITORY.
BUT IT BELONGS TO PEARL TANAKA.
TORCH IT AND LET HER KNOW WE'RE COMING.
SHE KNOWS THE ENDO TWINS ARE COMING.
AGAIN WITH THE FUCKING THIRD PERSON?

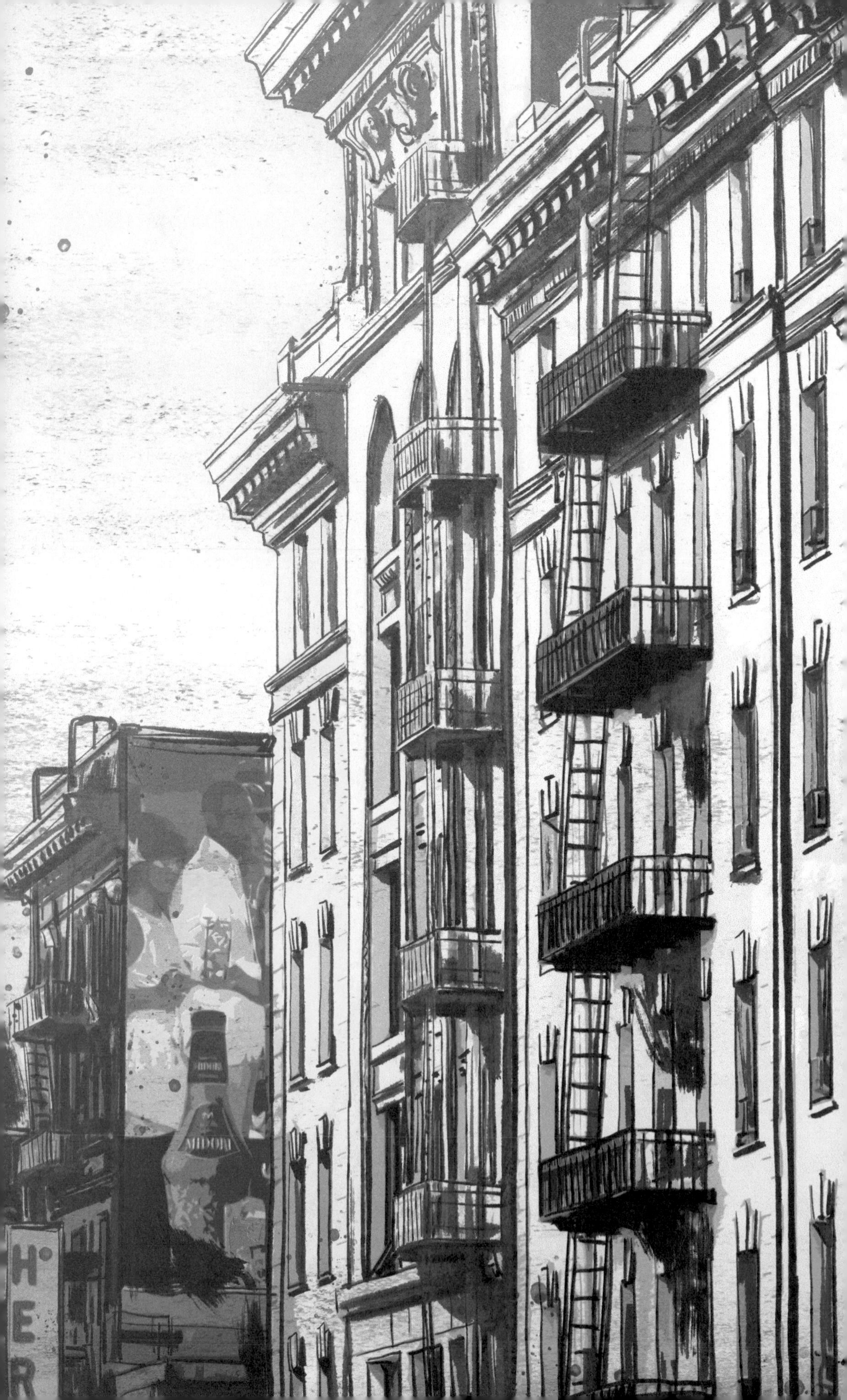
MIDORI
HER

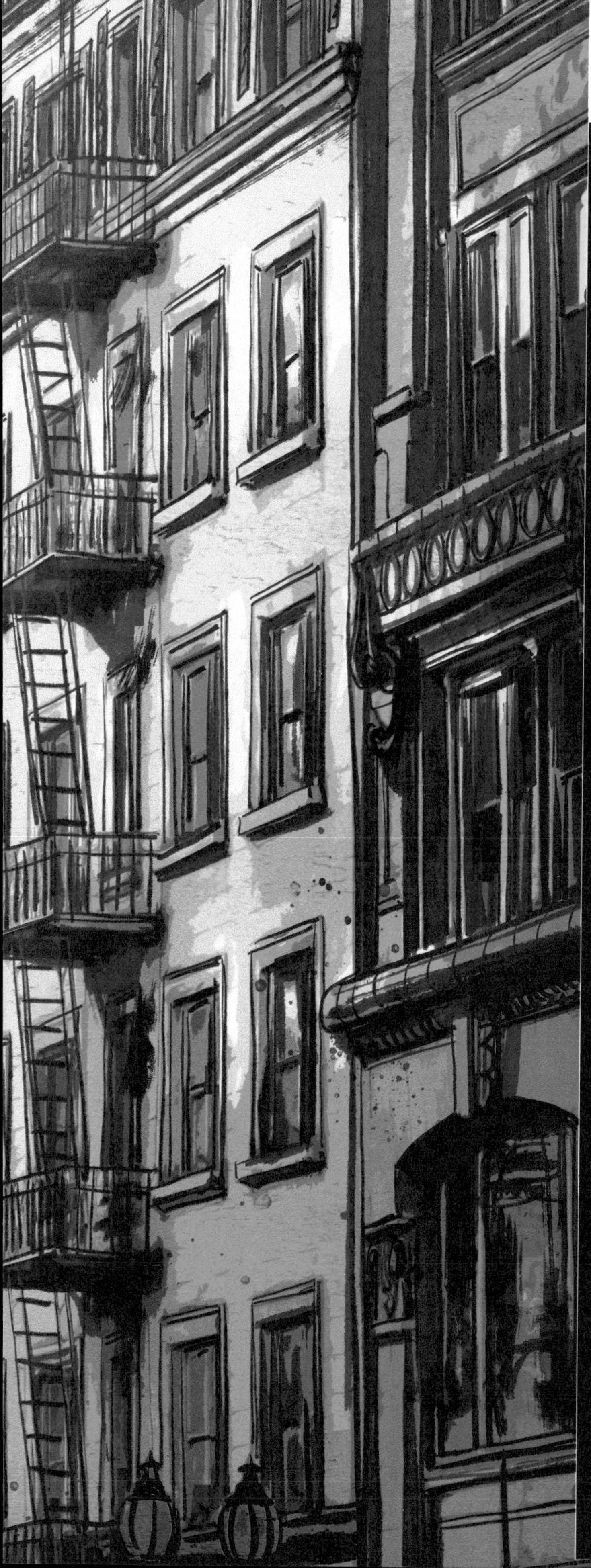

PEARL

PEARL IS A VERY TALENTED TATTOO ARTIST FOR ELITE MEMBERS OF THE YAKUZA IN SAN FRANCISCO, INCLUDING HER IMMEDIATE BOSS, MR. MIIKE. PEARL'S FATHER HAD PROTECTED HER FOR MANY YEARS BUT IS NO LONGER AROUND TO DO SO.

PEARL'S MOTHER, HER TEACHER, DIED RECENTLY. THE TRAUMA LED PEARL TO TATTOO HER SPECIAL ALBINO SKIN WITH AN EMPTY GUN. YOU CAN ONLY SEE THE ELABORATE, FULL-BODY TATTOO WHEN SHE IS FLUSHED WITH EXCITEMENT, EMOTION OR RAGE.

MR. MIIKE NOW EXPECTS PEARL TO BE A HIRED GUN FOR THE CLAN. THIS PUTS HER IN DIRECT CONFLICT WITH THE PORNOGRAPHY, EMPIRE, BUILDING ENDO TWINS AND REALLY SCREWS UP HER CHANCES WITH A FELLOW TATTOO ARTIST, RICK ARAKI, BECAUSE MIIKE WANTS HIM DEAD.

PEARL AND RICK DEFY THE CLAN TRADITIONS AND CONFRONT MR. MIIKE. THAT'S WHEN THE ENDO TWINS DECIDE TO DO THE SAME THING.

MMMM... MR. ARAKI, ARE YOU CREEPING ON ME WHILE I SLEEP?
CONFESSION!
UH-OH.

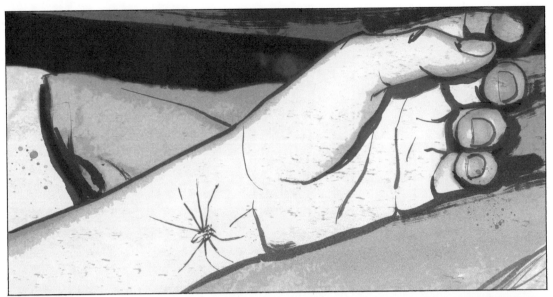

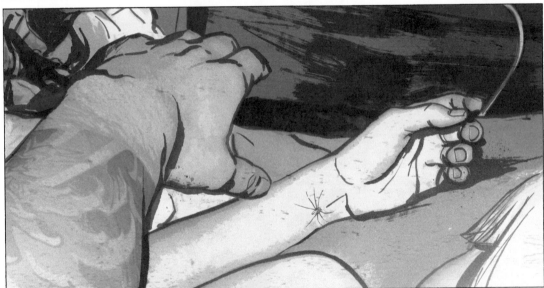

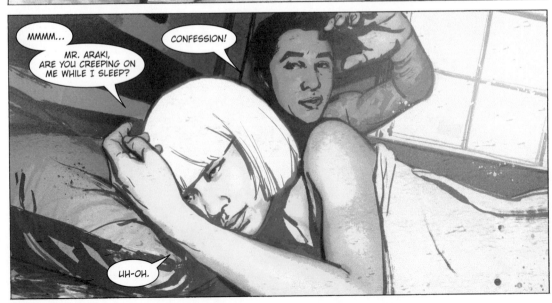

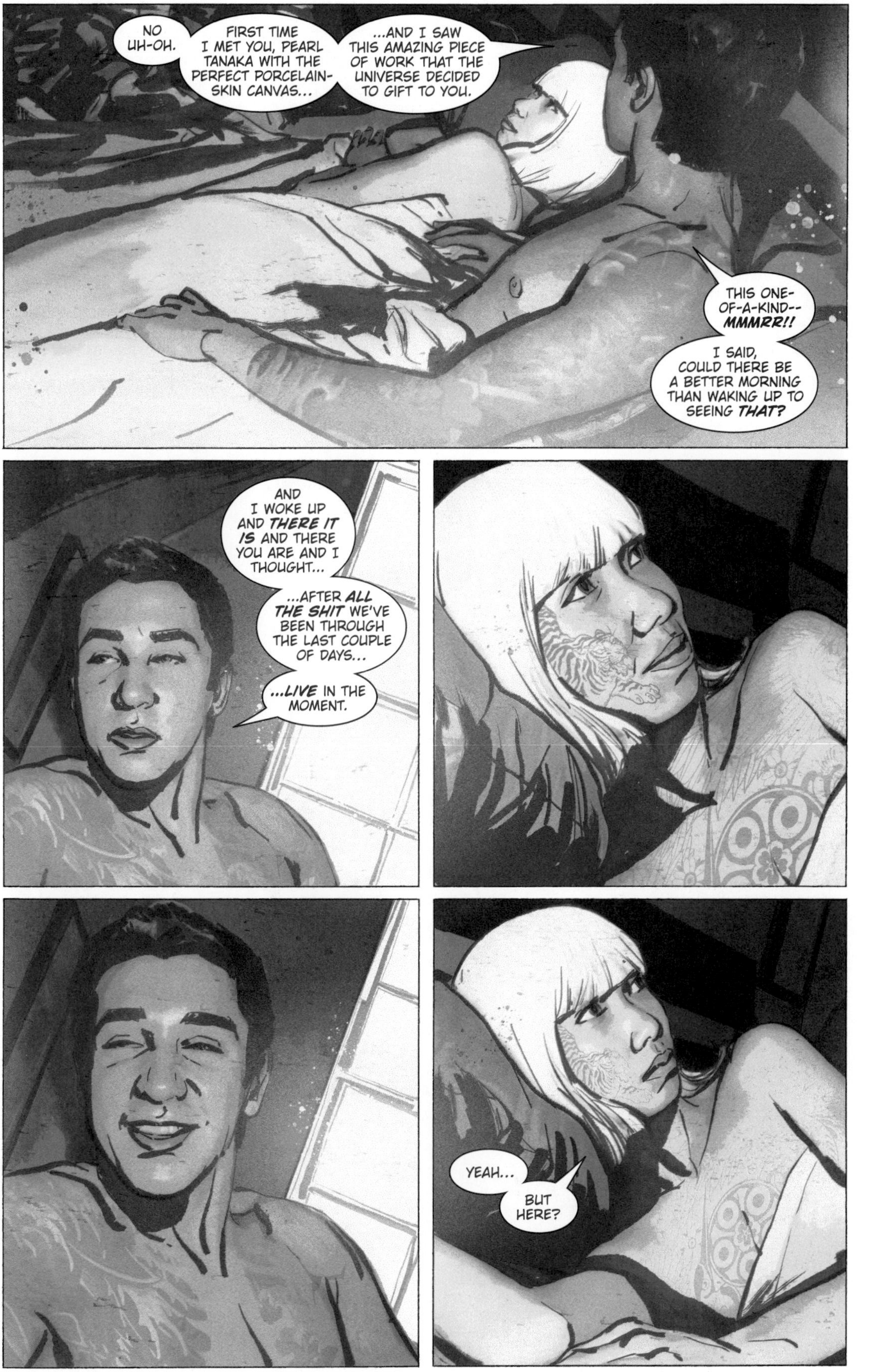
NO UH-OH.
FIRST TIME I MET YOU, PEARL TANAKA WITH THE PERFECT PORCELAIN-SKIN CANVAS...
...AND I SAW THIS AMAZING PIECE OF WORK THAT THE UNIVERSE DECIDED TO GIFT TO YOU.
THIS ONE-OF-A-KIND-- **MMMRR!!**
I SAID, COULD THERE BE A BETTER MORNING THAN WAKING UP TO SEEING ***THAT?***
AND I WOKE UP AND ***THERE IT IS*** AND THERE YOU ARE AND I THOUGHT...
...AFTER ***ALL THE SHIT*** WE'VE BEEN THROUGH THE LAST COUPLE OF DAYS...
...LIVE IN THE MOMENT.
YEAH...
BUT HERE?

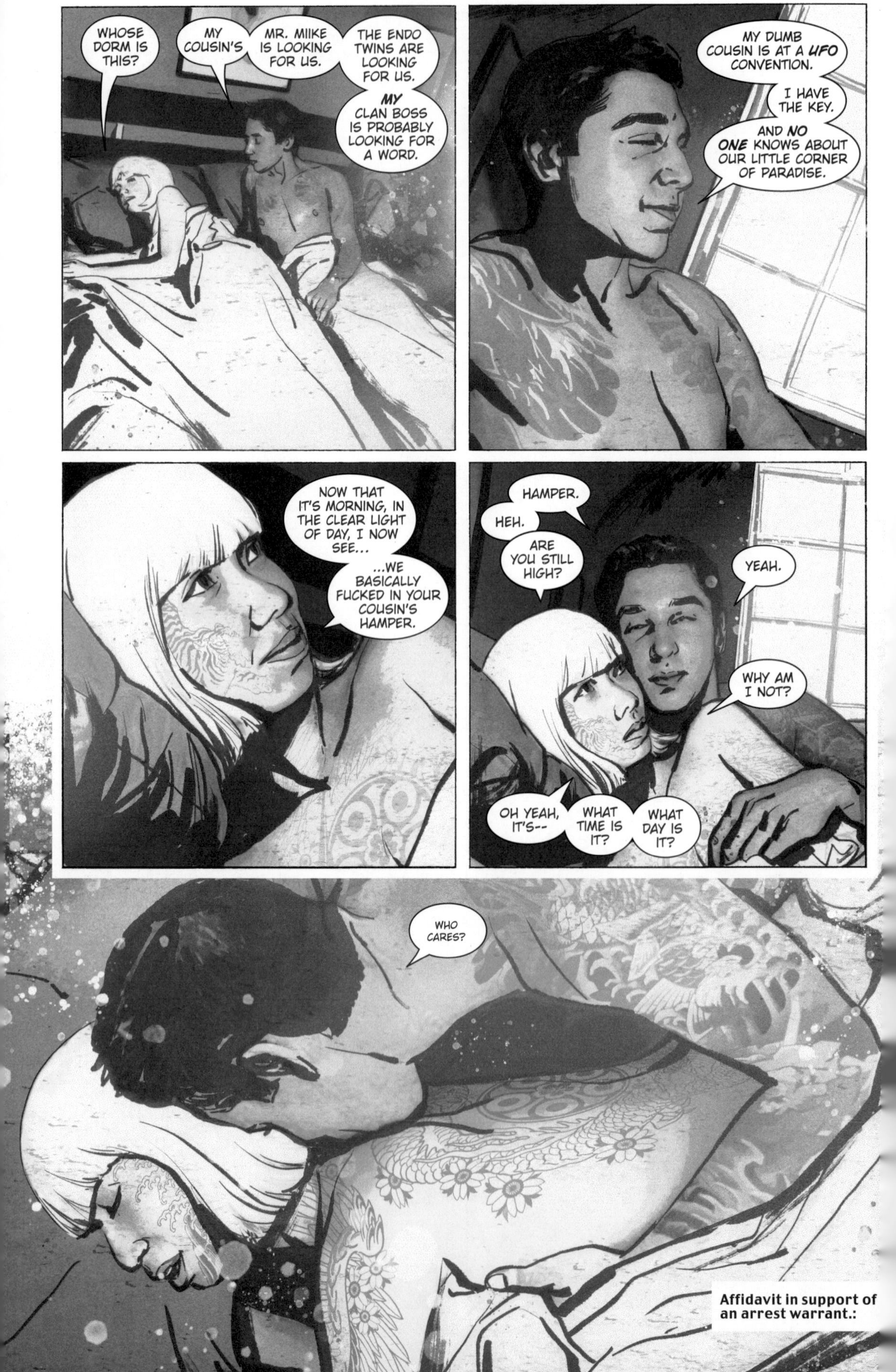
WHOSE DORM IS THIS?
MY COUSIN'S
MR. MIIKE IS LOOKING FOR US.
THE ENDO TWINS ARE LOOKING FOR US.
MY CLAN BOSS IS PROBABLY LOOKING FOR A WORD.
MY DUMB COUSIN IS AT A UFO CONVENTION.
I HAVE THE KEY.
AND NO ONE KNOWS ABOUT OUR LITTLE CORNER OF PARADISE.
NOW THAT IT'S MORNING, IN THE CLEAR LIGHT OF DAY, I NOW SEE...
...WE BASICALLY FUCKED IN YOUR COUSIN'S HAMPER.
HAMPER.
HEH.
ARE YOU STILL HIGH?
YEAH.
WHY AM I NOT?
OH YEAH, IT'S--
WHAT TIME IS IT?
WHAT DAY IS IT?
WHO CARES?
Affidavit in support of an arrest warrant.:

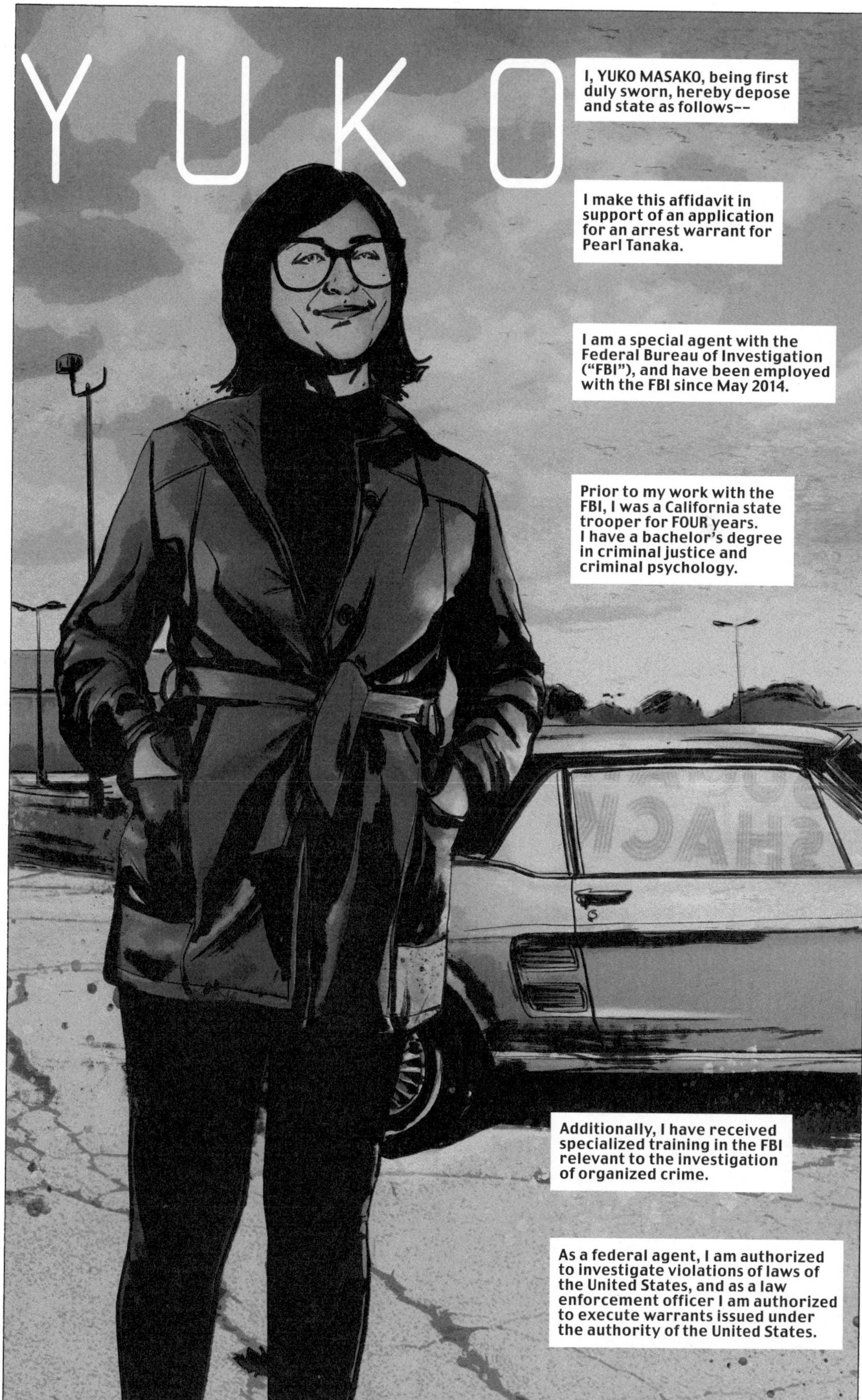
YUKO
I, YUKO MASAKO, being first duly sworn, hereby depose and state as follows--
I make this affidavit in support of an application for an arrest warrant for Pearl Tanaka.
I am a special agent with the Federal Bureau of Investigation ("FBI"), and have been employed with the FBI since May 2014.
Prior to my work with the FBI, I was a California state trooper for FOUR years. I have a bachelor's degree in criminal justice and criminal psychology.
Additionally, I have received specialized training in the FBI relevant to the investigation of organized crime.
As a federal agent, I am authorized to investigate violations of laws of the United States, and as a law enforcement officer I am authorized to execute warrants issued under the authority of the United States.

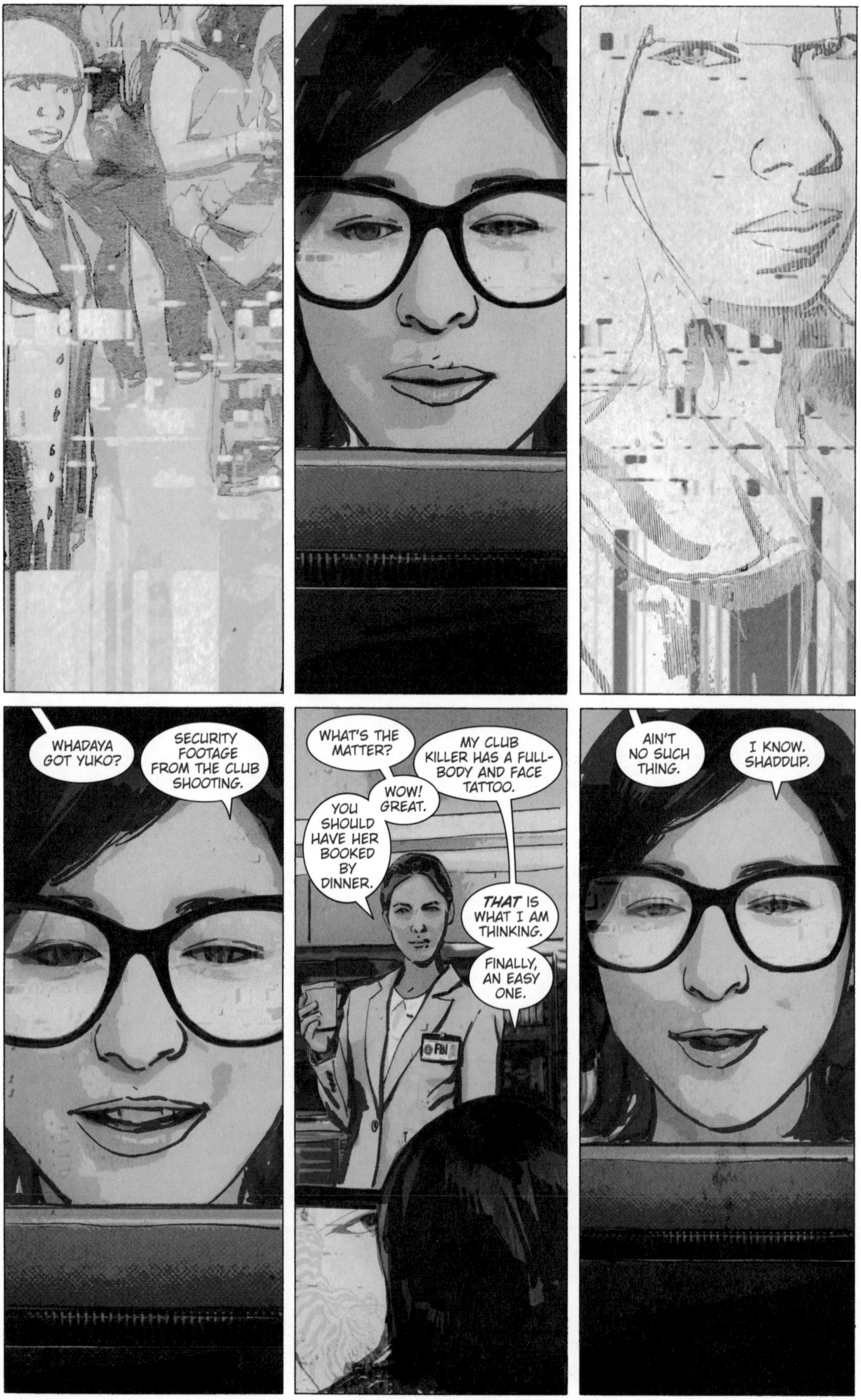
WHADAYA GOT YUKO?
SECURITY FOOTAGE FROM THE CLUB SHOOTING.
WHAT'S THE MATTER?
MY CLUB KILLER HAS A FULL-BODY AND FACE TATTOO.
WOW! GREAT.
YOU SHOULD HAVE HER BOOKED BY DINNER.
THAT IS WHAT I AM THINKING.
FINALLY, AN EASY ONE.
AIN'T NO SUCH THING.
I KNOW. SHADDUP.

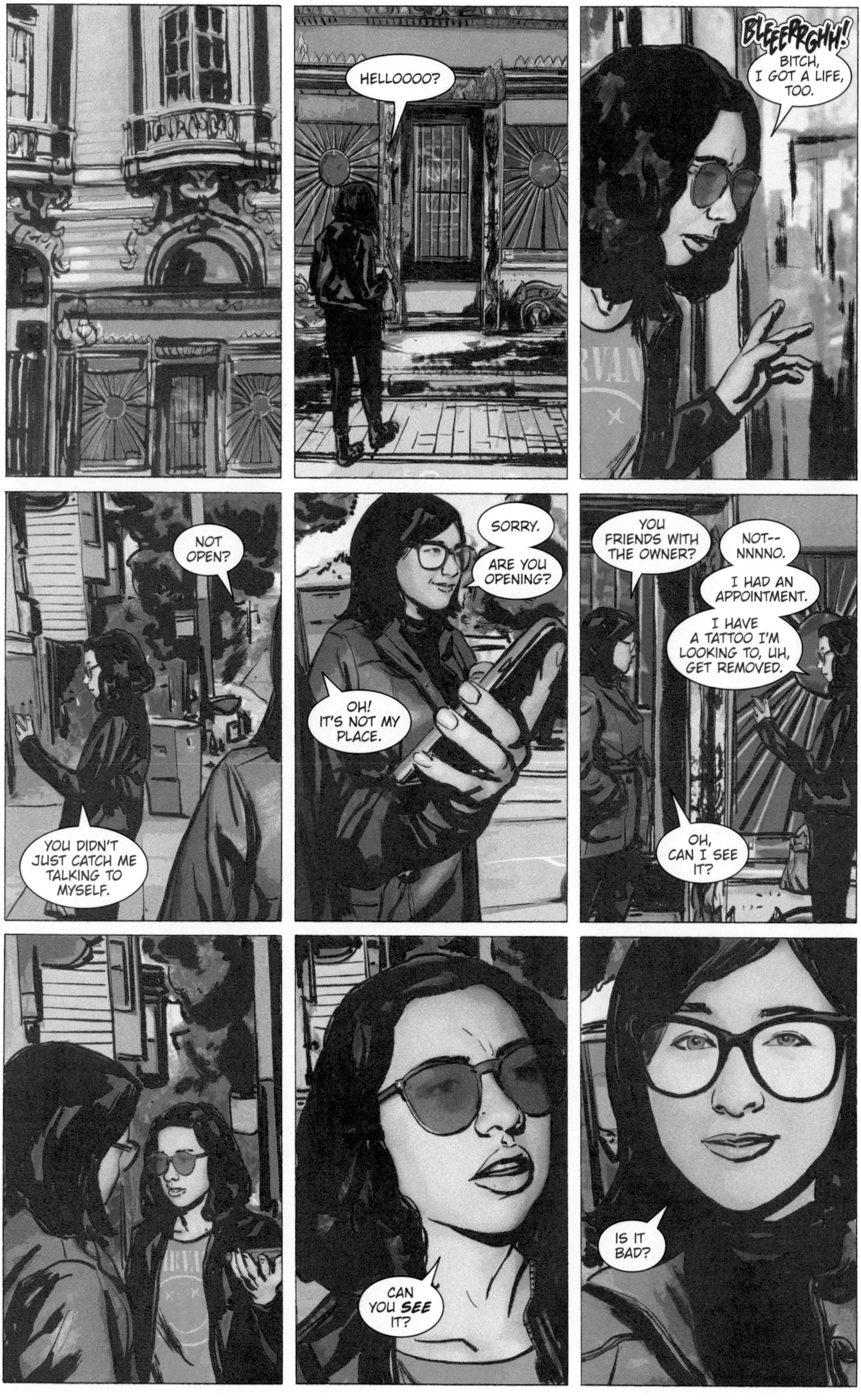
HELLOOOO?
BLEEERRGHH!
BITCH, I GOT A LIFE, TOO.
NOT OPEN?
YOU DIDN'T JUST CATCH ME TALKING TO MYSELF.
SORRY.
ARE YOU OPENING?
OH! IT'S NOT MY PLACE.
YOU FRIENDS WITH THE OWNER?
NOT-- NNNNO.
I HAD AN APPOINTMENT.
I HAVE A TATTOO I'M LOOKING TO, UH, GET REMOVED.
OH, CAN I SEE IT?
CAN YOU SEE IT?
IS IT BAD?

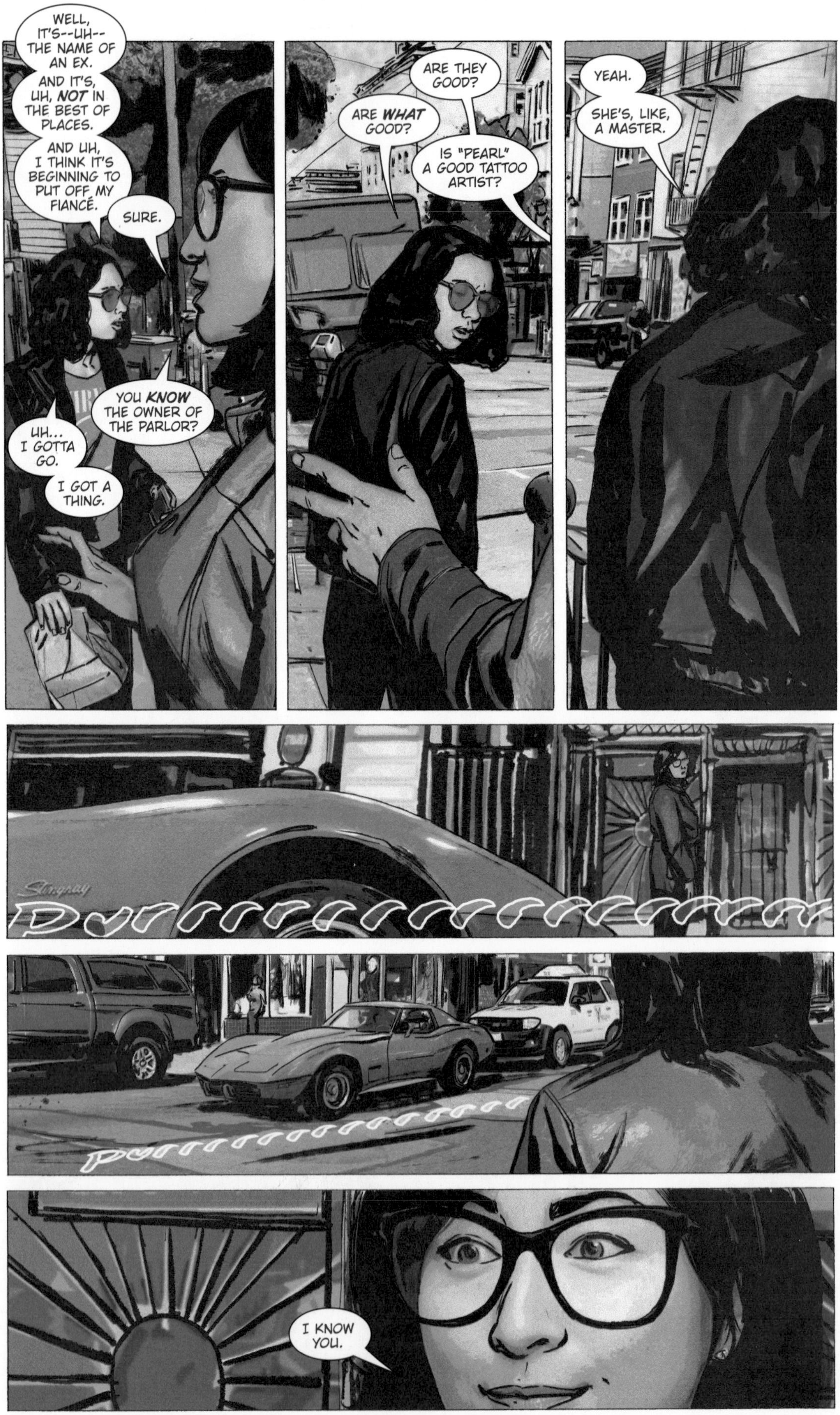
WELL, IT'S--UH-- THE NAME OF AN EX.
AND IT'S, UH, NOT IN THE BEST OF PLACES.
AND UH, I THINK IT'S BEGINNING TO PUT OFF MY FIANCÉ.
SURE.
YOU KNOW THE OWNER OF THE PARLOR?
UH... I GOTTA GO.
I GOT A THING.
ARE THEY GOOD?
ARE WHAT GOOD?
IS "PEARL" A GOOD TATTOO ARTIST?
YEAH.
SHE'S, LIKE, A MASTER.
Stingray
PURRRRRRRRRRRRRRRRRRRR
PURRRRRRRRRRRRRRRR
I KNOW YOU.

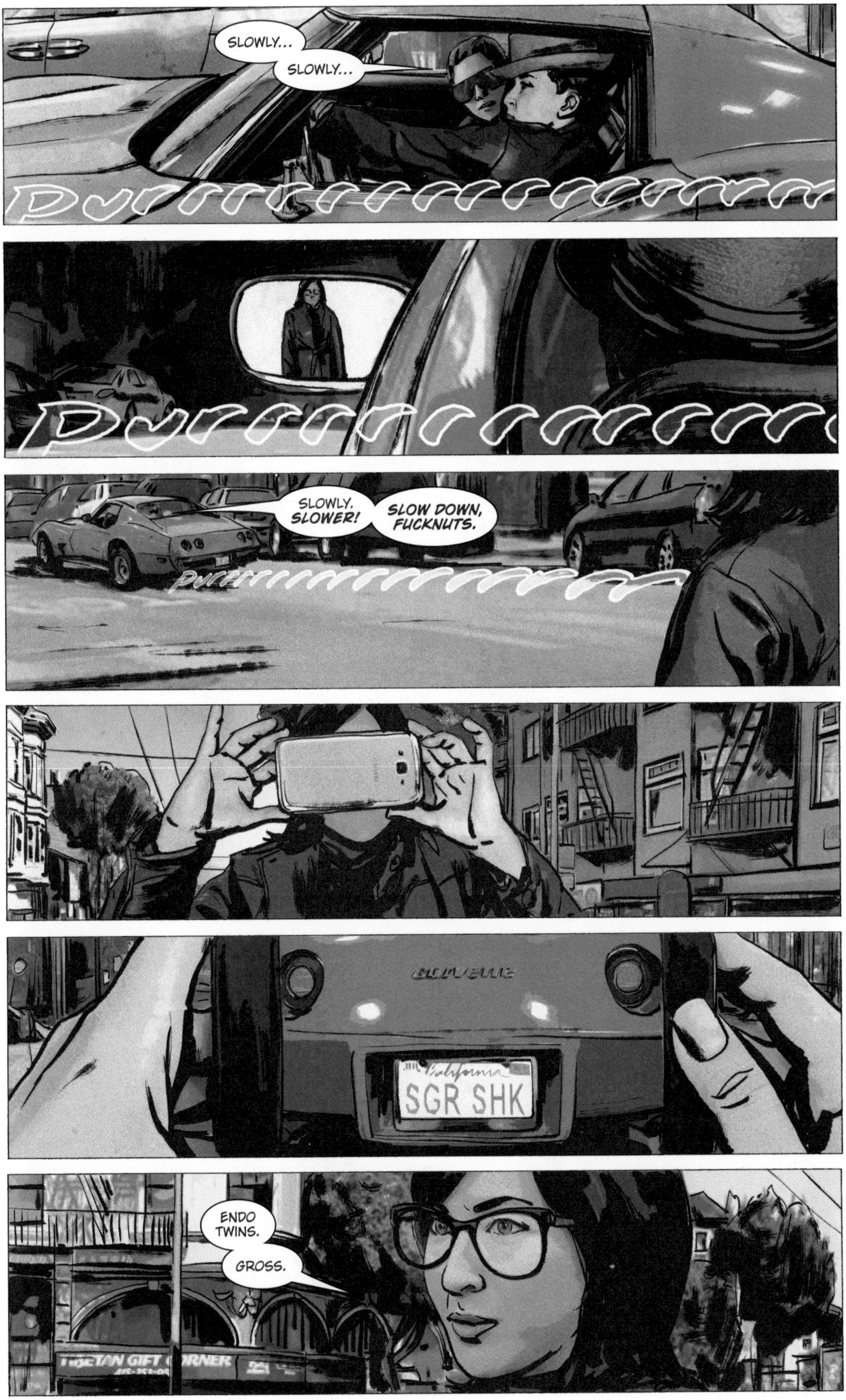
SLOWLY...
SLOWLY...
Purrrrrrrrrrrrrrrrr
Purrrrrrrrrrrrr
SLOWLY. SLOWER!
SLOW DOWN, FUCKNUTS.
Purrrrrrrrrrrrrrrrrrrr
SGR SHK
ENDO TWINS.
GROSS.
TIBETAN GIFT CORNER

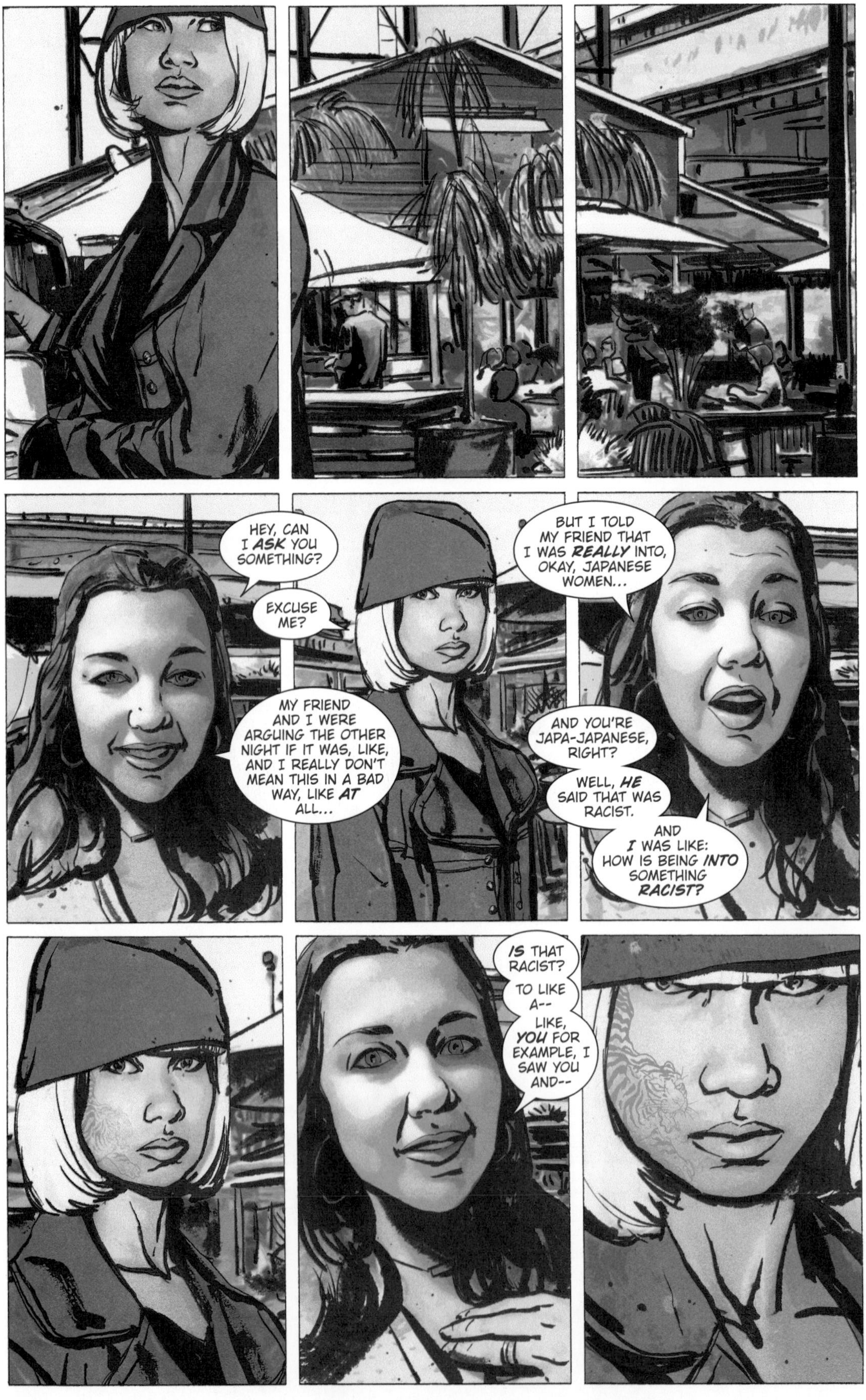
HEY, CAN I ASK YOU SOMETHING?
EXCUSE ME?
MY FRIEND AND I WERE ARGUING THE OTHER NIGHT IF IT WAS, LIKE, AND I REALLY DON'T MEAN THIS IN A BAD WAY, LIKE AT ALL...
BUT I TOLD MY FRIEND THAT I WAS REALLY INTO, OKAY, JAPANESE WOMEN...
AND YOU'RE JAPA-JAPANESE, RIGHT?
WELL, HE SAID THAT WAS RACIST.
AND I WAS LIKE: HOW IS BEING INTO SOMETHING RACIST?
IS THAT RACIST?
TO LIKE A--
LIKE, YOU FOR EXAMPLE, I SAW YOU AND--

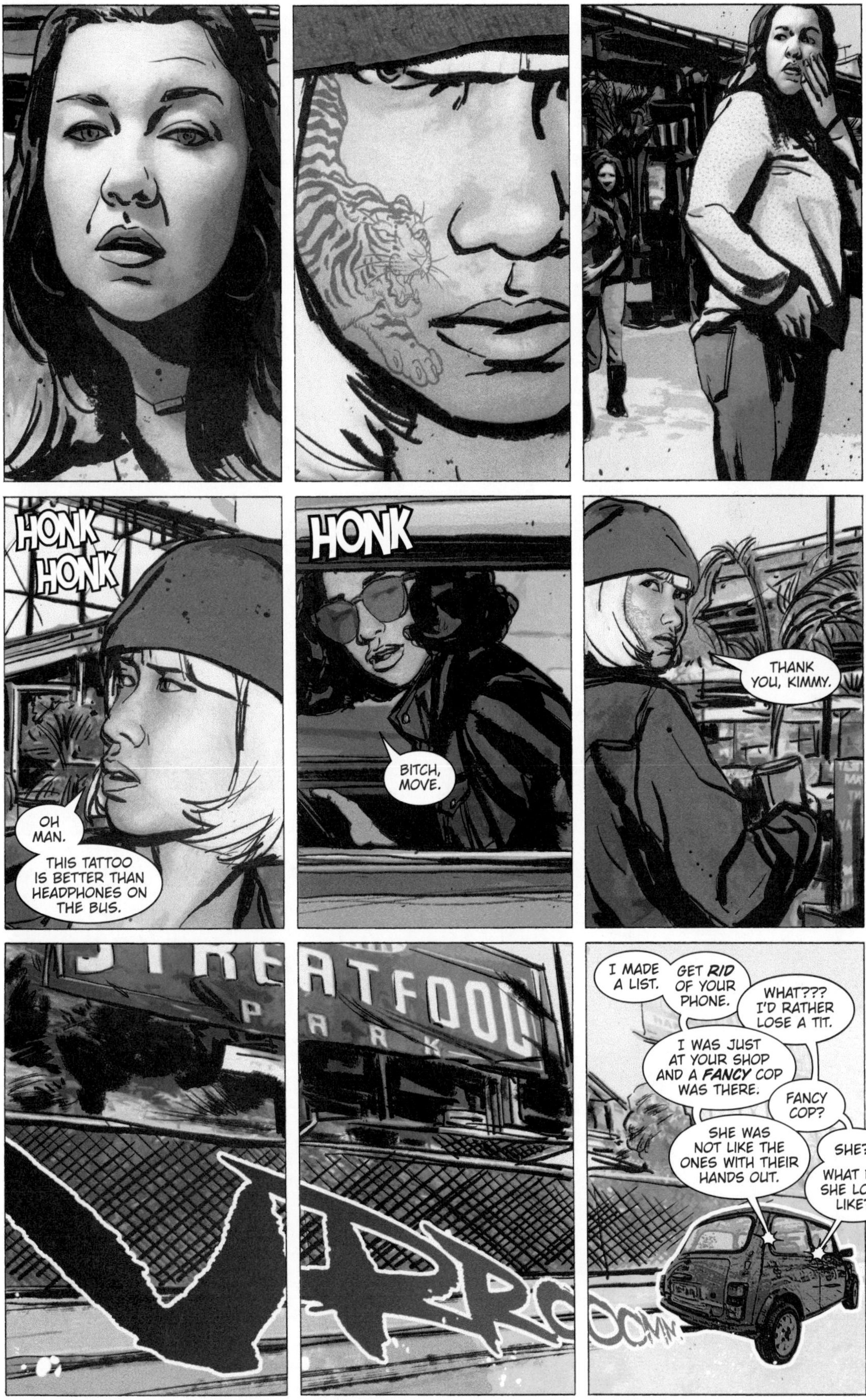
HONK
HONK
OH MAN.
THIS TATTOO IS BETTER THAN HEADPHONES ON THE BUS.
HONK
BITCH, MOVE.
THANK YOU, KIMMY.
ATFOOD
P A R K
I MADE A LIST.
GET RID OF YOUR PHONE.
WHAT??? I'D RATHER LOSE A TIT.
I WAS JUST AT YOUR SHOP AND A FANCY COP WAS THERE.
FANCY COP?
SHE WAS NOT LIKE THE ONES WITH THEIR HANDS OUT.
SHE?
WHAT DID SHE LOOK LIKE?

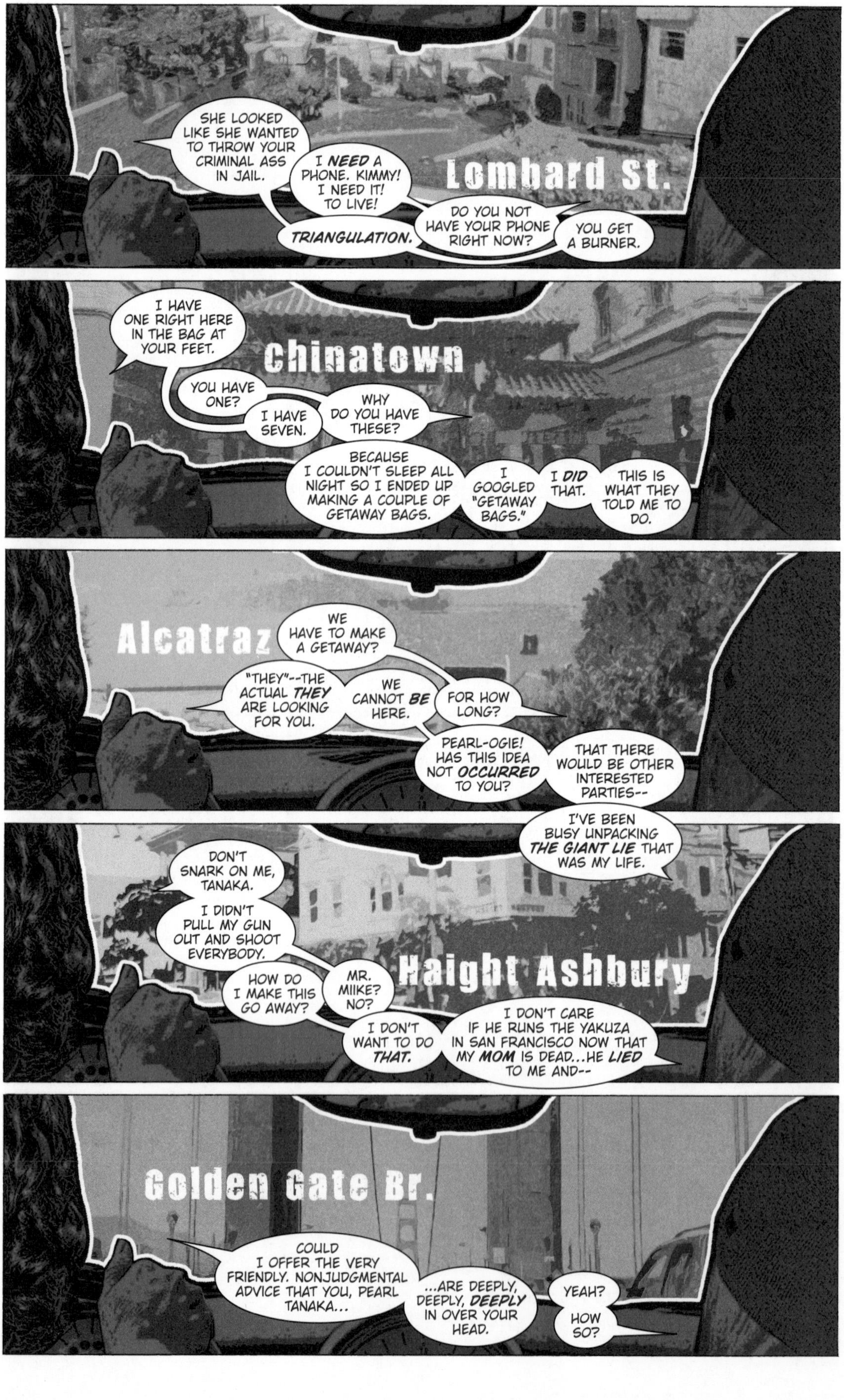
SHE LOOKED LIKE SHE WANTED TO THROW YOUR CRIMINAL ASS IN JAIL.
I **NEED** A PHONE. KIMMY! I NEED IT! TO LIVE!
Lombard St.
DO YOU NOT HAVE YOUR PHONE RIGHT NOW?
TRIANGULATION.
YOU GET A BURNER.
I HAVE ONE RIGHT HERE IN THE BAG AT YOUR FEET.
Chinatown
YOU HAVE ONE?
I HAVE SEVEN.
WHY DO YOU HAVE THESE?
BECAUSE I COULDN'T SLEEP ALL NIGHT SO I ENDED UP MAKING A COUPLE OF GETAWAY BAGS.
I GOOGLED "GETAWAY BAGS."
I **DID** THAT.
THIS IS WHAT THEY TOLD ME TO DO.
Alcatraz
WE HAVE TO MAKE A GETAWAY?
"THEY"--THE ACTUAL **THEY** ARE LOOKING FOR YOU.
WE CANNOT **BE** HERE.
FOR HOW LONG?
PEARL-OGIE! HAS THIS IDEA NOT **OCCURRED** TO YOU?
THAT THERE WOULD BE OTHER INTERESTED PARTIES--
I'VE BEEN BUSY UNPACKING **THE GIANT LIE** THAT WAS MY LIFE.
DON'T SNARK ON ME, TANAKA.
I DIDN'T PULL MY GUN OUT AND SHOOT EVERYBODY.
Haight Ashbury
HOW DO I MAKE THIS GO AWAY?
MR. MIIKE? NO?
I DON'T WANT TO DO **THAT.**
I DON'T CARE IF HE RUNS THE YAKUZA IN SAN FRANCISCO NOW THAT MY **MOM** IS DEAD...HE **LIED** TO ME AND--
Golden Gate Br.
COULD I OFFER THE VERY FRIENDLY. NONJUDGMENTAL ADVICE THAT YOU, PEARL TANAKA...
...ARE DEEPLY, DEEPLY, **DEEPLY** IN OVER YOUR HEAD.
YEAH?
HOW SO?

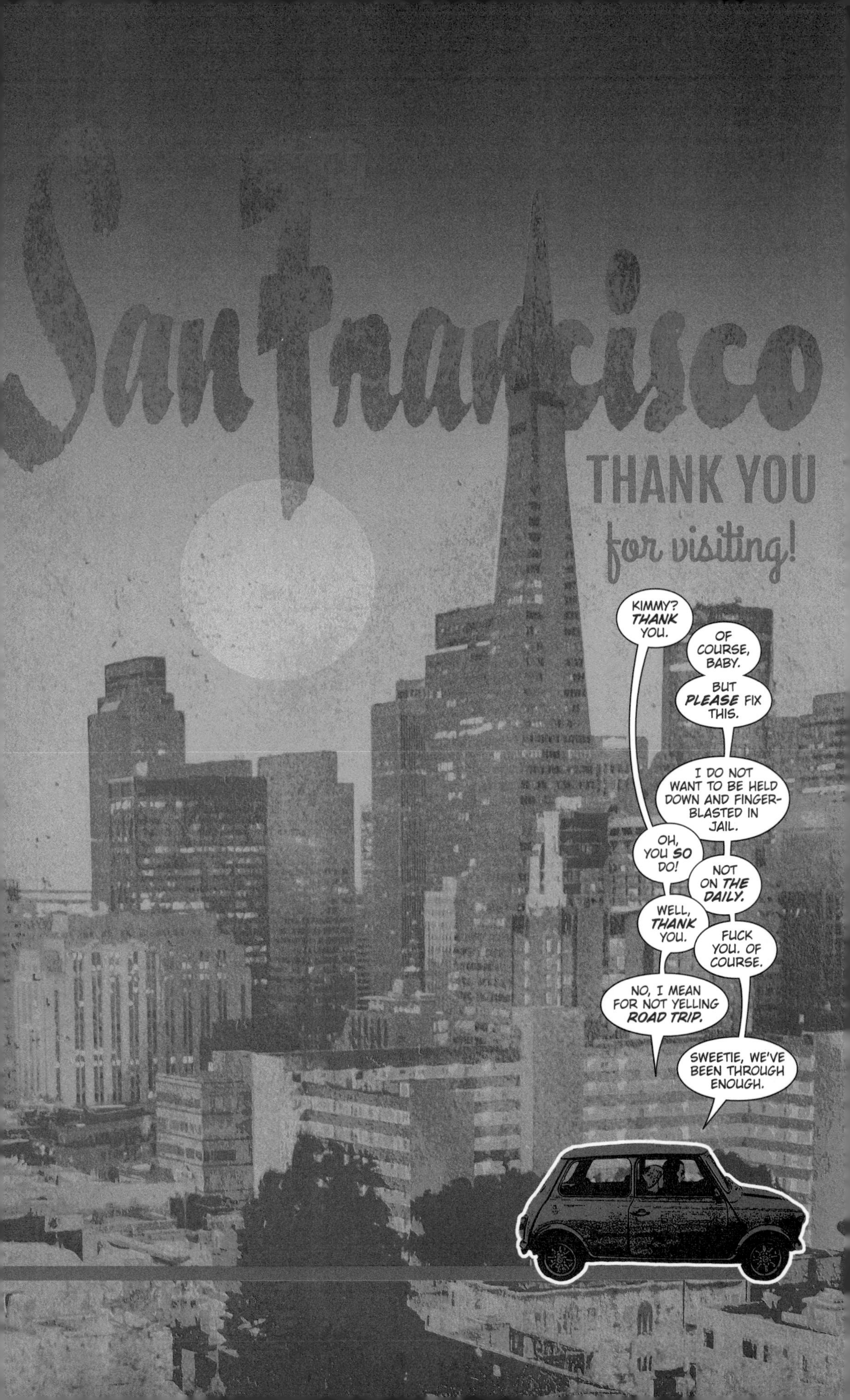
San Francisco
THANK YOU
for visiting!
KIMMY? THANK YOU.
OF COURSE, BABY.
BUT PLEASE FIX THIS.
I DO NOT WANT TO BE HELD DOWN AND FINGER-BLASTED IN JAIL.
OH, YOU SO DO!
NOT ON THE DAILY.
WELL, THANK YOU.
FUCK YOU. OF COURSE.
NO, I MEAN FOR NOT YELLING ROAD TRIP.
SWEETIE, WE'VE BEEN THROUGH ENOUGH.

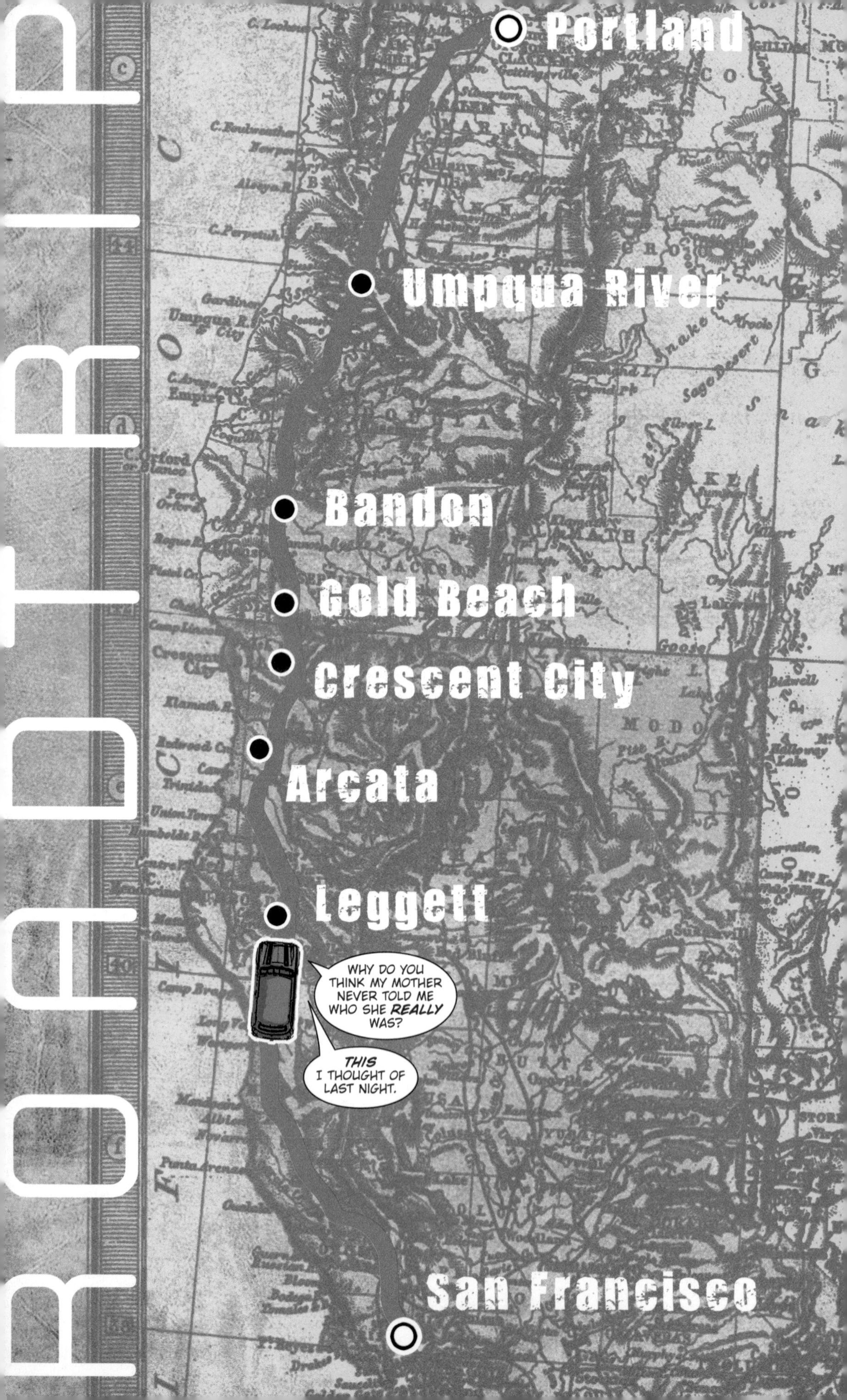
ROAD TRIP
Portland
Umpqua River
Bandon
Gold Beach
Crescent City
Arcata
Leggett
WHY DO YOU THINK MY MOTHER NEVER TOLD ME WHO SHE *REALLY* WAS?
THIS I THOUGHT OF LAST NIGHT.
San Francisco

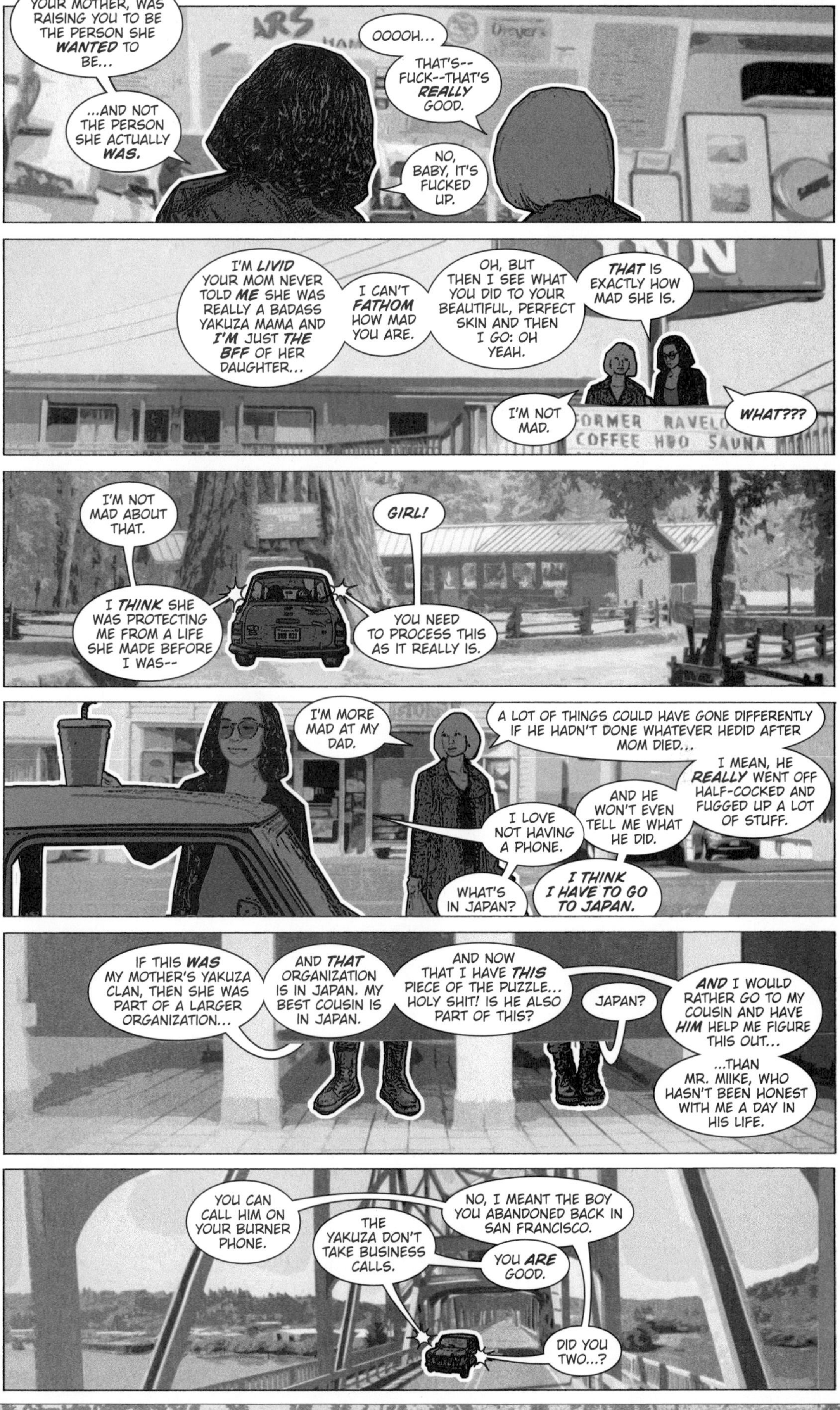
I THINK SHE, YOUR MOTHER, WAS RAISING YOU TO BE THE PERSON SHE *WANTED* TO BE...
...AND NOT THE PERSON SHE ACTUALLY *WAS.*
OOOOH...
THAT'S--FUCK--THAT'S *REALLY* GOOD.
NO, BABY, IT'S FUCKED UP.
I'M *LIVID* YOUR MOM NEVER TOLD *ME* SHE WAS REALLY A BADASS YAKUZA MAMA AND *I'M* JUST *THE BFF* OF HER DAUGHTER...
I CAN'T *FATHOM* HOW MAD YOU ARE.
OH, BUT THEN I SEE WHAT YOU DID TO YOUR BEAUTIFUL, PERFECT SKIN AND THEN I GO: OH YEAH.
THAT IS EXACTLY HOW MAD SHE IS.
I'M NOT MAD.
WHAT???
I'M NOT MAD ABOUT THAT.
I *THINK* SHE WAS PROTECTING ME FROM A LIFE SHE MADE BEFORE I WAS--
GIRL!
YOU NEED TO PROCESS THIS AS IT REALLY IS.
I'M MORE MAD AT MY DAD.
A LOT OF THINGS COULD HAVE GONE DIFFERENTLY IF HE HADN'T DONE WHATEVER HEDID AFTER MOM DIED...
I MEAN, HE *REALLY* WENT OFF HALF-COCKED AND FUGGED UP A LOT OF STUFF.
AND HE WON'T EVEN TELL ME WHAT HE DID.
I LOVE NOT HAVING A PHONE.
I THINK I HAVE TO GO TO JAPAN.
WHAT'S IN JAPAN?
IF THIS *WAS* MY MOTHER'S YAKUZA CLAN, THEN SHE WAS PART OF A LARGER ORGANIZATION...
AND *THAT* ORGANIZATION IS IN JAPAN. MY BEST COUSIN IS IN JAPAN.
AND NOW THAT I HAVE *THIS* PIECE OF THE PUZZLE... HOLY SHIT! IS HE ALSO PART OF THIS?
JAPAN?
AND I WOULD RATHER GO TO MY COUSIN AND HAVE *HIM* HELP ME FIGURE THIS OUT...
...THAN MR. MIIKE, WHO HASN'T BEEN HONEST WITH ME A DAY IN HIS LIFE.
YOU CAN CALL HIM ON YOUR BURNER PHONE.
THE YAKUZA DON'T TAKE BUSINESS CALLS.
NO, I MEANT THE BOY YOU ABANDONED BACK IN SAN FRANCISCO.
YOU *ARE* GOOD.
DID YOU TWO...?

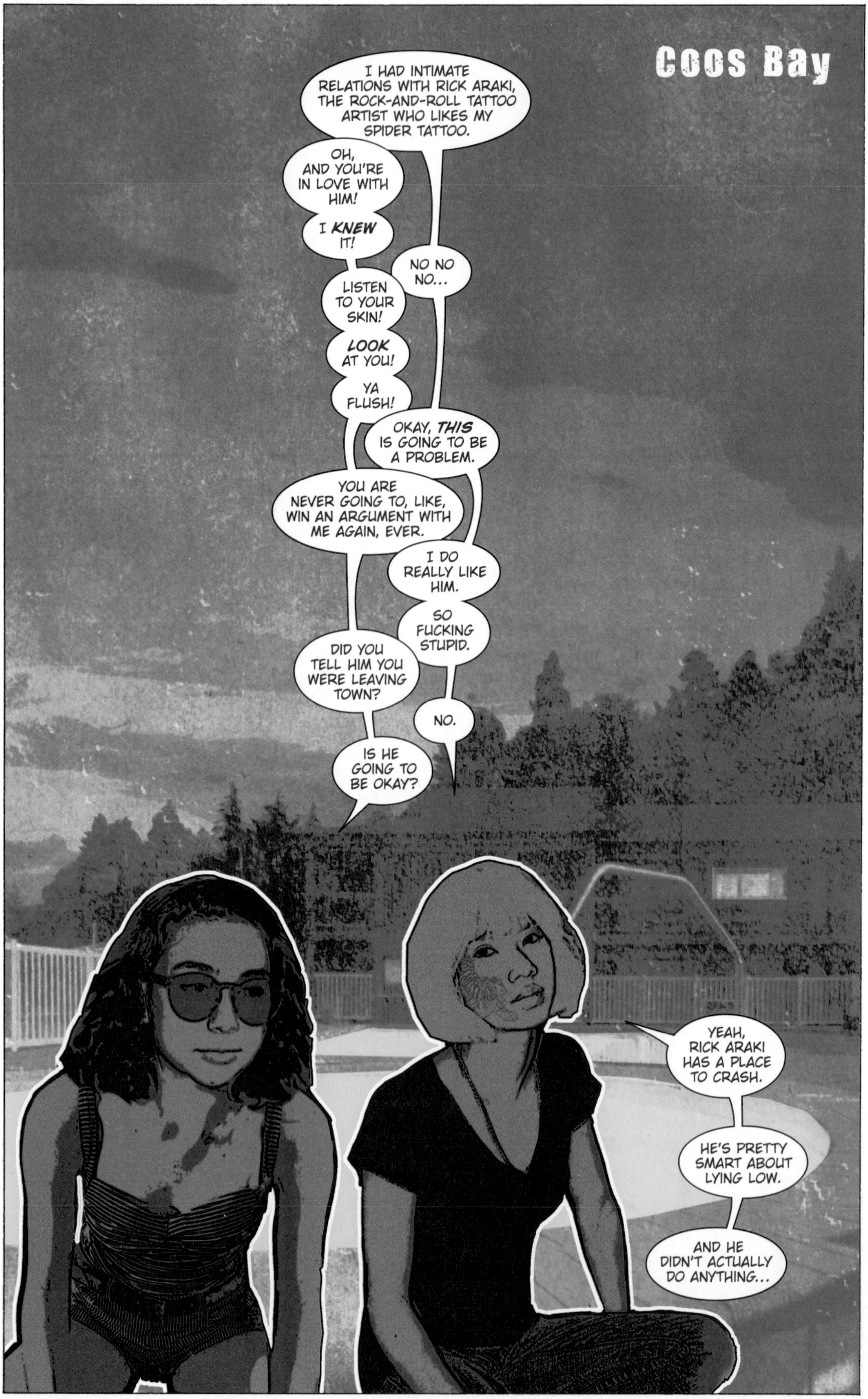
Coos Bay
I HAD INTIMATE RELATIONS WITH RICK ARAKI, THE ROCK-AND-ROLL TATTOO ARTIST WHO LIKES MY SPIDER TATTOO.
OH, AND YOU'RE IN LOVE WITH HIM!
I *KNEW* IT!
NO NO NO...
LISTEN TO YOUR SKIN!
LOOK AT YOU!
YA FLUSH!
OKAY, *THIS* IS GOING TO BE A PROBLEM.
YOU ARE NEVER GOING TO, LIKE, WIN AN ARGUMENT WITH ME AGAIN, EVER.
I DO REALLY LIKE HIM.
SO FUCKING STUPID.
DID YOU TELL HIM YOU WERE LEAVING TOWN?
NO.
IS HE GOING TO BE OKAY?
YEAH, RICK ARAKI HAS A PLACE TO CRASH.
HE'S PRETTY SMART ABOUT LYING LOW.
AND HE DIDN'T ACTUALLY DO ANYTHING...

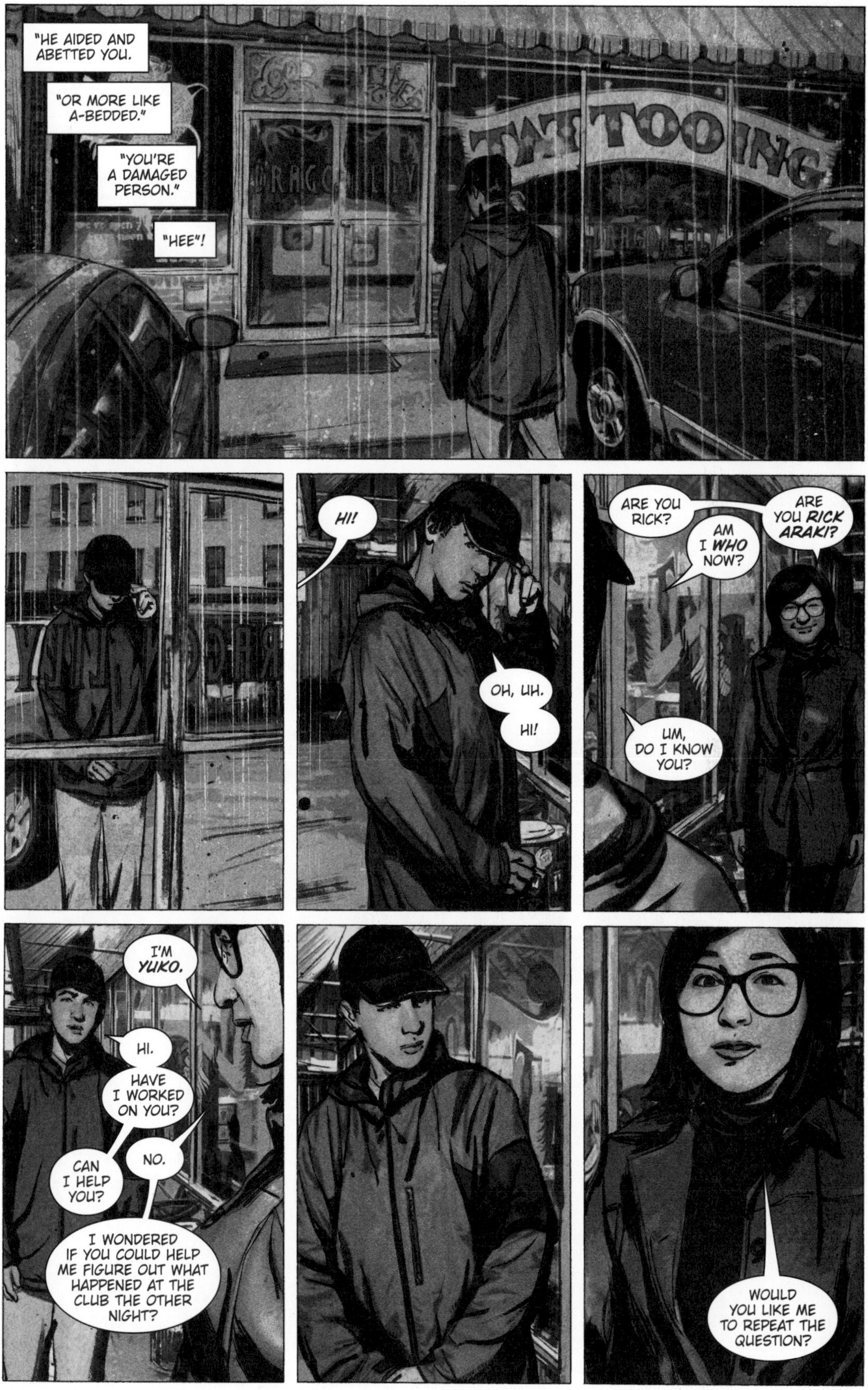
"HE AIDED AND ABETTED YOU.
"OR MORE LIKE A-BEDDED."
"YOU'RE A DAMAGED PERSON."
"HEE"!
TATTOOING
HI!
OH, UH.
HI!
ARE YOU RICK?
ARE YOU RICK ARAKI?
AM I WHO NOW?
UM, DO I KNOW YOU?
I'M YUKO.
HI.
HAVE I WORKED ON YOU?
NO.
CAN I HELP YOU?
I WONDERED IF YOU COULD HELP ME FIGURE OUT WHAT HAPPENED AT THE CLUB THE OTHER NIGHT?
WOULD YOU LIKE ME TO REPEAT THE QUESTION?

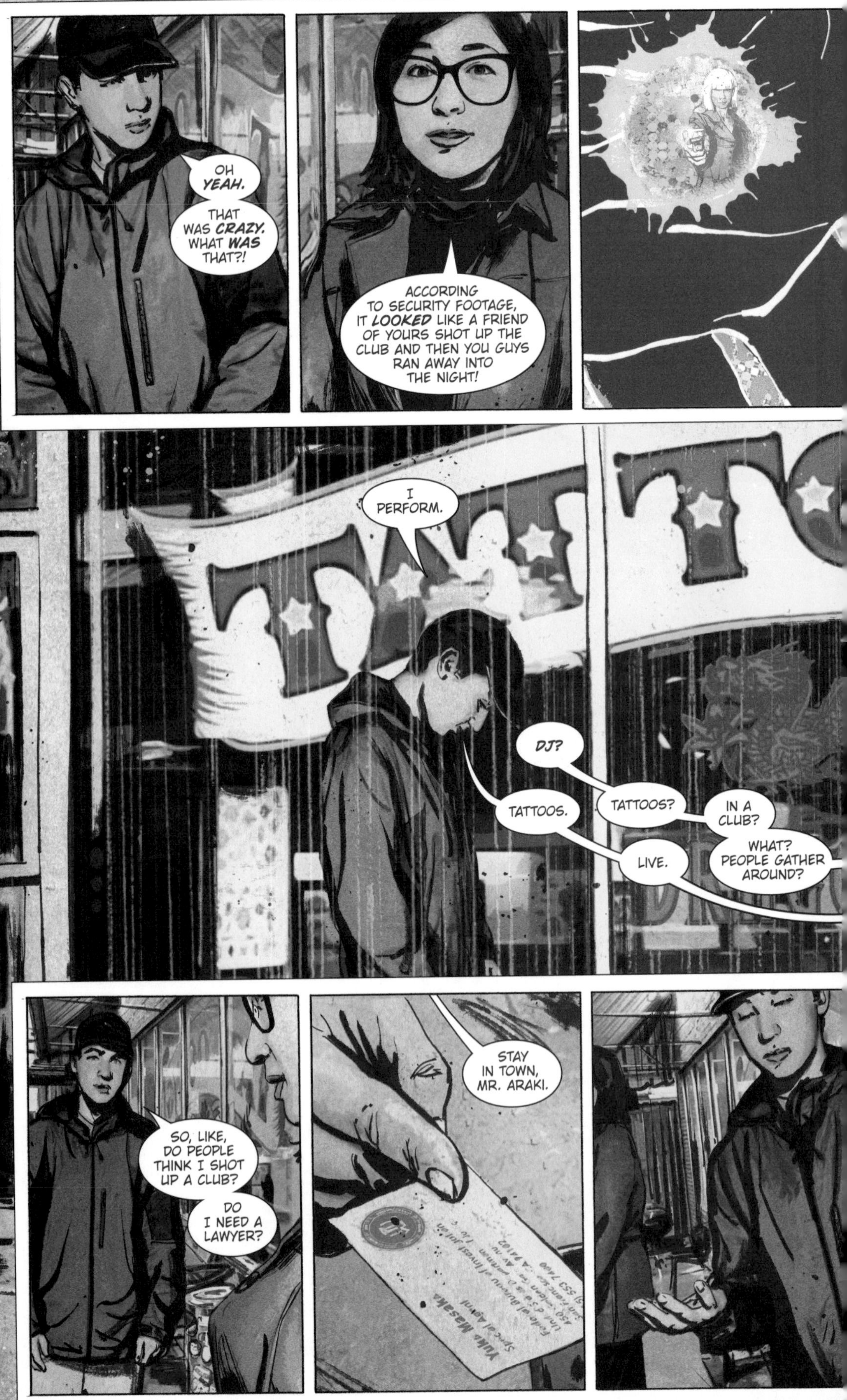

OH *YEAH.*
THAT WAS *CRAZY.* WHAT *WAS* THAT?!
ACCORDING TO SECURITY FOOTAGE, IT *LOOKED* LIKE A FRIEND OF YOURS SHOT UP THE CLUB AND THEN YOU GUYS RAN AWAY INTO THE NIGHT!
I PERFORM.
DJ?
TATTOOS.
TATTOOS?
IN A CLUB?
WHAT? PEOPLE GATHER AROUND?
LIVE.
SO, LIKE, DO PEOPLE THINK I SHOT UP A CLUB?
DO I NEED A LAWYER?
STAY IN TOWN, MR. ARAKI.

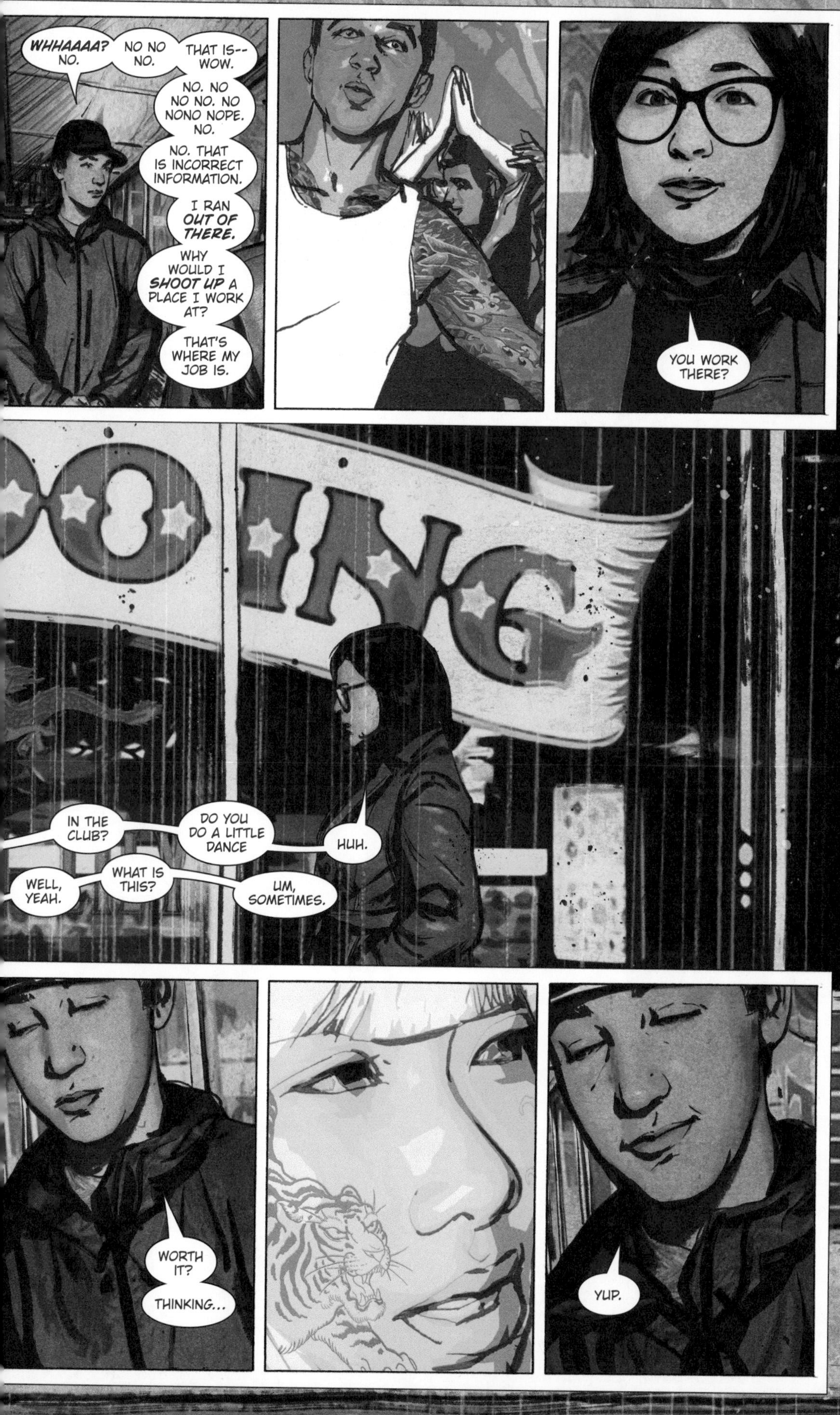

WHHAAAA? NO.
NO NO NO.
THAT IS-- WOW.
NO. NO NO NO. NO NONO NOPE. NO.
NO. THAT IS INCORRECT INFORMATION.
I RAN OUT OF THERE.
WHY WOULD I SHOOT UP A PLACE I WORK AT?
THAT'S WHERE MY JOB IS.
YOU WORK THERE?
ING
HUH.
DO YOU DO A LITTLE DANCE
IN THE CLUB?
UM, SOMETIMES.
WHAT IS THIS?
WELL, YEAH.
WORTH IT?
THINKING...
YUP.

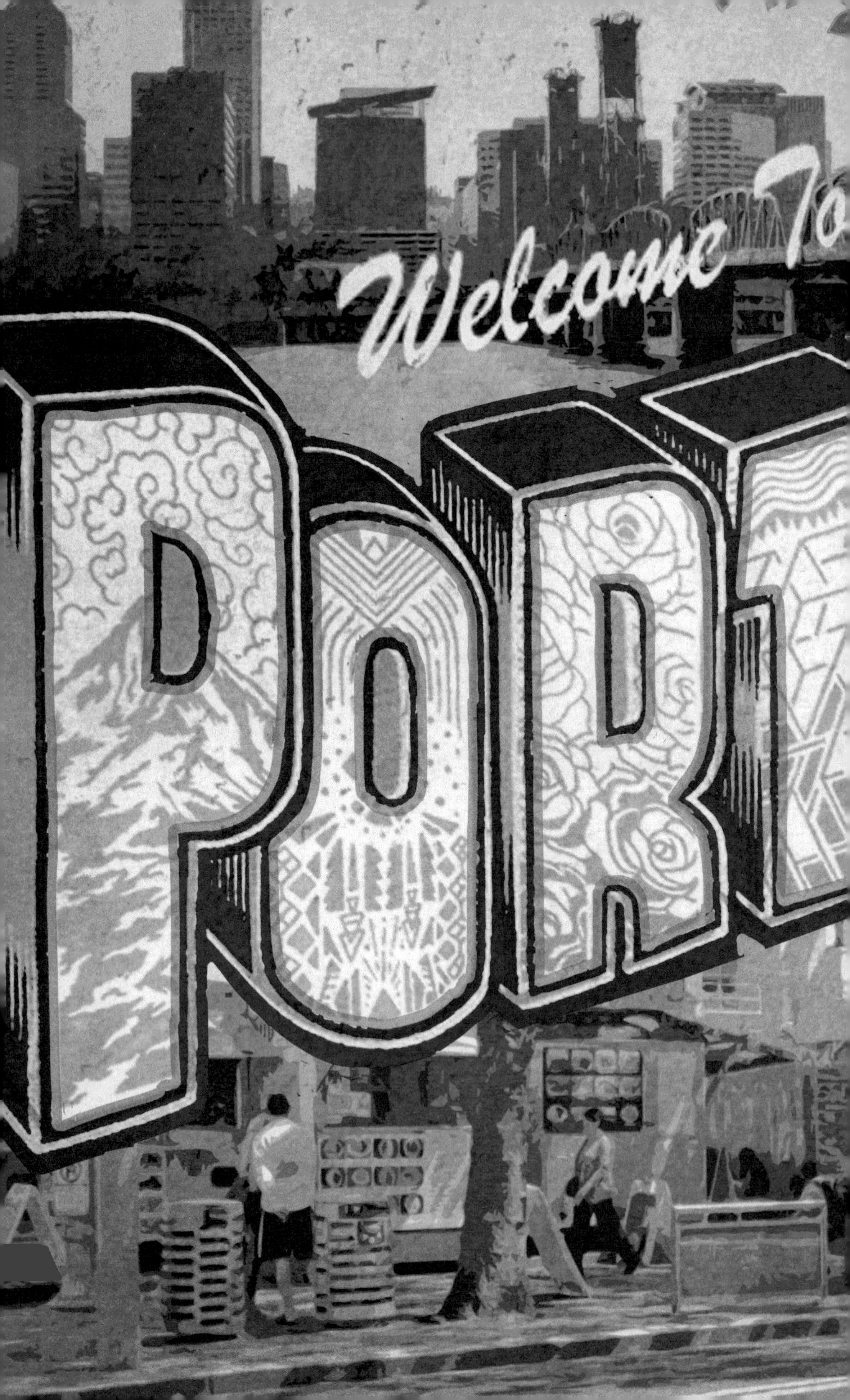
Welcome To
POR

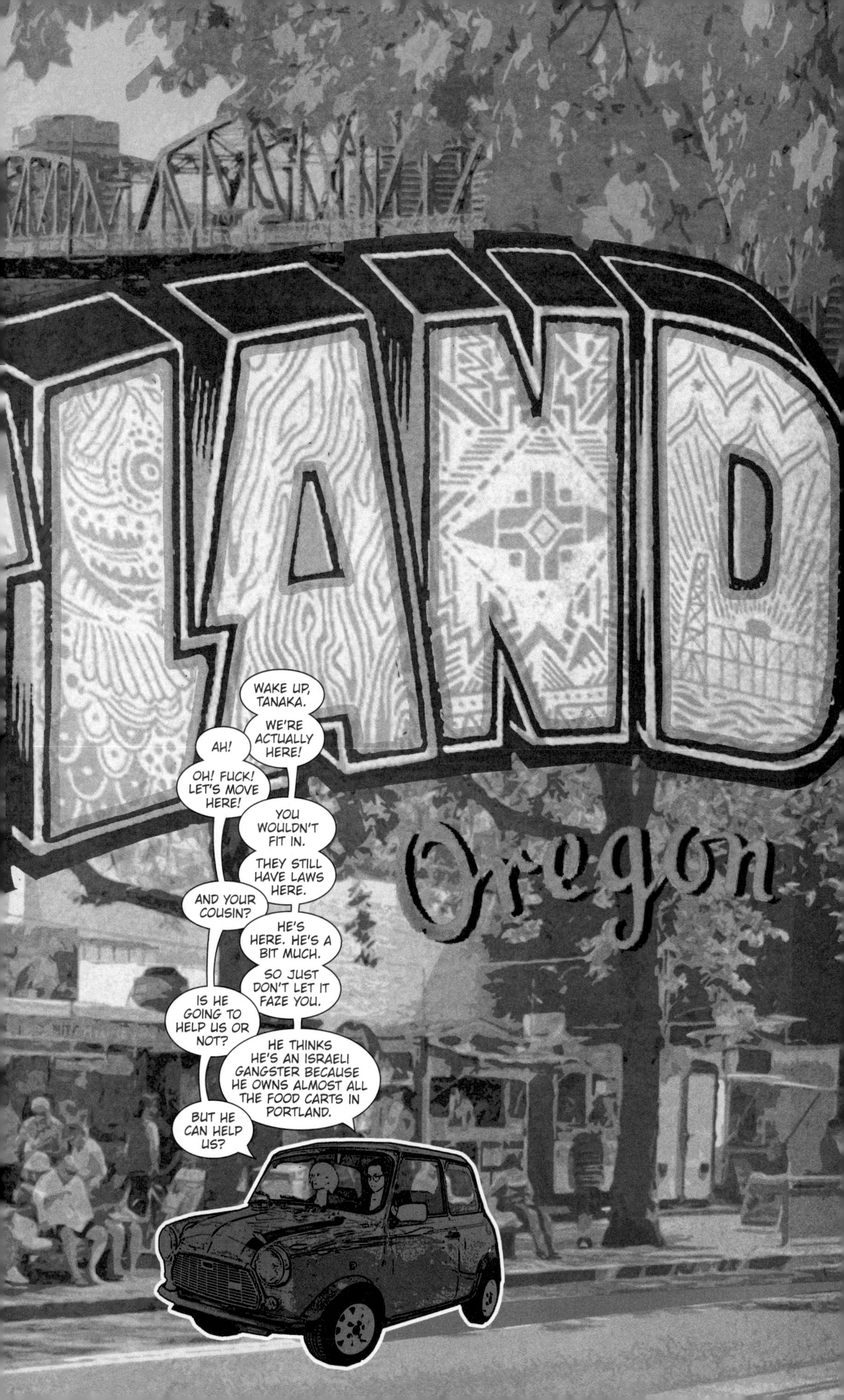
LAND
Oregon
WAKE UP, TANAKA.
WE'RE ACTUALLY HERE!
AH!
OH! FUCK! LET'S MOVE HERE!
YOU WOULDN'T FIT IN.
THEY STILL HAVE LAWS HERE.
AND YOUR COUSIN?
HE'S HERE. HE'S A BIT MUCH.
SO JUST DON'T LET IT FAZE YOU.
IS HE GOING TO HELP US OR NOT?
HE THINKS HE'S AN ISRAELI GANGSTER BECAUSE HE OWNS ALMOST ALL THE FOOD CARTS IN PORTLAND.
BUT HE CAN HELP US?

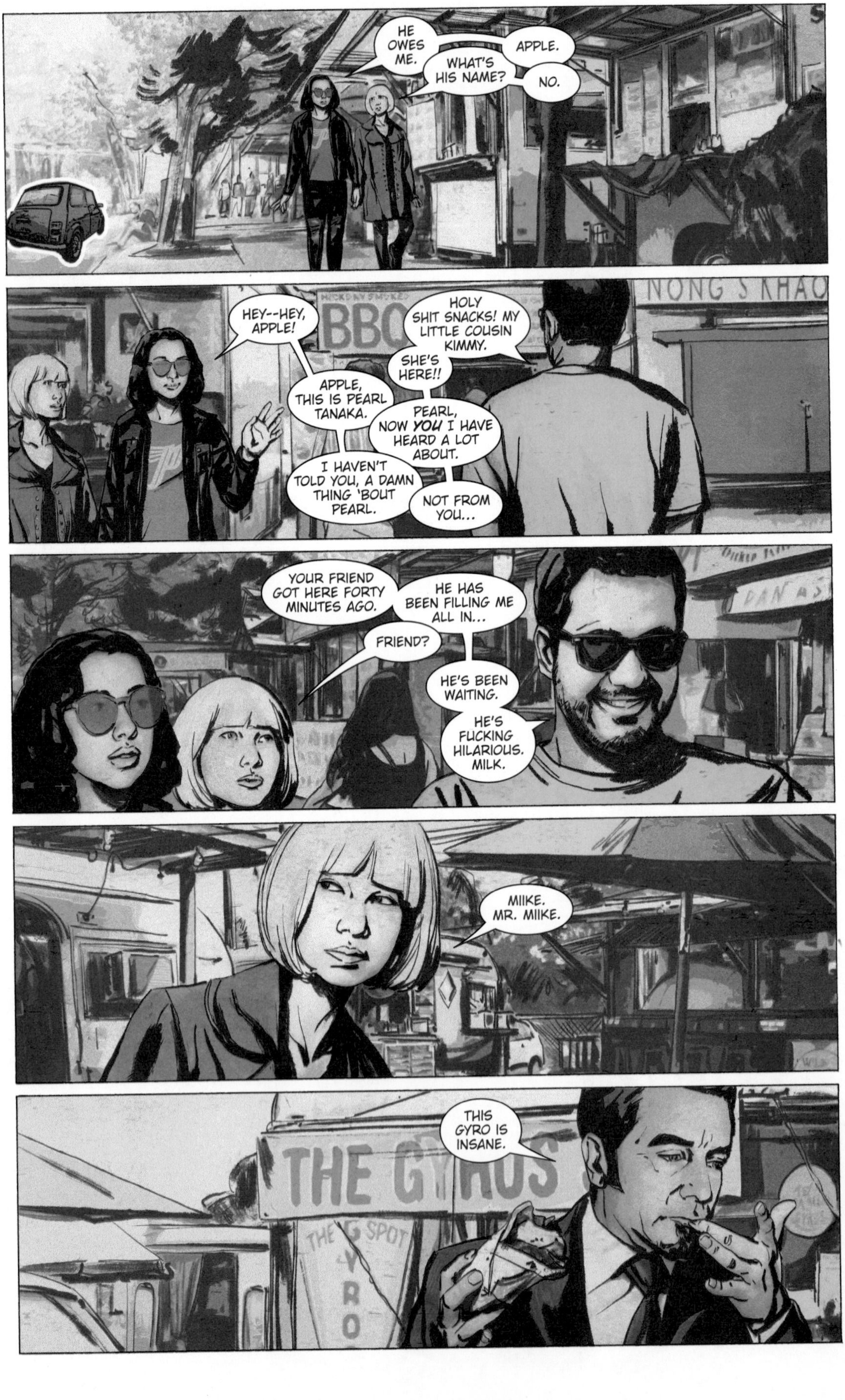
HE OWES ME.
APPLE.
WHAT'S HIS NAME?
NO.
BBQ
NONG S KHAO
HEY--HEY, APPLE!
HOLY SHIT SNACKS! MY LITTLE COUSIN KIMMY.
SHE'S HERE!!
APPLE, THIS IS PEARL TANAKA.
PEARL, NOW *YOU* I HAVE HEARD A LOT ABOUT.
I HAVEN'T TOLD YOU, A DAMN THING 'BOUT PEARL.
NOT FROM YOU...
YOUR FRIEND GOT HERE FORTY MINUTES AGO.
HE HAS BEEN FILLING ME ALL IN...
FRIEND?
HE'S BEEN WAITING.
HE'S FUCKING HILARIOUS. MILK.
MIIKE. MR. MIIKE.
THE GYROS
THIS GYRO IS INSANE.

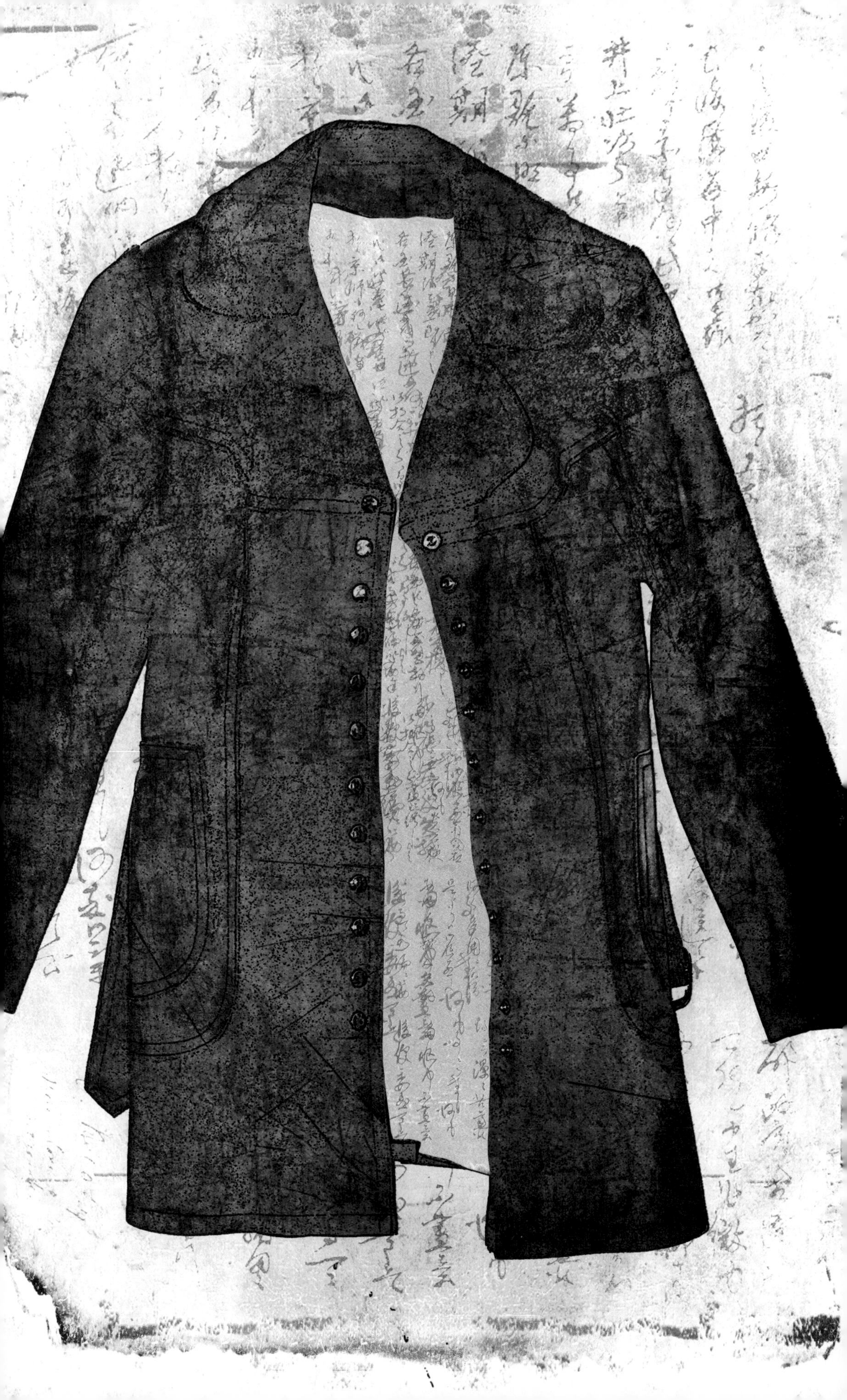

Variant cover art for issue #8
by TULA LOTAY

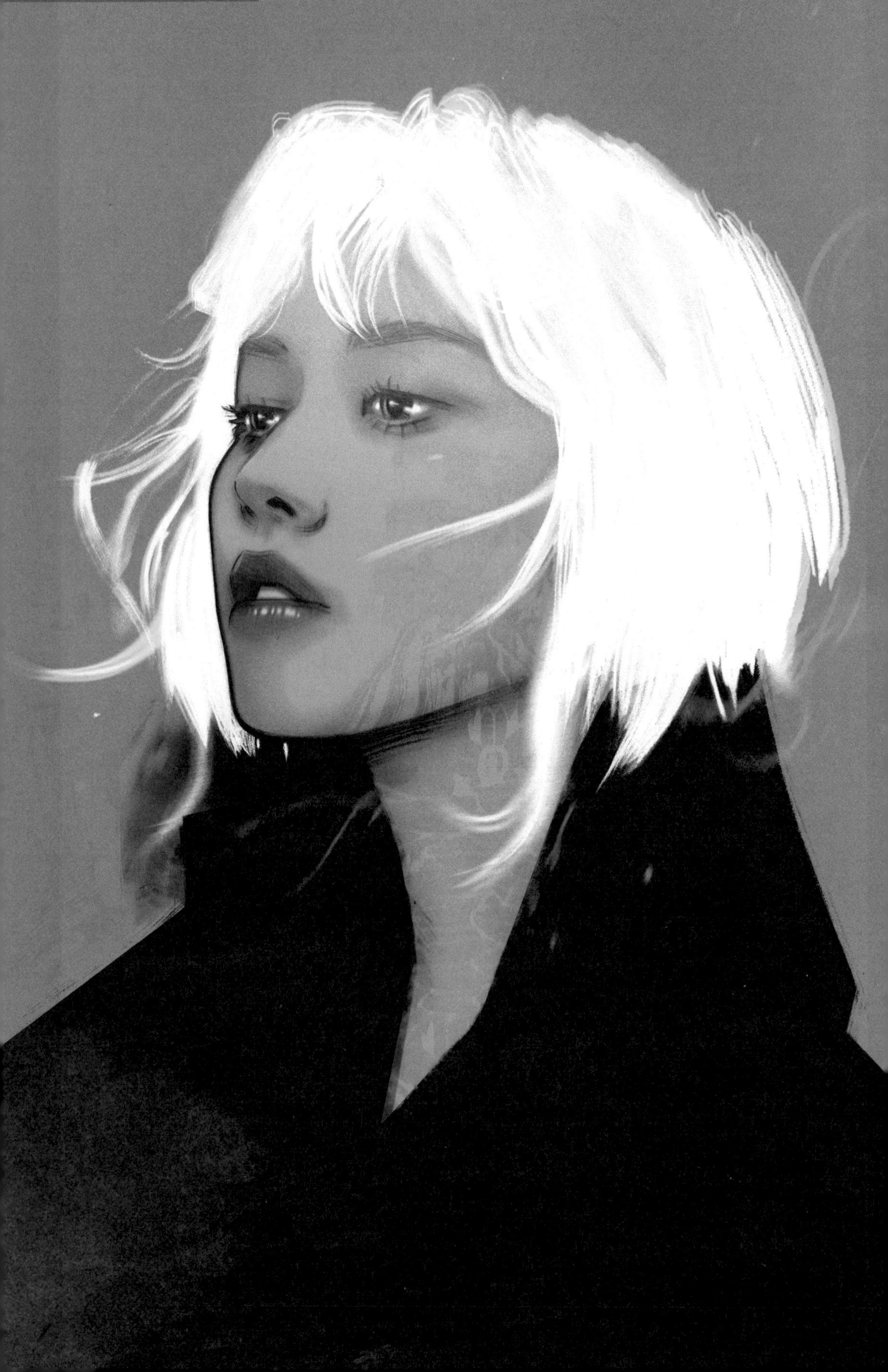

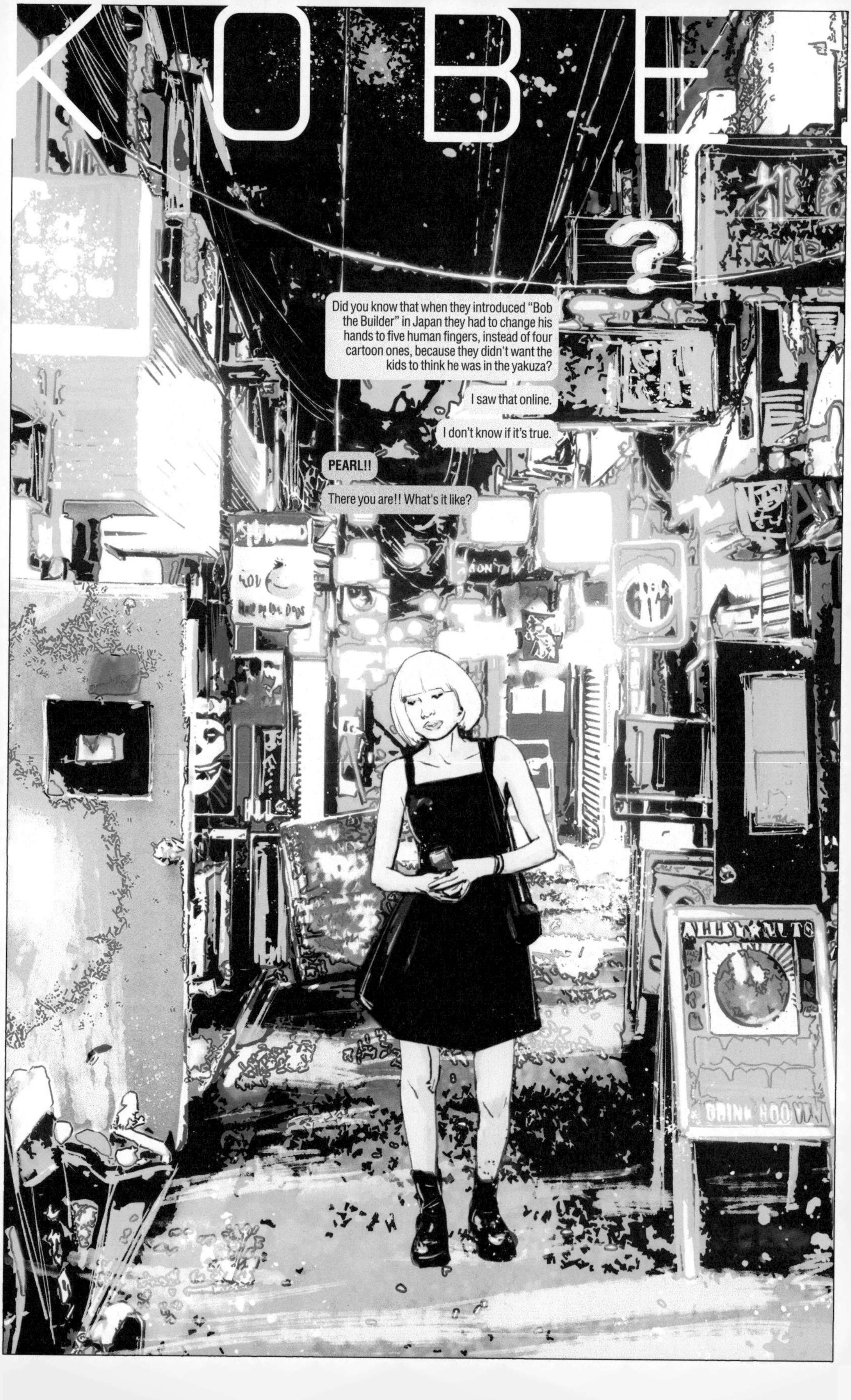
KOBE
Did you know that when they introduced "Bob the Builder" in Japan they had to change his hands to five human fingers, instead of four cartoon ones, because they didn't want the kids to think he was in the yakuza?
I saw that online.
I don't know if it's true.
PEARL!!
There you are!! What's it like?

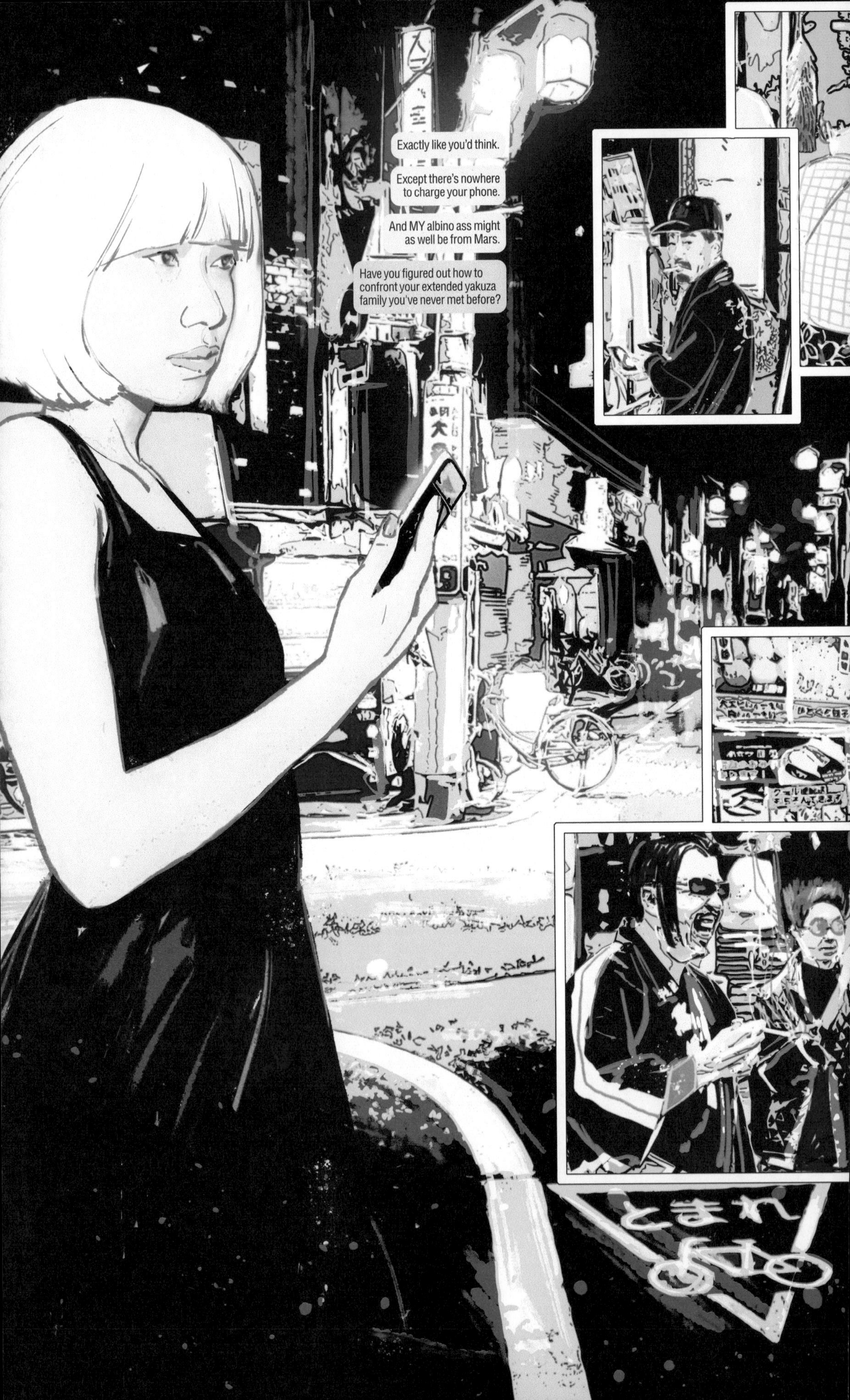

Exactly like you'd think.
Except there's nowhere to charge your phone.
And MY albino ass might as well be from Mars.
Have you figured out how to confront your extended yakuza family you've never met before?
とまれ

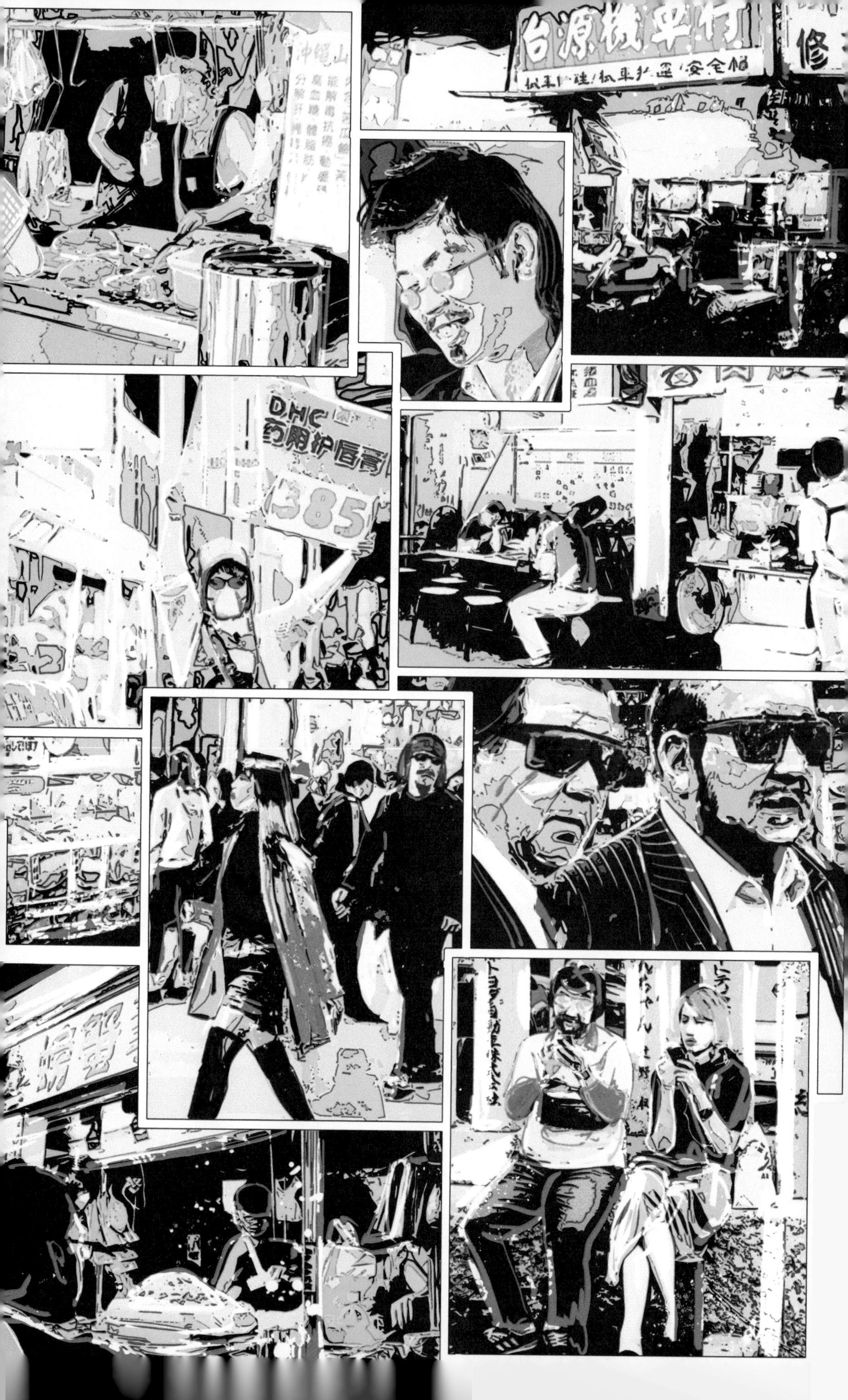

台源機車行
修
DHC
药用护唇膏
385

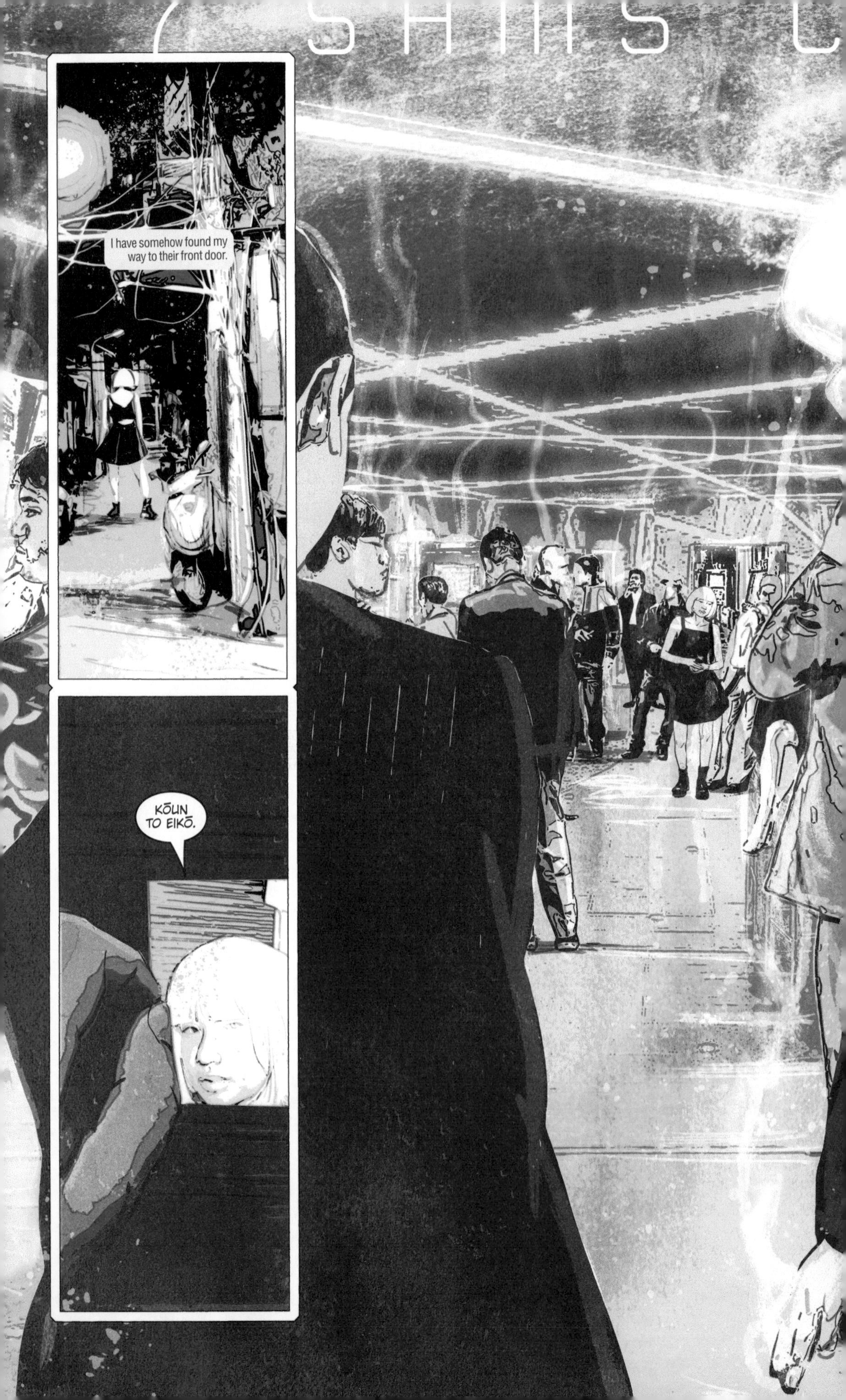
I have somehow found my way to their front door.
KŌUN TO EIKŌ.

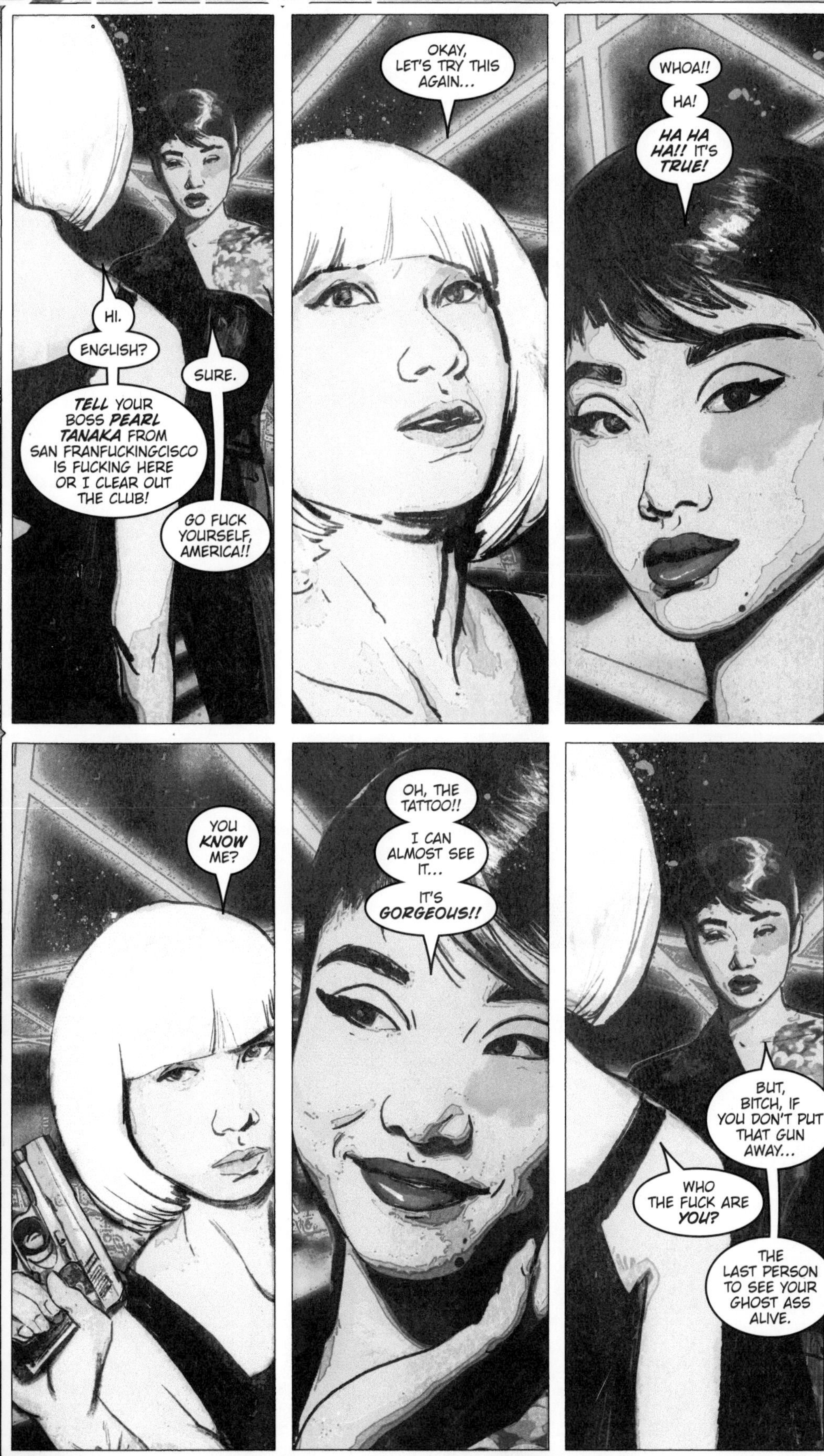
HI.
ENGLISH?
SURE.
TELL YOUR BOSS PEARL TANAKA FROM SAN FRANFUCKINGCISCO IS FUCKING HERE OR I CLEAR OUT THE CLUB!
GO FUCK YOURSELF, AMERICA!!
OKAY, LET'S TRY THIS AGAIN...
WHOA!!
HA!
HA HA HA!! IT'S TRUE!
YOU KNOW ME?
OH, THE TATTOO!!
I CAN ALMOST SEE IT...
IT'S GORGEOUS!!
BUT, BITCH, IF YOU DON'T PUT THAT GUN AWAY...
WHO THE FUCK ARE YOU?
THE LAST PERSON TO SEE YOUR GHOST ASS ALIVE.

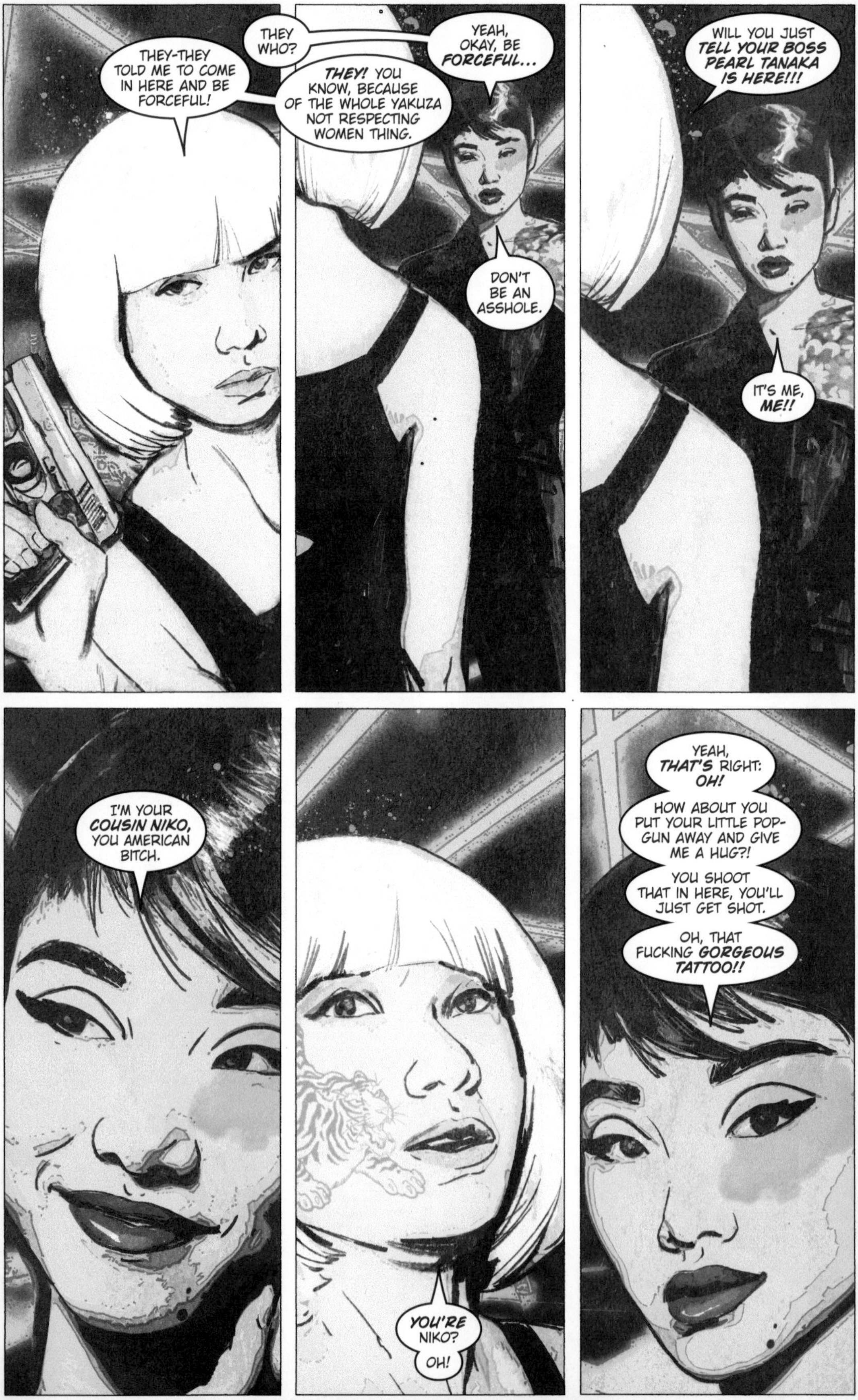
THEY-THEY TOLD ME TO COME IN HERE AND BE FORCEFUL!
THEY WHO?
YEAH, OKAY, BE FORCEFUL...
THEY! YOU KNOW, BECAUSE OF THE WHOLE YAKUZA NOT RESPECTING WOMEN THING.
DON'T BE AN ASSHOLE.
WILL YOU JUST TELL YOUR BOSS PEARL TANAKA IS HERE!!!
IT'S ME, ME!!
I'M YOUR COUSIN NIKO, YOU AMERICAN BITCH.
YOU'RE NIKO?
OH!
YEAH, THAT'S RIGHT: OH!
HOW ABOUT YOU PUT YOUR LITTLE POP-GUN AWAY AND GIVE ME A HUG?!
YOU SHOOT THAT IN HERE, YOU'LL JUST GET SHOT.
OH, THAT FUCKING GORGEOUS TATTOO!!

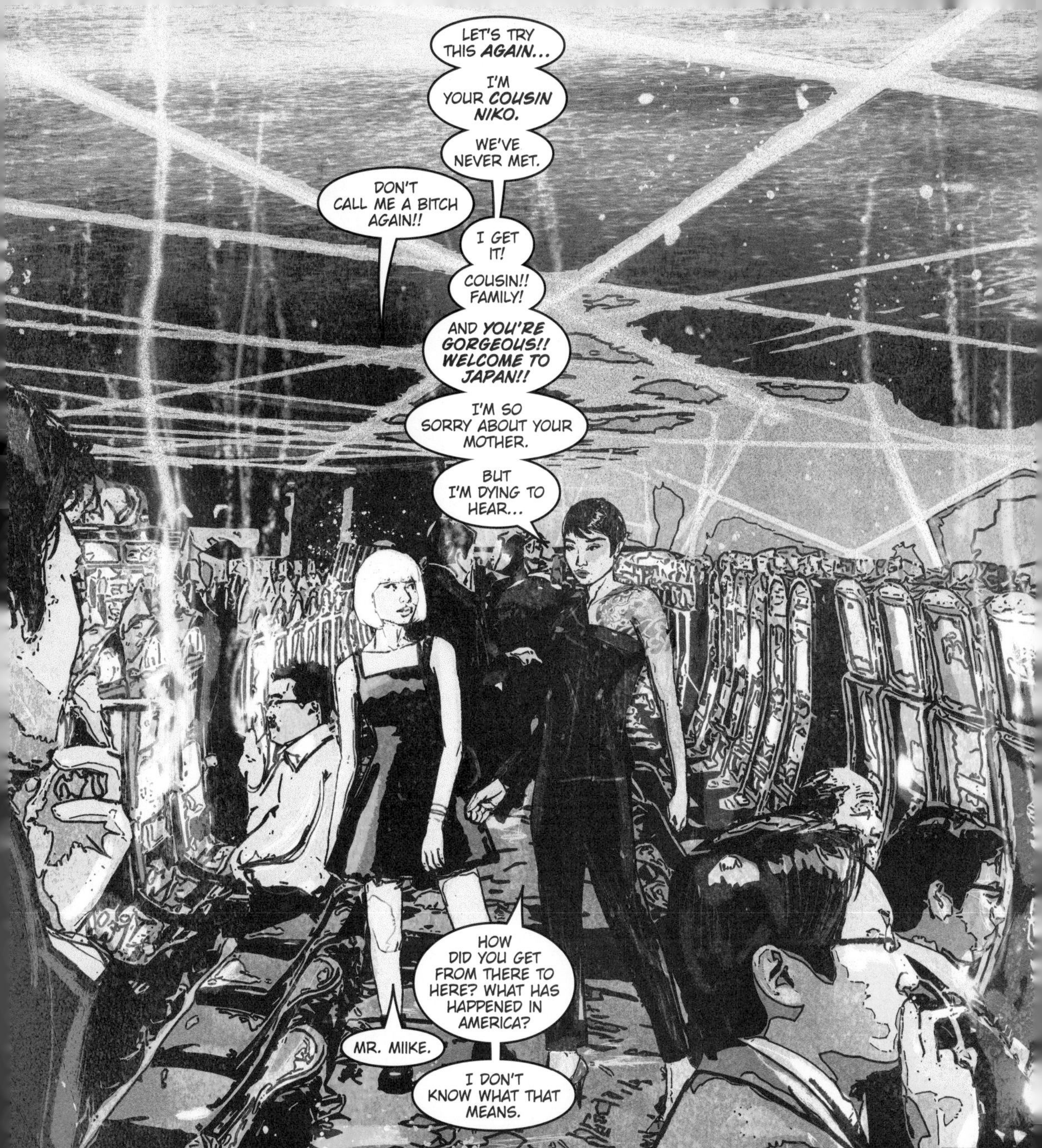
LET'S TRY THIS AGAIN...
I'M YOUR COUSIN NIKO.
WE'VE NEVER MET.
DON'T CALL ME A BITCH AGAIN!!
I GET IT!
COUSIN!! FAMILY!
AND YOU'RE GORGEOUS!! WELCOME TO JAPAN!!
I'M SO SORRY ABOUT YOUR MOTHER.
BUT I'M DYING TO HEAR...
HOW DID YOU GET FROM THERE TO HERE? WHAT HAS HAPPENED IN AMERICA?
MR. MIIKE.
I DON'T KNOW WHAT THAT MEANS.

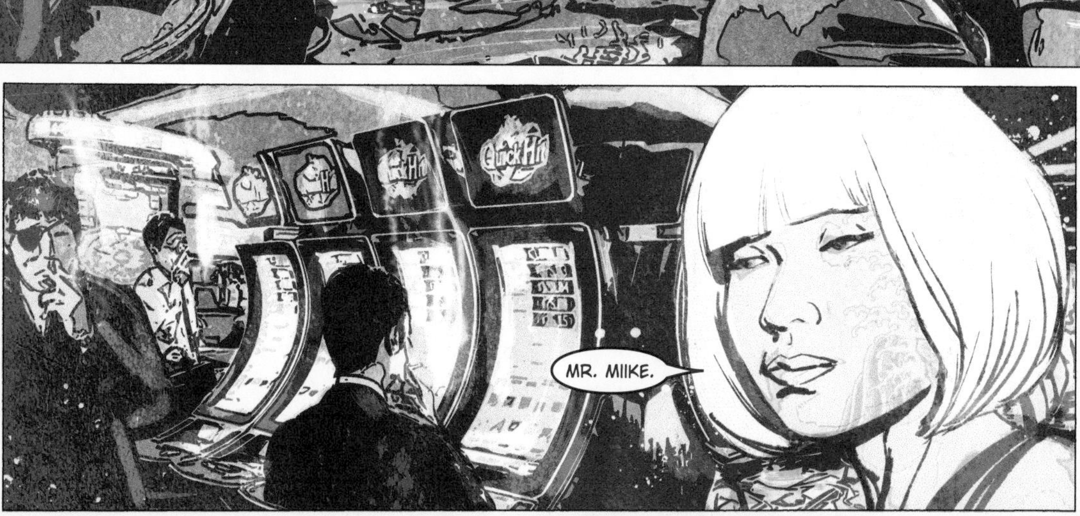
MR. MIIKE.

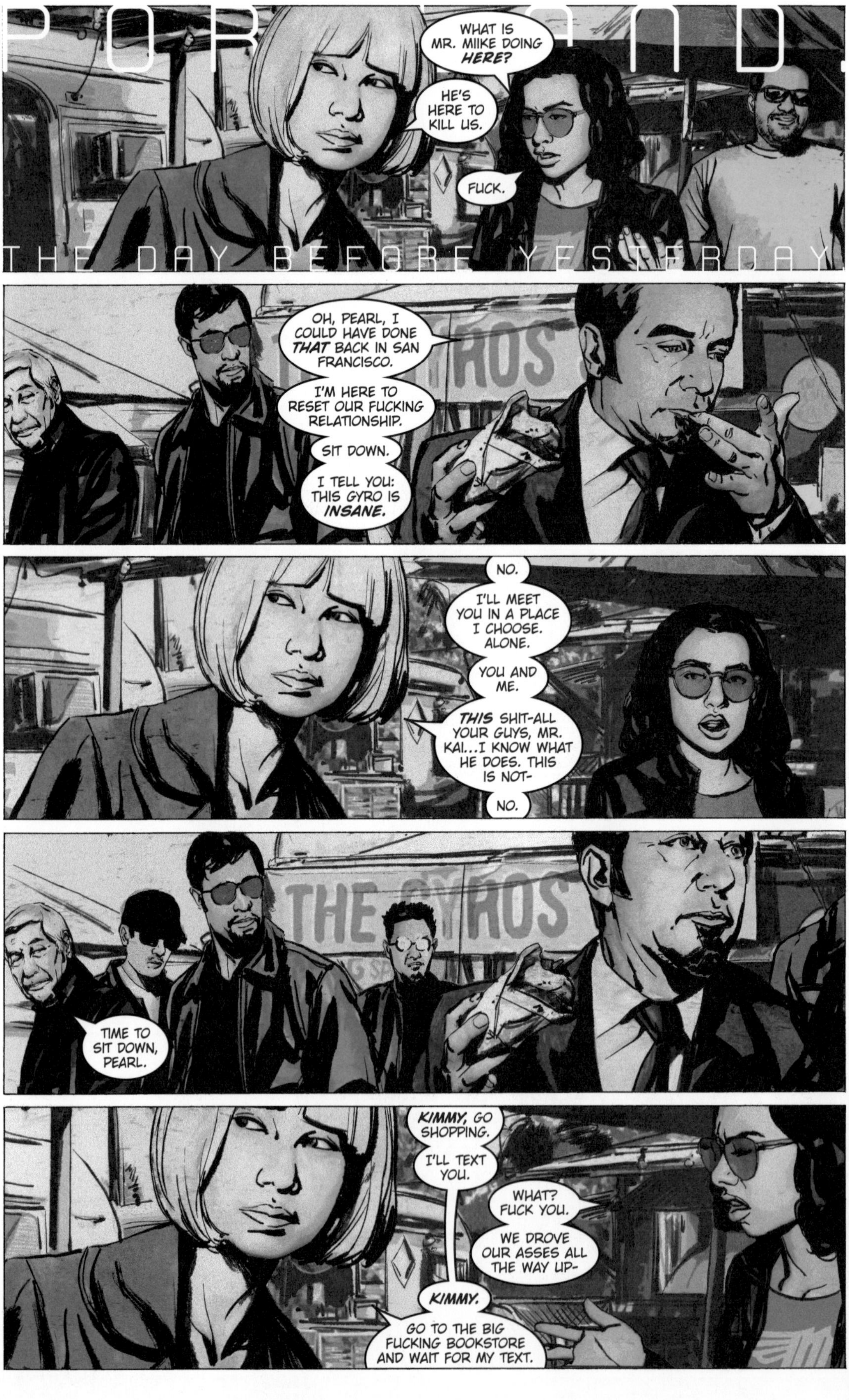
PORTLAND.
WHAT IS MR. MIIKE DOING HERE?
HE'S HERE TO KILL US.
FUCK.
THE DAY BEFORE YESTERDAY
OH, PEARL, I COULD HAVE DONE THAT BACK IN SAN FRANCISCO.
I'M HERE TO RESET OUR FUCKING RELATIONSHIP.
SIT DOWN.
I TELL YOU: THIS GYRO IS INSANE.
NO.
I'LL MEET YOU IN A PLACE I CHOOSE. ALONE.
YOU AND ME.
THIS SHIT-ALL YOUR GUYS, MR. KAI...I KNOW WHAT HE DOES. THIS IS NOT-
NO.
THE GYROS
TIME TO SIT DOWN, PEARL.
KIMMY, GO SHOPPING.
I'LL TEXT YOU.
WHAT? FUCK YOU.
WE DROVE OUR ASSES ALL THE WAY UP-
KIMMY.
GO TO THE BIG FUCKING BOOKSTORE AND WAIT FOR MY TEXT.

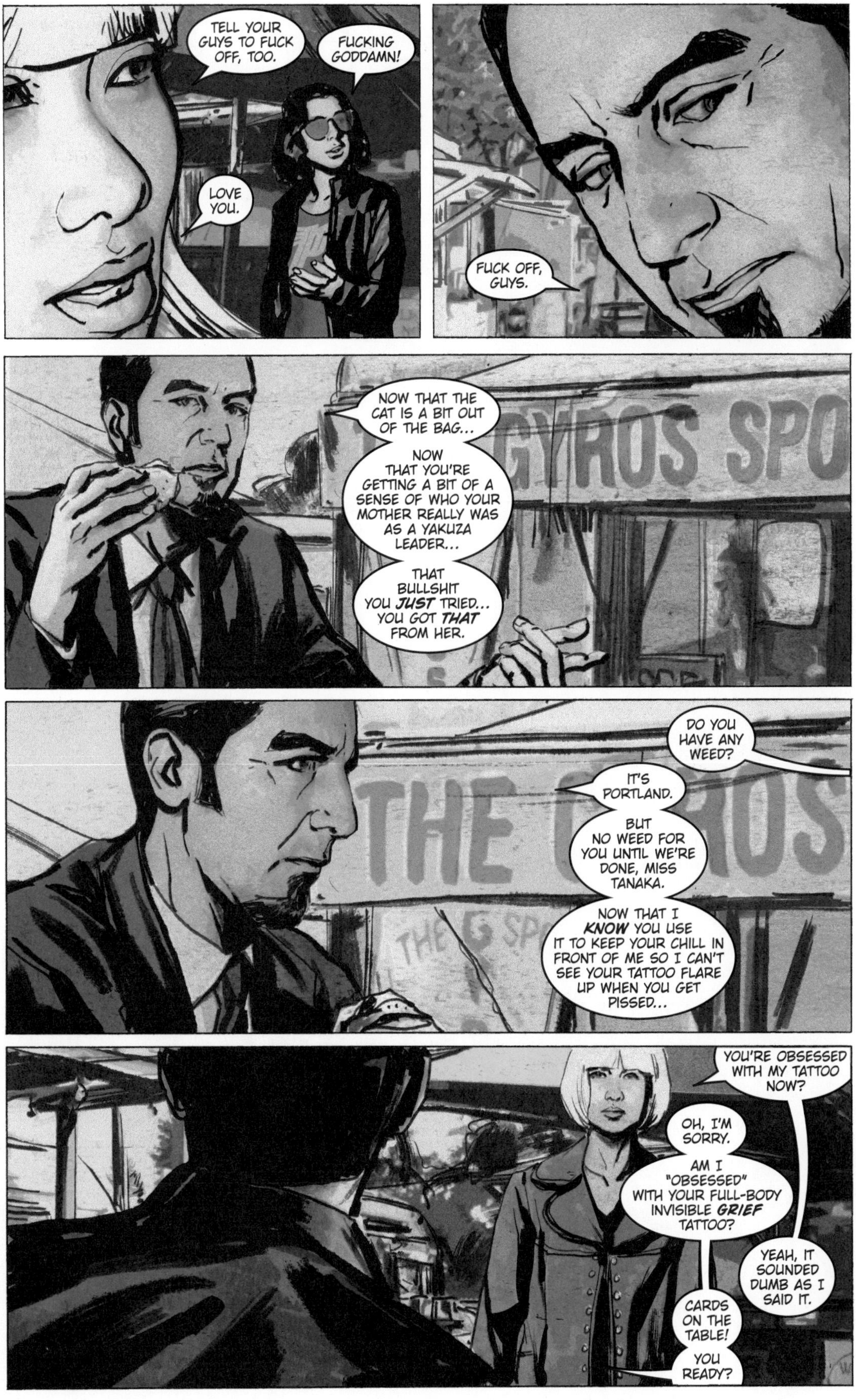
TELL YOUR GUYS TO FUCK OFF, TOO.
FUCKING GODDAMN!
LOVE YOU.
FUCK OFF, GUYS.
NOW THAT THE CAT IS A BIT OUT OF THE BAG...
NOW THAT YOU'RE GETTING A BIT OF A SENSE OF WHO YOUR MOTHER REALLY WAS AS A YAKUZA LEADER...
THAT BULLSHIT YOU *JUST* TRIED... YOU GOT *THAT* FROM HER.
GYROS SPO
DO YOU HAVE ANY WEED?
IT'S PORTLAND.
BUT NO WEED FOR YOU UNTIL WE'RE DONE, MISS TANAKA.
NOW THAT I *KNOW* YOU USE IT TO KEEP YOUR CHILL IN FRONT OF ME SO I CAN'T SEE YOUR TATTOO FLARE UP WHEN YOU GET PISSED...
YOU'RE OBSESSED WITH MY TATTOO NOW?
OH, I'M SORRY.
AM I "OBSESSED" WITH YOUR FULL-BODY INVISIBLE *GRIEF* TATTOO?
YEAH, IT SOUNDED DUMB AS I SAID IT.
CARDS ON THE TABLE!
YOU READY?

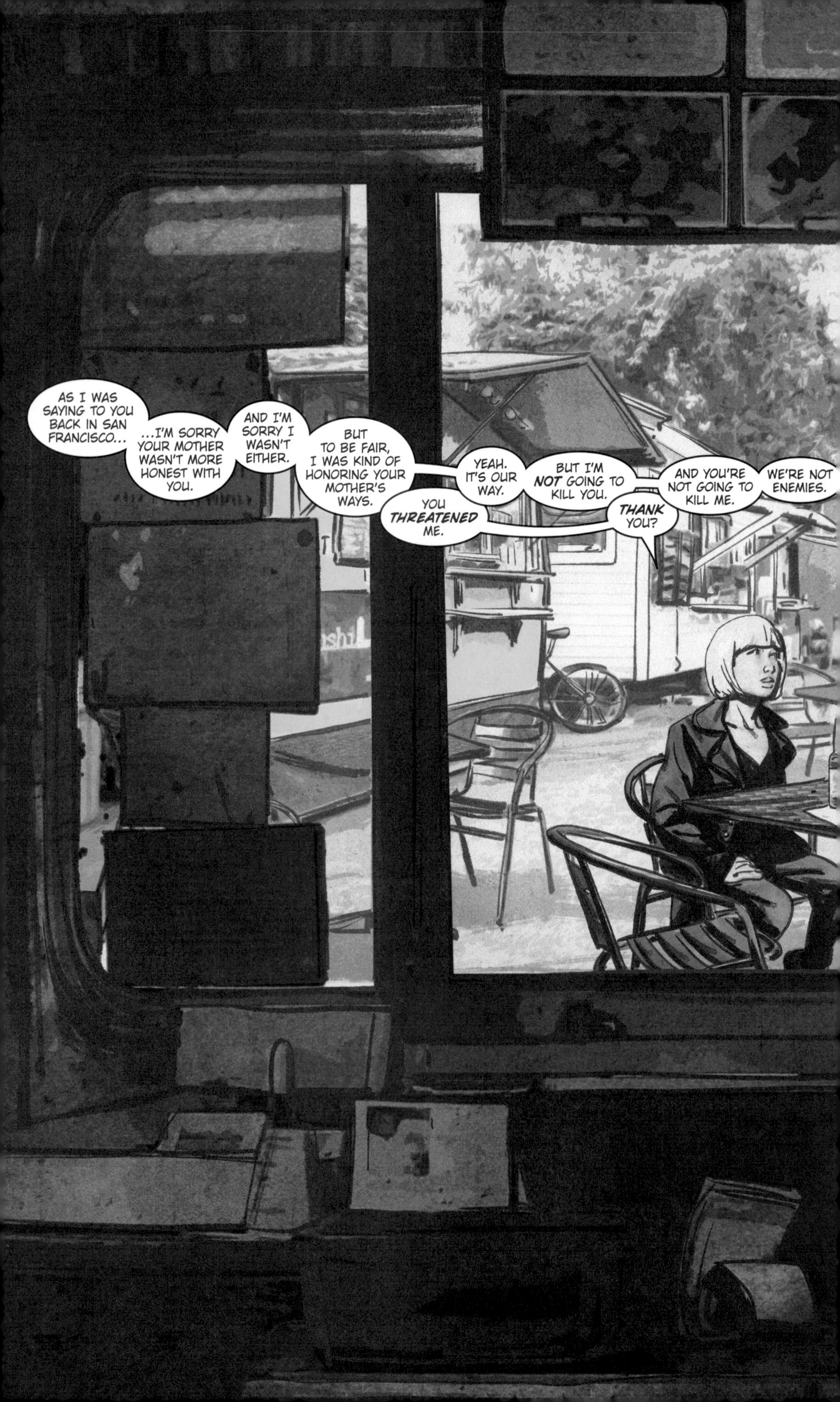
AS I WAS SAYING TO YOU BACK IN SAN FRANCISCO...
...I'M SORRY YOUR MOTHER WASN'T MORE HONEST WITH YOU.
AND I'M SORRY I WASN'T EITHER.
BUT TO BE FAIR, I WAS KIND OF HONORING YOUR MOTHER'S WAYS.
YOU *THREATENED* ME.
YEAH. IT'S OUR WAY.
BUT I'M *NOT* GOING TO KILL YOU.
THANK YOU?
AND YOU'RE NOT GOING TO KILL ME.
WE'RE NOT ENEMIES.

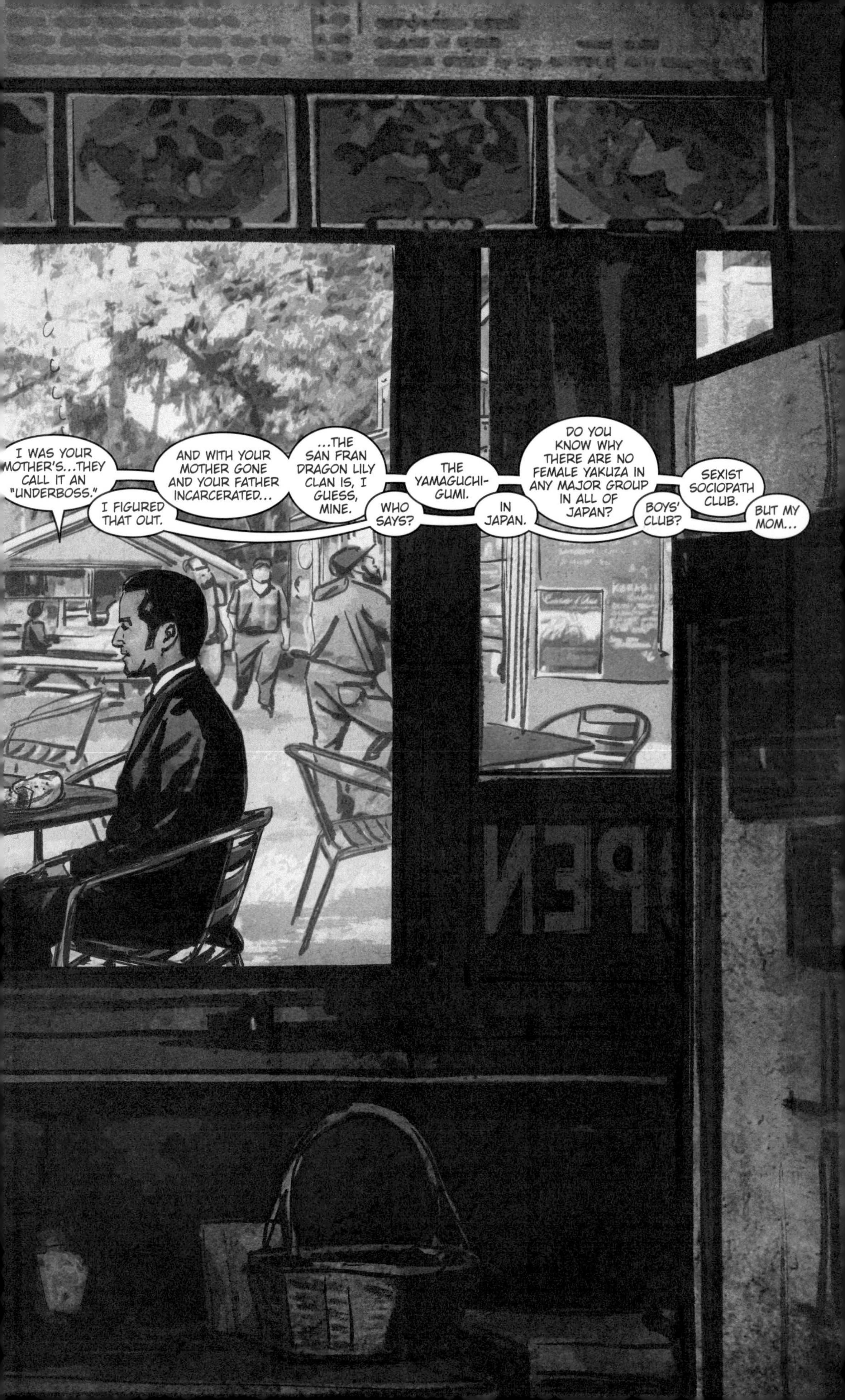
I WAS YOUR MOTHER'S...THEY CALL IT AN "UNDERBOSS."
I FIGURED THAT OUT.
AND WITH YOUR MOTHER GONE AND YOUR FATHER INCARCERATED...
...THE SAN FRAN DRAGON LILY CLAN IS, I GUESS, MINE.
WHO SAYS?
THE YAMAGUCHI-GUMI.
IN JAPAN.
DO YOU KNOW WHY THERE ARE NO FEMALE YAKUZA IN ANY MAJOR GROUP IN ALL OF JAPAN?
BOYS' CLUB?
SEXIST SOCIOPATH CLUB.
BUT MY MOM...

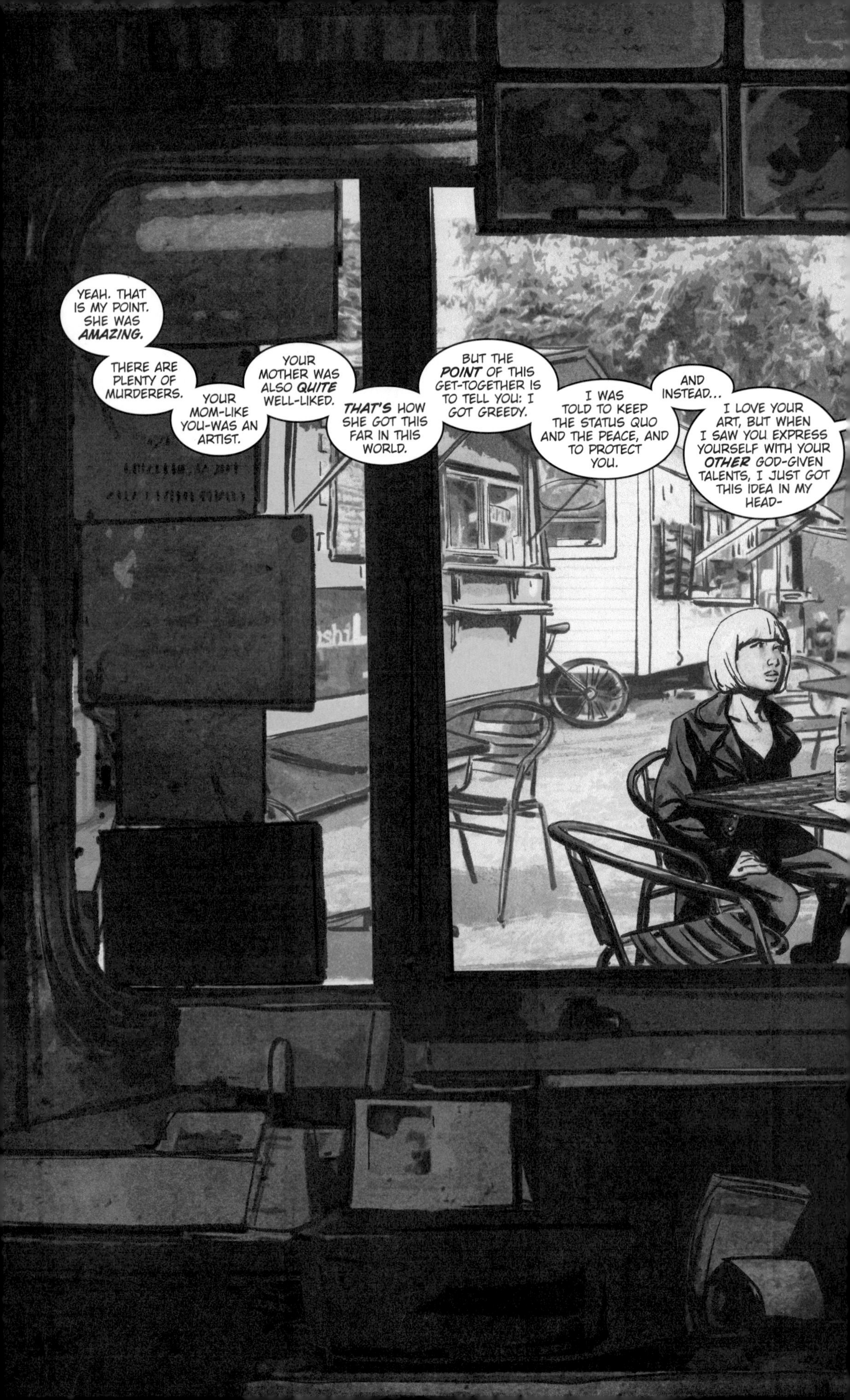

YEAH. THAT IS MY POINT. SHE WAS **AMAZING.**
THERE ARE PLENTY OF MURDERERS.
YOUR MOM-LIKE YOU-WAS AN ARTIST.
YOUR MOTHER WAS ALSO **QUITE** WELL-LIKED.
THAT'S HOW SHE GOT THIS FAR IN THIS WORLD.
BUT THE **POINT** OF THIS GET-TOGETHER IS TO TELL YOU: I GOT GREEDY.
I WAS TOLD TO KEEP THE STATUS QUO AND THE PEACE, AND TO PROTECT YOU.
AND INSTEAD...
I LOVE YOUR ART, BUT WHEN I SAW YOU EXPRESS YOURSELF WITH YOUR **OTHER** GOD-GIVEN TALENTS, I JUST GOT THIS IDEA IN MY HEAD-

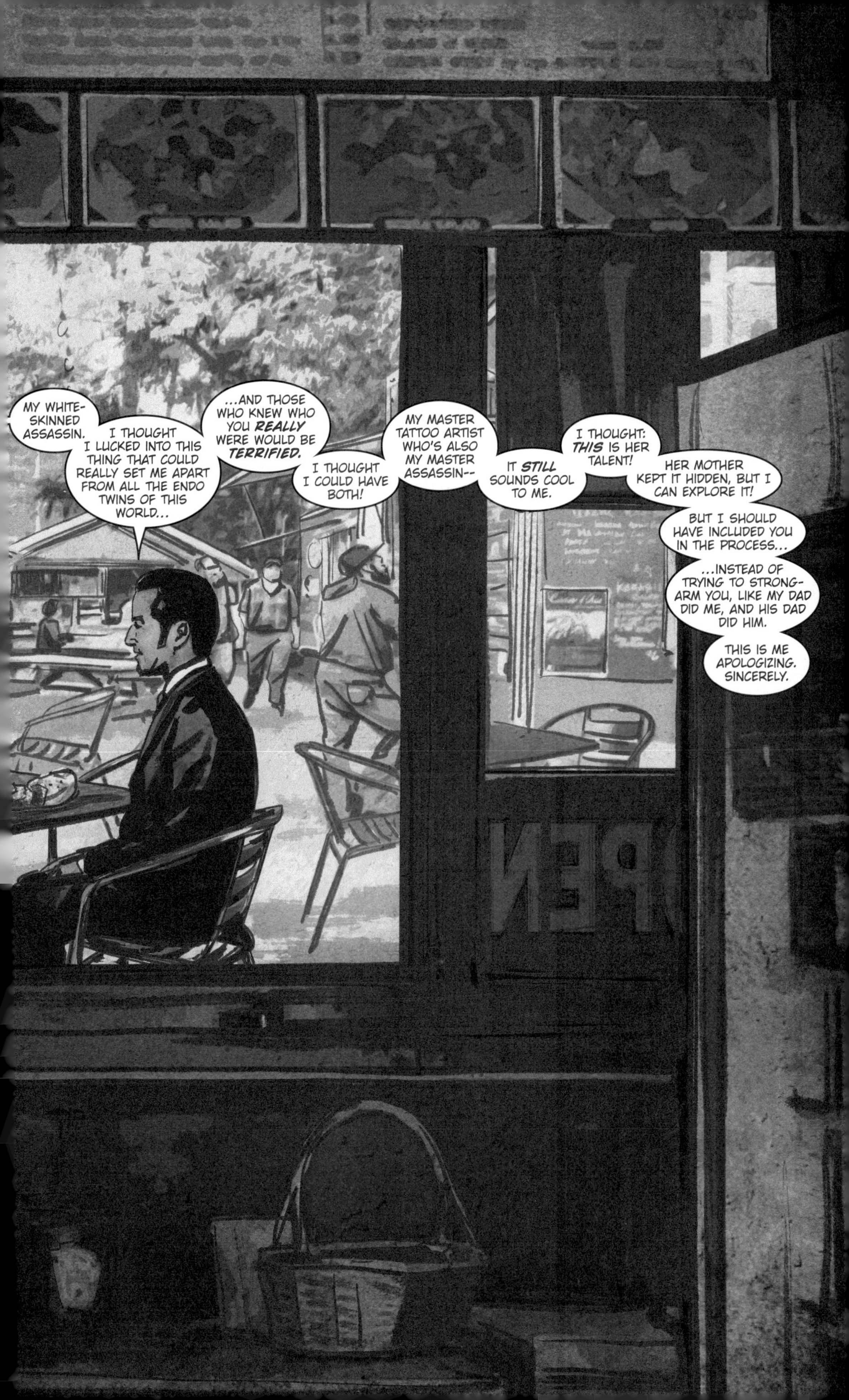
MY WHITE-SKINNED ASSASSIN.
I THOUGHT I LUCKED INTO THIS THING THAT COULD REALLY SET ME APART FROM ALL THE ENDO TWINS OF THIS WORLD...
...AND THOSE WHO KNEW WHO YOU **REALLY** WERE WOULD BE ***TERRIFIED.***
I THOUGHT I COULD HAVE BOTH!
MY MASTER TATTOO ARTIST WHO'S ALSO MY MASTER ASSASSIN--
IT ***STILL*** SOUNDS COOL TO ME.
I THOUGHT: ***THIS*** IS HER TALENT!
HER MOTHER KEPT IT HIDDEN, BUT I CAN EXPLORE IT!
BUT I SHOULD HAVE INCLUDED YOU IN THE PROCESS...
...INSTEAD OF TRYING TO STRONG-ARM YOU, LIKE MY DAD DID ME, AND HIS DAD DID HIM.
THIS IS ME APOLOGIZING. SINCERELY.

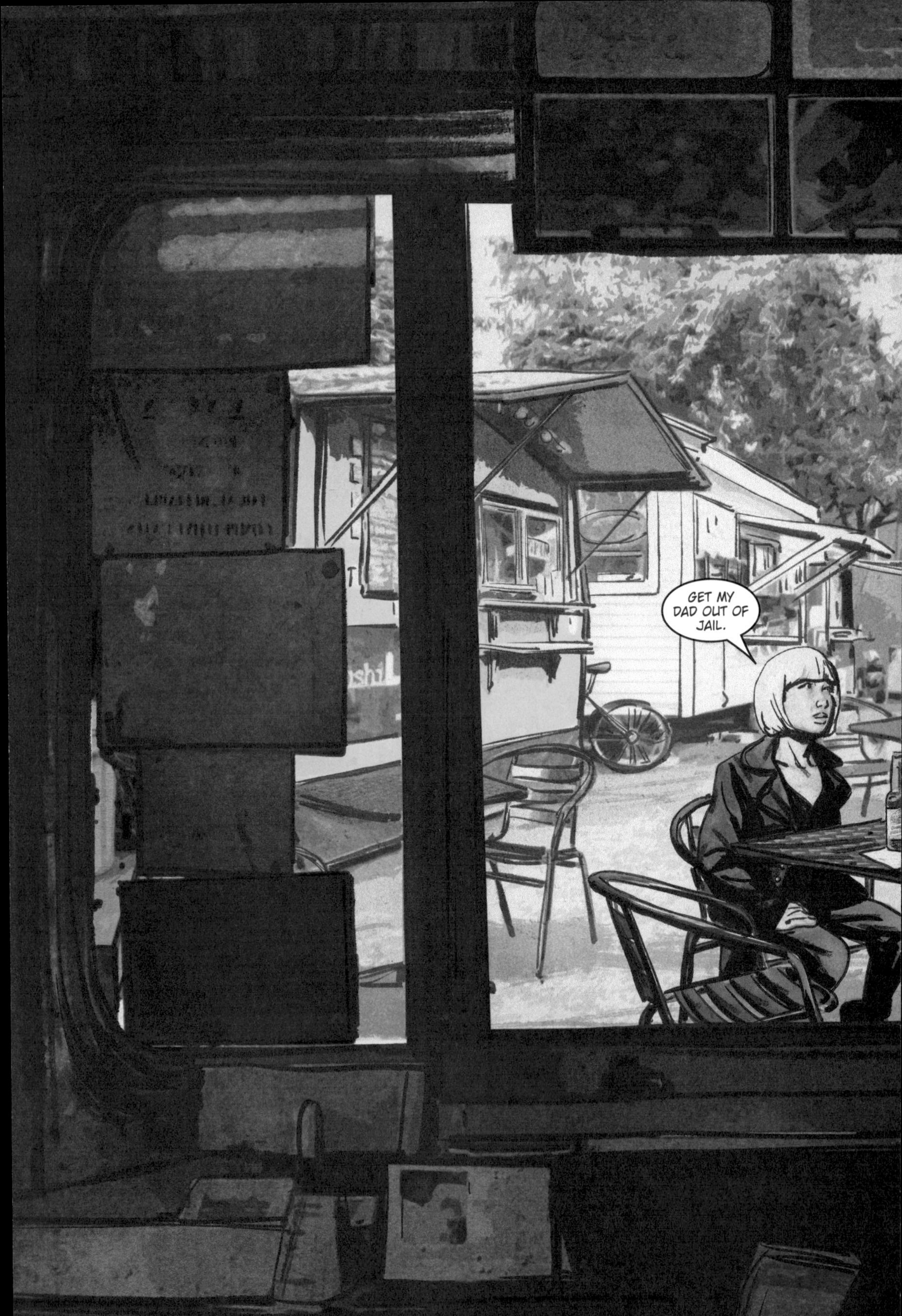
GET MY DAD OUT OF JAIL.

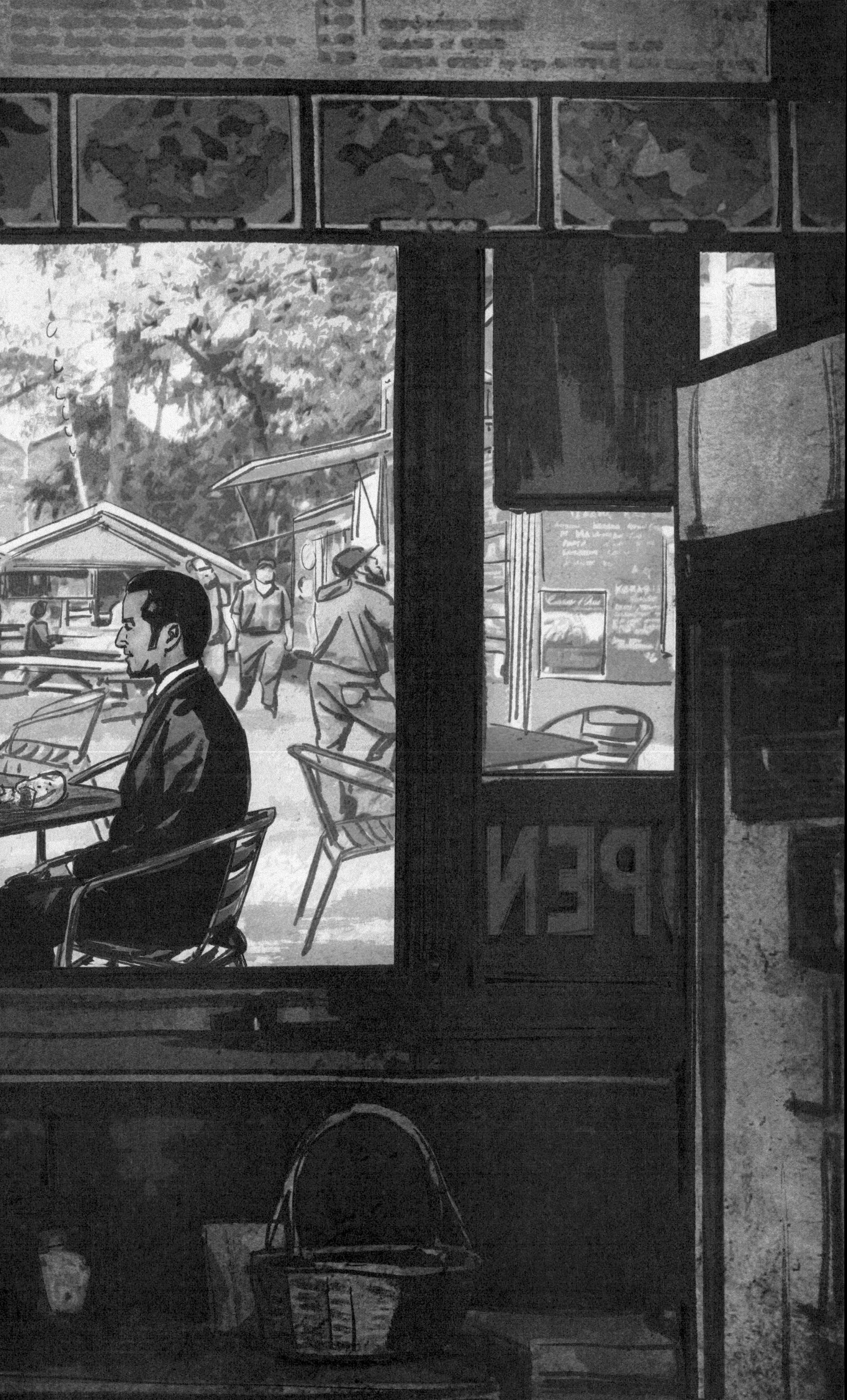

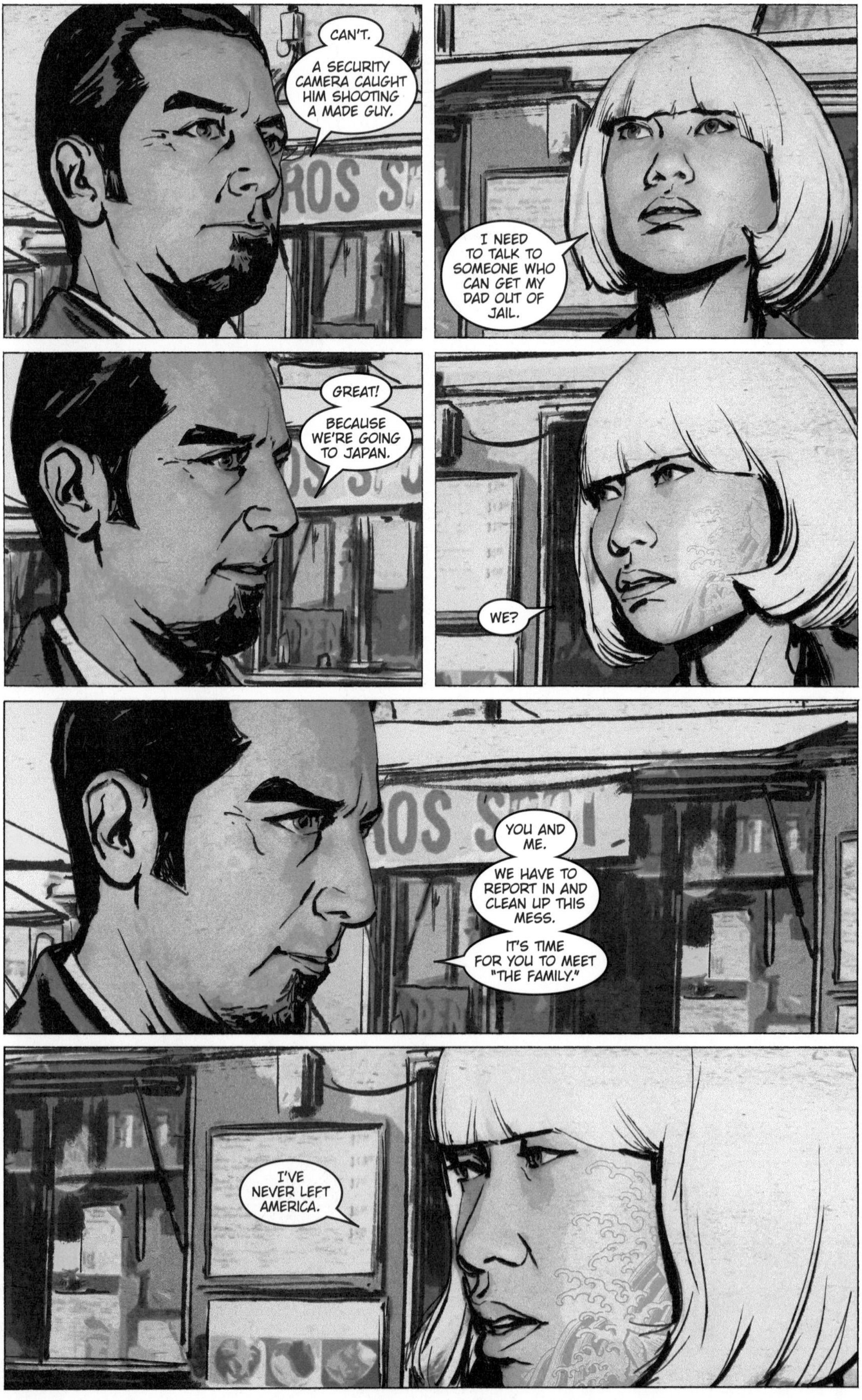
CAN'T.
A SECURITY CAMERA CAUGHT HIM SHOOTING A MADE GUY.
I NEED TO TALK TO SOMEONE WHO CAN GET MY DAD OUT OF JAIL.
GREAT!
BECAUSE WE'RE GOING TO JAPAN.
WE?
YOU AND ME.
WE HAVE TO REPORT IN AND CLEAN UP THIS MESS.
IT'S TIME FOR YOU TO MEET "THE FAMILY."
I'VE NEVER LEFT AMERICA.

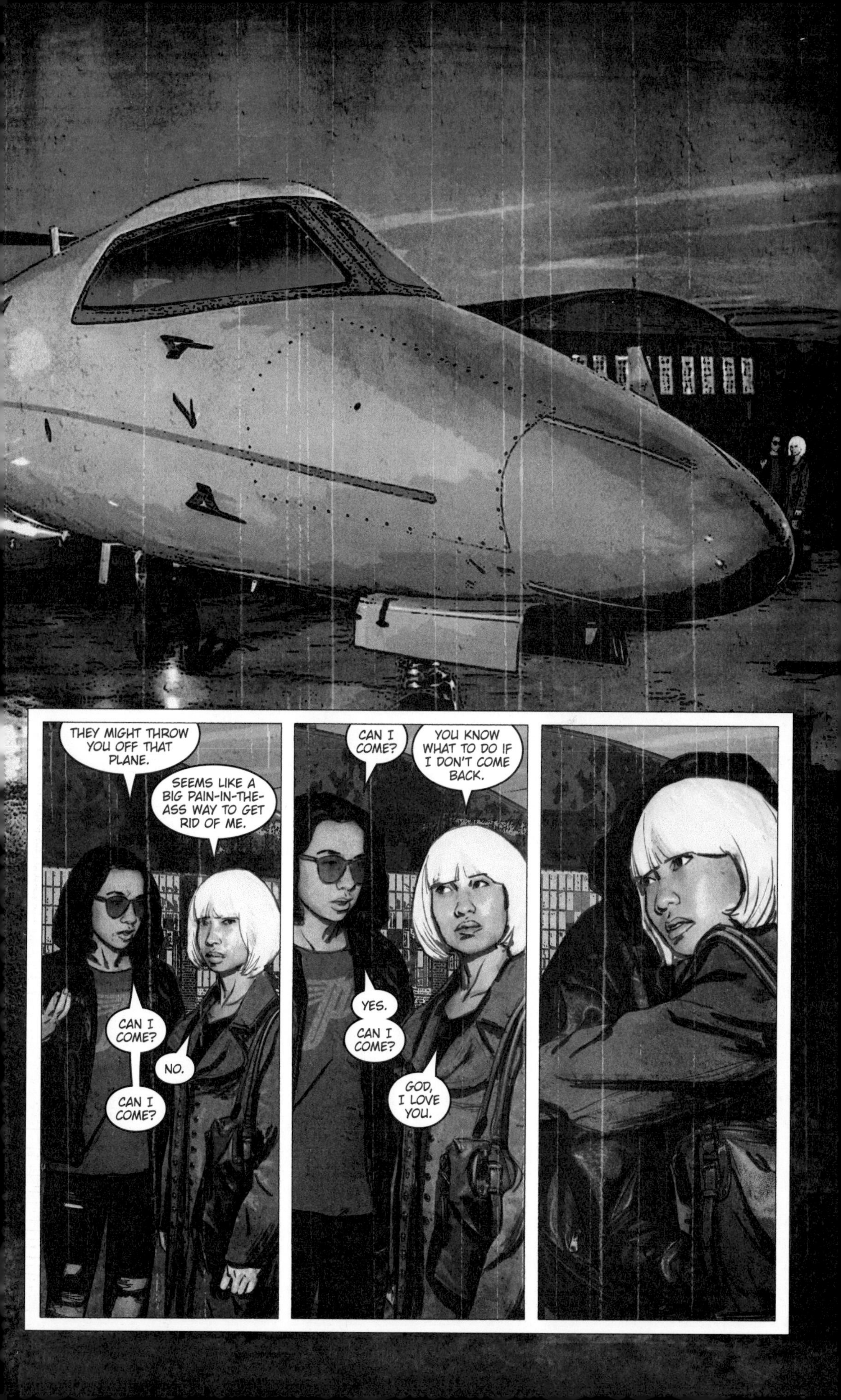
THEY MIGHT THROW YOU OFF THAT PLANE.
SEEMS LIKE A BIG PAIN-IN-THE-ASS WAY TO GET RID OF ME.
CAN I COME?
NO.
CAN I COME?
CAN I COME?
YOU KNOW WHAT TO DO IF I DON'T COME BACK.
YES.
CAN I COME?
GOD, I LOVE YOU.

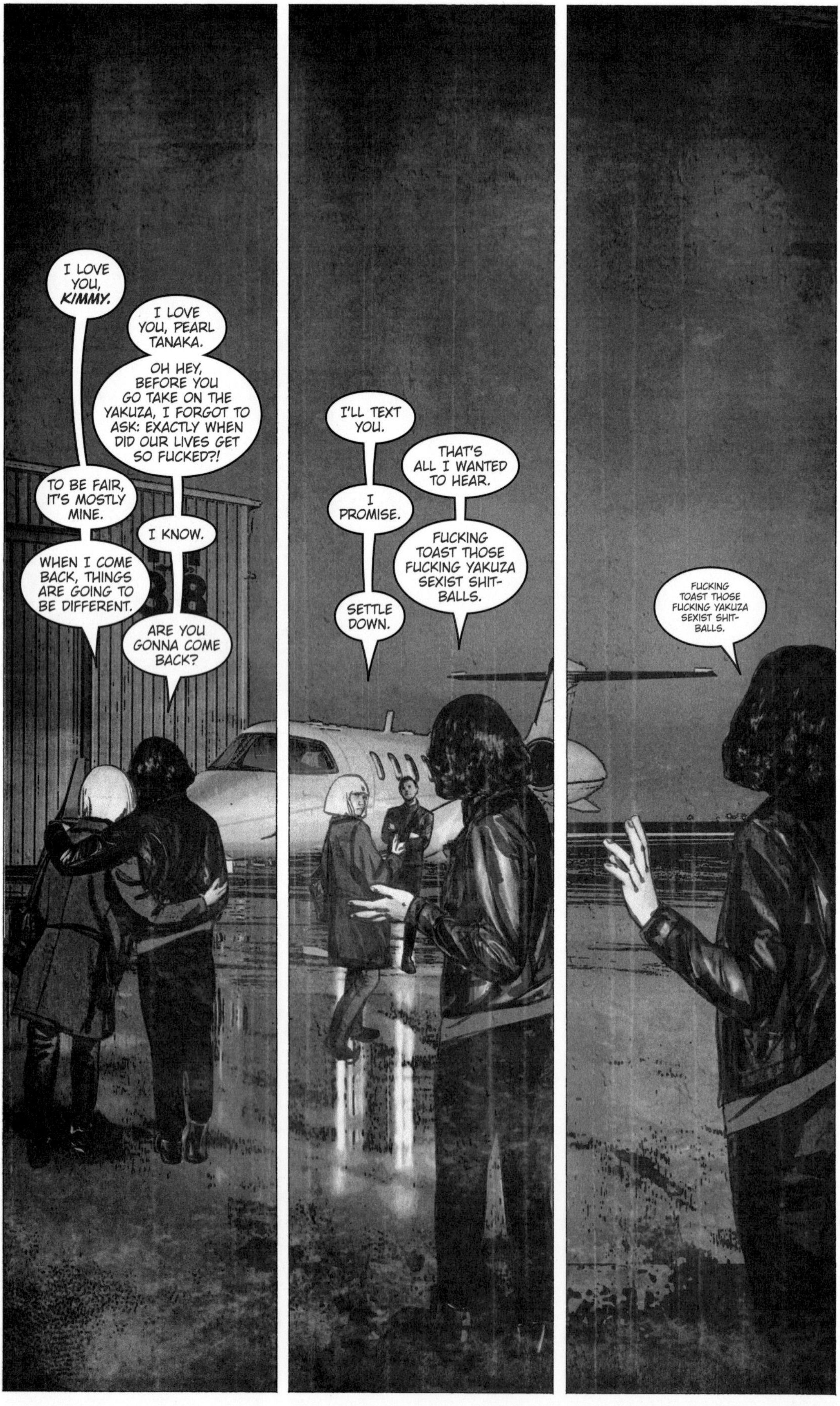
I LOVE YOU, *KIMMY.*
I LOVE YOU, PEARL TANAKA.
OH HEY, BEFORE YOU GO TAKE ON THE YAKUZA, I FORGOT TO ASK: EXACTLY WHEN DID OUR LIVES GET SO FUCKED?!
TO BE FAIR, IT'S MOSTLY MINE.
I KNOW.
WHEN I COME BACK, THINGS ARE GOING TO BE DIFFERENT.
ARE YOU GONNA COME BACK?
I'LL TEXT YOU.
I PROMISE.
SETTLE DOWN.
THAT'S ALL I WANTED TO HEAR.
FUCKING TOAST THOSE FUCKING YAKUZA SEXIST SHIT-BALLS.
FUCKING TOAST THOSE FUCKING YAKUZA SEXIST SHIT-BALLS.

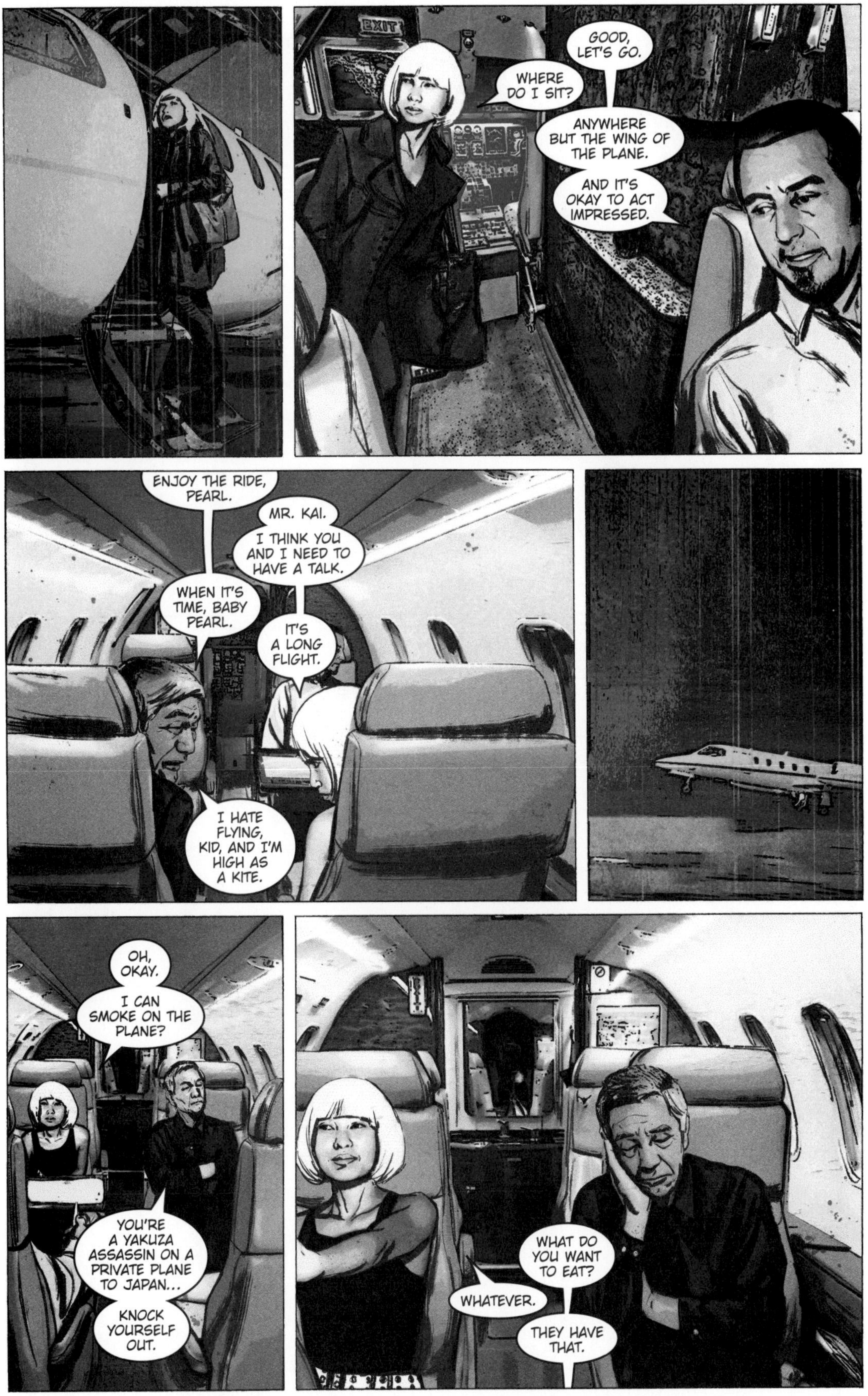
WHERE DO I SIT?
GOOD, LET'S GO.
ANYWHERE BUT THE WING OF THE PLANE.
AND IT'S OKAY TO ACT IMPRESSED.
ENJOY THE RIDE, PEARL.
MR. KAI.
I THINK YOU AND I NEED TO HAVE A TALK.
WHEN IT'S TIME, BABY PEARL.
IT'S A LONG FLIGHT.
I HATE FLYING, KID, AND I'M HIGH AS A KITE.
OH, OKAY.
I CAN SMOKE ON THE PLANE?
YOU'RE A YAKUZA ASSASSIN ON A PRIVATE PLANE TO JAPAN...
KNOCK YOURSELF OUT.
WHAT DO YOU WANT TO EAT?
WHATEVER.
THEY HAVE THAT.

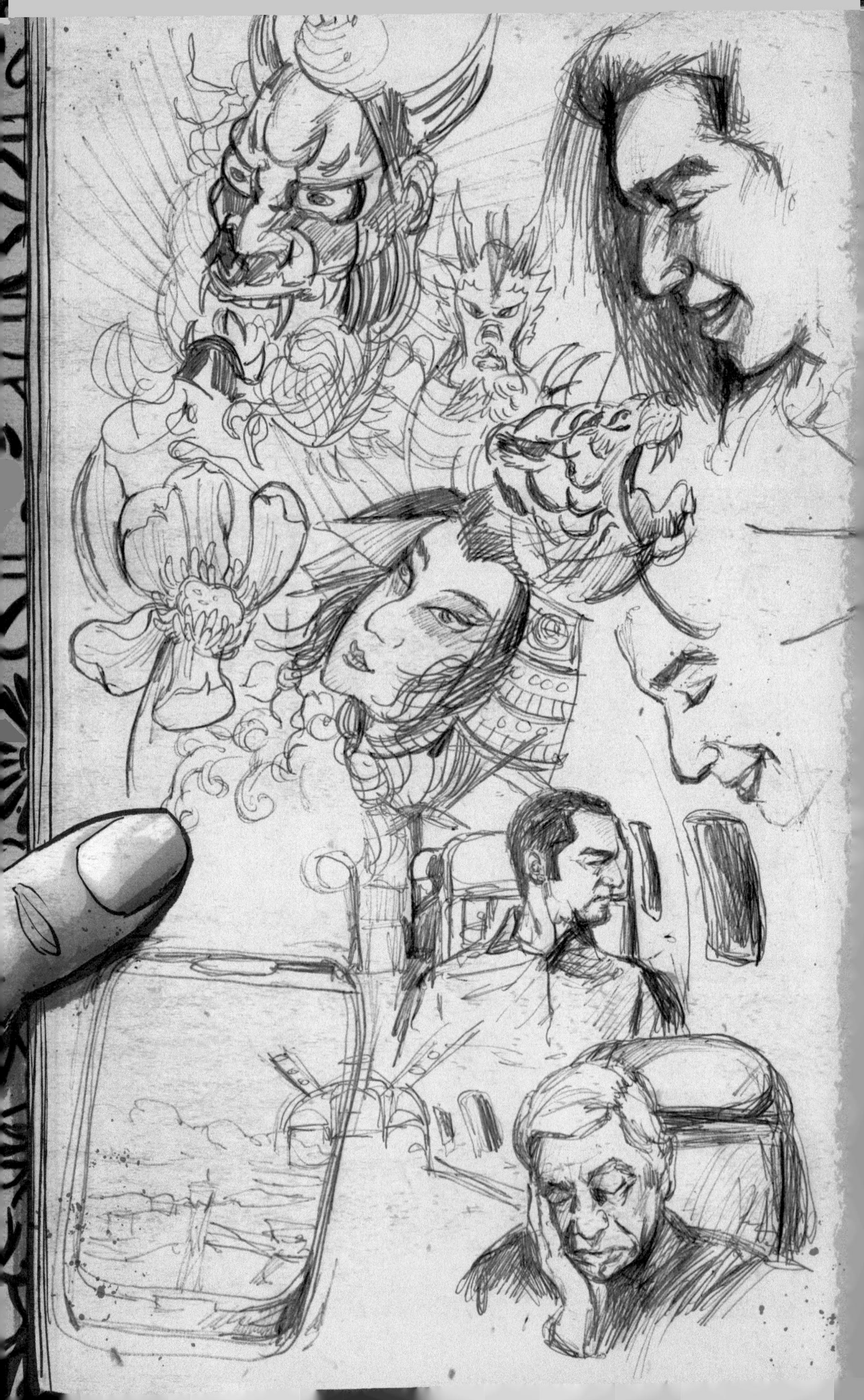

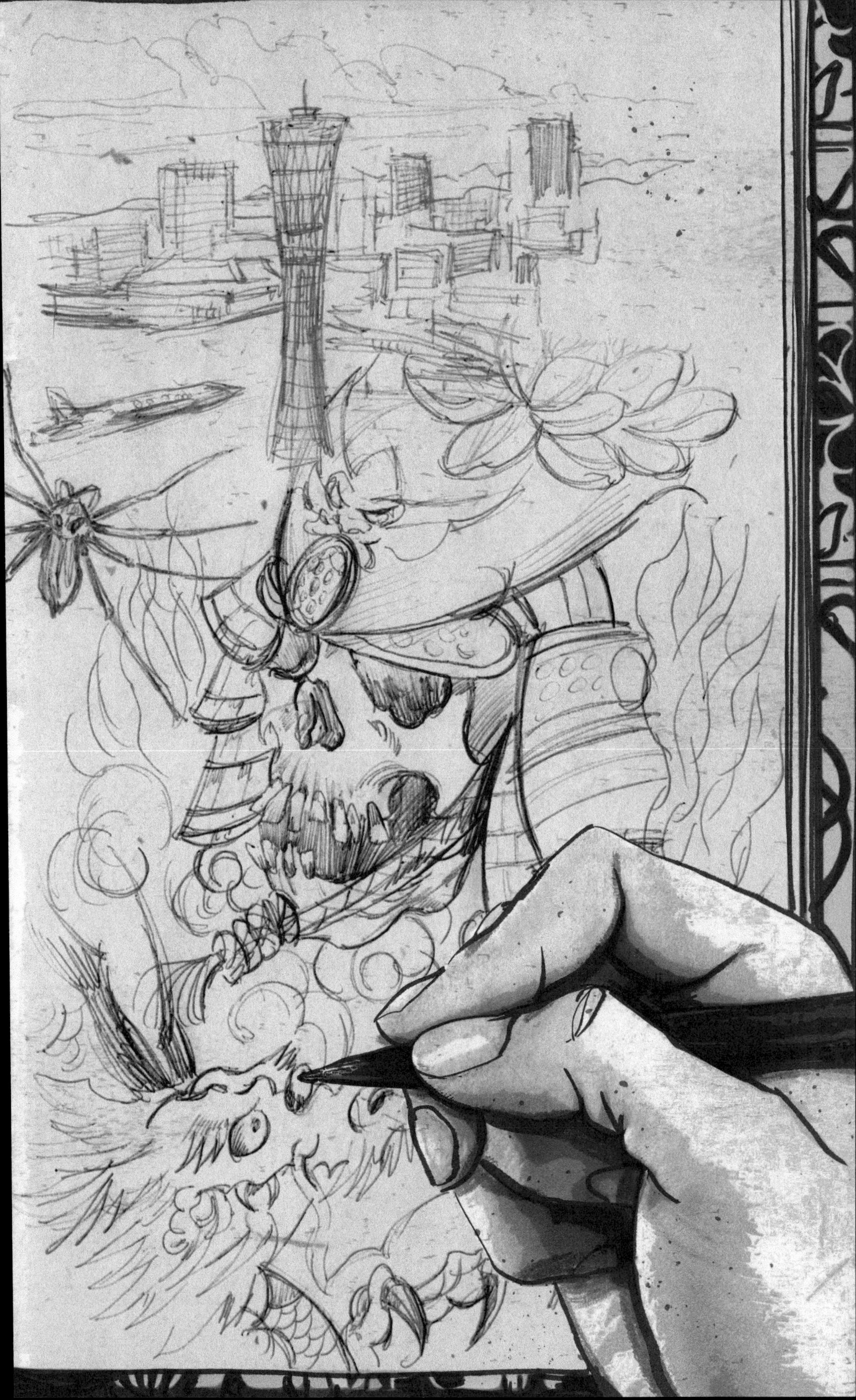

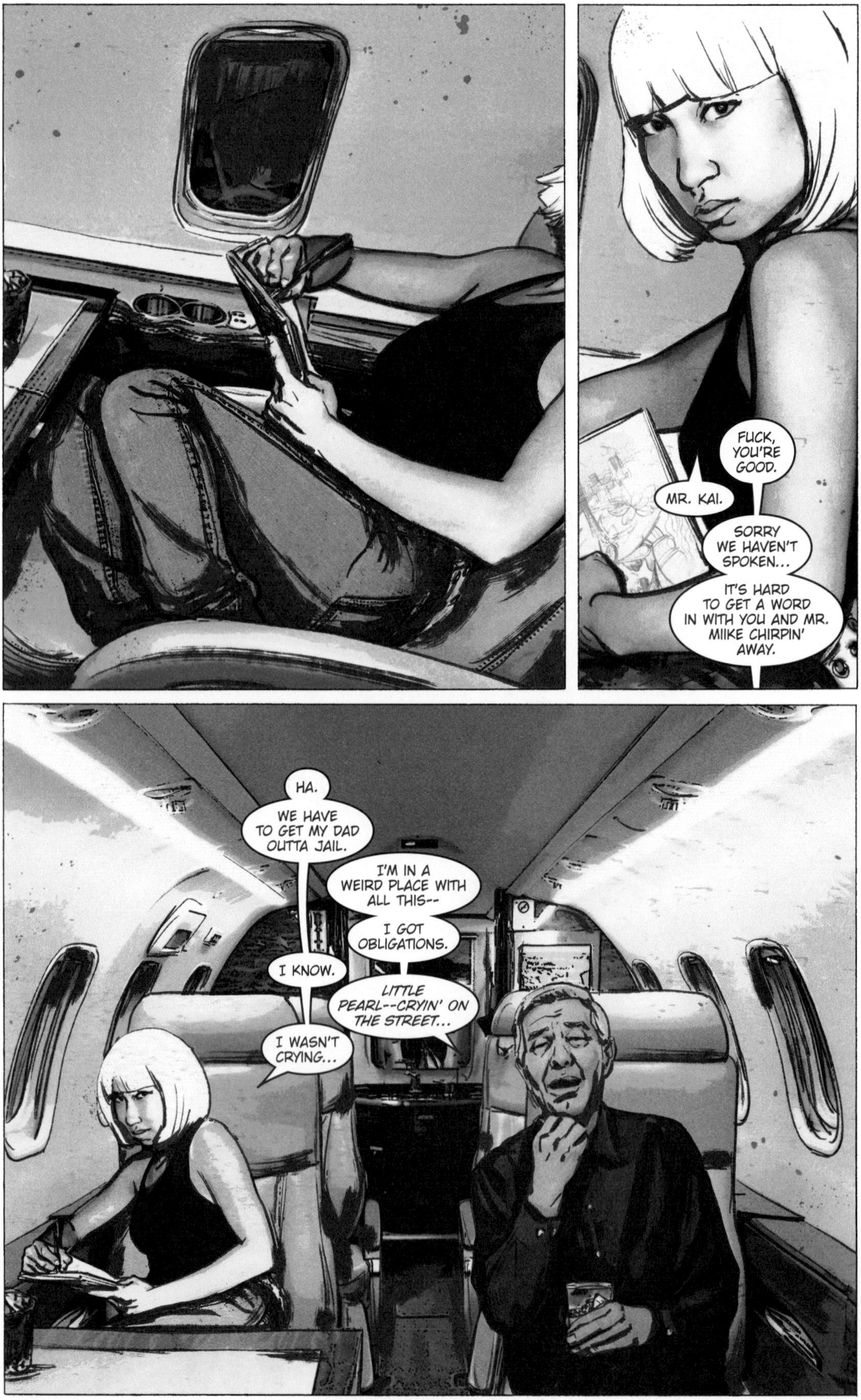
FUCK, YOU'RE GOOD.
MR. KAI.
SORRY WE HAVEN'T SPOKEN...
IT'S HARD TO GET A WORD IN WITH YOU AND MR. MIIKE CHIRPIN' AWAY.
HA.
WE HAVE TO GET MY DAD OUTTA JAIL.
I'M IN A WEIRD PLACE WITH ALL THIS--
I GOT OBLIGATIONS.
I KNOW.
LITTLE PEARL--CRYIN' ON THE STREET...
I WASN'T CRYING...

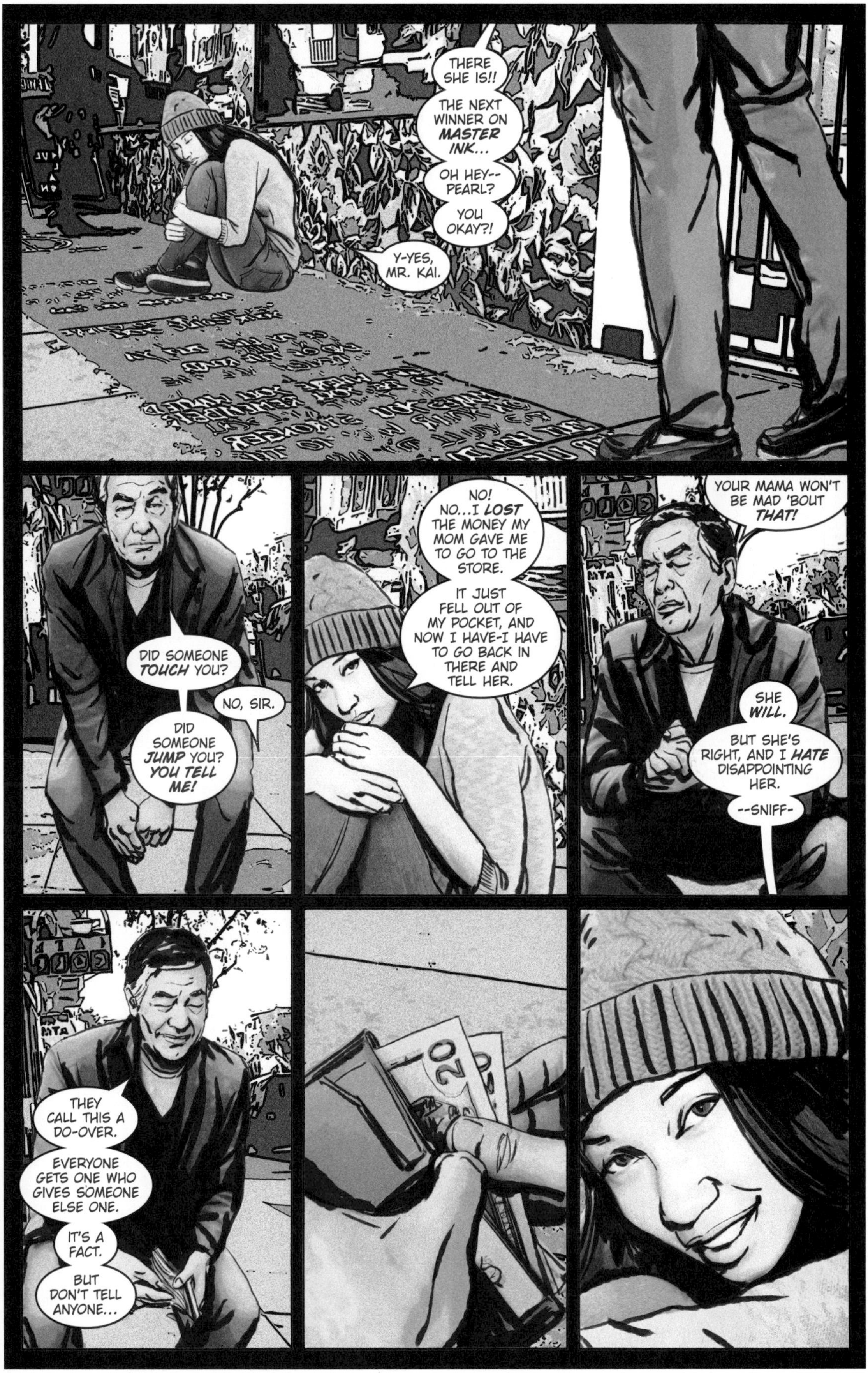

THERE SHE IS!!
THE NEXT WINNER ON MASTER INK...
OH HEY-- PEARL?
YOU OKAY?!
Y-YES, MR. KAI.
DID SOMEONE TOUCH YOU?
NO, SIR.
DID SOMEONE JUMP YOU? YOU TELL ME!
NO! NO...I LOST THE MONEY MY MOM GAVE ME TO GO TO THE STORE.
IT JUST FELL OUT OF MY POCKET, AND NOW I HAVE-I HAVE TO GO BACK IN THERE AND TELL HER.
YOUR MAMA WON'T BE MAD 'BOUT THAT!
SHE WILL.
BUT SHE'S RIGHT, AND I HATE DISAPPOINTING HER.
--SNIFF-
THEY CALL THIS A DO-OVER.
EVERYONE GETS ONE WHO GIVES SOMEONE ELSE ONE.
IT'S A FACT.
BUT DON'T TELL ANYONE...

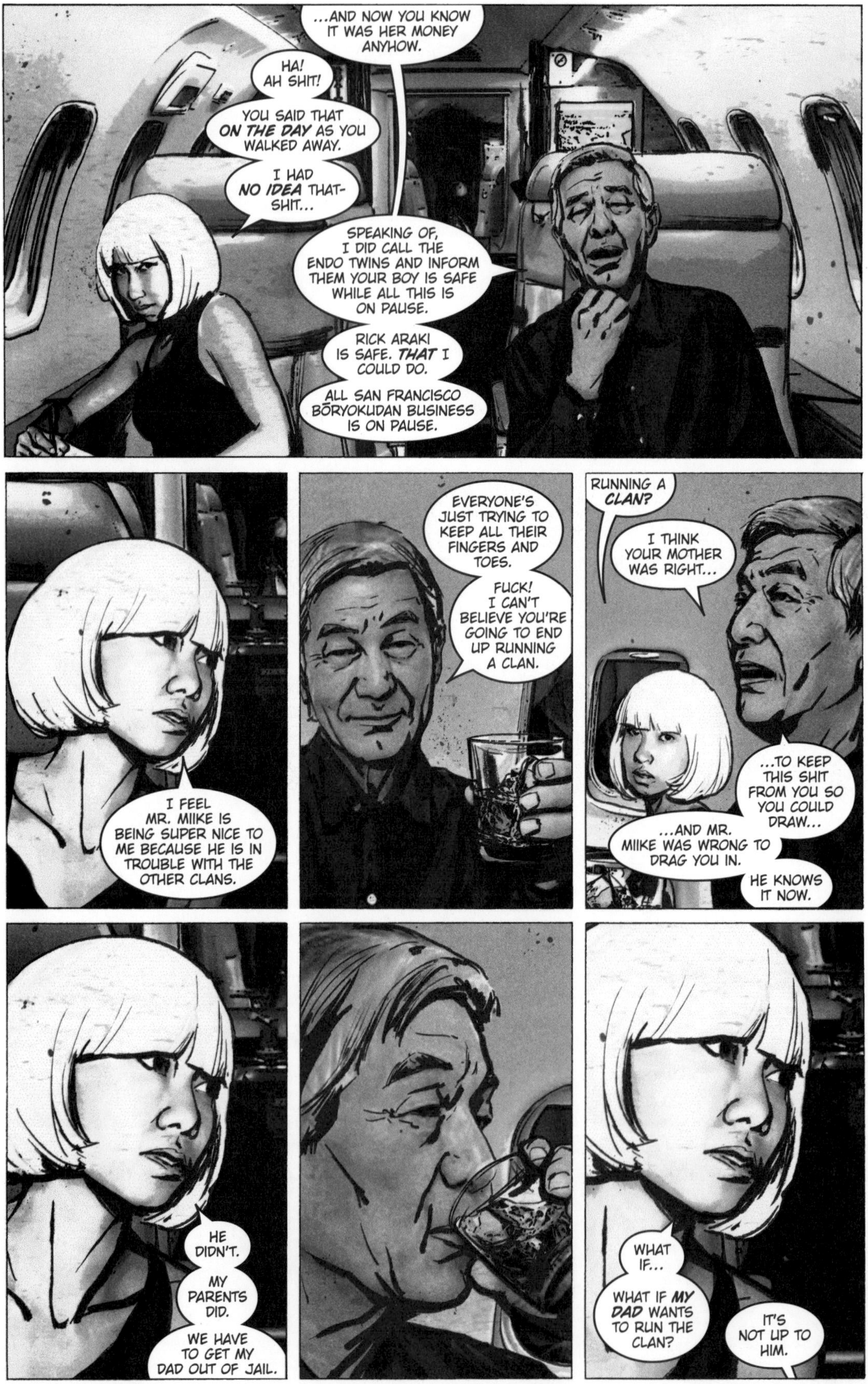
...AND NOW YOU KNOW IT WAS HER MONEY ANYHOW.
HA! AH SHIT!
YOU SAID THAT ON THE DAY AS YOU WALKED AWAY.
I HAD NO IDEA THAT-SHIT...
SPEAKING OF, I DID CALL THE ENDO TWINS AND INFORM THEM YOUR BOY IS SAFE WHILE ALL THIS IS ON PAUSE.
RICK ARAKI IS SAFE. THAT I COULD DO.
ALL SAN FRANCISCO BŌRYOKUDAN BUSINESS IS ON PAUSE.
I FEEL MR. MIIKE IS BEING SUPER NICE TO ME BECAUSE HE IS IN TROUBLE WITH THE OTHER CLANS.
EVERYONE'S JUST TRYING TO KEEP ALL THEIR FINGERS AND TOES.
FUCK! I CAN'T BELIEVE YOU'RE GOING TO END UP RUNNING A CLAN.
RUNNING A CLAN?
I THINK YOUR MOTHER WAS RIGHT...
...TO KEEP THIS SHIT FROM YOU SO YOU COULD DRAW...
...AND MR. MIIKE WAS WRONG TO DRAG YOU IN.
HE KNOWS IT NOW.
HE DIDN'T.
MY PARENTS DID.
WE HAVE TO GET MY DAD OUT OF JAIL.
WHAT IF...
WHAT IF MY DAD WANTS TO RUN THE CLAN?
IT'S NOT UP TO HIM.

'KAY?

NOT UP TO HIM. NOT UP TO YOU.

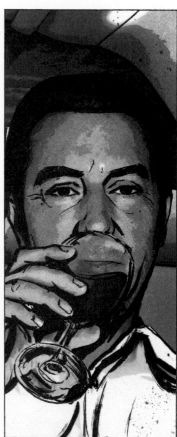

WHEN YOU GET TO KOBE...

...GO DIRECTLY TO YOUR COUSIN *NIKO.*

I'VE BEEN TEXTING HER.

WHEN YOU GO IN THERE, THOUGH-- LISTEN, EVEN WITH YOUR COUSIN...

THESE OLD-SCHOOL YAKUZA AND THESE NEW-SCHOOL YAKUZA...

YOU KNOW WHAT THEY HAVE IN COMMON?

TATTOOS?

ISSUES WITH WOMEN.

LIKE YOU'VE *NEVER* EXPERIENCED.

THEY WILL NOT SEE YOU AS A HUMAN BEING--

YOU GOTTA *GO IN THERE* AND *SHOW* THEM WHO YOU ARE--

WITH THE FUCKIN' *DRAGON SPIRIT* OF YOUR MOTHER GUIDING YOU.

I AM NOT SHITTIN' YOU. YOU GO IN THERE WITH...

...DRAGON FIRE.

"DRAGON FUCKING FIRE."

MR. MIIKE.

I DON'T KNOW WHAT THAT MEANS.

FUHHHCCCKKKKK...

<YOU MADE OF GLASS, HONEY!!>

<YOU WANT ME TO SHINE YOU?!>

<I DO, I WANT TO SHINE YOUR SHININESS.>

IT'S AMAZING. I DON'T SPEAK A WORD OF JAPANESE BUT I CAN TELL-

7 SINS CASINO

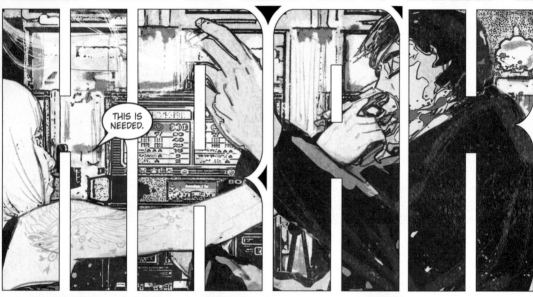

THIS IS NEEDED.

WWHHOOAAA!!

COME WITH ME, TANAKA!

I'LL INTRODUCE YOU TO HE WHO KNOWS ALL ABOUT WHAT'S GOING ON-

DO NOT FUCKING TOUCH ME!

WHAT DID HE FUCKING CALL ME?

BABYDOLL-FACE, YOU CAN'T FREAK OUT EVERY TIME SOMEONE RUNS UP AGAINST YOU IN A PLACE LIKE-

YOU.

RICK, WHAT ARE YOU DOING HERE?

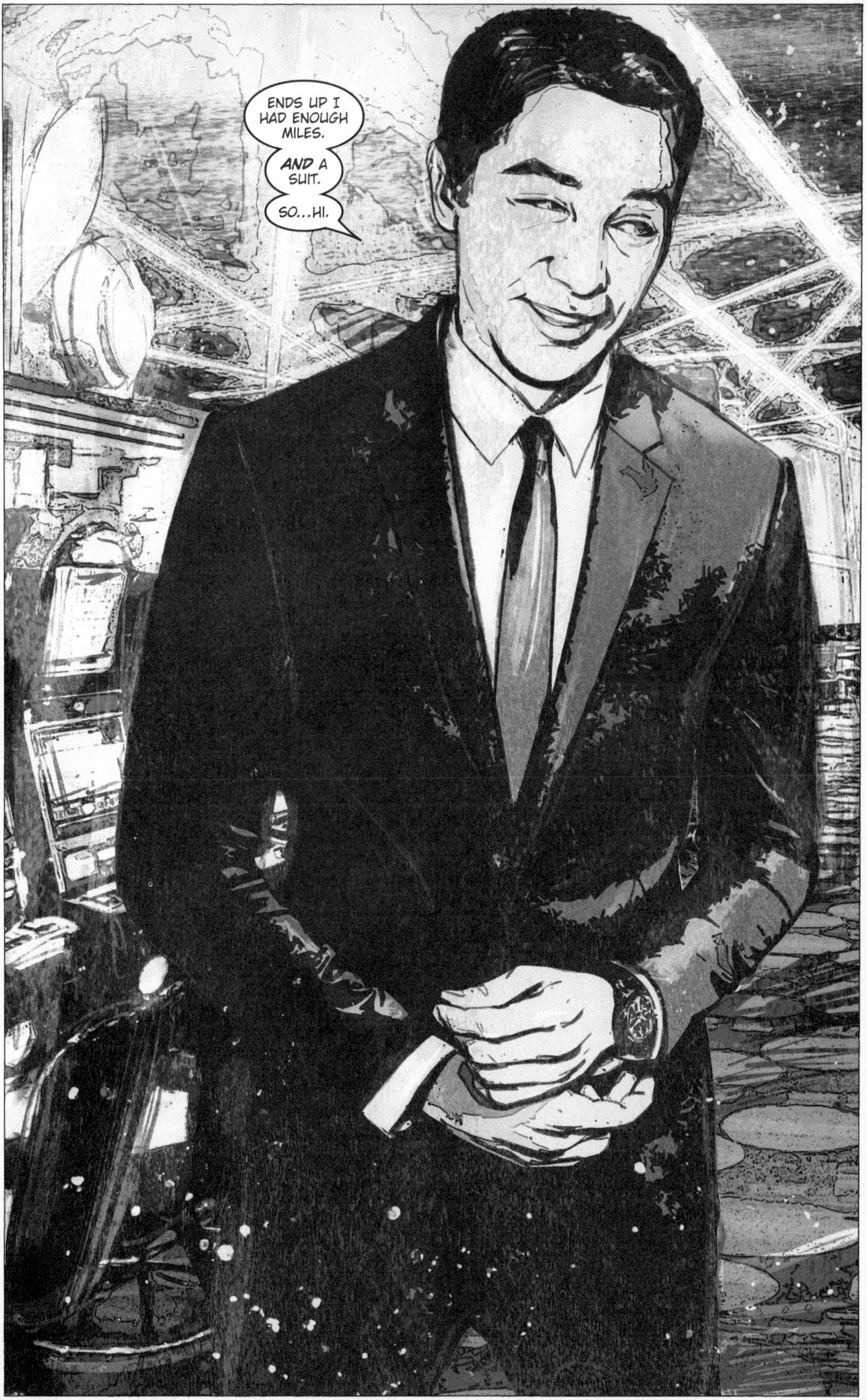
ENDS UP I HAD ENOUGH MILES.
AND A SUIT.
SO...HI.

真珠

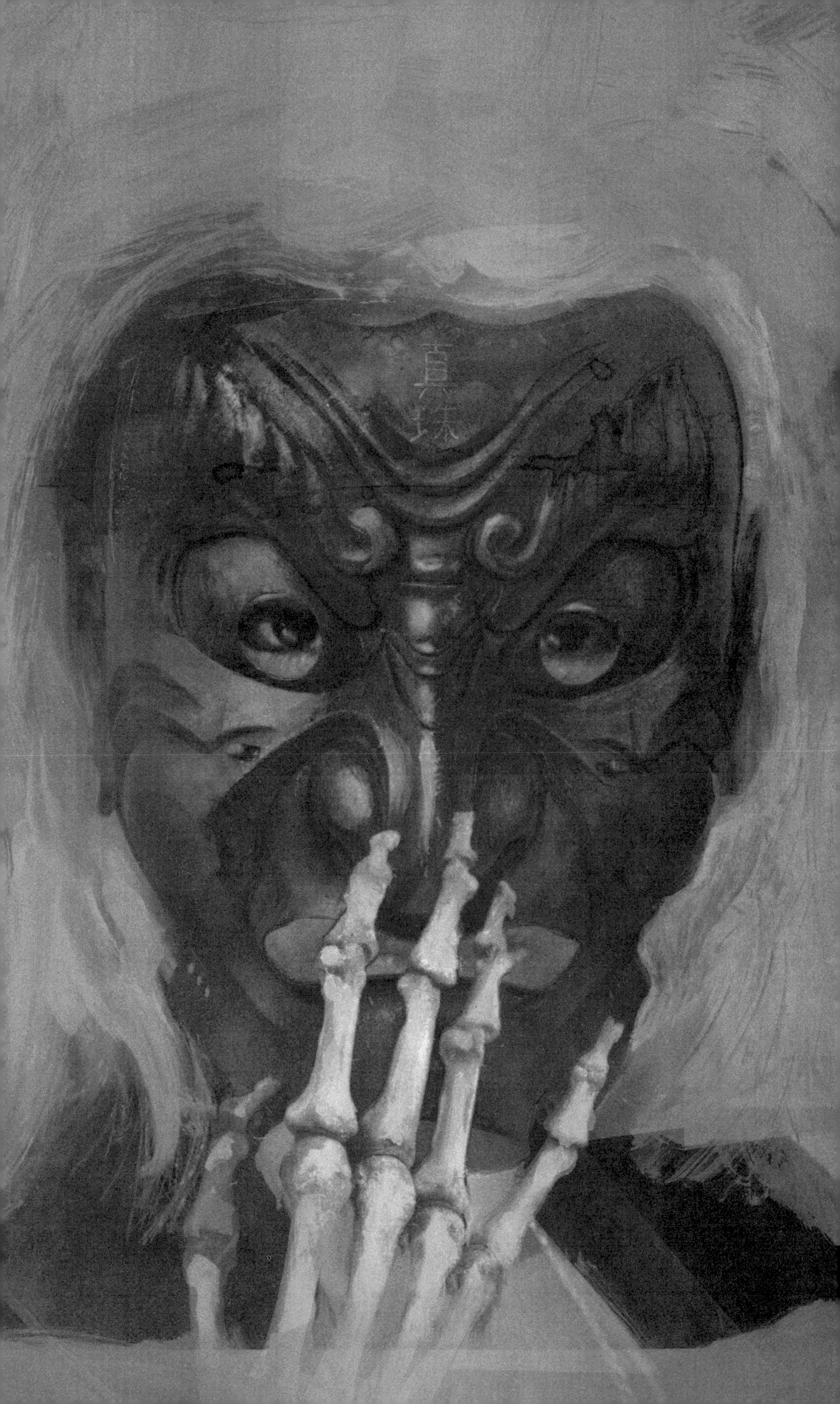

Variant cover art for issue #9
by KENT WILLIAMS

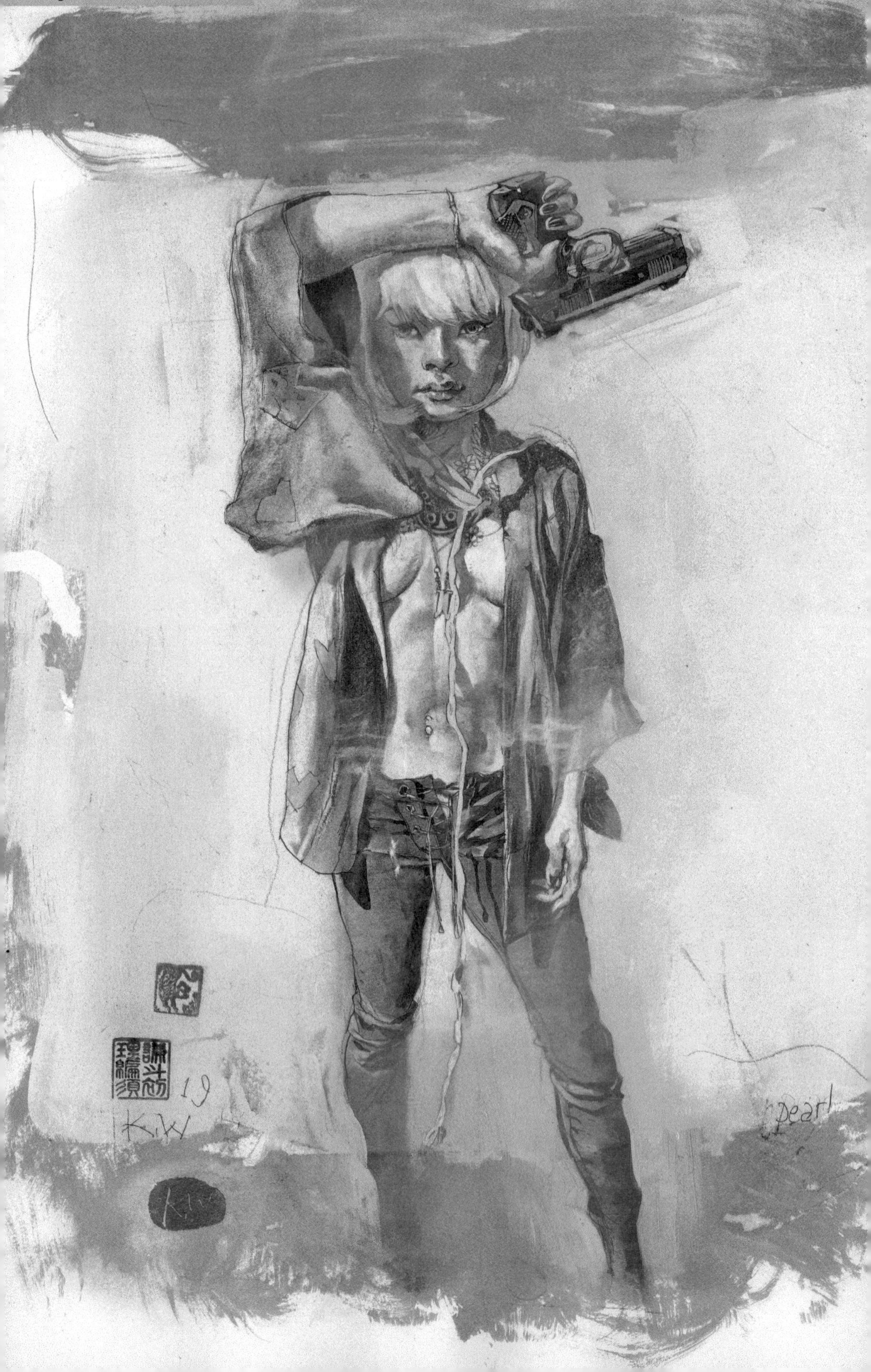
Pearl

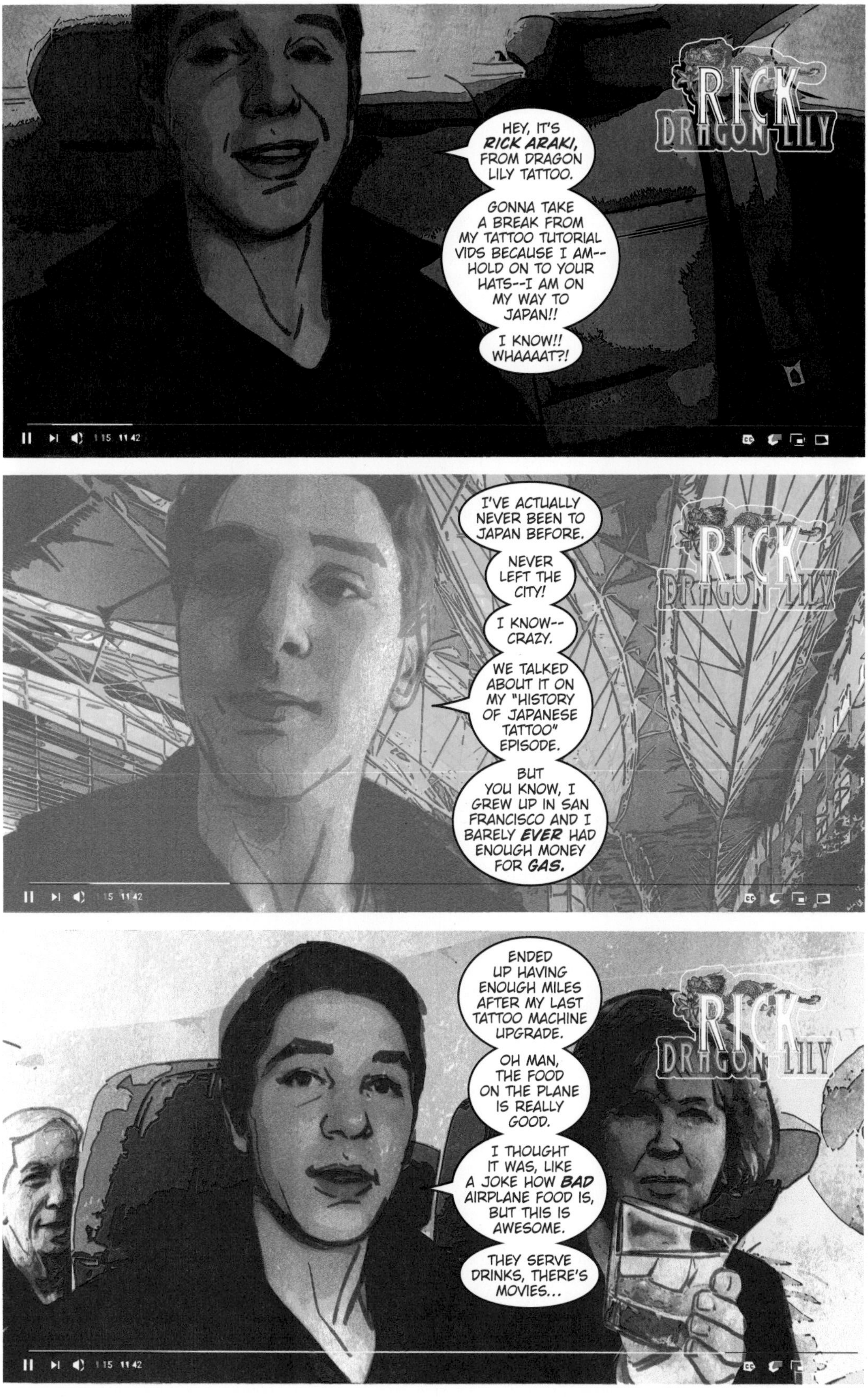

HEY, IT'S **RICK ARAKI,** FROM DRAGON LILY TATTOO.
GONNA TAKE A BREAK FROM MY TATTOO TUTORIAL VIDS BECAUSE I AM--HOLD ON TO YOUR HATS--I AM ON MY WAY TO JAPAN!!
I KNOW!! WHAAAAT?!
I'VE ACTUALLY NEVER BEEN TO JAPAN BEFORE.
NEVER LEFT THE CITY!
I KNOW--CRAZY.
WE TALKED ABOUT IT ON MY "HISTORY OF JAPANESE TATTOO" EPISODE.
BUT YOU KNOW, I GREW UP IN SAN FRANCISCO AND I BARELY ***EVER*** HAD ENOUGH MONEY FOR ***GAS.***
ENDED UP HAVING ENOUGH MILES AFTER MY LAST TATTOO MACHINE UPGRADE.
OH MAN, THE FOOD ON THE PLANE IS REALLY GOOD.
I THOUGHT IT WAS, LIKE A JOKE HOW ***BAD*** AIRPLANE FOOD IS, BUT THIS IS AWESOME.
THEY SERVE DRINKS, THERE'S MOVIES...

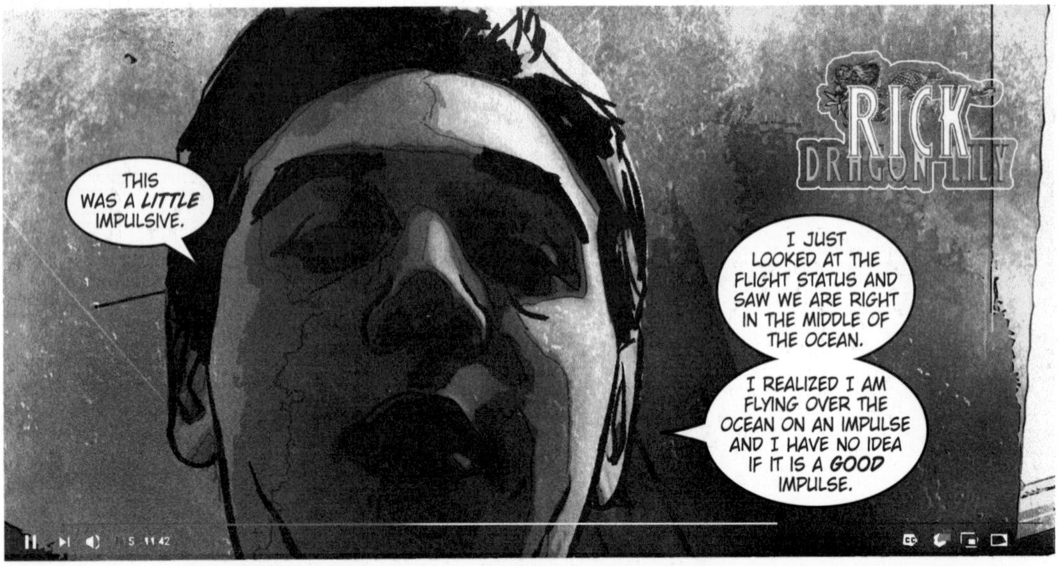
RICK DRAGON LILY
THIS WAS A *LITTLE* IMPULSIVE.
I JUST LOOKED AT THE FLIGHT STATUS AND SAW WE ARE RIGHT IN THE MIDDLE OF THE OCEAN.
I REALIZED I AM FLYING OVER THE OCEAN ON AN IMPULSE AND I HAVE NO IDEA IF IT IS A ***GOOD*** IMPULSE.

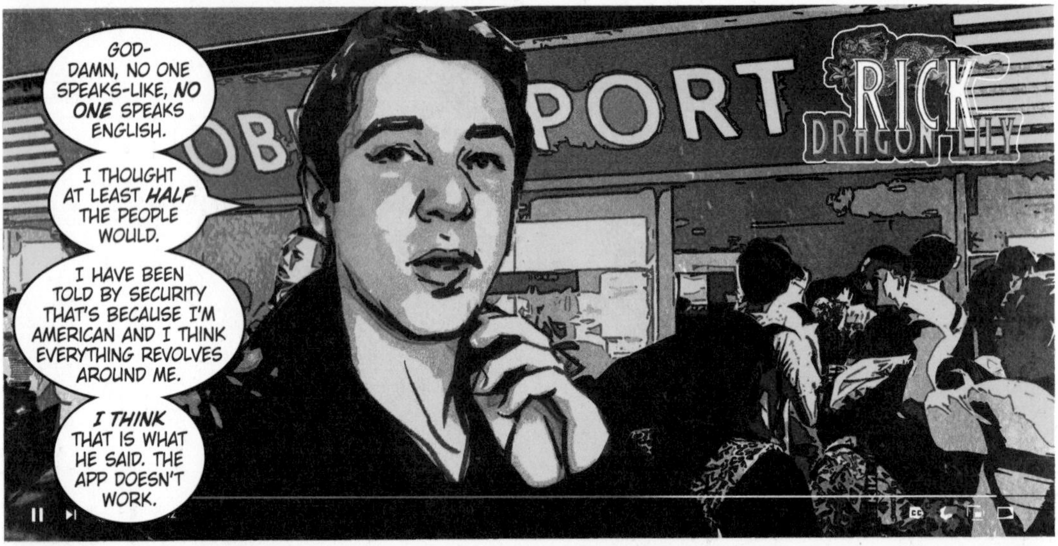
RICK DRAGON LILY
GOD-DAMN, NO ONE SPEAKS-LIKE, ***NO ONE*** SPEAKS ENGLISH.
I THOUGHT AT LEAST ***HALF*** THE PEOPLE WOULD.
I HAVE BEEN TOLD BY SECURITY THAT'S BECAUSE I'M AMERICAN AND I THINK EVERYTHING REVOLVES AROUND ME.
I THINK THAT IS WHAT HE SAID. THE APP DOESN'T WORK.

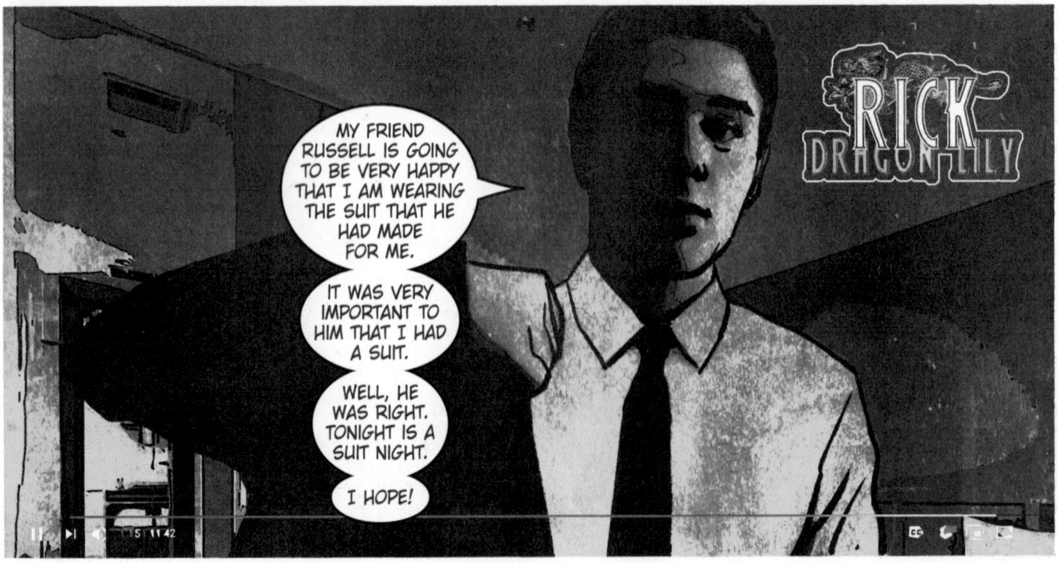
RICK DRAGON LILY
MY FRIEND RUSSELL IS GOING TO BE VERY HAPPY THAT I AM WEARING THE SUIT THAT HE HAD MADE FOR ME.
IT WAS VERY IMPORTANT TO HIM THAT I HAD A SUIT.
WELL, HE WAS RIGHT. TONIGHT IS A SUIT NIGHT.
I HOPE!

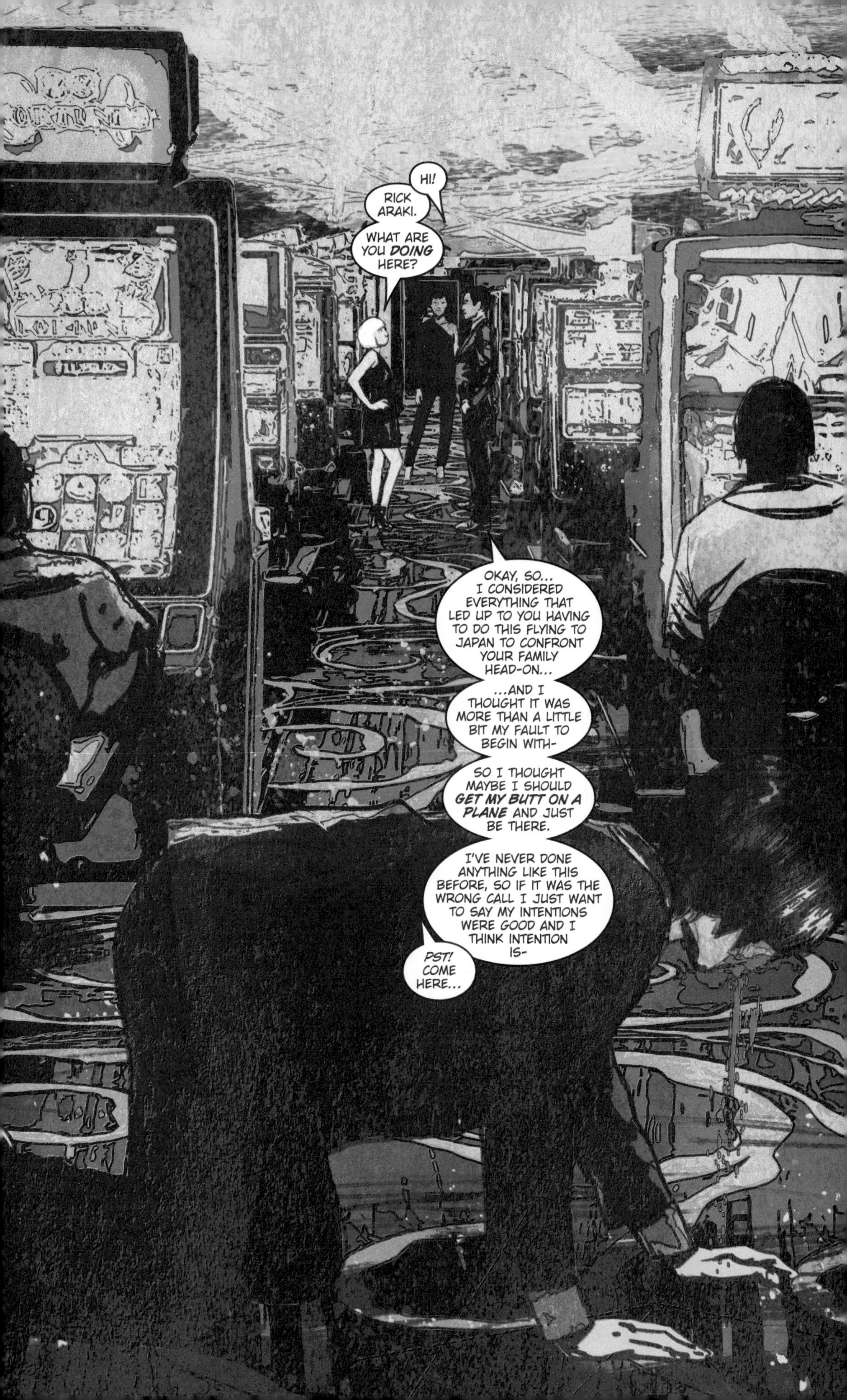

HI!
RICK ARAKI.
WHAT ARE YOU DOING HERE?
OKAY, SO... I CONSIDERED EVERYTHING THAT LED UP TO YOU HAVING TO DO THIS FLYING TO JAPAN TO CONFRONT YOUR FAMILY HEAD-ON...
...AND I THOUGHT IT WAS MORE THAN A LITTLE BIT MY FAULT TO BEGIN WITH-
SO I THOUGHT MAYBE I SHOULD GET MY BUTT ON A PLANE AND JUST BE THERE.
I'VE NEVER DONE ANYTHING LIKE THIS BEFORE, SO IF IT WAS THE WRONG CALL I JUST WANT TO SAY MY INTENTIONS WERE GOOD AND I THINK INTENTION IS-
PST! COME HERE...

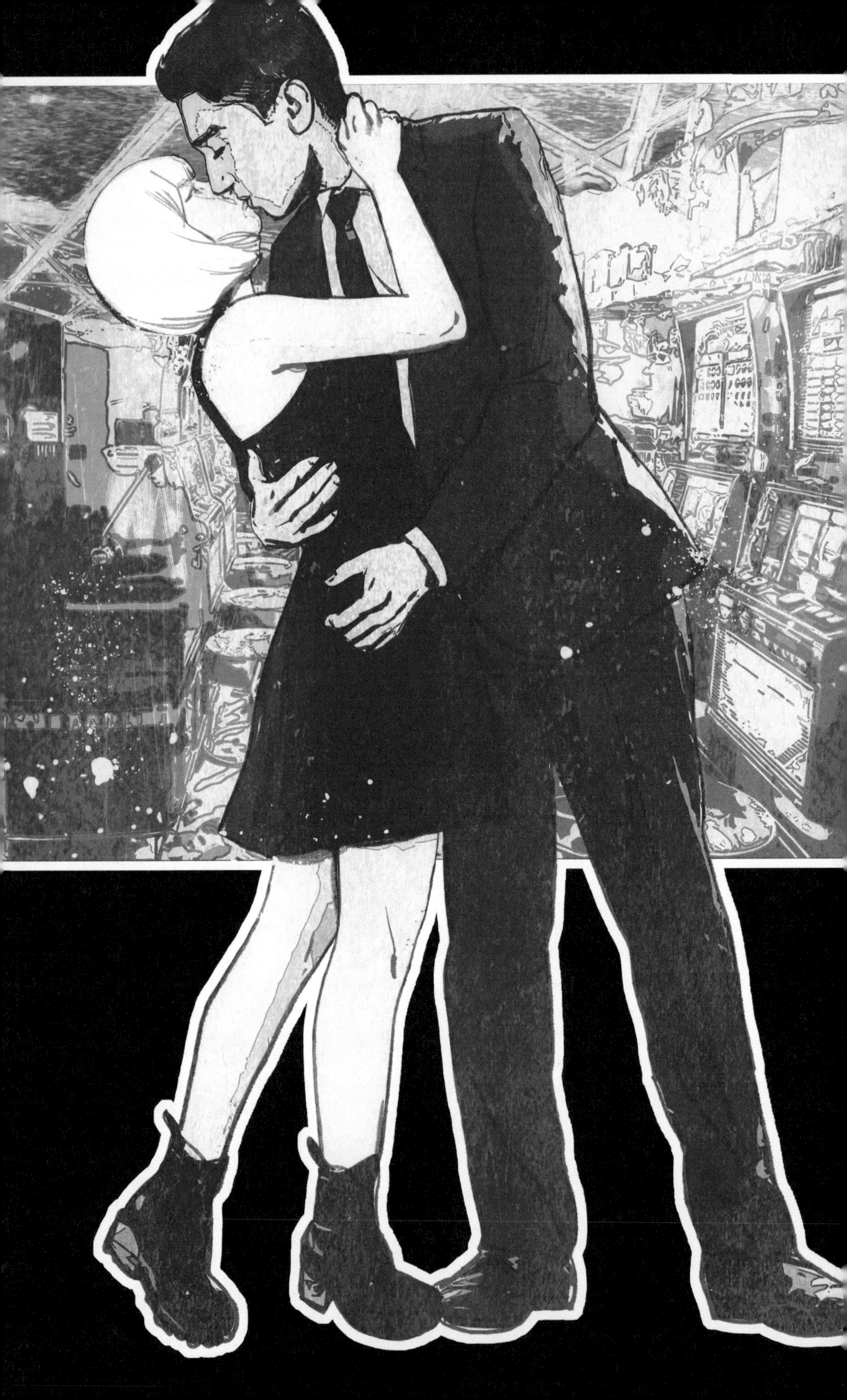

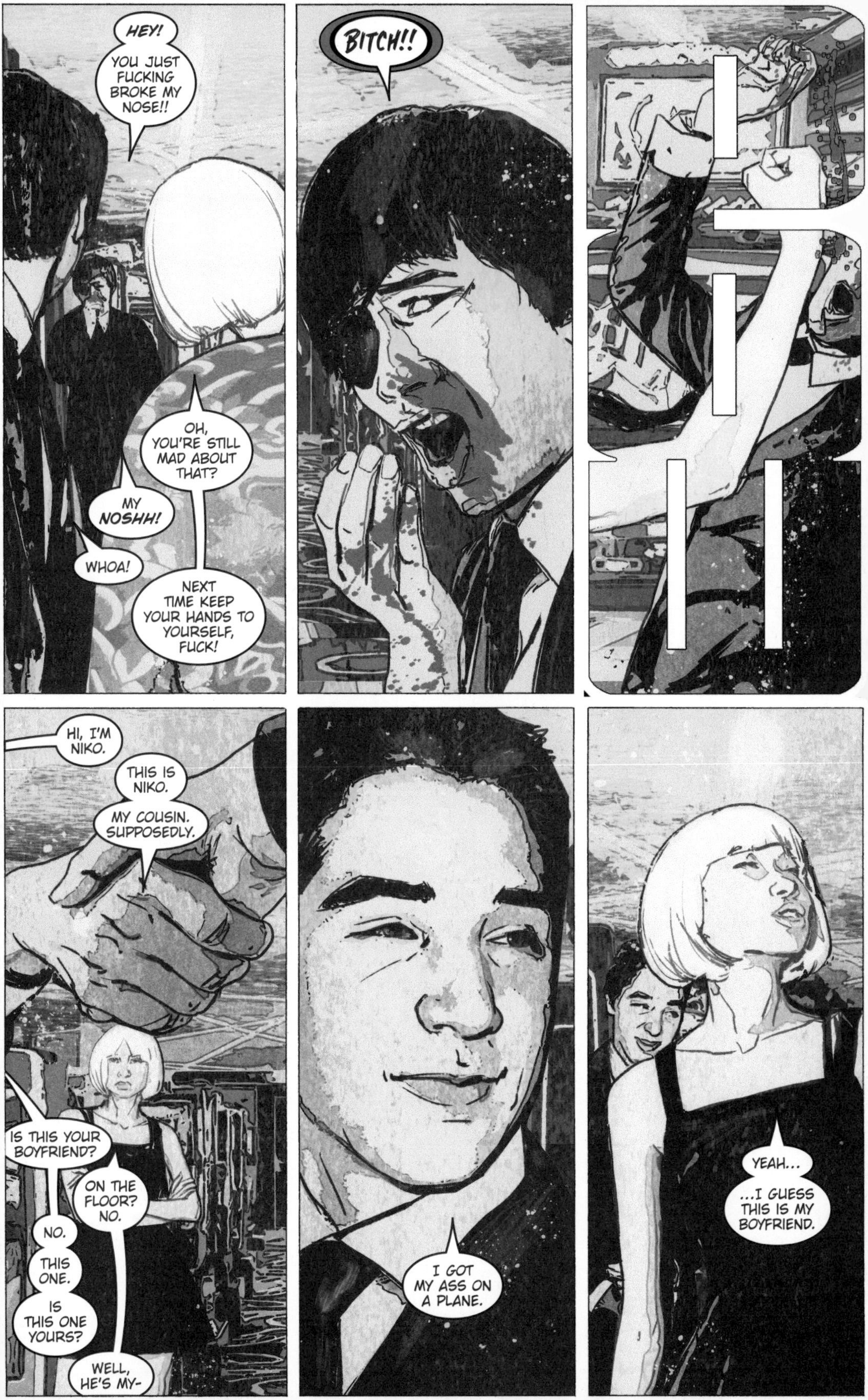
HEY!
YOU JUST FUCKING BROKE MY NOSE!!
OH, YOU'RE STILL MAD ABOUT THAT?
MY NOSHH!
WHOA!
NEXT TIME KEEP YOUR HANDS TO YOURSELF, FUCK!
BITCH!!
HI, I'M NIKO.
THIS IS NIKO.
MY COUSIN. SUPPOSEDLY.
IS THIS YOUR BOYFRIEND?
ON THE FLOOR? NO.
NO.
THIS ONE.
IS THIS ONE YOURS?
WELL, HE'S MY-
I GOT MY ASS ON A PLANE.
YEAH...
...I GUESS THIS IS MY BOYFRIEND.

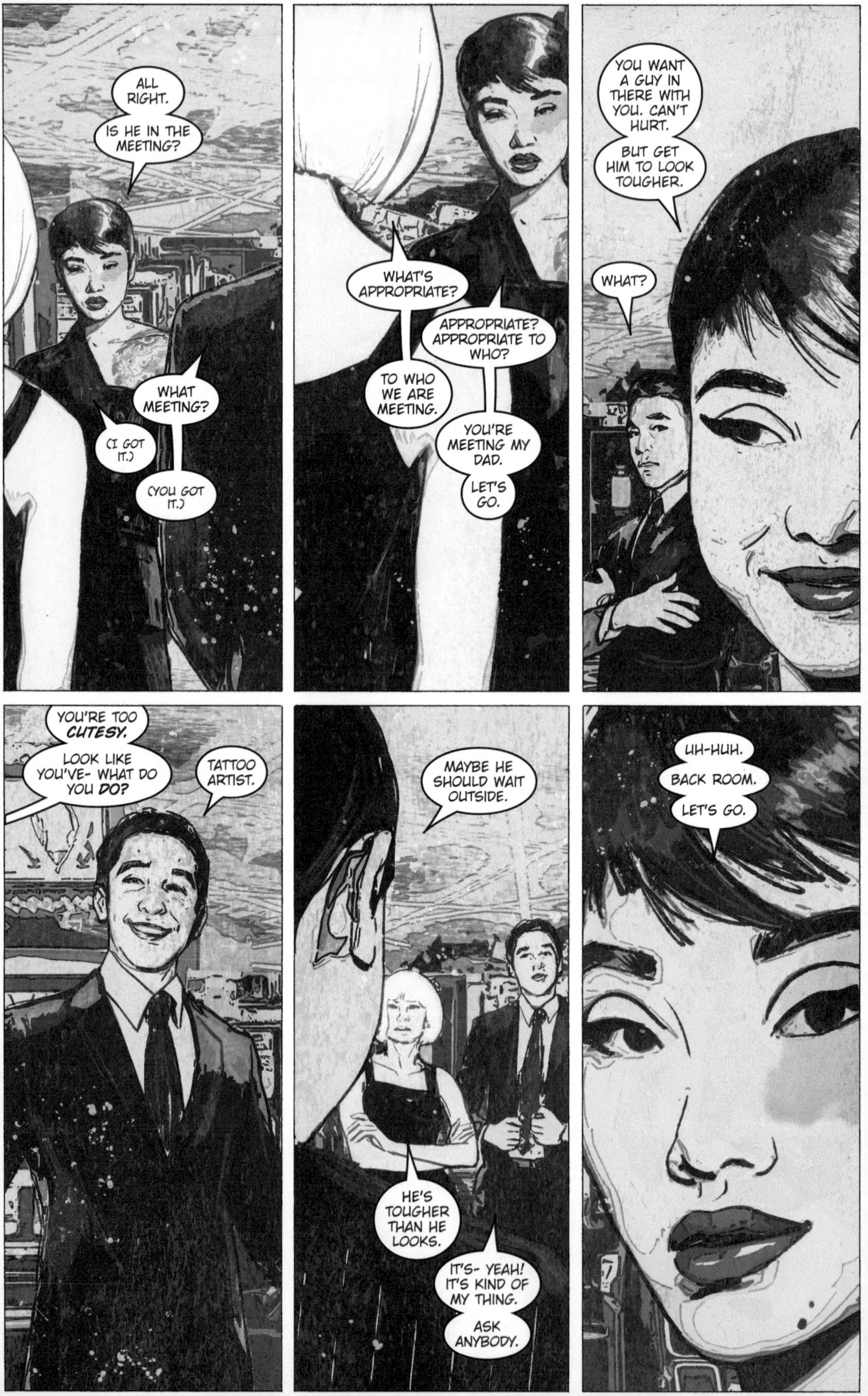
ALL RIGHT.
IS HE IN THE MEETING?
WHAT MEETING?
(I GOT IT.)
(YOU GOT IT.)
WHAT'S APPROPRIATE?
APPROPRIATE? APPROPRIATE TO WHO?
TO WHO WE ARE MEETING.
YOU'RE MEETING MY DAD.
LET'S GO.
YOU WANT A GUY IN THERE WITH YOU. CAN'T HURT.
BUT GET HIM TO LOOK TOUGHER.
WHAT?
YOU'RE TOO CUTESY.
LOOK LIKE YOU'VE- WHAT DO YOU DO?
TATTOO ARTIST.
MAYBE HE SHOULD WAIT OUTSIDE.
HE'S TOUGHER THAN HE LOOKS.
IT'S- YEAH! IT'S KIND OF MY THING.
ASK ANYBODY.
UH-HUH.
BACK ROOM.
LET'S GO.

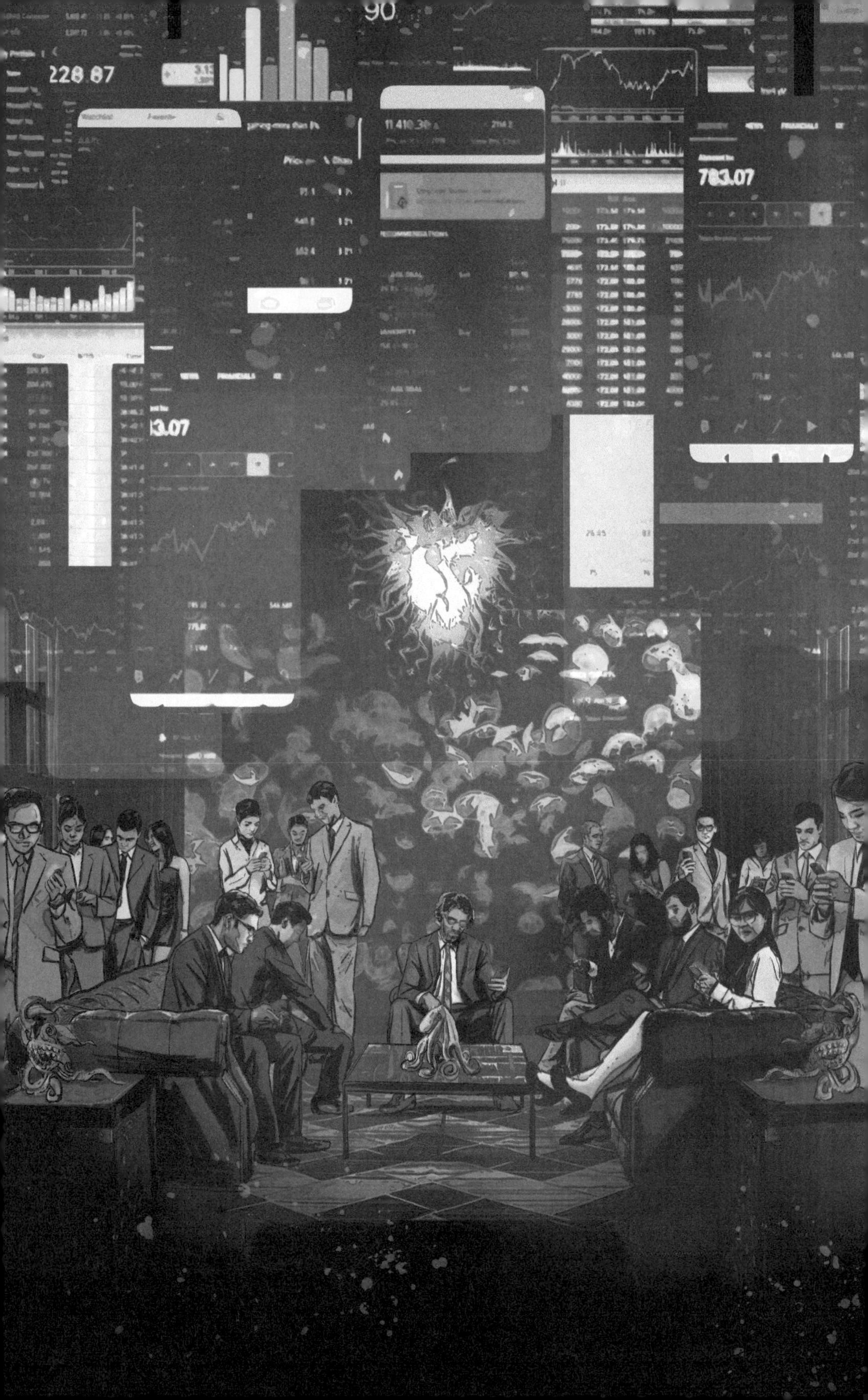
228.87
783.07

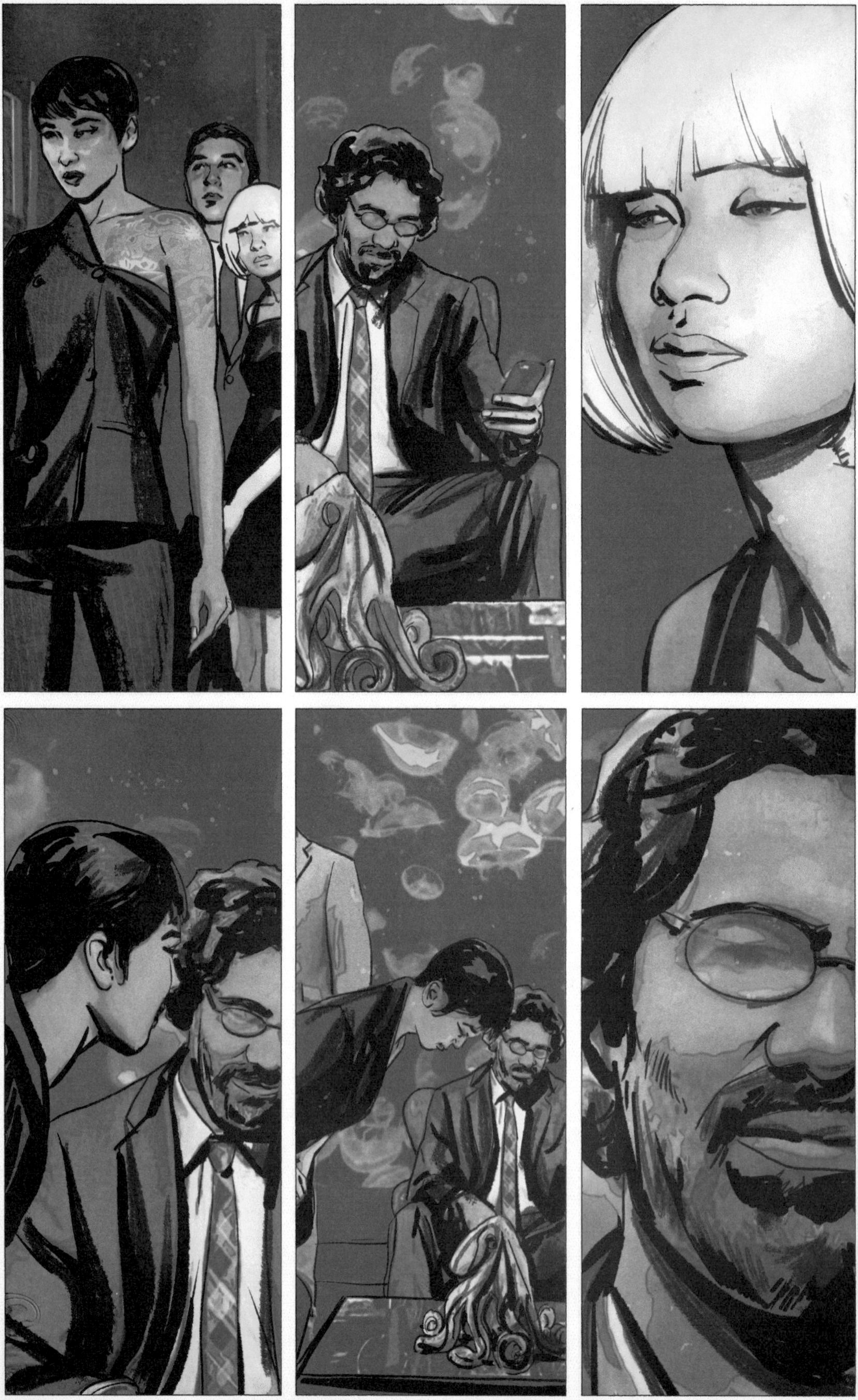

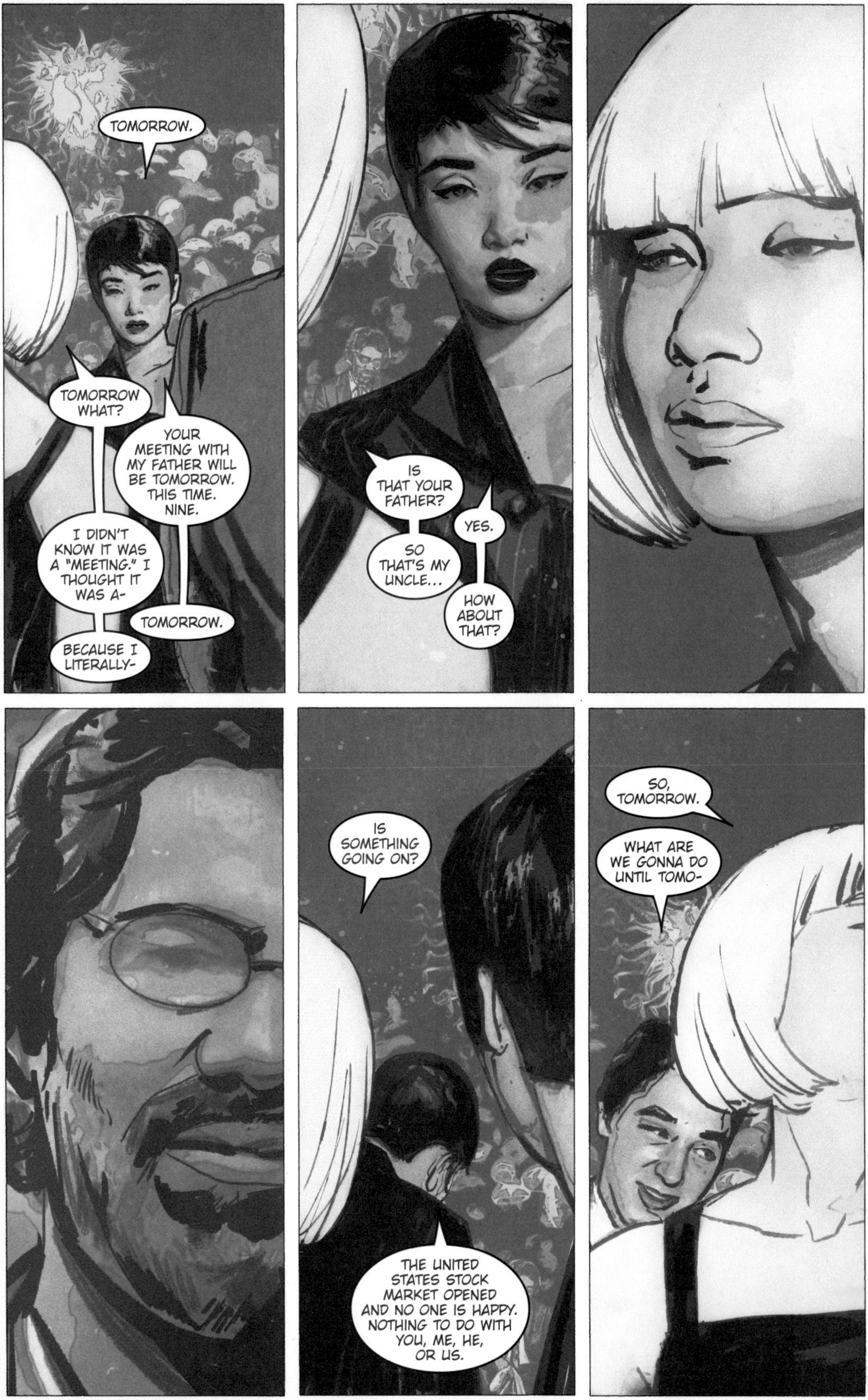
TOMORROW.
TOMORROW WHAT?
YOUR MEETING WITH MY FATHER WILL BE TOMORROW. THIS TIME. NINE.
I DIDN'T KNOW IT WAS A "MEETING." I THOUGHT IT WAS A-
TOMORROW.
BECAUSE I LITERALLY-
IS THAT YOUR FATHER?
YES.
SO THAT'S MY UNCLE...
HOW ABOUT THAT?
IS SOMETHING GOING ON?
THE UNITED STATES STOCK MARKET OPENED AND NO ONE IS HAPPY. NOTHING TO DO WITH YOU, ME, HE, OR US.
SO, TOMORROW.
WHAT ARE WE GONNA DO UNTIL TOMO-

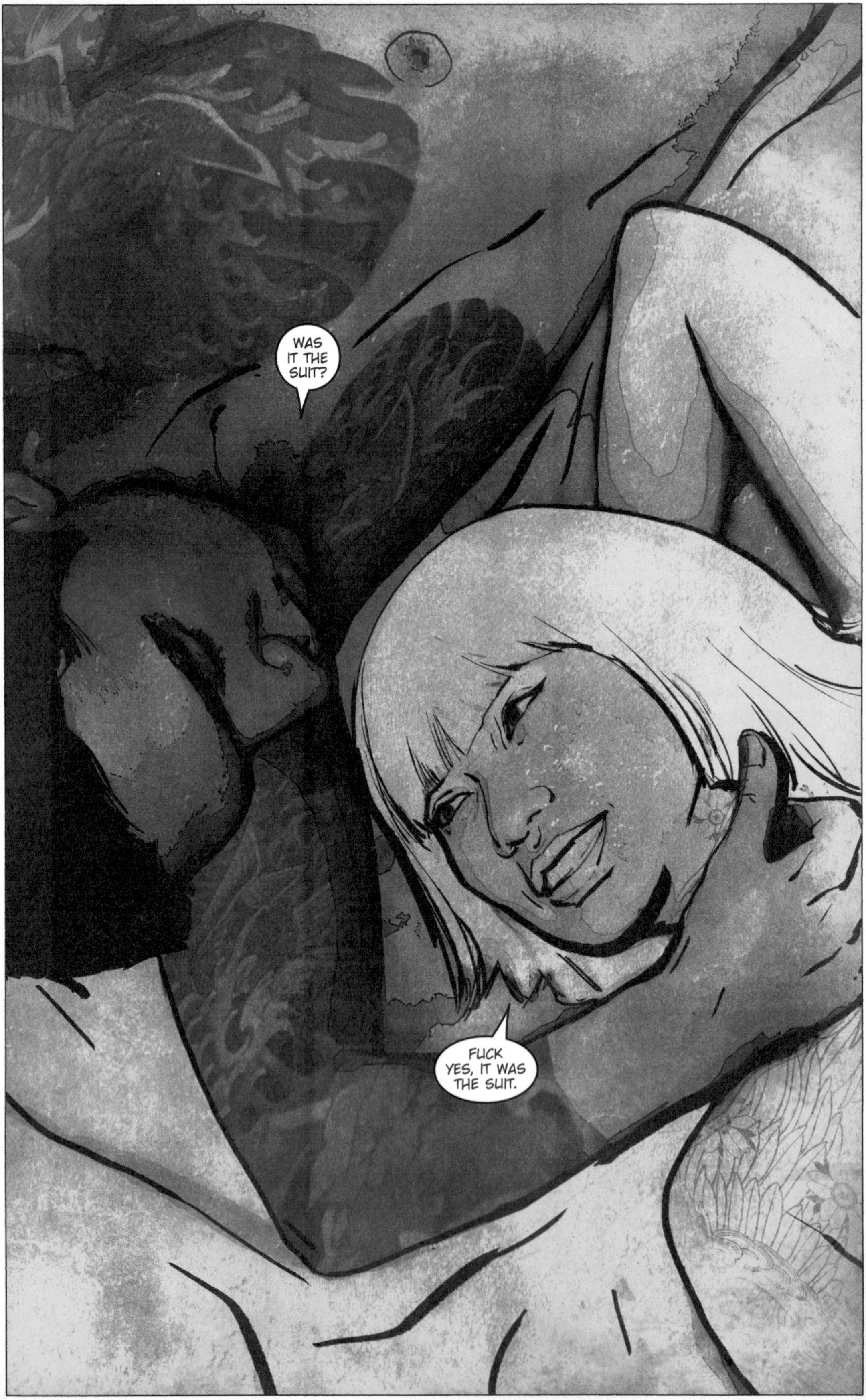
WAS IT THE SUIT?
FUCK YES, IT WAS THE SUIT.

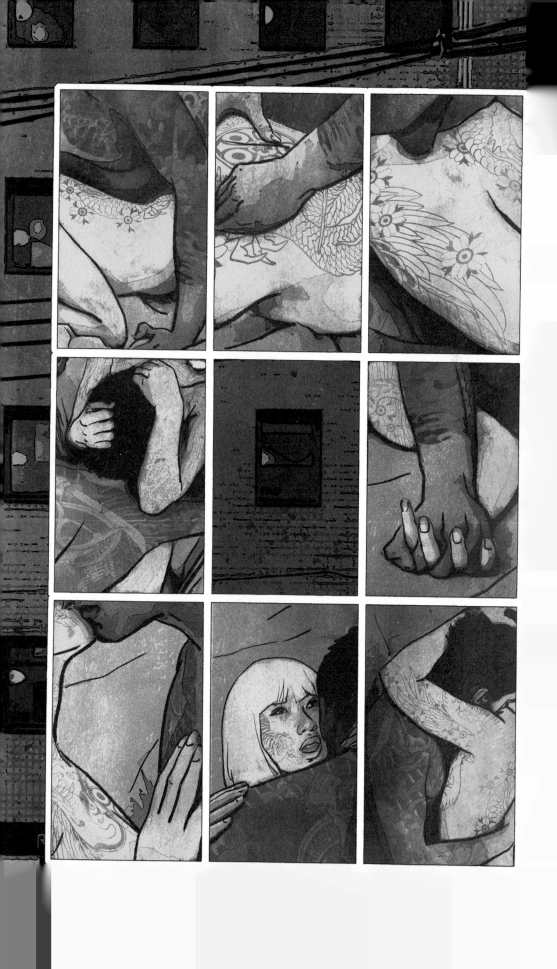

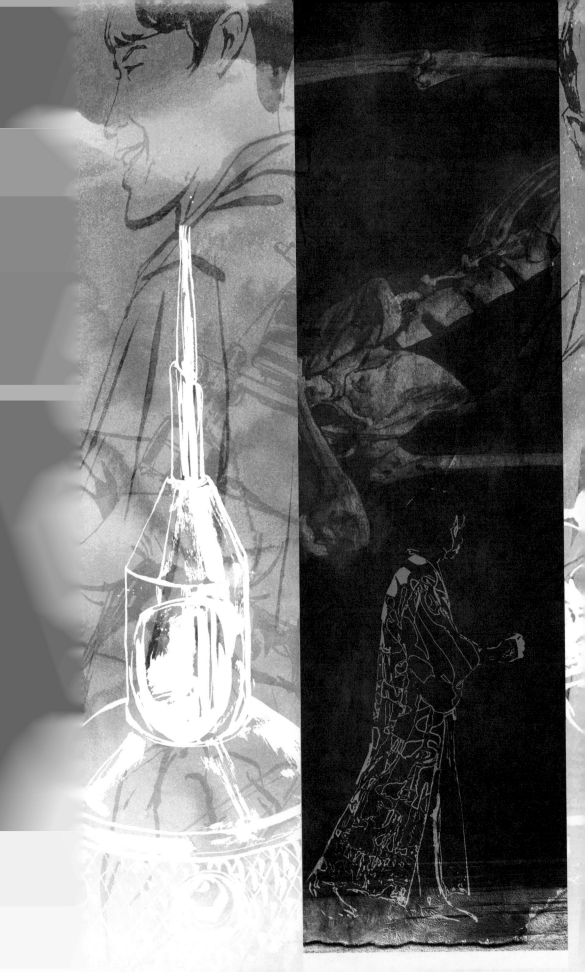

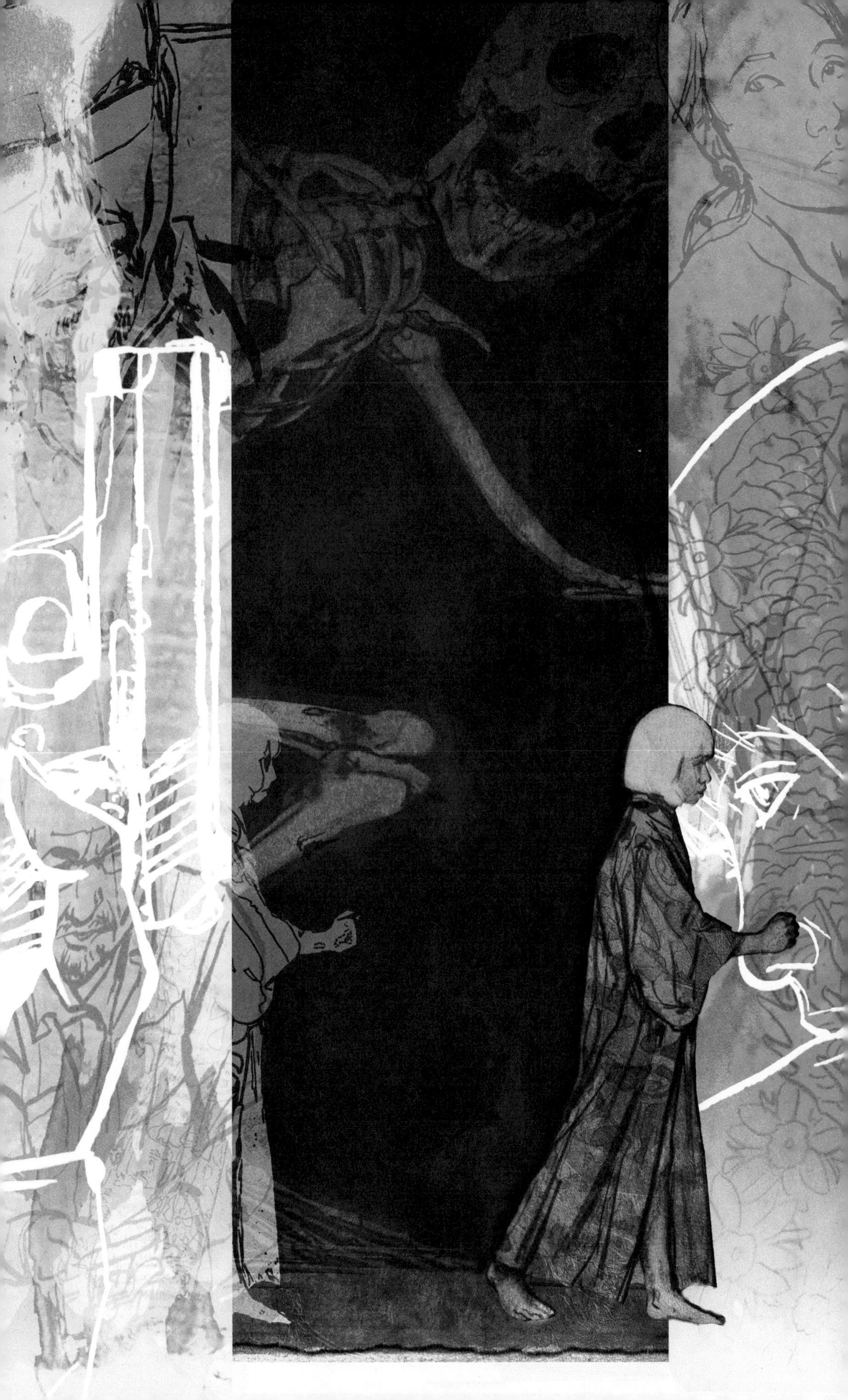

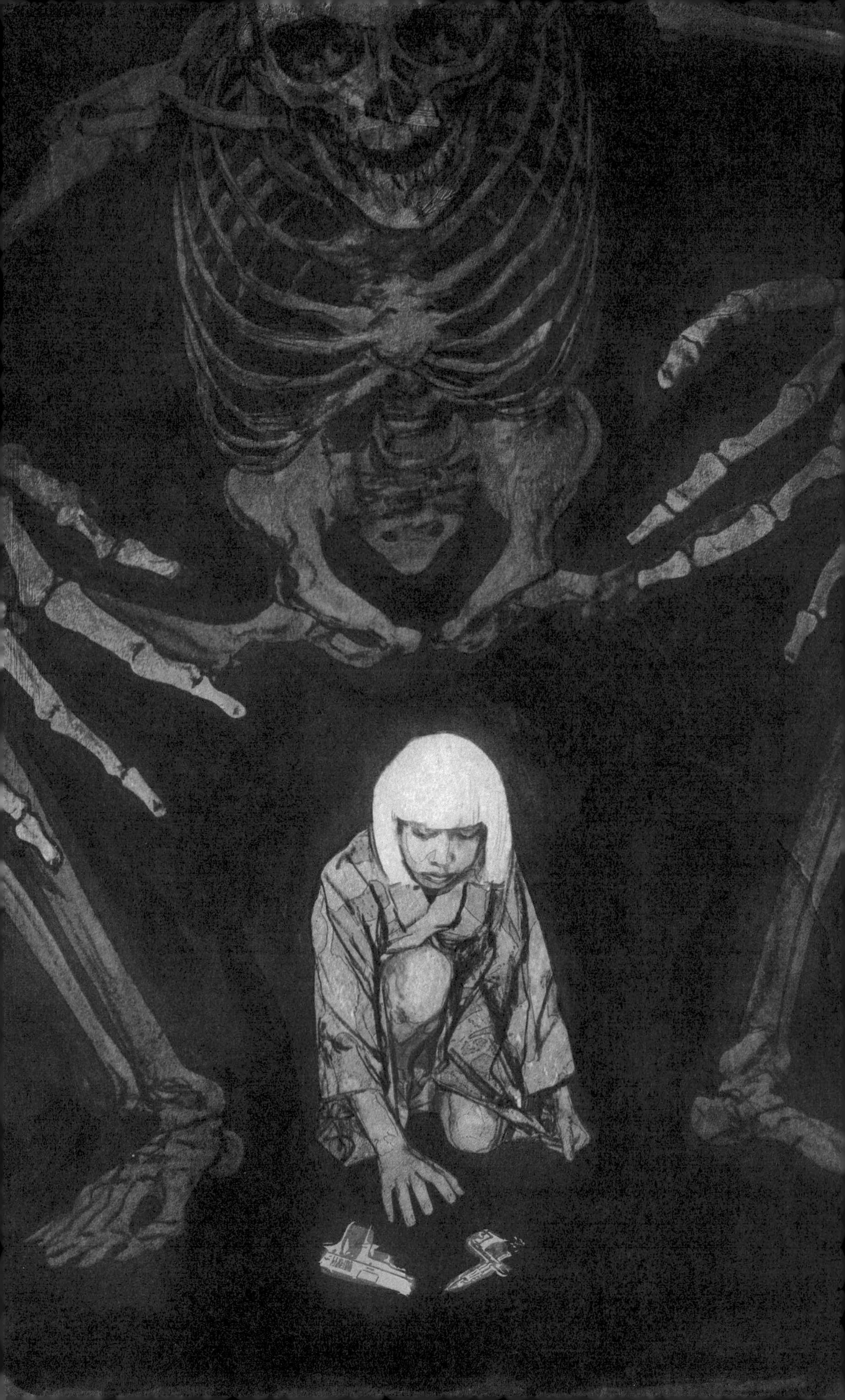

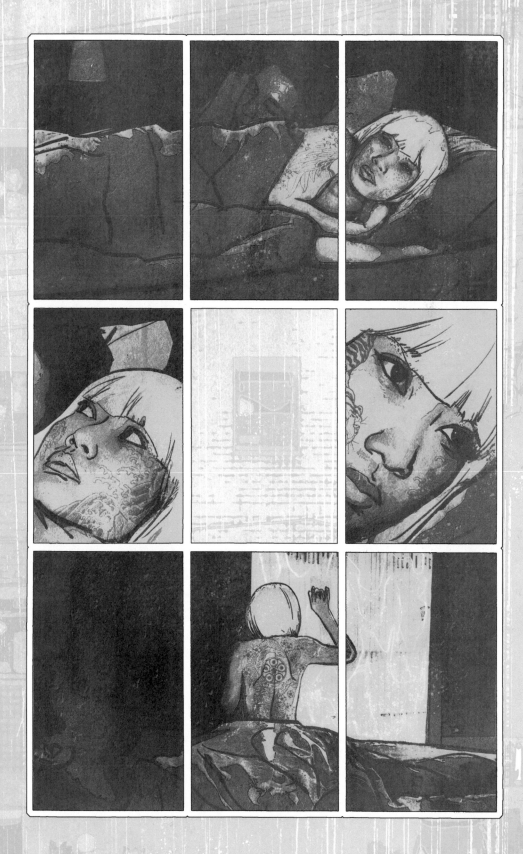

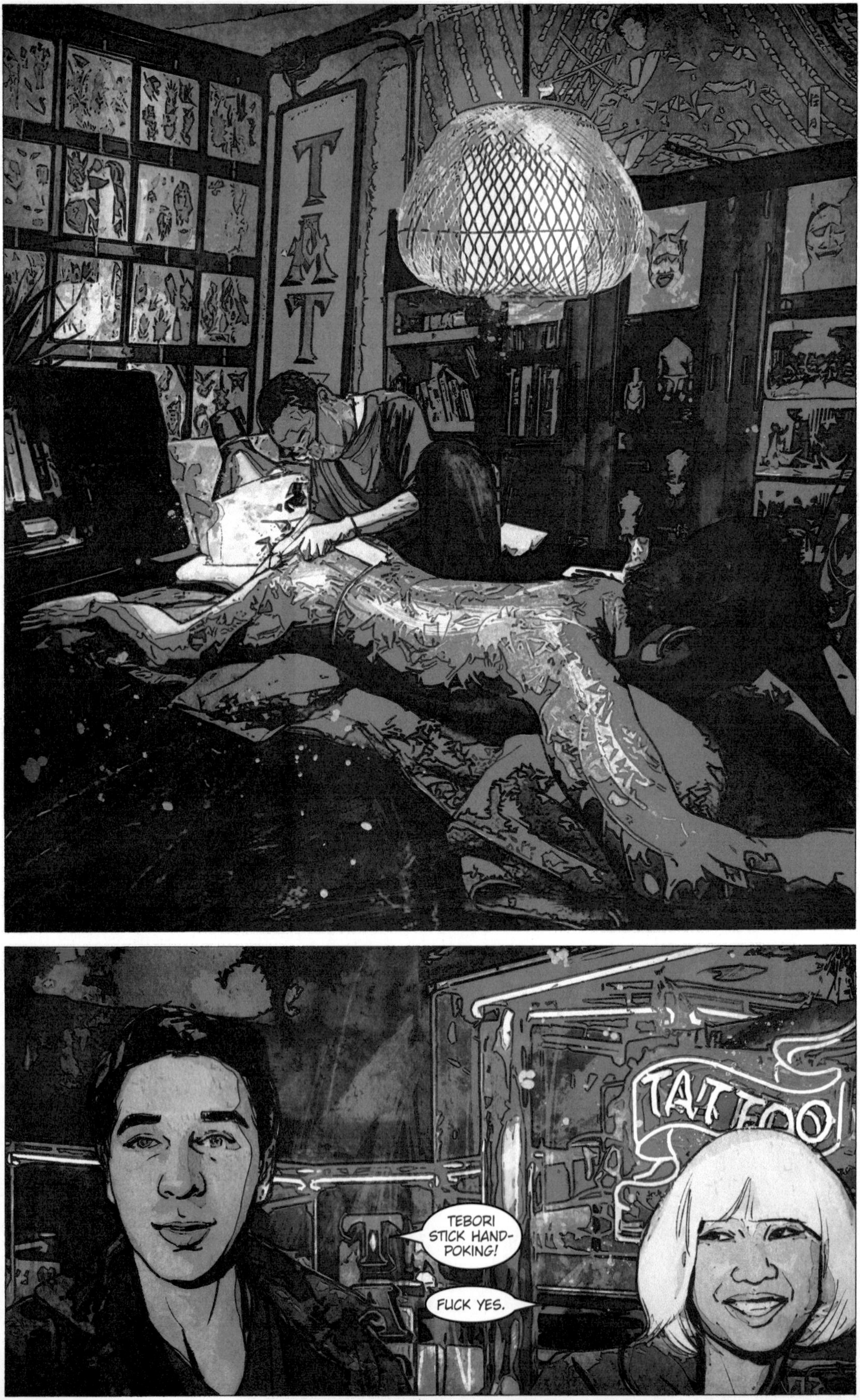
TATTOO
TEBORI STICK HAND-POKING!
FUCK YES.

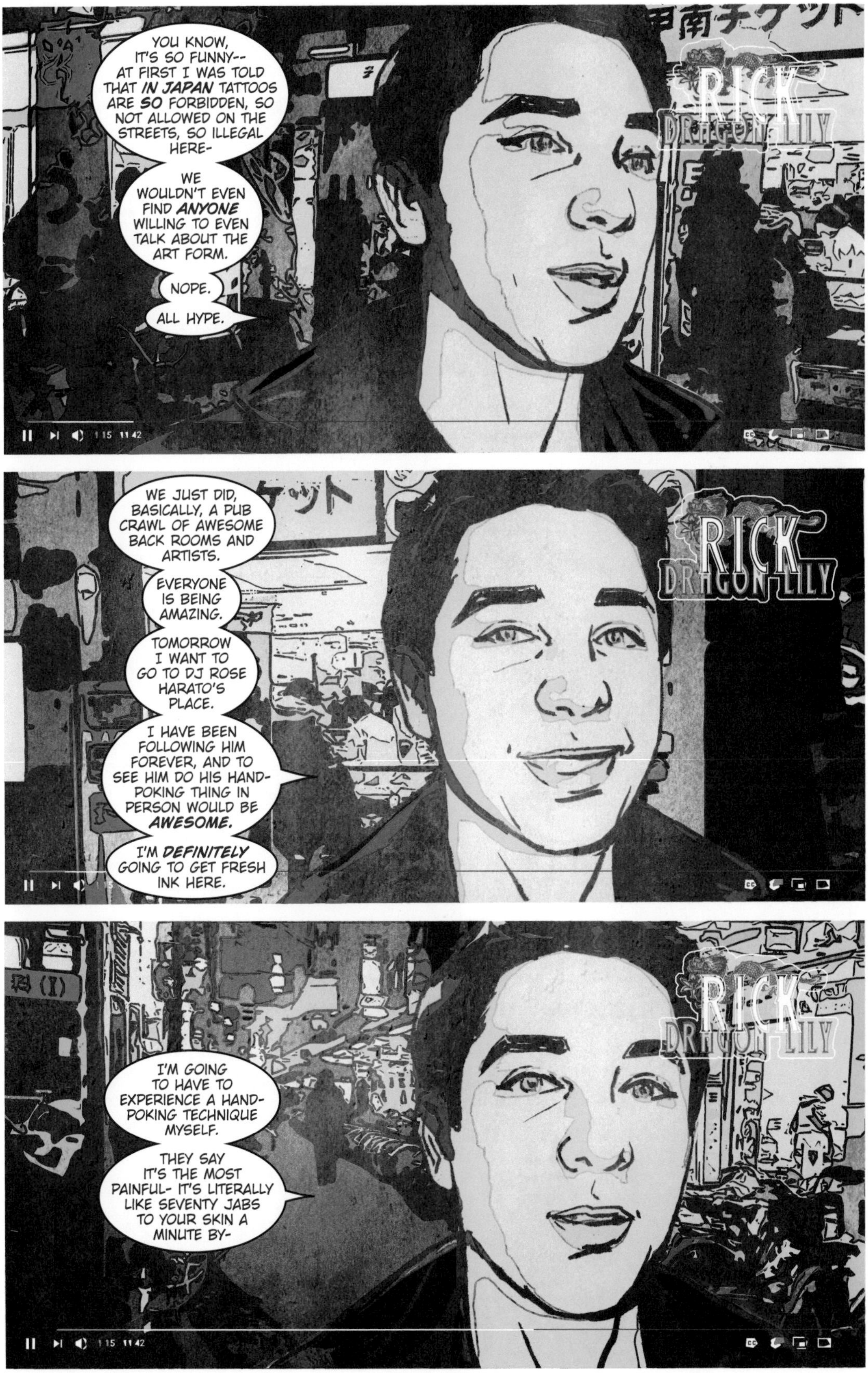
RICK DRAGON LILY
YOU KNOW, IT'S SO FUNNY-- AT FIRST I WAS TOLD THAT *IN JAPAN* TATTOOS ARE *SO* FORBIDDEN, SO NOT ALLOWED ON THE STREETS, SO ILLEGAL HERE-
WE WOULDN'T EVEN FIND *ANYONE* WILLING TO EVEN TALK ABOUT THE ART FORM.
NOPE.
ALL HYPE.
RICK DRAGON LILY
WE JUST DID, BASICALLY, A PUB CRAWL OF AWESOME BACK ROOMS AND ARTISTS.
EVERYONE IS BEING AMAZING.
TOMORROW I WANT TO GO TO DJ ROSE HARATO'S PLACE.
I HAVE BEEN FOLLOWING HIM FOREVER, AND TO SEE HIM DO HIS HAND-POKING THING IN PERSON WOULD BE *AWESOME.*
I'M *DEFINITELY* GOING TO GET FRESH INK HERE.
RICK DRAGON LILY
I'M GOING TO HAVE TO EXPERIENCE A HAND-POKING TECHNIQUE MYSELF.
THEY SAY IT'S THE MOST PAINFUL- IT'S LITERALLY LIKE SEVENTY JABS TO YOUR SKIN A MINUTE BY-

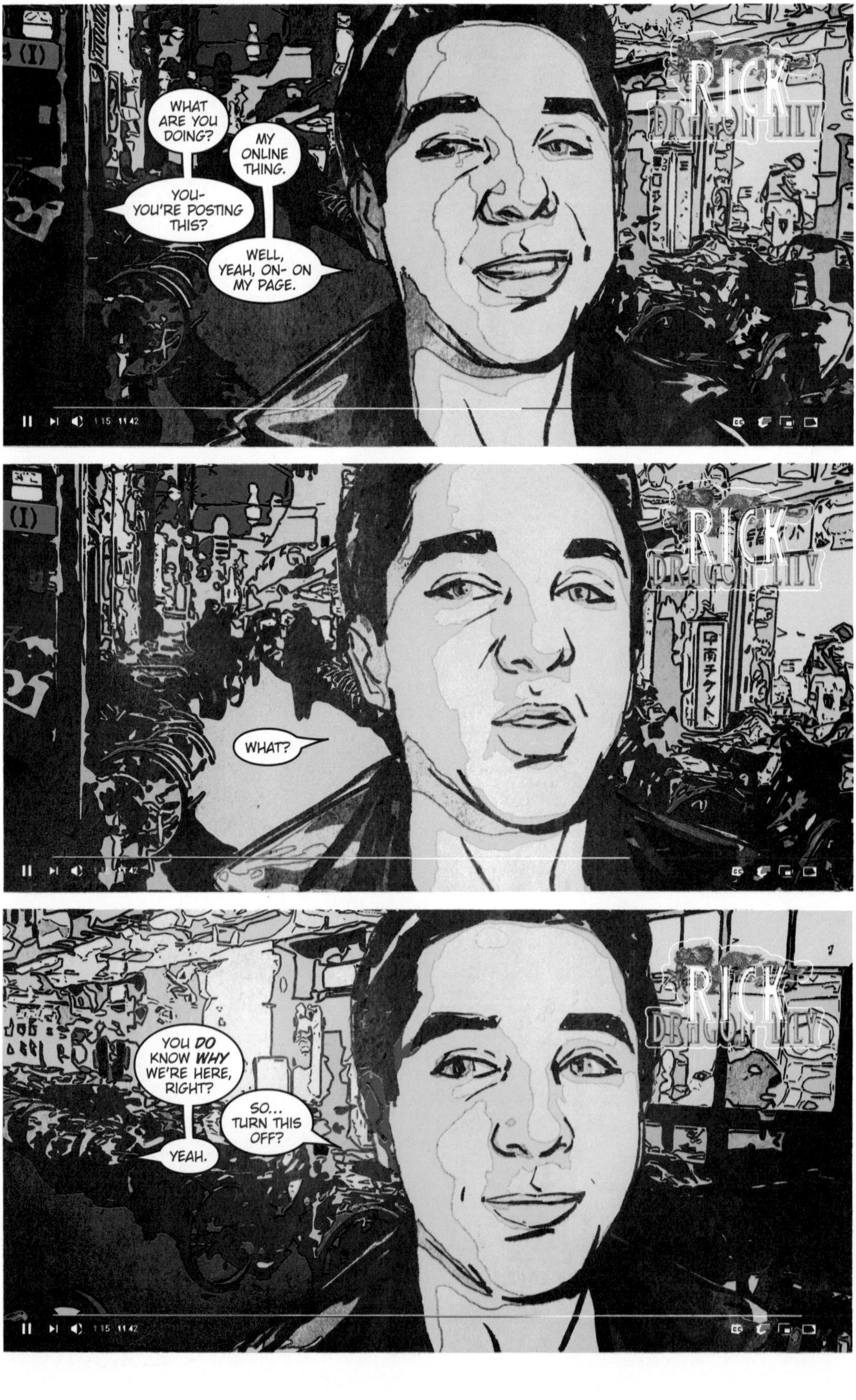
RICK
DRAGON LILY
WHAT ARE YOU DOING?
MY ONLINE THING.
YOU- YOU'RE POSTING THIS?
WELL, YEAH, ON- ON MY PAGE.
RICK
DRAGON LILY
WHAT?
RICK
DRAGON LILY
YOU **DO** KNOW **WHY** WE'RE HERE, RIGHT?
SO... TURN THIS OFF?
YEAH.

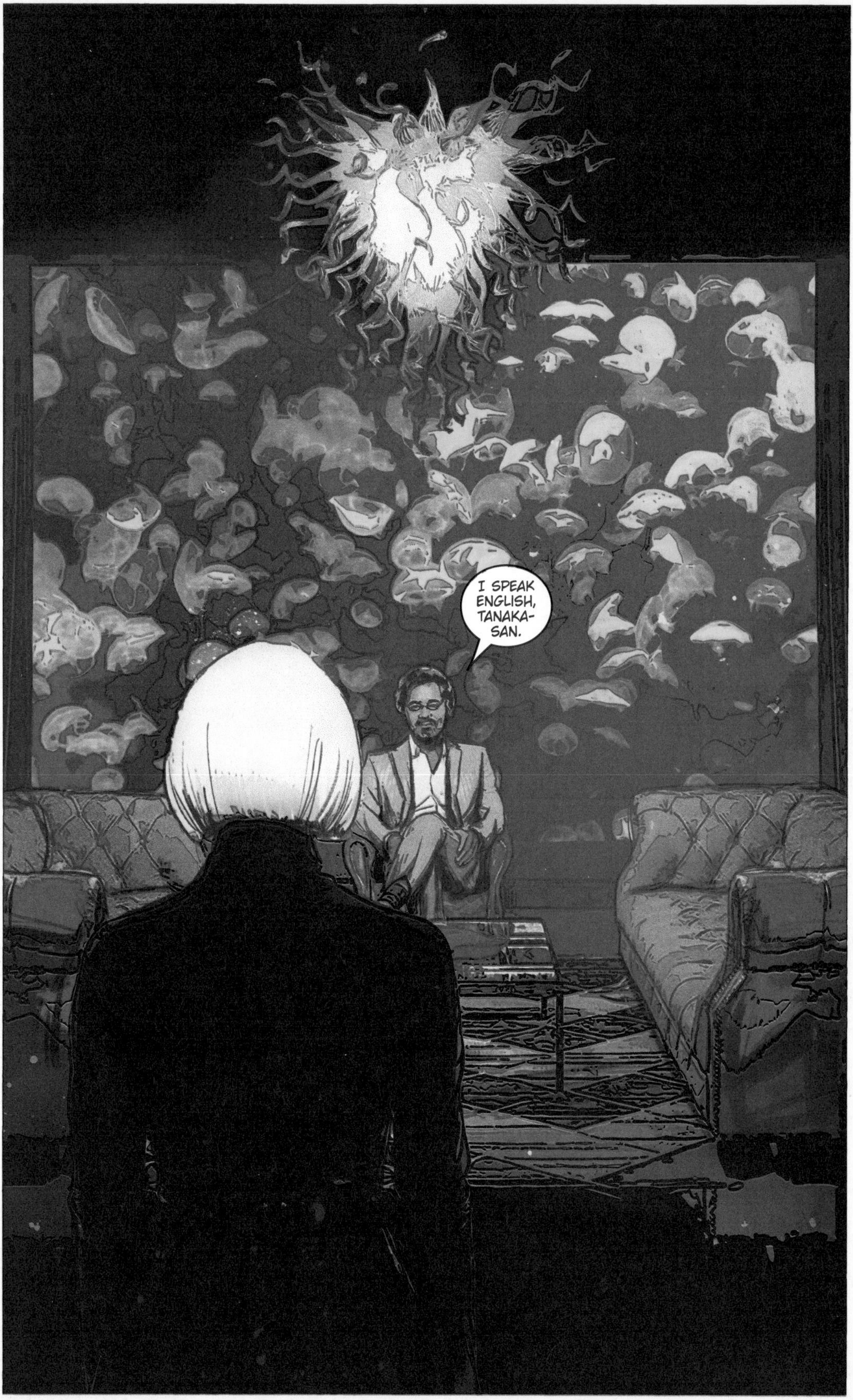
I SPEAK ENGLISH, TANAKA-SAN.

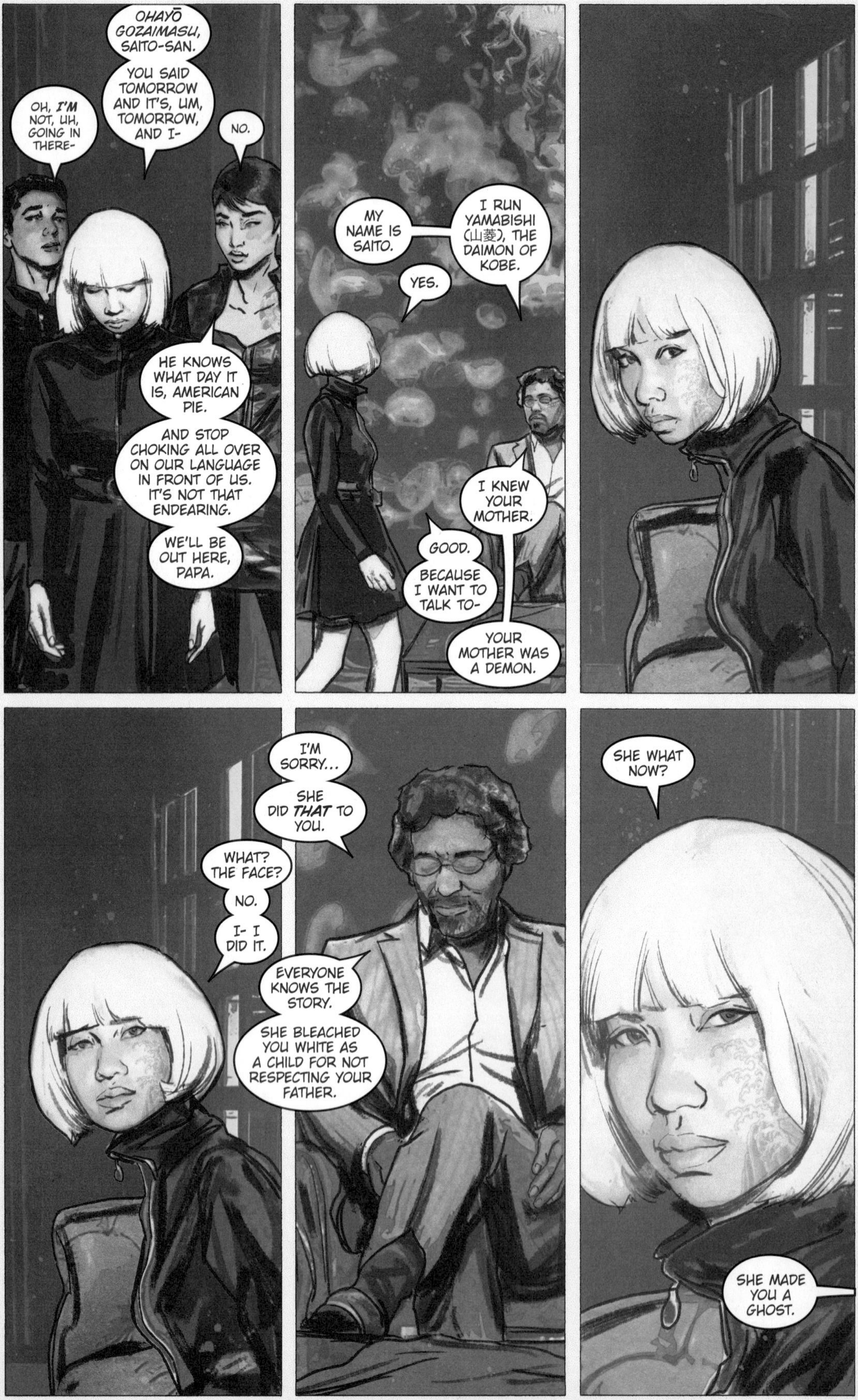
OHAYŌ GOZAIMASU, SAITO-SAN.
YOU SAID TOMORROW AND IT'S, UM, TOMORROW, AND I-
OH, *I'M* NOT, UH, GOING IN THERE-
NO.
HE KNOWS WHAT DAY IT IS, AMERICAN PIE.
AND STOP CHOKING ALL OVER ON OUR LANGUAGE IN FRONT OF US. IT'S NOT THAT ENDEARING.
WE'LL BE OUT HERE, PAPA.
MY NAME IS SAITO.
I RUN YAMABISHI (山菱), THE DAIMON OF KOBE.
YES.
I KNEW YOUR MOTHER.
GOOD.
BECAUSE I WANT TO TALK TO-
YOUR MOTHER WAS A DEMON.
I'M SORRY...
SHE DID *THAT* TO YOU.
WHAT? THE FACE?
NO.
I- I DID IT.
EVERYONE KNOWS THE STORY.
SHE BLEACHED YOU WHITE AS A CHILD FOR NOT RESPECTING YOUR FATHER.
SHE WHAT NOW?
SHE MADE YOU A GHOST.

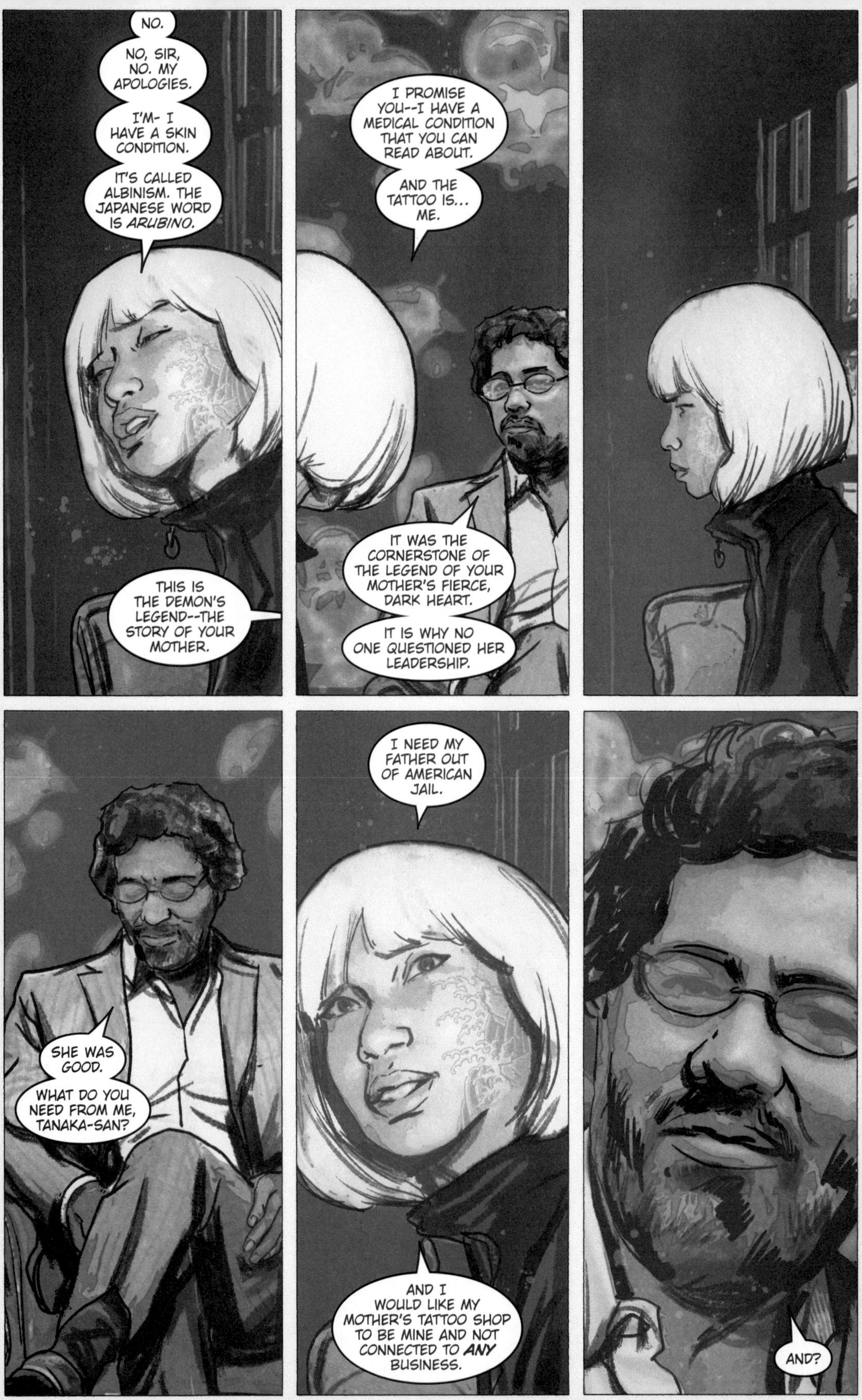

NO.
NO, SIR, NO. MY APOLOGIES.
I'M- I HAVE A SKIN CONDITION.
IT'S CALLED ALBINISM. THE JAPANESE WORD IS *ARUBINO*.
THIS IS THE DEMON'S LEGEND--THE STORY OF YOUR MOTHER.
I PROMISE YOU--I HAVE A MEDICAL CONDITION THAT YOU CAN READ ABOUT.
AND THE TATTOO IS... ME.
IT WAS THE CORNERSTONE OF THE LEGEND OF YOUR MOTHER'S FIERCE, DARK HEART.
IT IS WHY NO ONE QUESTIONED HER LEADERSHIP.
SHE WAS GOOD.
WHAT DO YOU NEED FROM ME, TANAKA-SAN?
I NEED MY FATHER OUT OF AMERICAN JAIL.
AND I WOULD LIKE MY MOTHER'S TATTOO SHOP TO BE MINE AND NOT CONNECTED TO ***ANY*** BUSINESS.
AND?

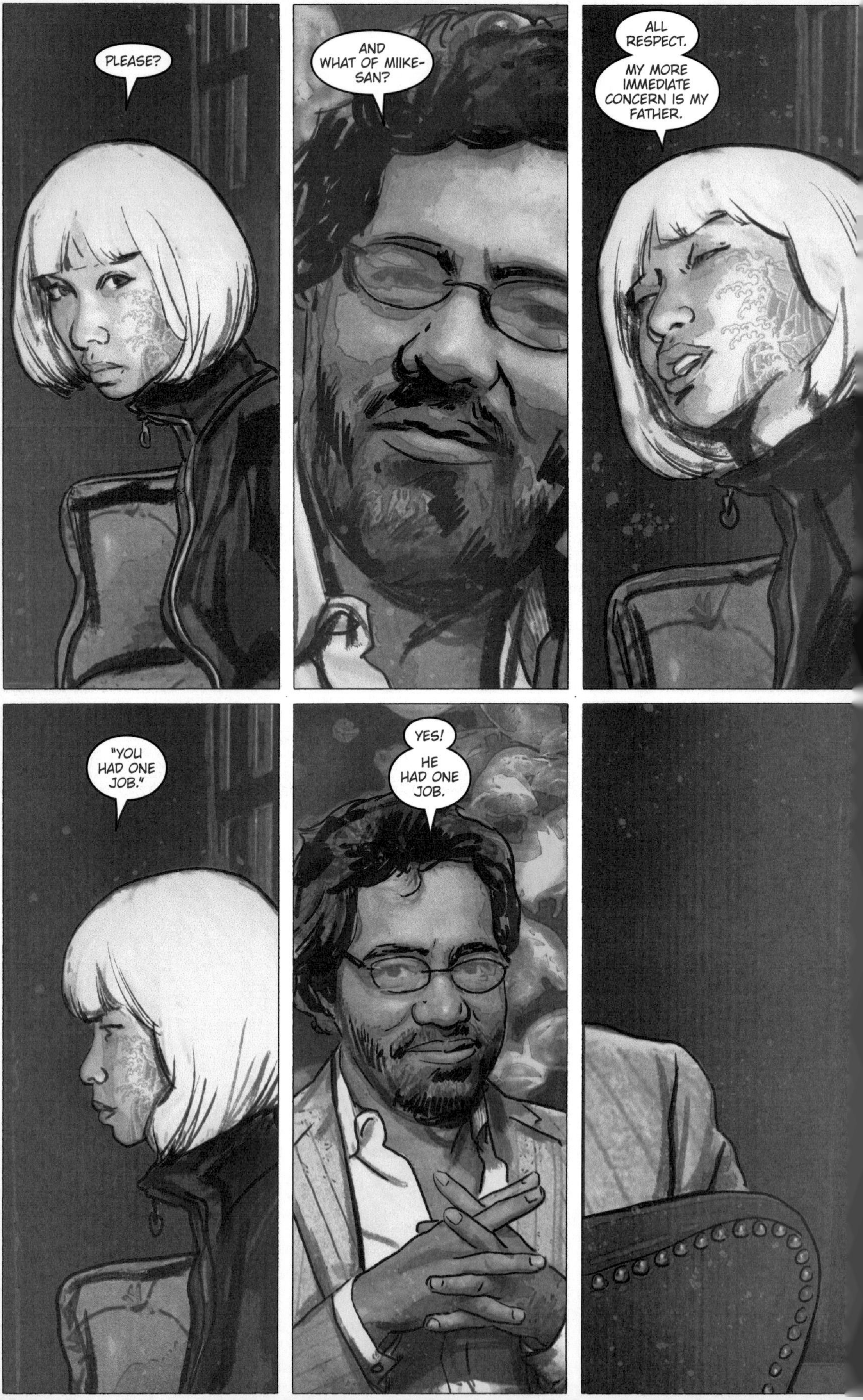
PLEASE?
AND WHAT OF MIIKE-SAN?
ALL RESPECT.
MY MORE IMMEDIATE CONCERN IS MY FATHER.
"YOU HAD ONE JOB."
YES!
HE HAD ONE JOB.

WE ARE HERE TO DISCUSS THE BETRAYAL.

HE BETRAYED YOUR MOTHER AND YOUR FATHER.

SHE IS DEAD BY THE HAND OF AN ENEMY.

THEY SAY IN AMERICA, TO A MIIKE-SAN, THEY SAY--

"YOU HAVE THE JOB."

IF I MAY REQUEST FROM YOU, SAITO-SAN...

I AM *VERY* FRUSTRATED...

WHAT WOULD *YOU* DO WITH MIIKE-SAN IF YOU FOUND YOURSELF IN MY PLACE?

I APPRECIATE THE SEARCH FOR WISDOM IN THE FACE OF A NEW CHALLENGE--

--WHO DOESN'T LIKE A NEW CHALLENGE?!

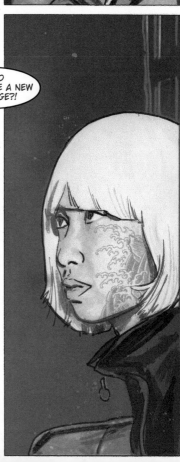

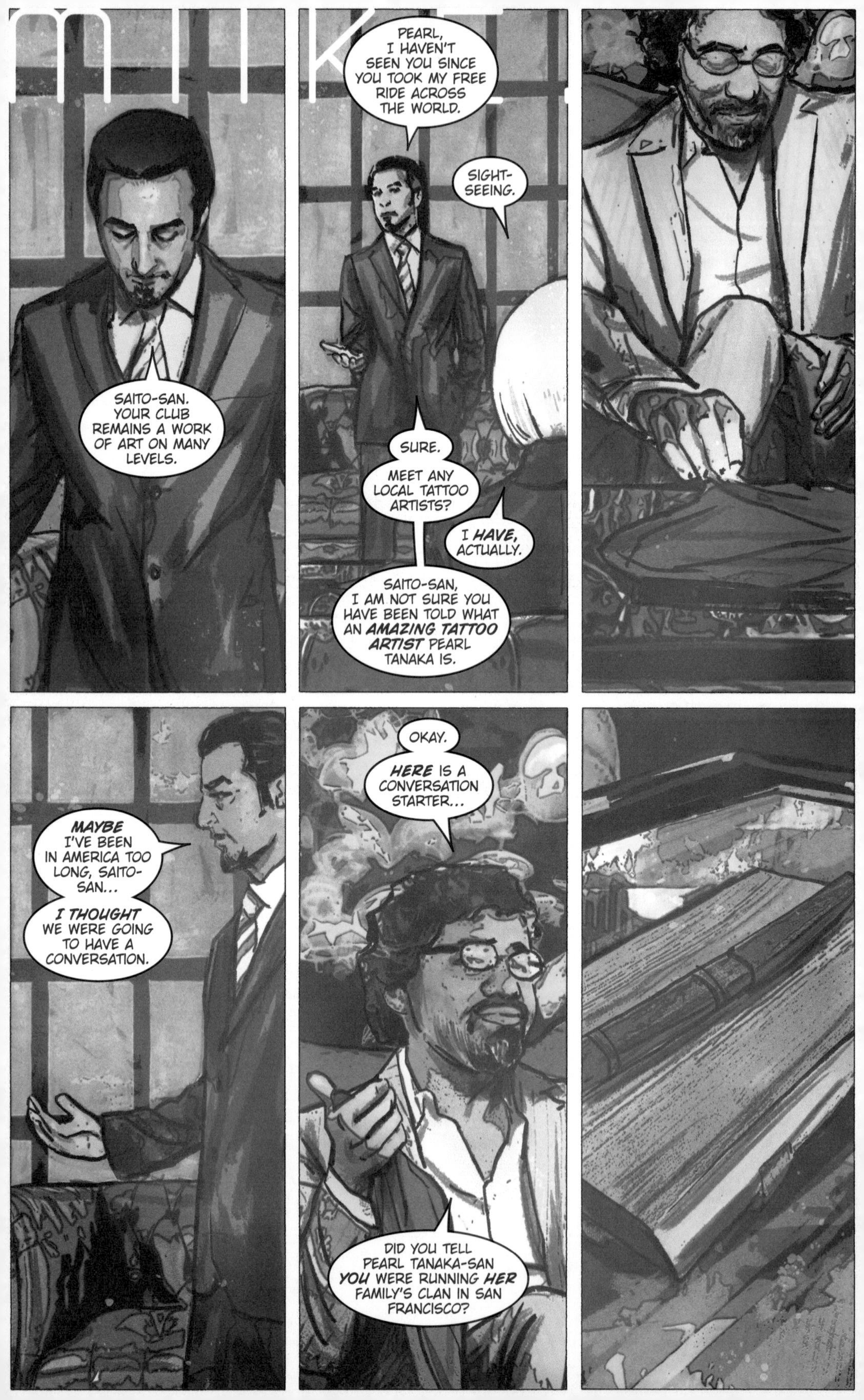
SAITO-SAN. YOUR CLUB REMAINS A WORK OF ART ON MANY LEVELS.
PEARL, I HAVEN'T SEEN YOU SINCE YOU TOOK MY FREE RIDE ACROSS THE WORLD.
SIGHT-SEEING.
SURE.
MEET ANY LOCAL TATTOO ARTISTS?
I *HAVE,* ACTUALLY.
SAITO-SAN, I AM NOT SURE YOU HAVE BEEN TOLD WHAT AN ***AMAZING TATTOO ARTIST*** PEARL TANAKA IS.
MAYBE I'VE BEEN IN AMERICA TOO LONG, SAITO-SAN...
I THOUGHT WE WERE GOING TO HAVE A CONVERSATION.
OKAY.
HERE IS A CONVERSATION STARTER...
DID YOU TELL PEARL TANAKA-SAN ***YOU*** WERE RUNNING ***HER*** FAMILY'S CLAN IN SAN FRANCISCO?

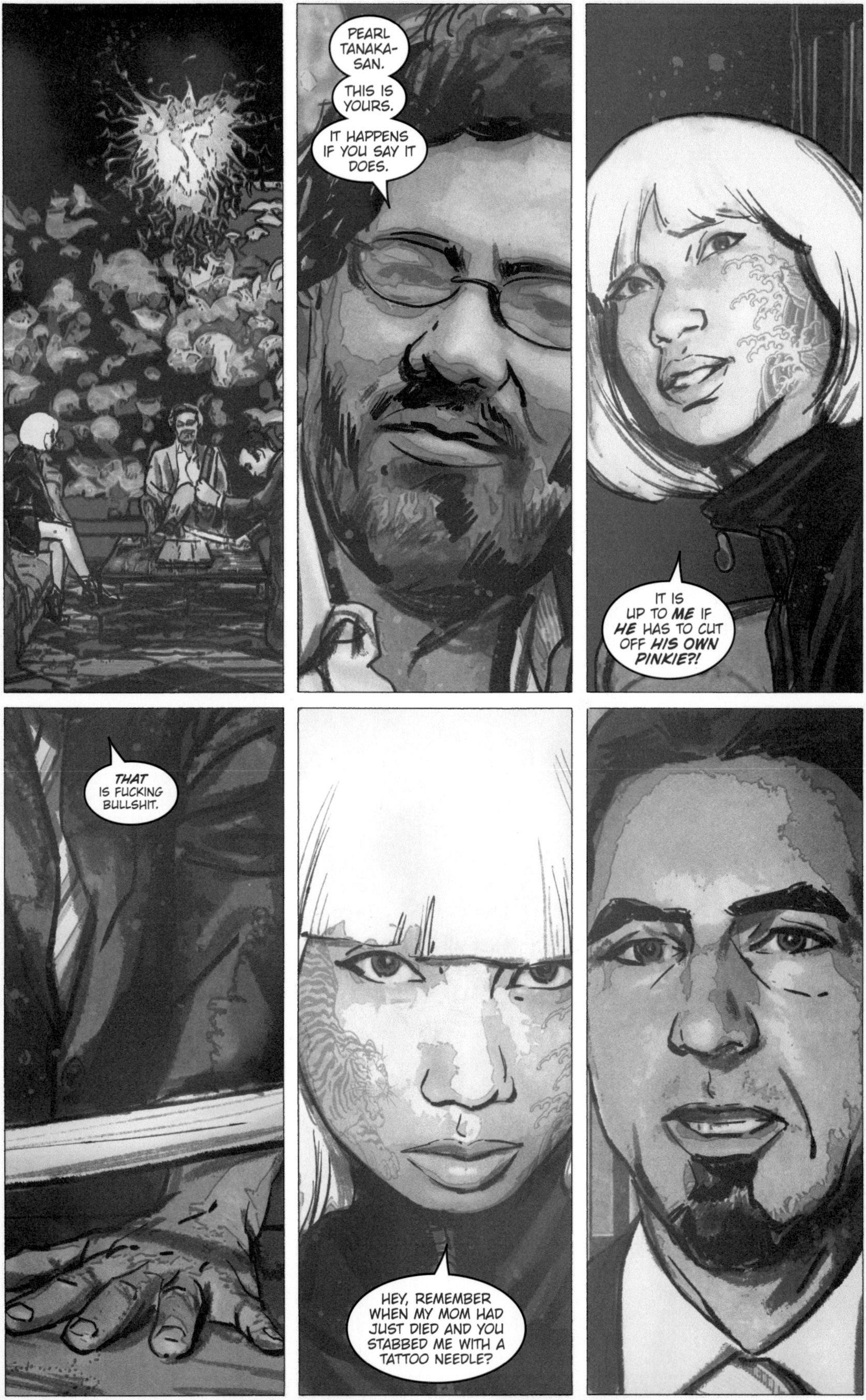
PEARL TANAKA-SAN.
THIS IS YOURS.
IT HAPPENS IF YOU SAY IT DOES.
IT IS UP TO ME IF HE HAS TO CUT OFF HIS OWN PINKIE?!
THAT IS FUCKING BULLSHIT.
HEY, REMEMBER WHEN MY MOM HAD JUST DIED AND YOU STABBED ME WITH A TATTOO NEEDLE?

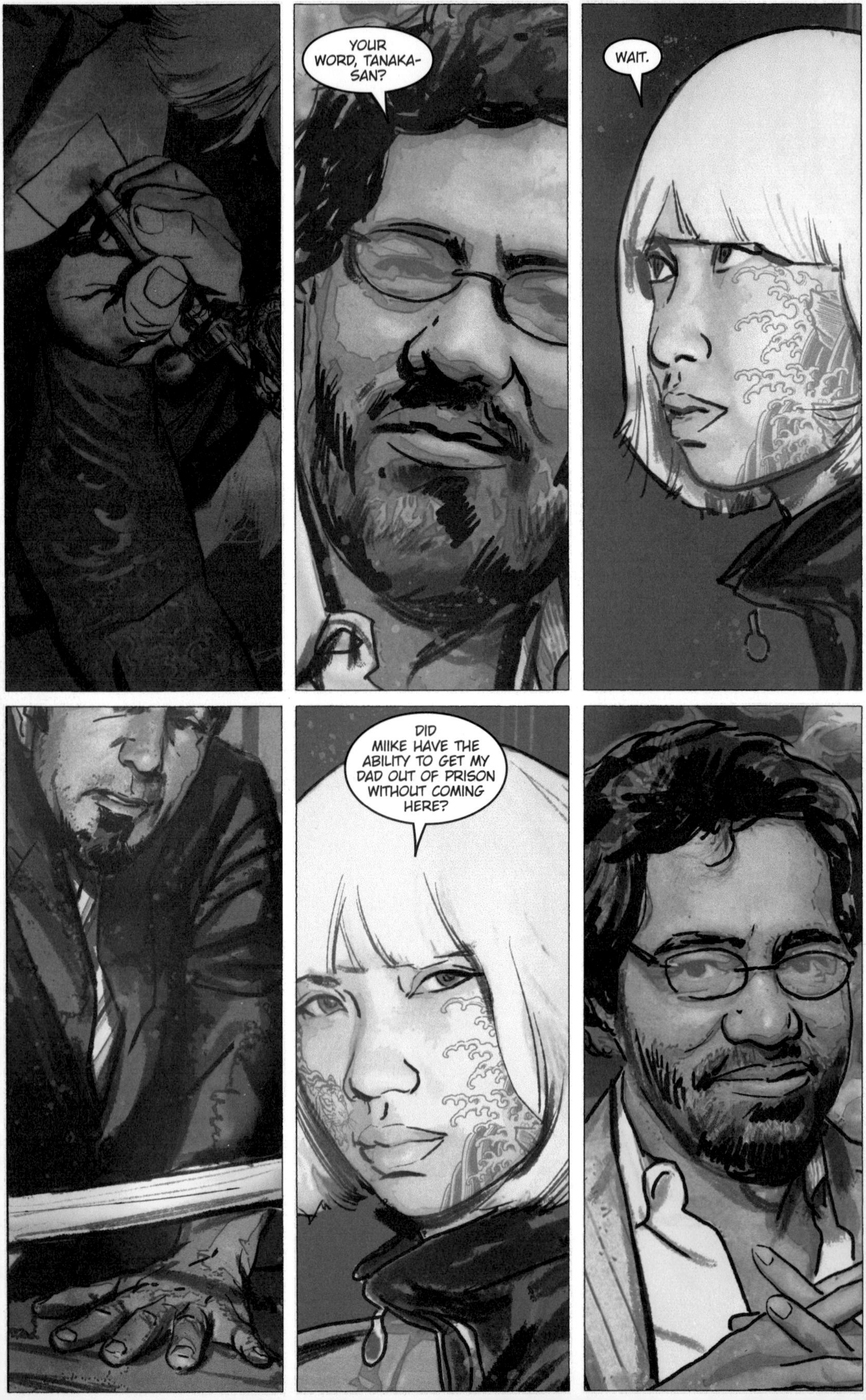
YOUR WORD, TANAKA-SAN?
WAIT.
DID MIIKE HAVE THE ABILITY TO GET MY DAD OUT OF PRISON WITHOUT COMING HERE?

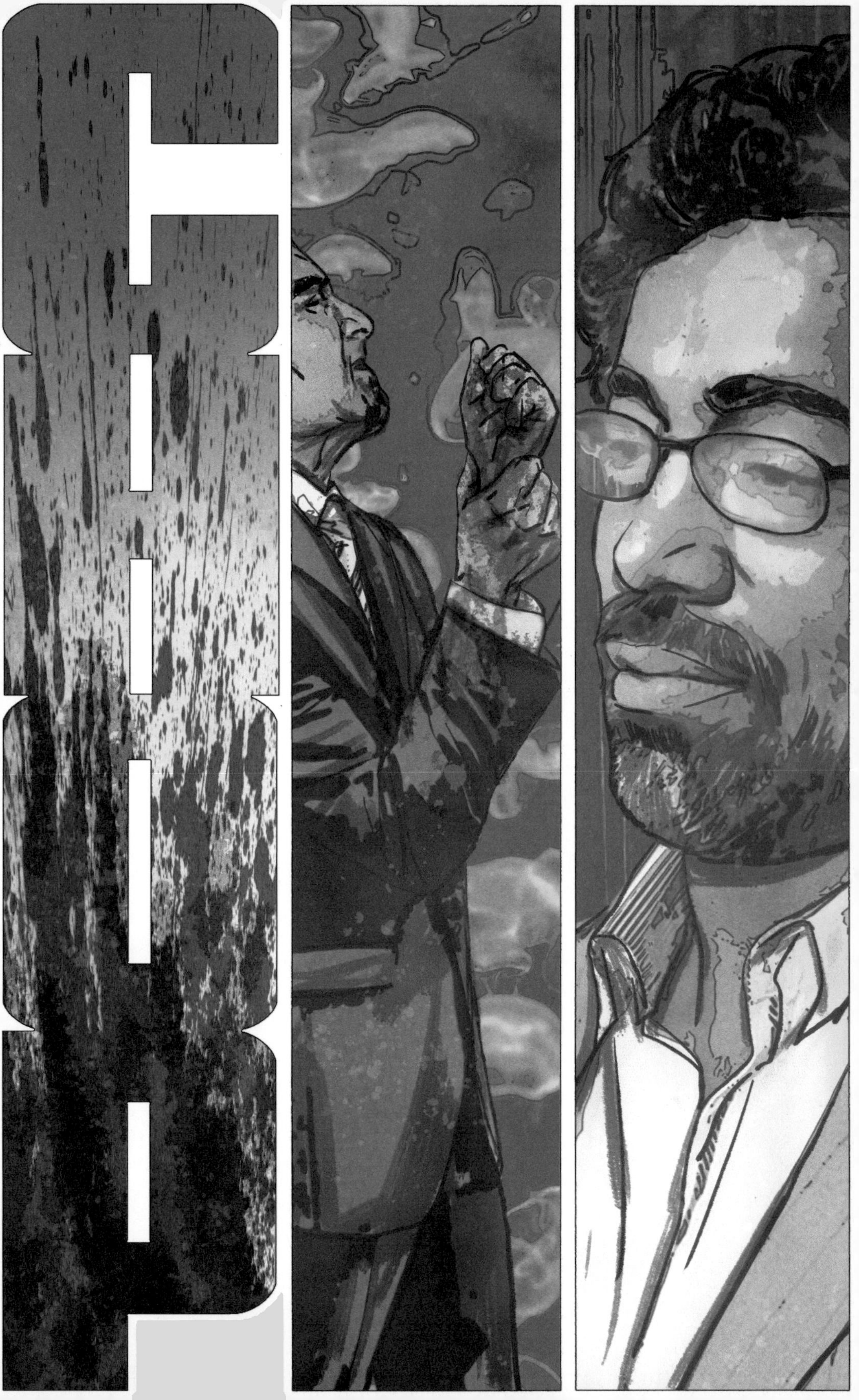

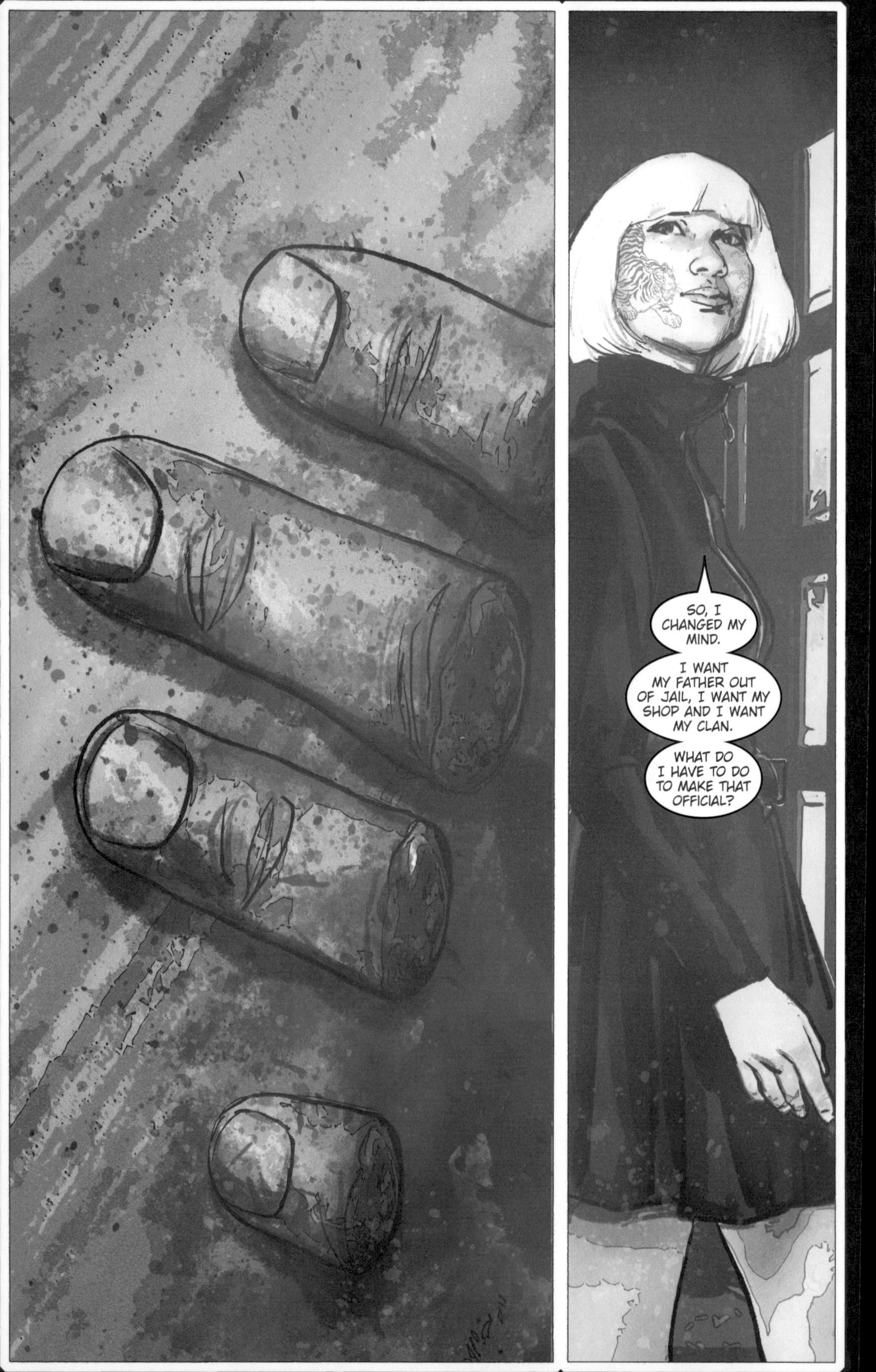
SO, I CHANGED MY MIND.
I WANT MY FATHER OUT OF JAIL, I WANT MY SHOP AND I WANT MY CLAN.
WHAT DO I HAVE TO DO TO MAKE THAT OFFICIAL?

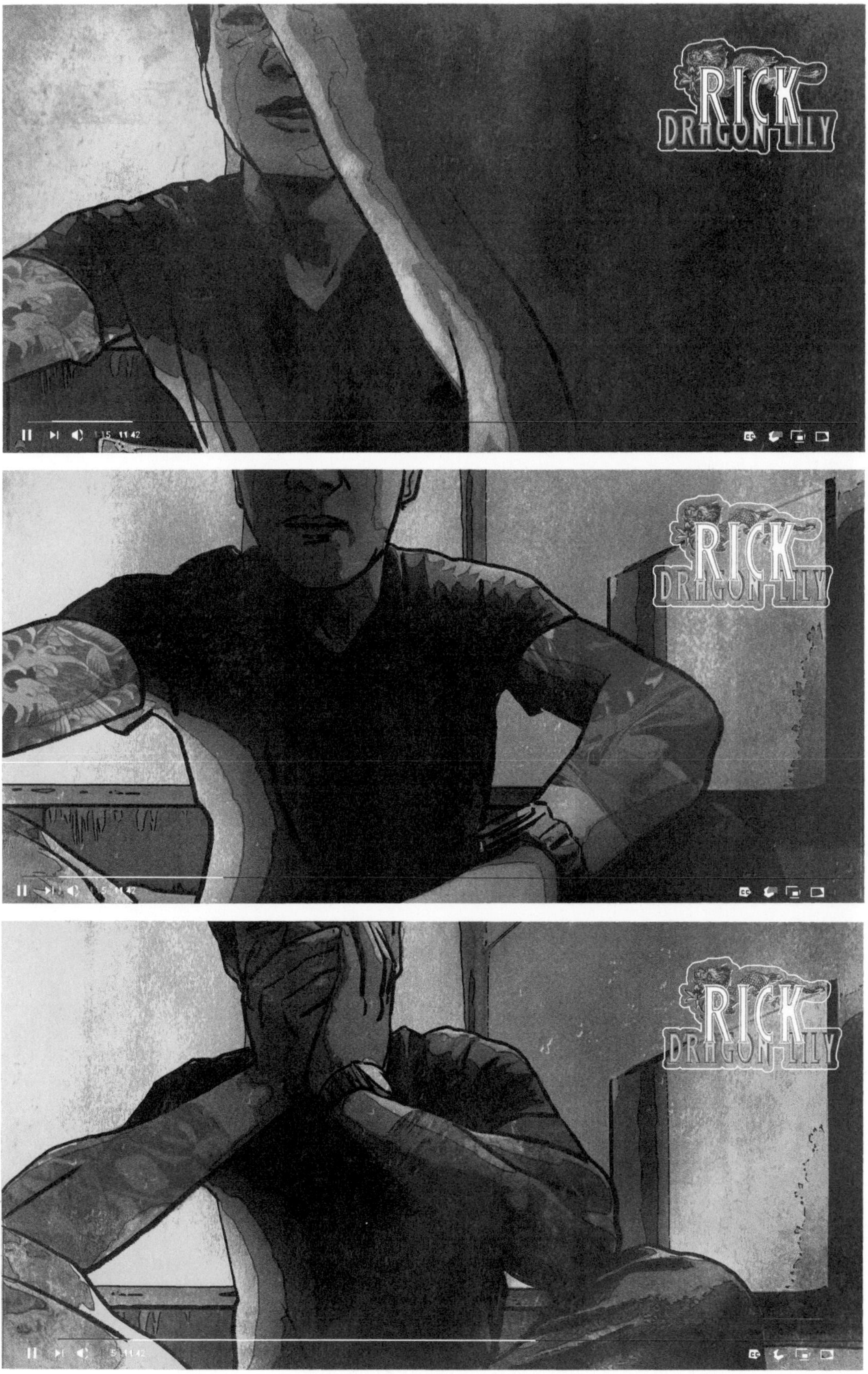
RICK
DRAGON LILY
RICK
DRAGON LILY
RICK
DRAGON LILY

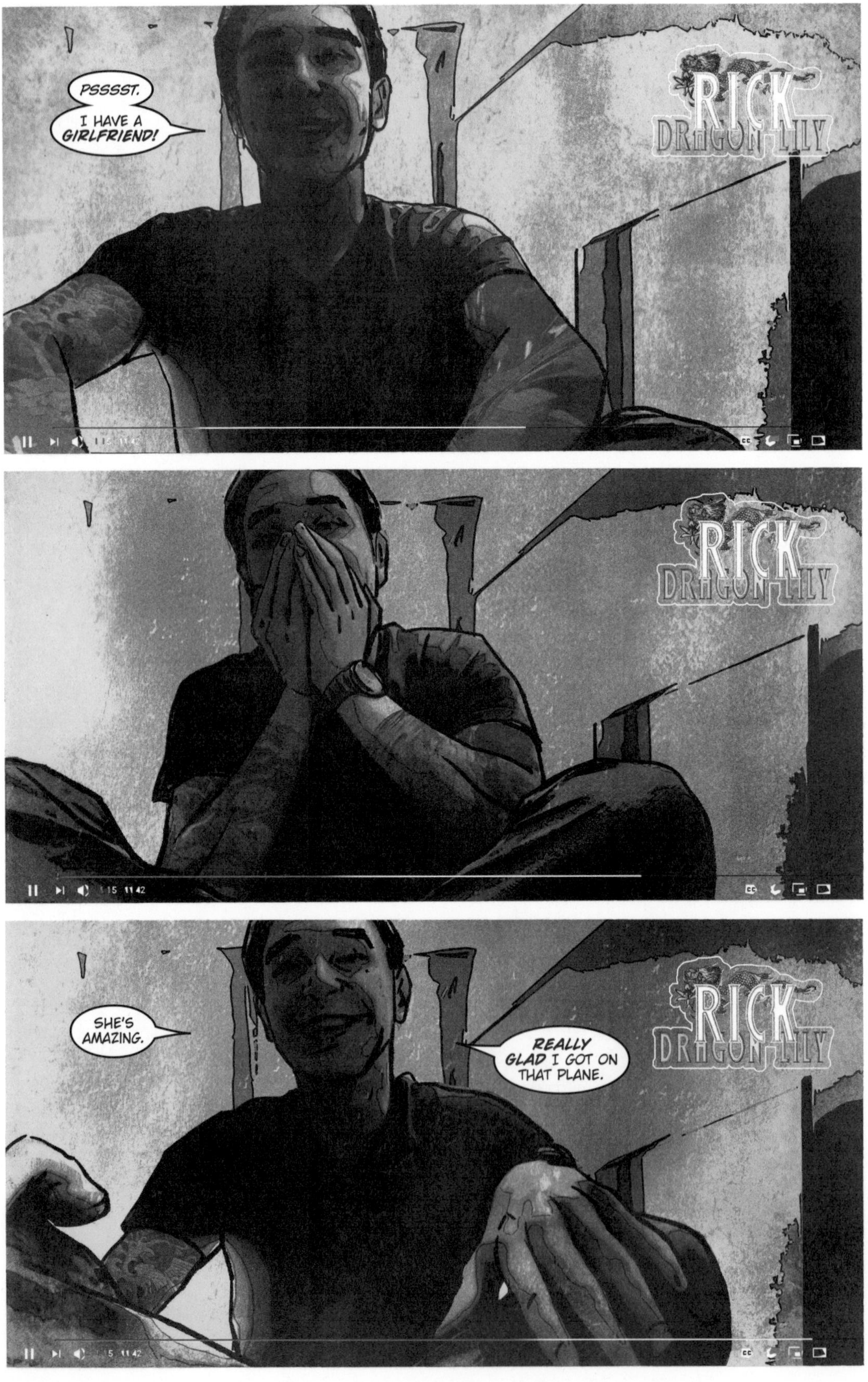
PSSSST.
I HAVE A GIRLFRIEND!
RICK
DRAGON LILY
SHE'S AMAZING.
REALLY GLAD I GOT ON THAT PLANE.

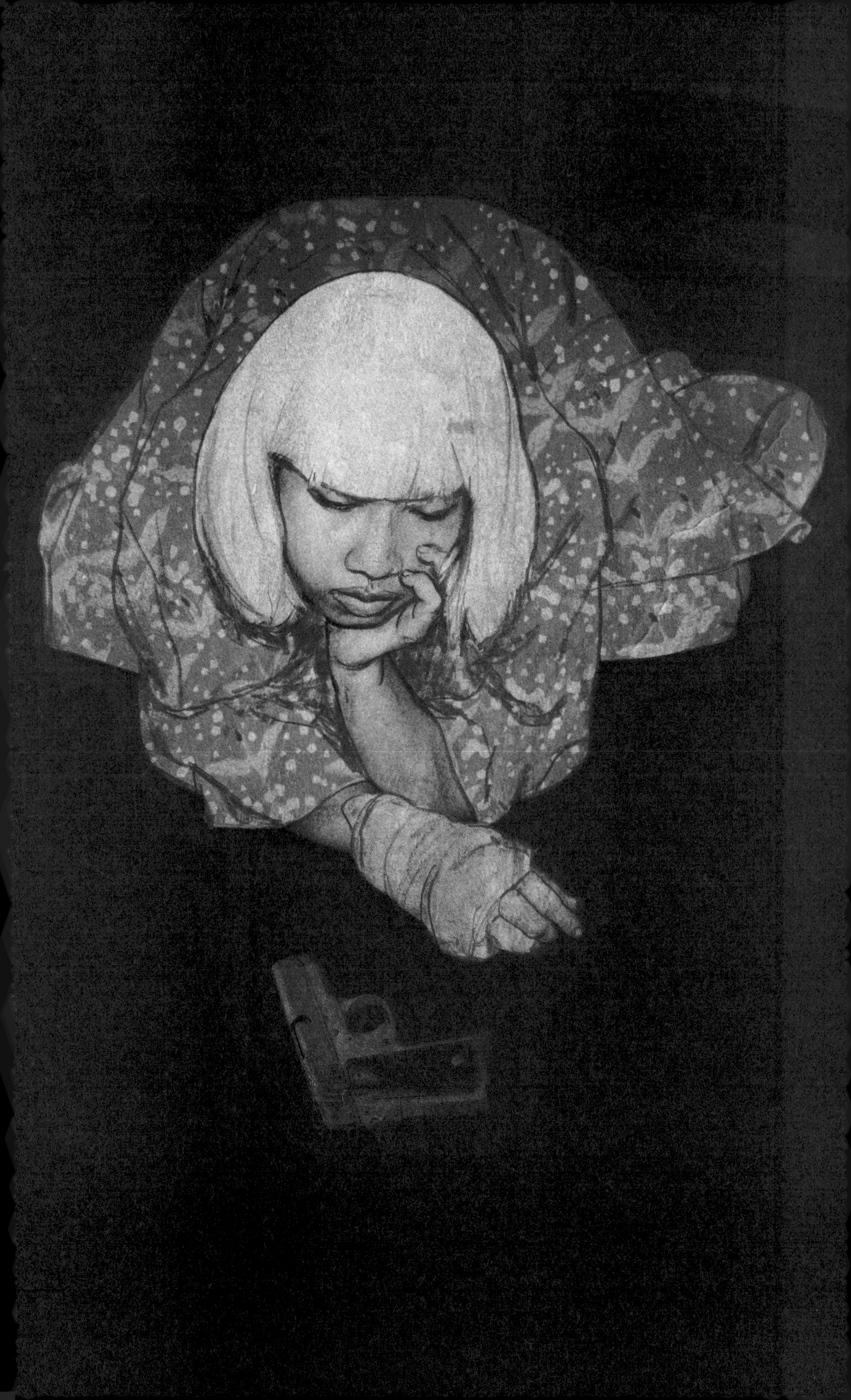

Variant cover art for issue #10
by GEORGE PRATT

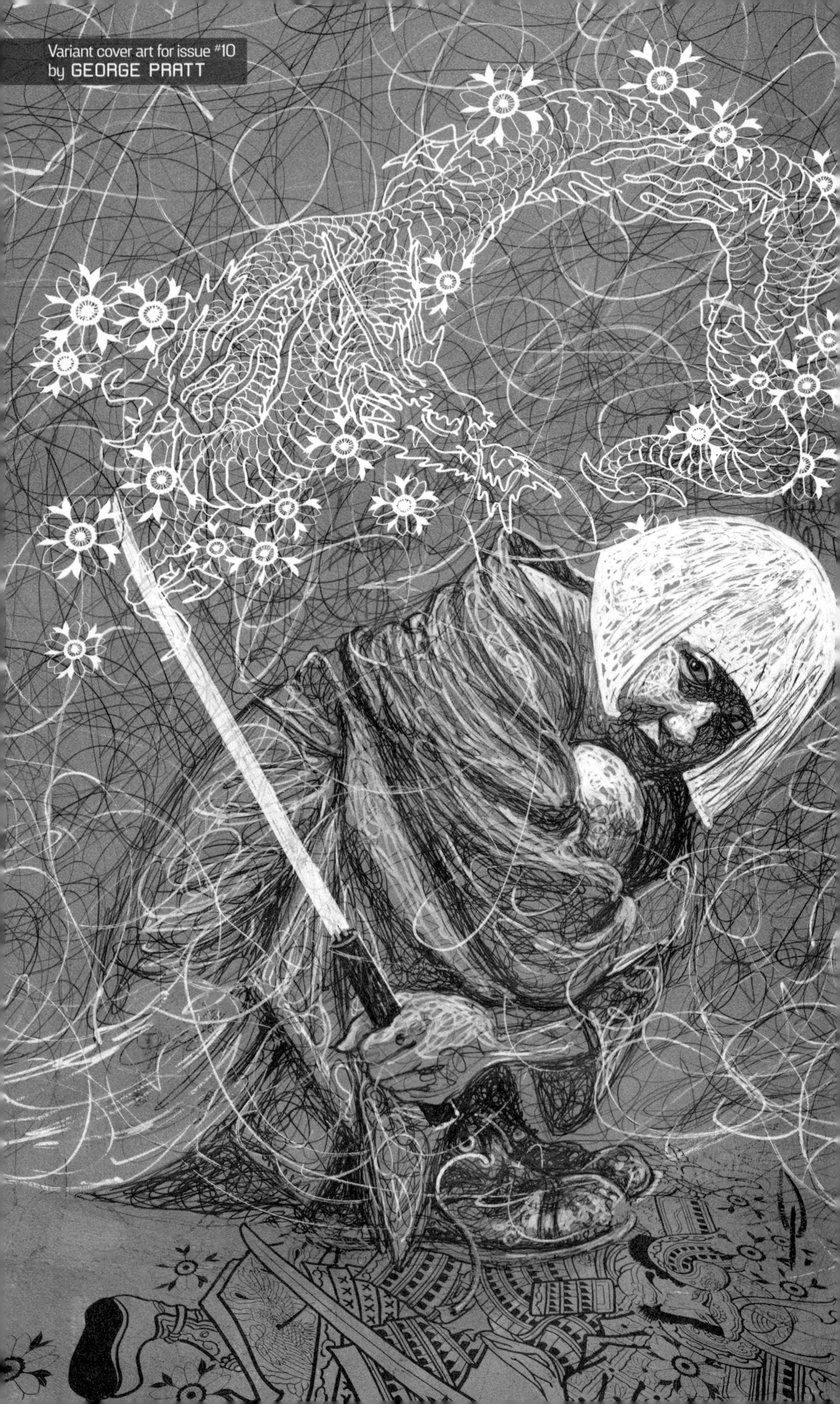

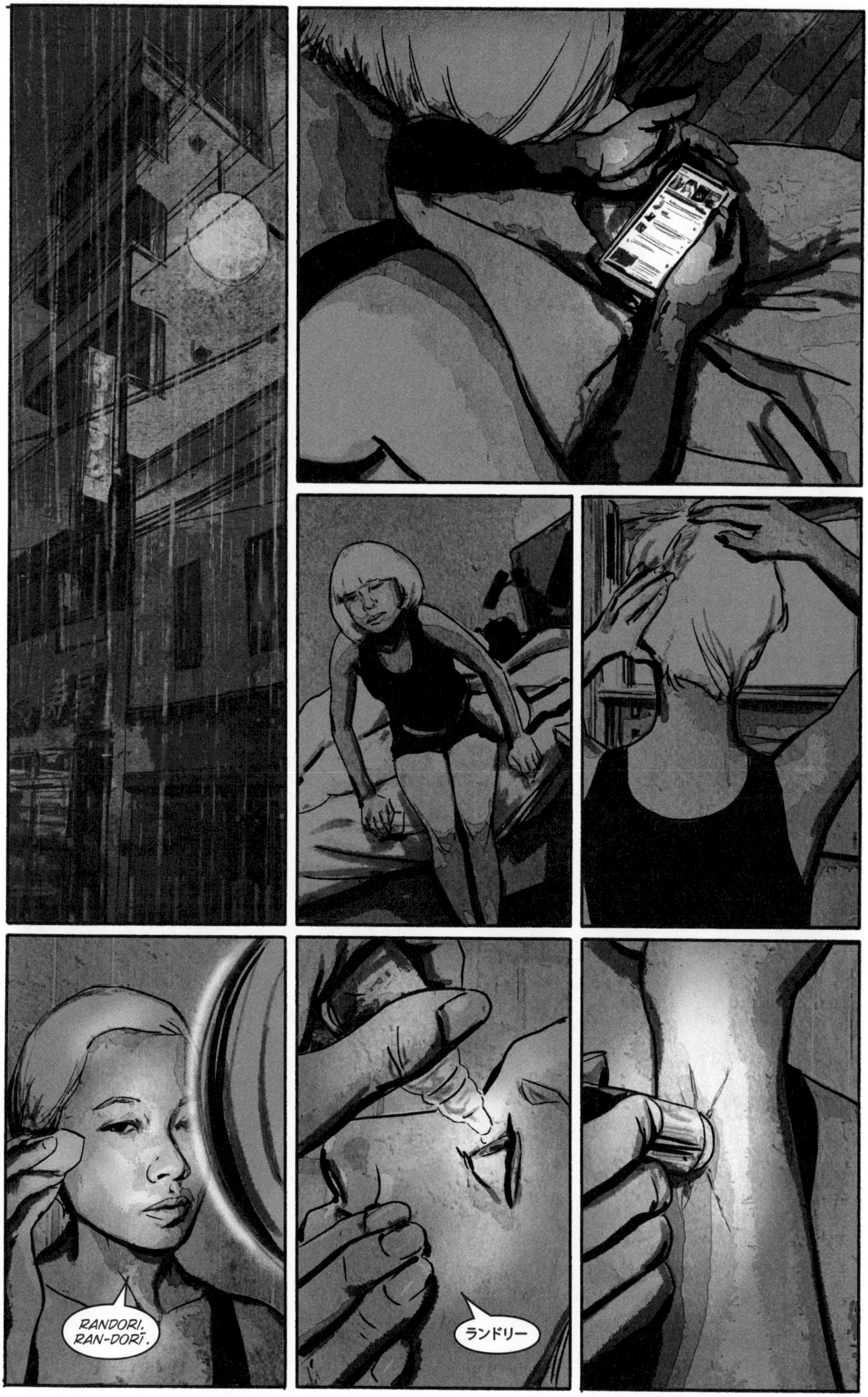
RANDORI.
RAN-DORĪ.
ランドリー

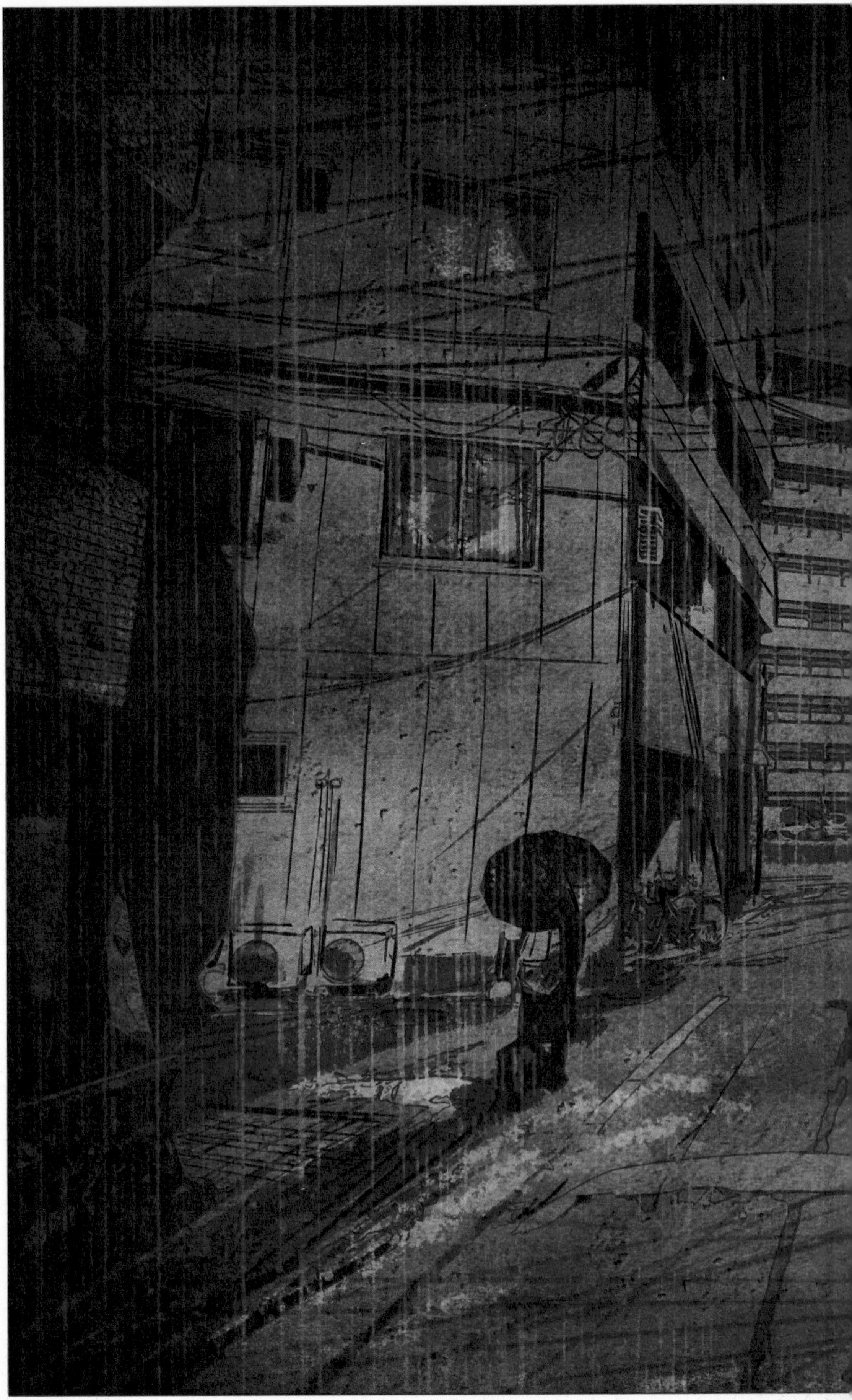

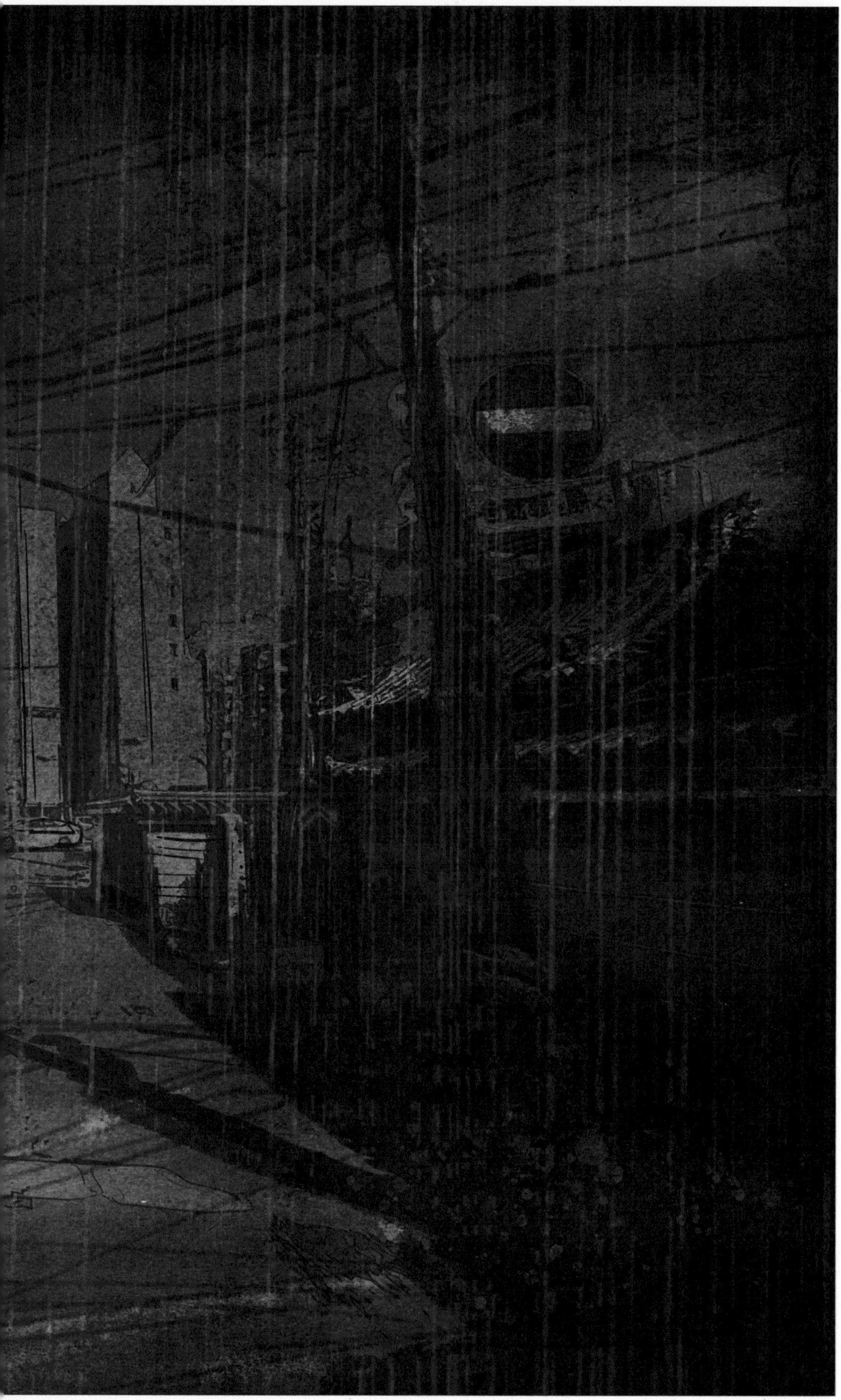

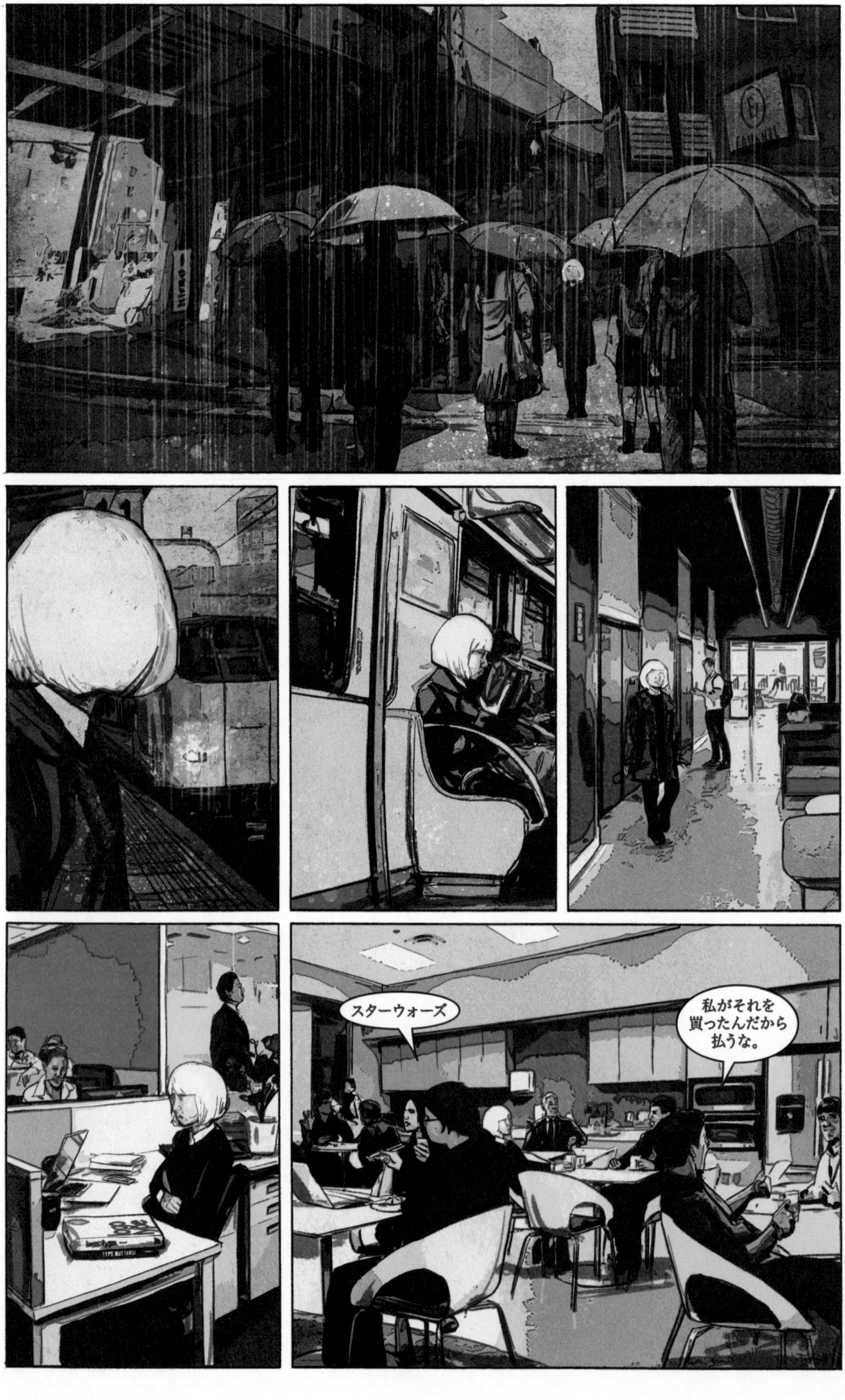
スターウォーズ
私がそれを買ったんだから払うな。

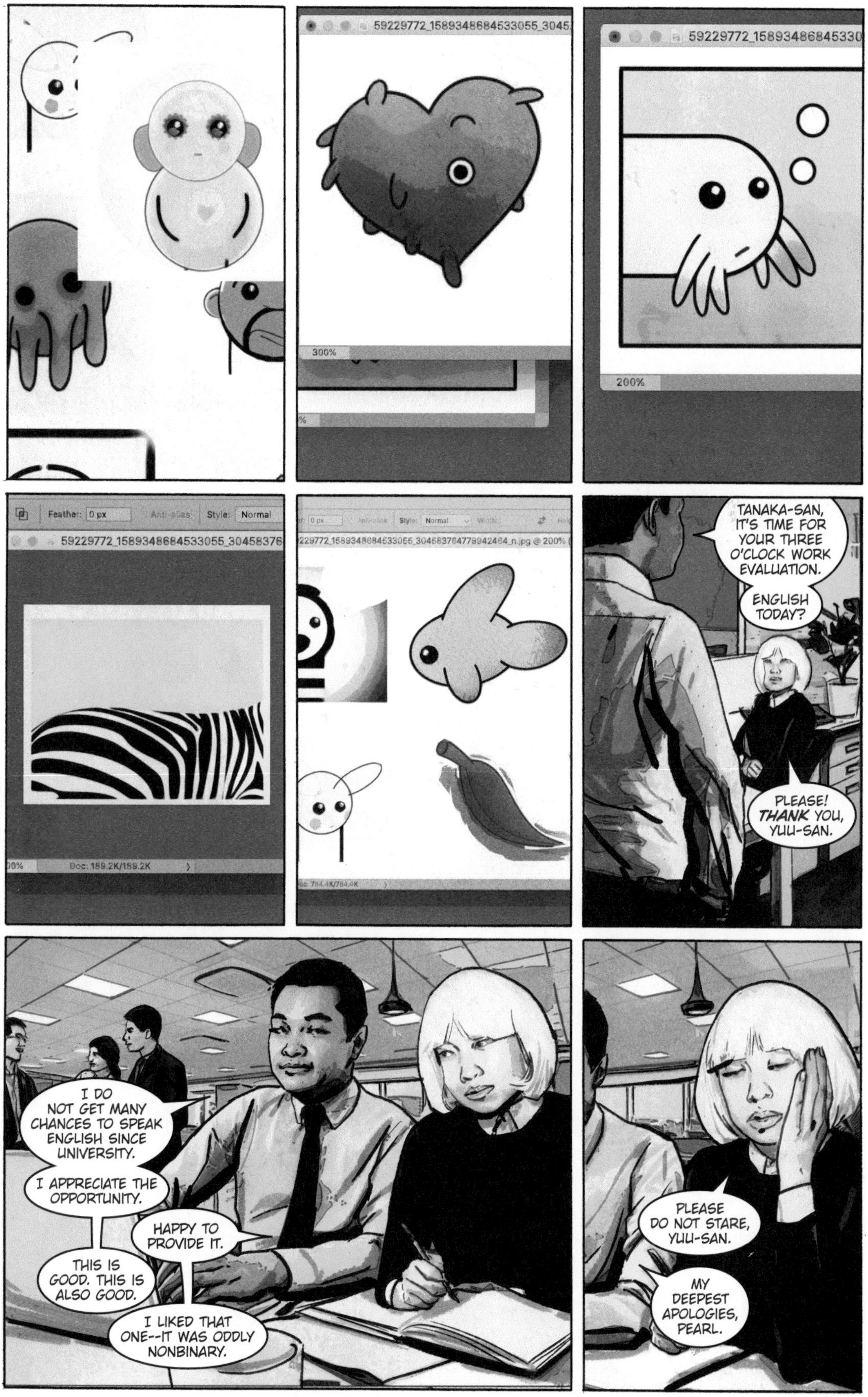
59229772_1589348684533055_3045
59229772_15893486845330
300%
200%
Feather: 0 px
Anti-alias
Style: Normal
59229772_1589348684533055_30458376
Doc: 189.2K/189.2K
Doc: 784.4K/784.4K
TANAKA-SAN, IT'S TIME FOR YOUR THREE O'CLOCK WORK EVALUATION.
ENGLISH TODAY?
PLEASE! *THANK* YOU, YUU-SAN.
I DO NOT GET MANY CHANCES TO SPEAK ENGLISH SINCE UNIVERSITY.
I APPRECIATE THE OPPORTUNITY.
HAPPY TO PROVIDE IT.
THIS IS GOOD. THIS IS ALSO GOOD.
I LIKED THAT ONE--IT WAS ODDLY NONBINARY.
PLEASE DO NOT STARE, YUU-SAN.
MY DEEPEST APOLOGIES, PEARL.

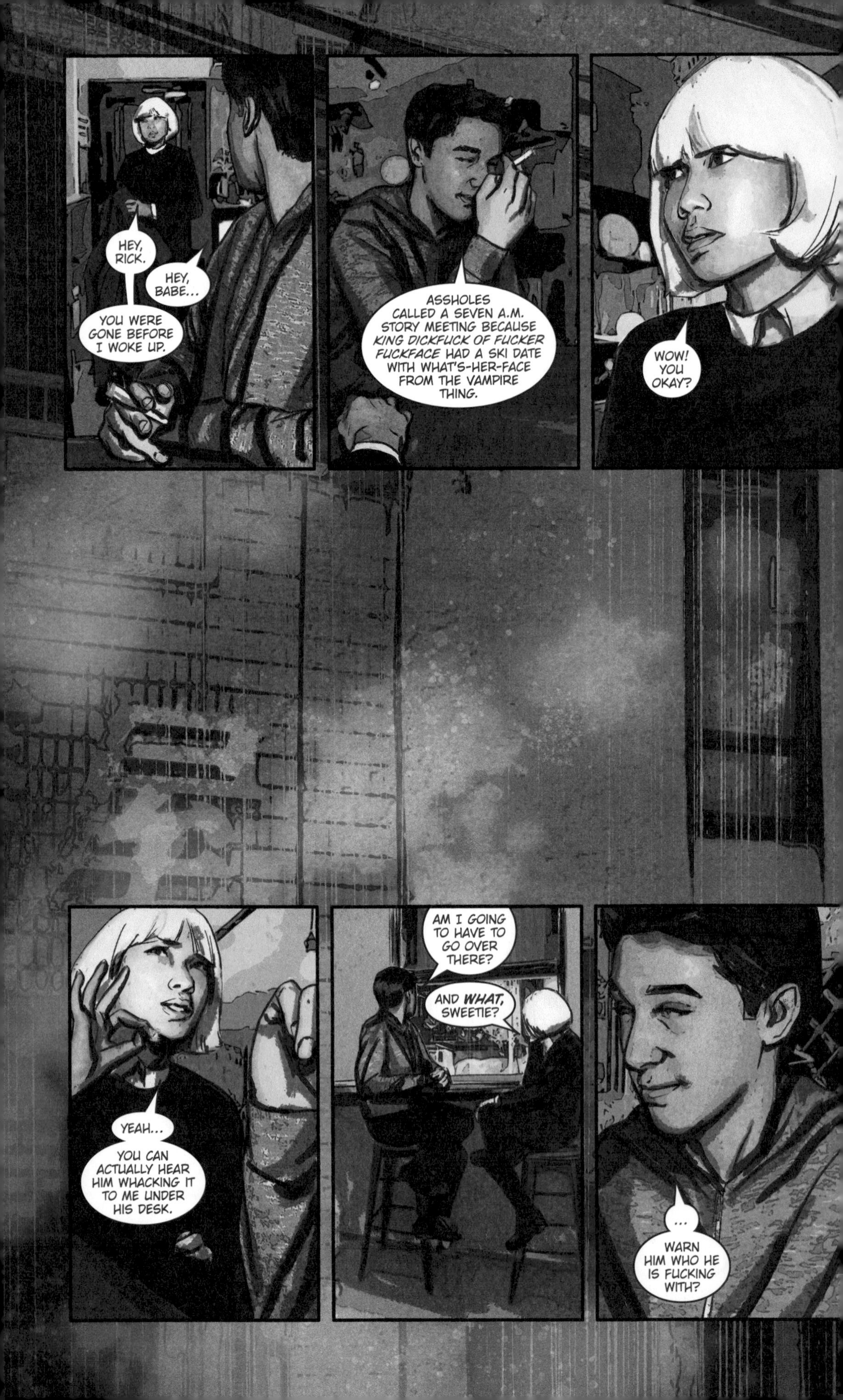
HEY, RICK.
HEY, BABE...
YOU WERE GONE BEFORE I WOKE UP.
ASSHOLES CALLED A SEVEN A.M. STORY MEETING BECAUSE *KING DICKFUCK OF FUCKER FUCKFACE* HAD A SKI DATE WITH WHAT'S-HER-FACE FROM THE VAMPIRE THING.
WOW! YOU OKAY?
YEAH...
YOU CAN ACTUALLY HEAR HIM WHACKING IT TO ME UNDER HIS DESK.
AM I GOING TO HAVE TO GO OVER THERE?
AND ***WHAT,*** SWEETIE?
...
WARN HIM WHO HE IS FUCKING WITH?

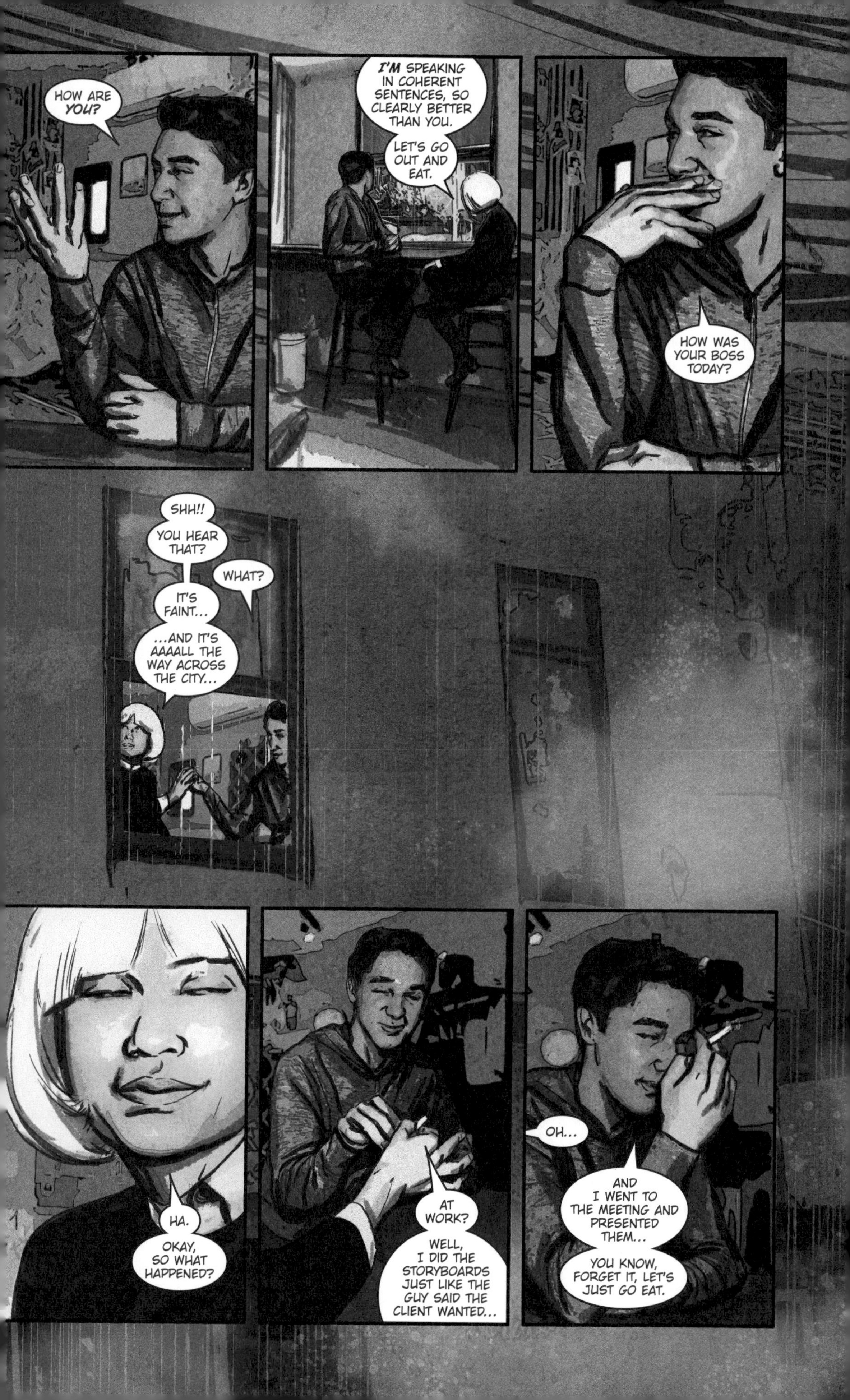
HOW ARE YOU?
I'M SPEAKING IN COHERENT SENTENCES, SO CLEARLY BETTER THAN YOU.
LET'S GO OUT AND EAT.
HOW WAS YOUR BOSS TODAY?
SHH!!
YOU HEAR THAT?
WHAT?
IT'S FAINT...
...AND IT'S AAAALL THE WAY ACROSS THE CITY...
HA.
OKAY, SO WHAT HAPPENED?
AT WORK?
WELL, I DID THE STORYBOARDS JUST LIKE THE GUY SAID THE CLIENT WANTED...
OH...
AND I WENT TO THE MEETING AND PRESENTED THEM...
YOU KNOW, FORGET IT, LET'S JUST GO EAT.

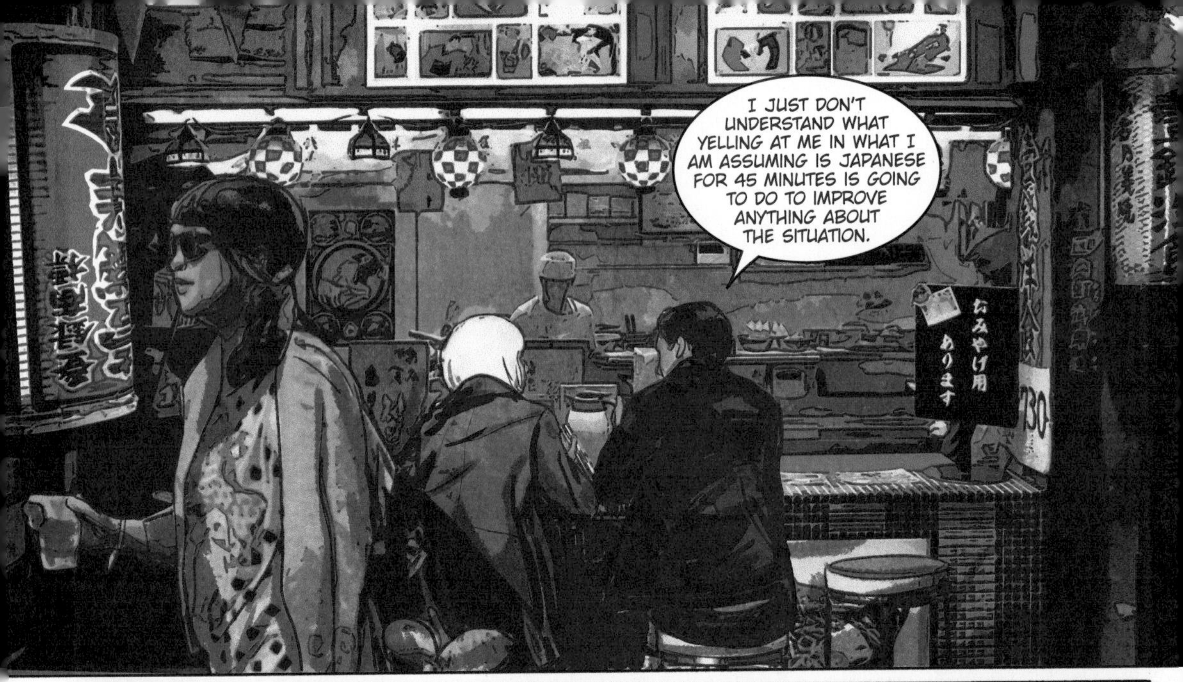
I JUST DON'T UNDERSTAND WHAT YELLING AT ME IN WHAT I AM ASSUMING IS JAPANESE FOR 45 MINUTES IS GOING TO DO TO IMPROVE ANYTHING ABOUT THE SITUATION.
おみやげ用
あります

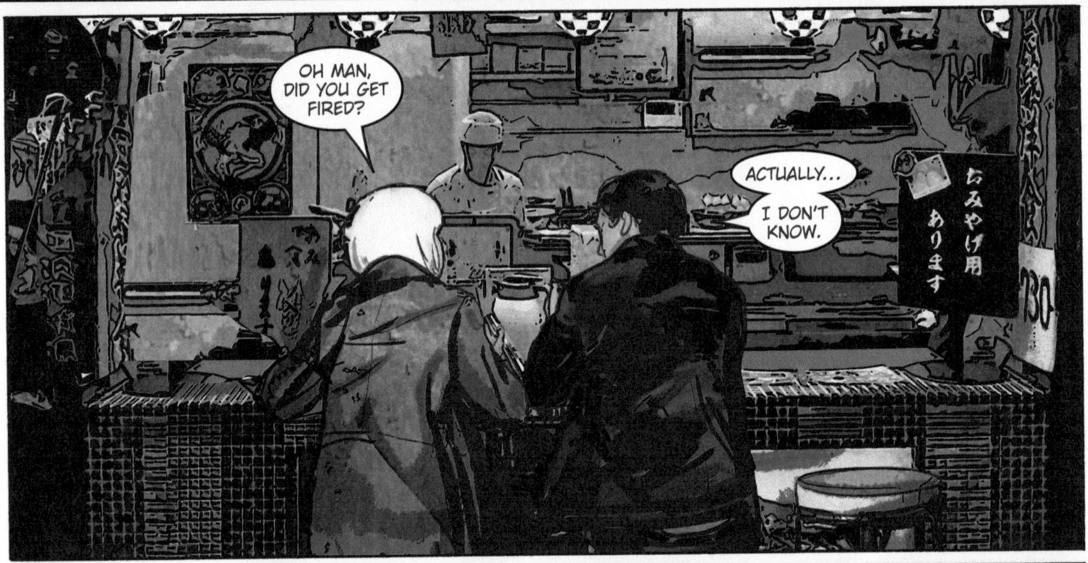
OH MAN, DID YOU GET FIRED?
ACTUALLY...
I DON'T KNOW.
おみやげ用
あります

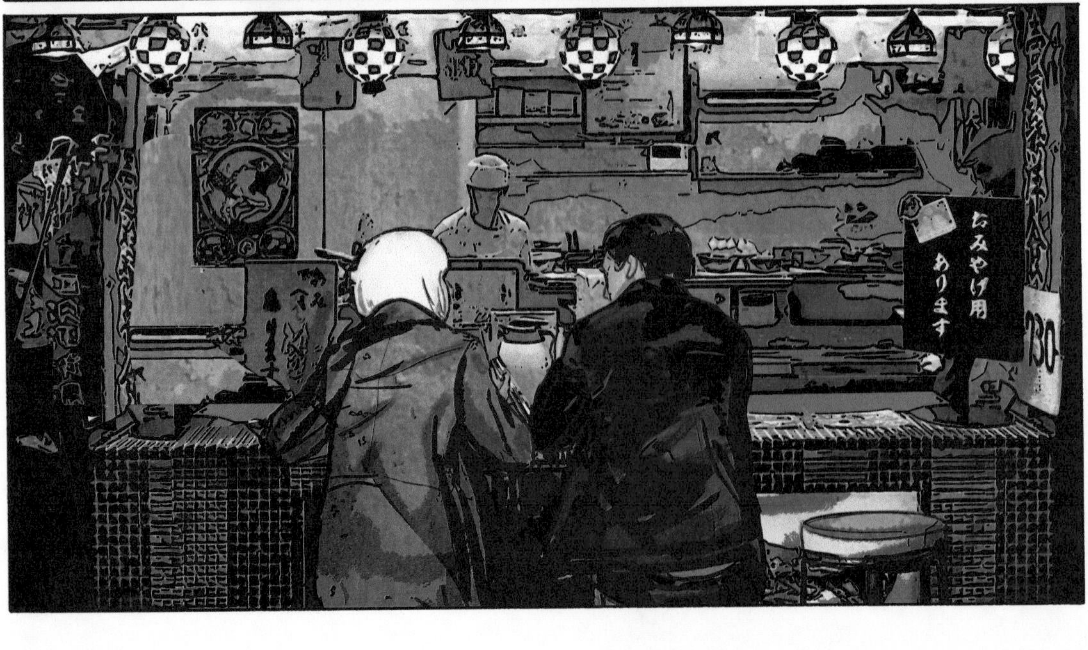
おみやげ用
あります

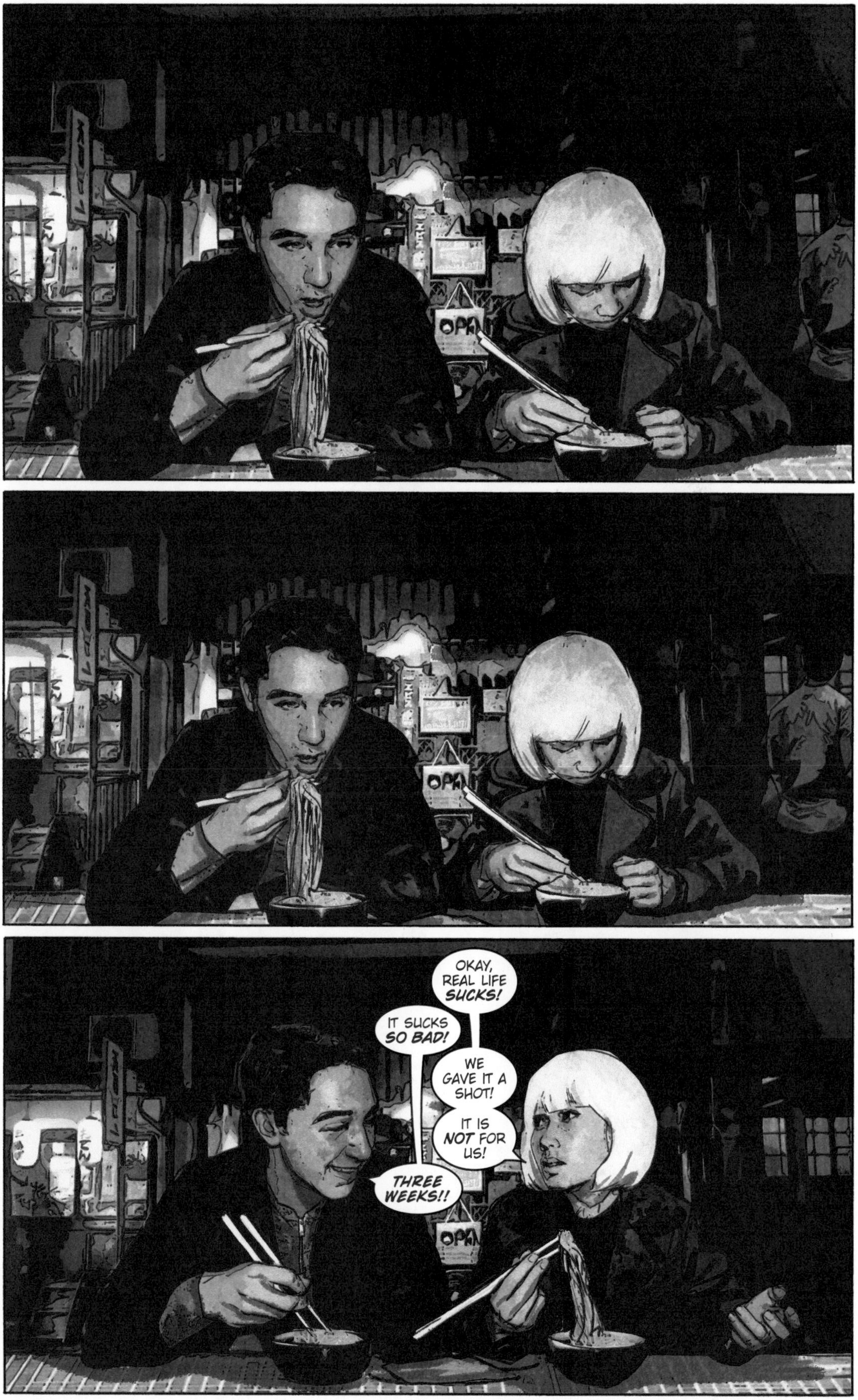
OKAY, REAL LIFE SUCKS!
IT SUCKS SO BAD!
WE GAVE IT A SHOT!
IT IS NOT FOR US!
THREE WEEKS!!

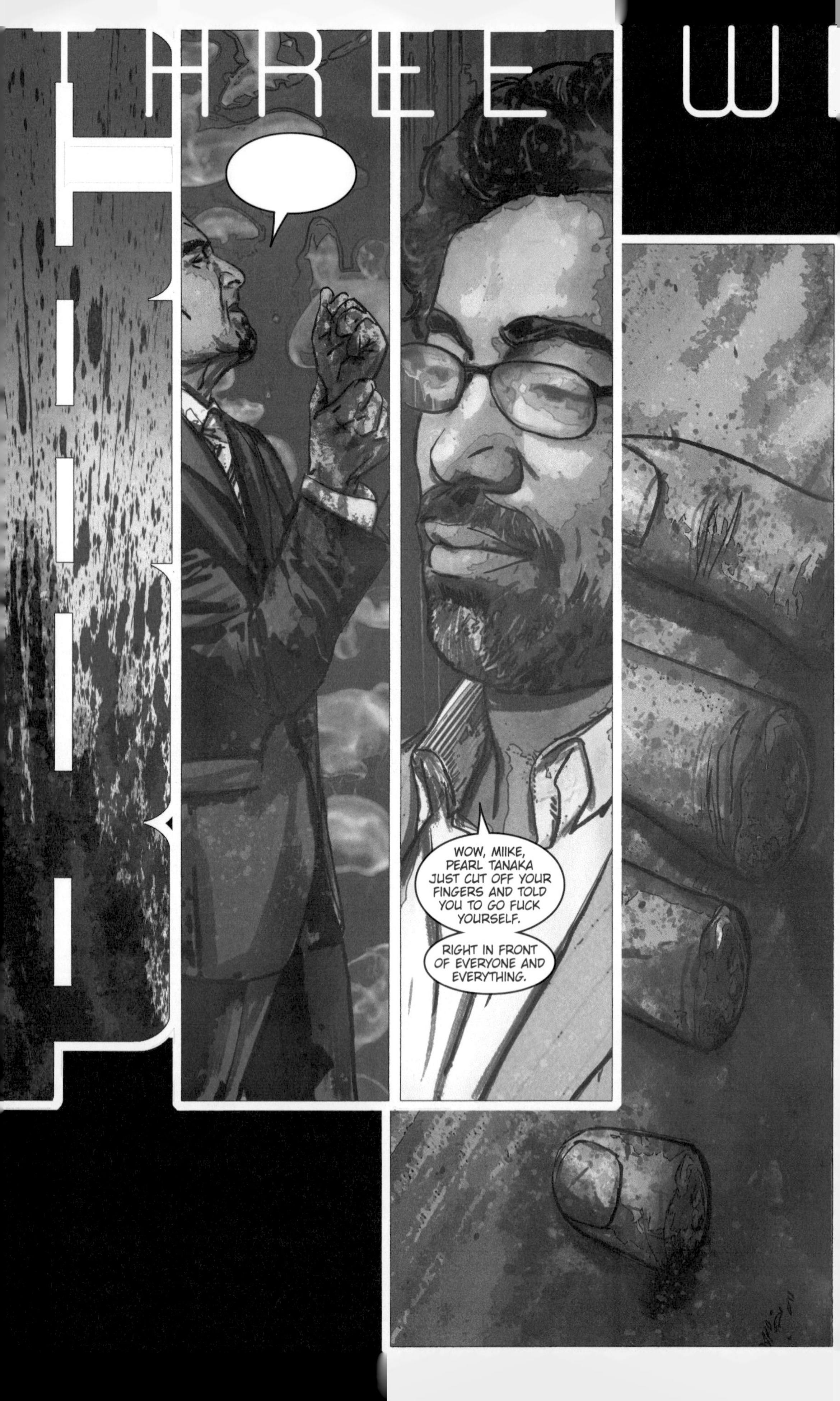
THREE WI
WOW, MIIKE, PEARL TANAKA JUST CUT OFF YOUR FINGERS AND TOLD YOU TO GO FUCK YOURSELF.
RIGHT IN FRONT OF EVERYONE AND EVERYTHING.

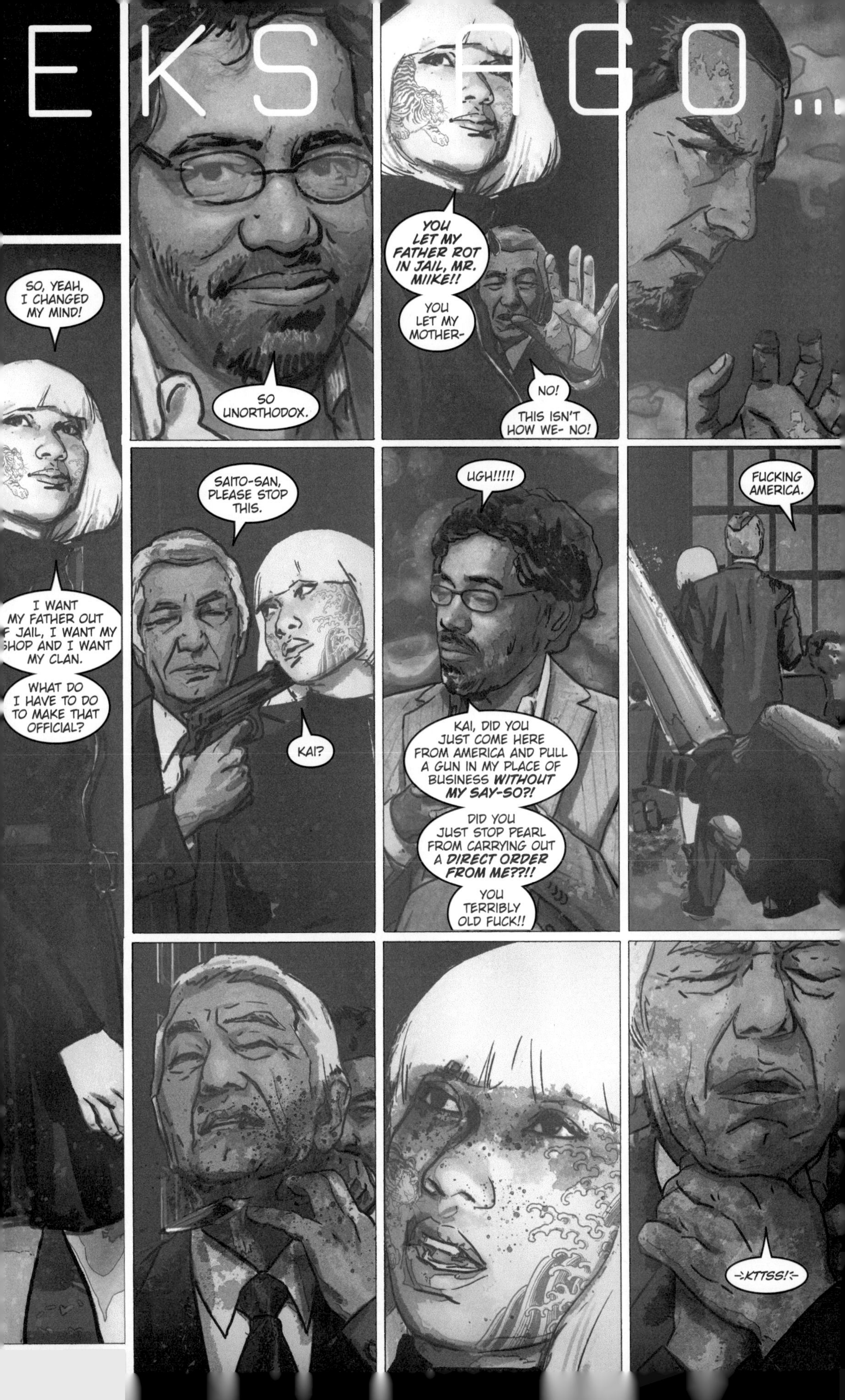

EKS AGO...
SO, YEAH, I CHANGED MY MIND!
SO UNORTHODOX.
YOU LET MY FATHER ROT IN JAIL, MR. MIIKE!!
YOU LET MY MOTHER-
NO!
THIS ISN'T HOW WE- NO!
I WANT MY FATHER OUT F JAIL, I WANT MY SHOP AND I WANT MY CLAN.
WHAT DO I HAVE TO DO TO MAKE THAT OFFICIAL?
SAITO-SAN, PLEASE STOP THIS.
KAI?
UGH!!!!!
KAI, DID YOU JUST COME HERE FROM AMERICA AND PULL A GUN IN MY PLACE OF BUSINESS WITHOUT MY SAY-SO?!
DID YOU JUST STOP PEARL FROM CARRYING OUT A DIRECT ORDER FROM ME??!!
YOU TERRIBLY OLD FUCK!!
FUCKING AMERICA.
-KTTSS!-

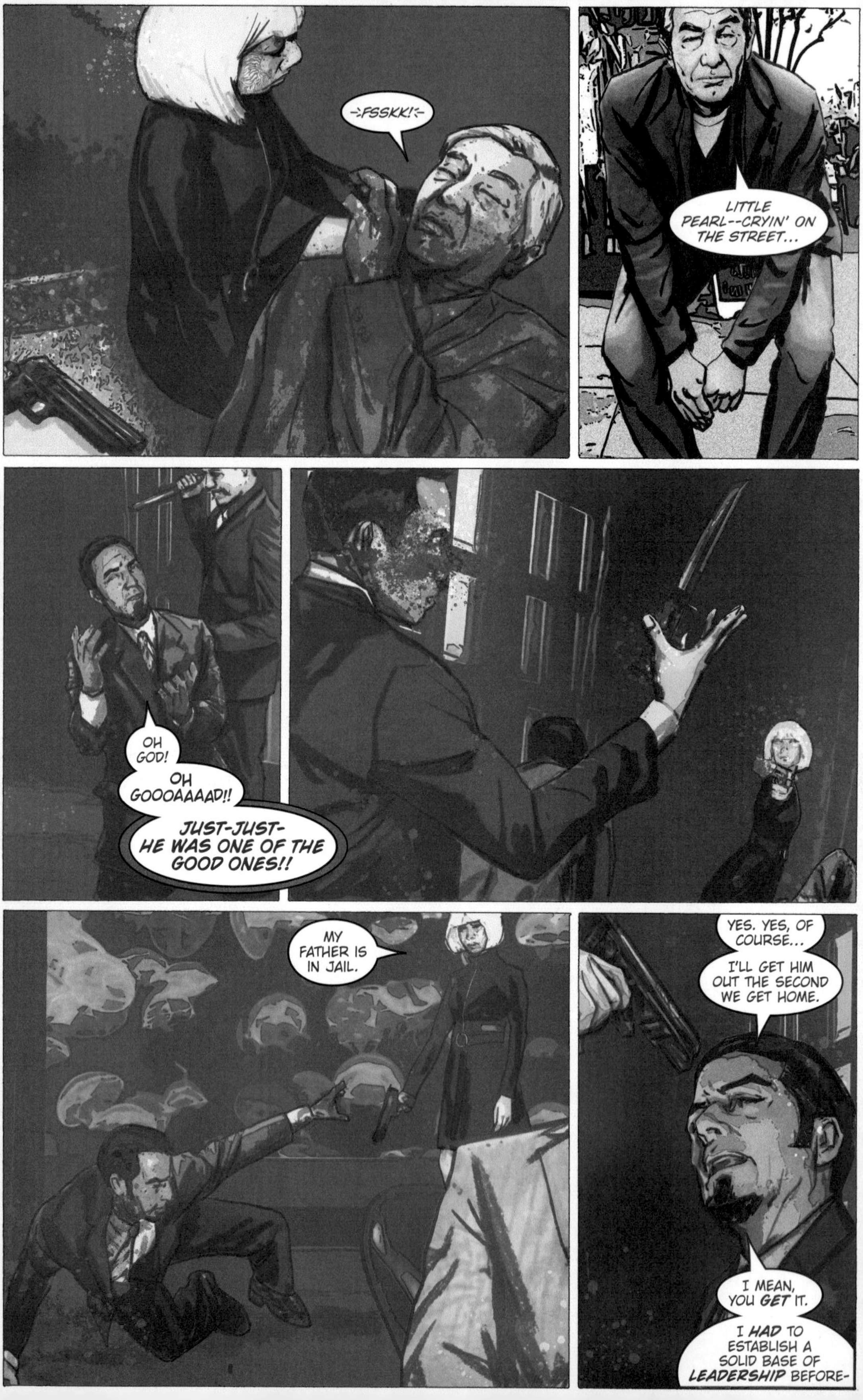
-FSSKK!-
LITTLE PEARL--CRYIN' ON THE STREET...
OH GOD!
OH GOOOAAAAD!!
JUST-JUST- HE WAS ONE OF THE GOOD ONES!!
MY FATHER IS IN JAIL.
YES. YES, OF COURSE...
I'LL GET HIM OUT THE SECOND WE GET HOME.
I MEAN, YOU GET IT.
I HAD TO ESTABLISH A SOLID BASE OF LEADERSHIP BEFORE-

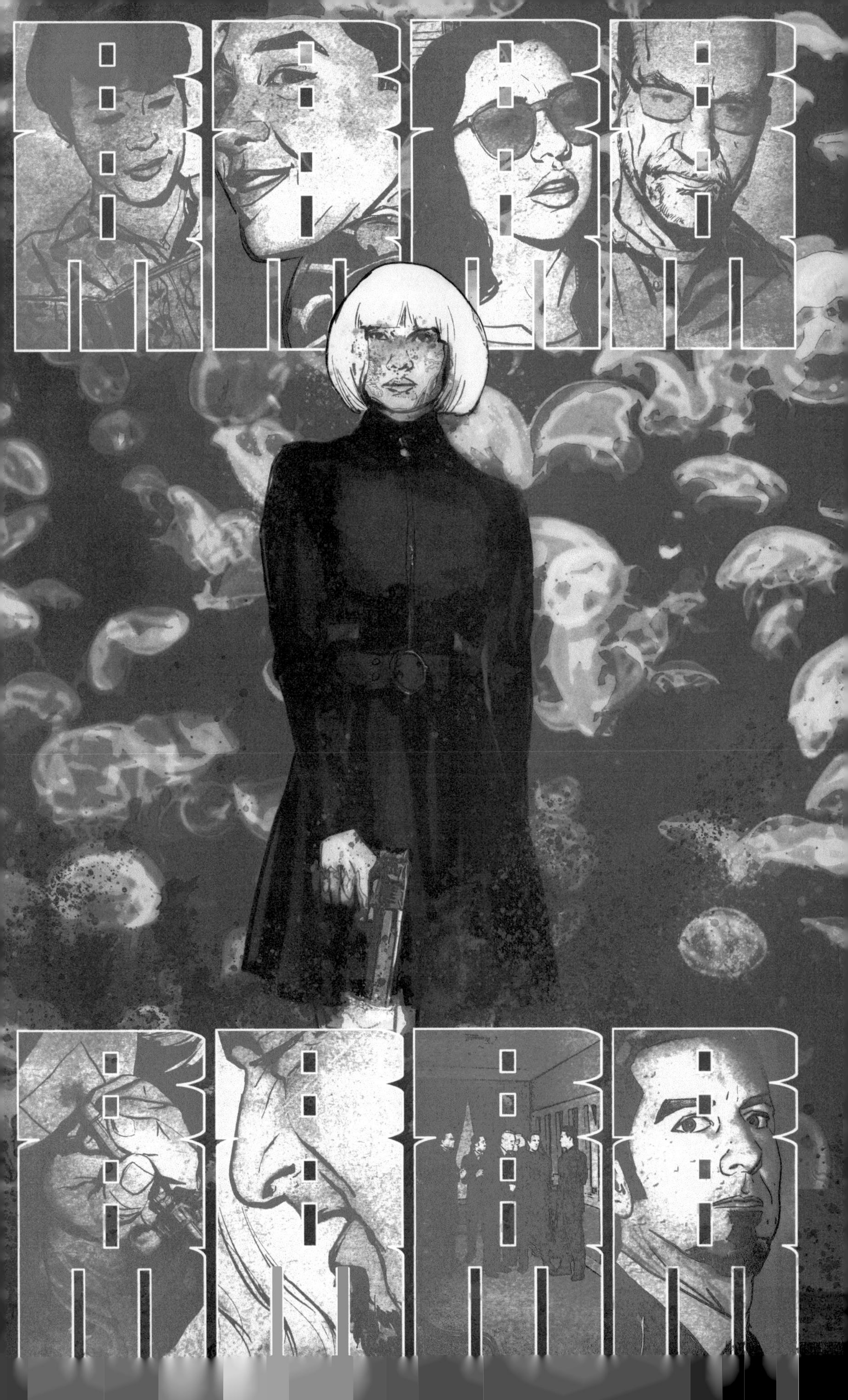

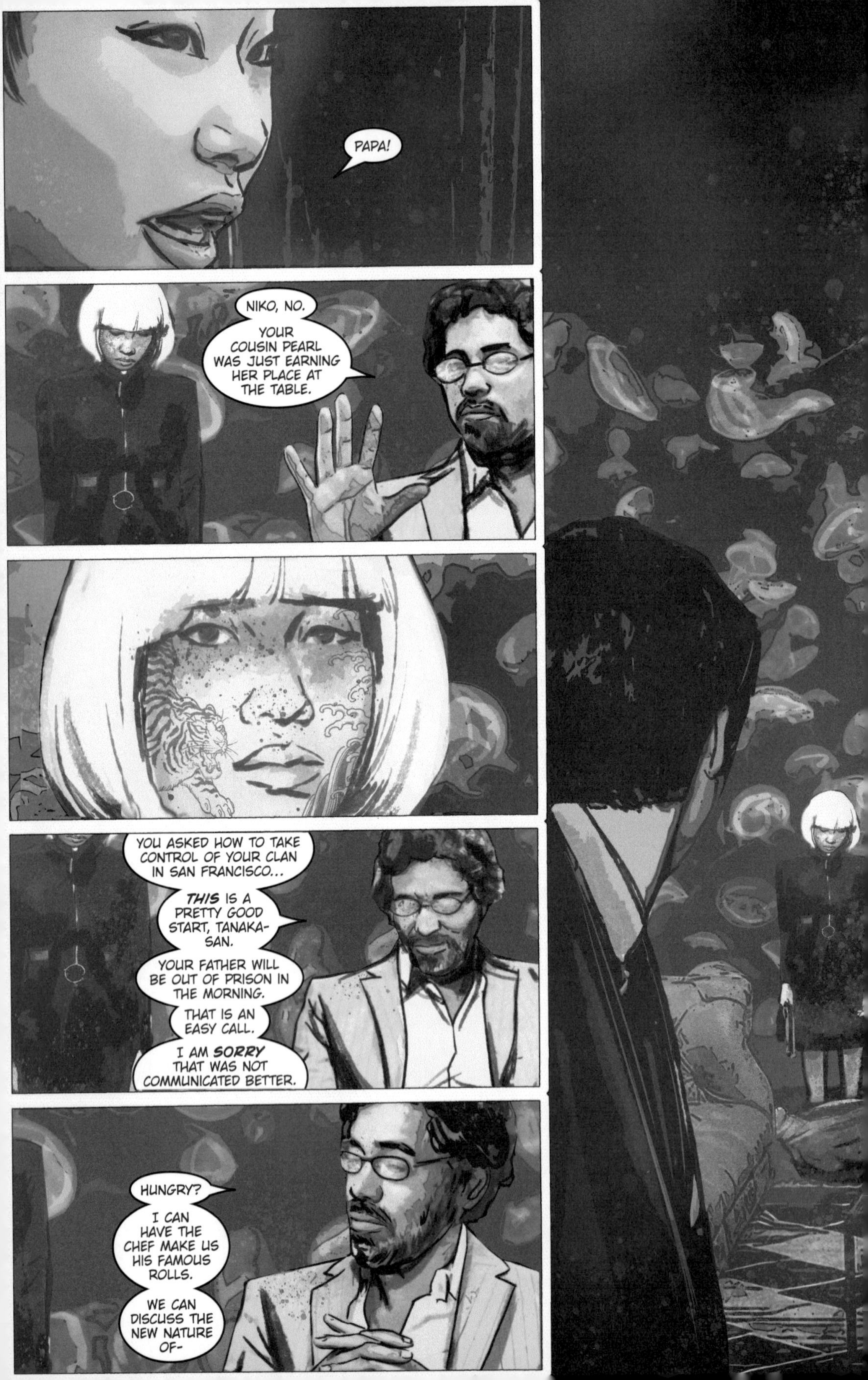
PAPA!
NIKO, NO.
YOUR COUSIN PEARL WAS JUST EARNING HER PLACE AT THE TABLE.
YOU ASKED HOW TO TAKE CONTROL OF YOUR CLAN IN SAN FRANCISCO...
THIS IS A PRETTY GOOD START, TANAKA-SAN.
YOUR FATHER WILL BE OUT OF PRISON IN THE MORNING.
THAT IS AN EASY CALL.
I AM **SORRY** THAT WAS NOT COMMUNICATED BETTER.
HUNGRY?
I CAN HAVE THE CHEF MAKE US HIS FAMOUS ROLLS.
WE CAN DISCUSS THE NEW NATURE OF-

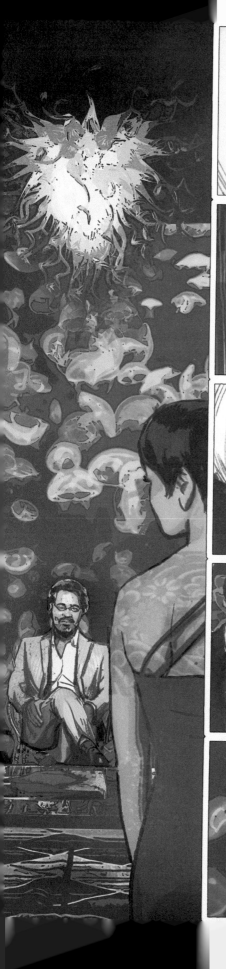

PEARL?

PEARL, LET'S GO. WE— WE SHOULDN'T BE HERE.

BIKKURI!

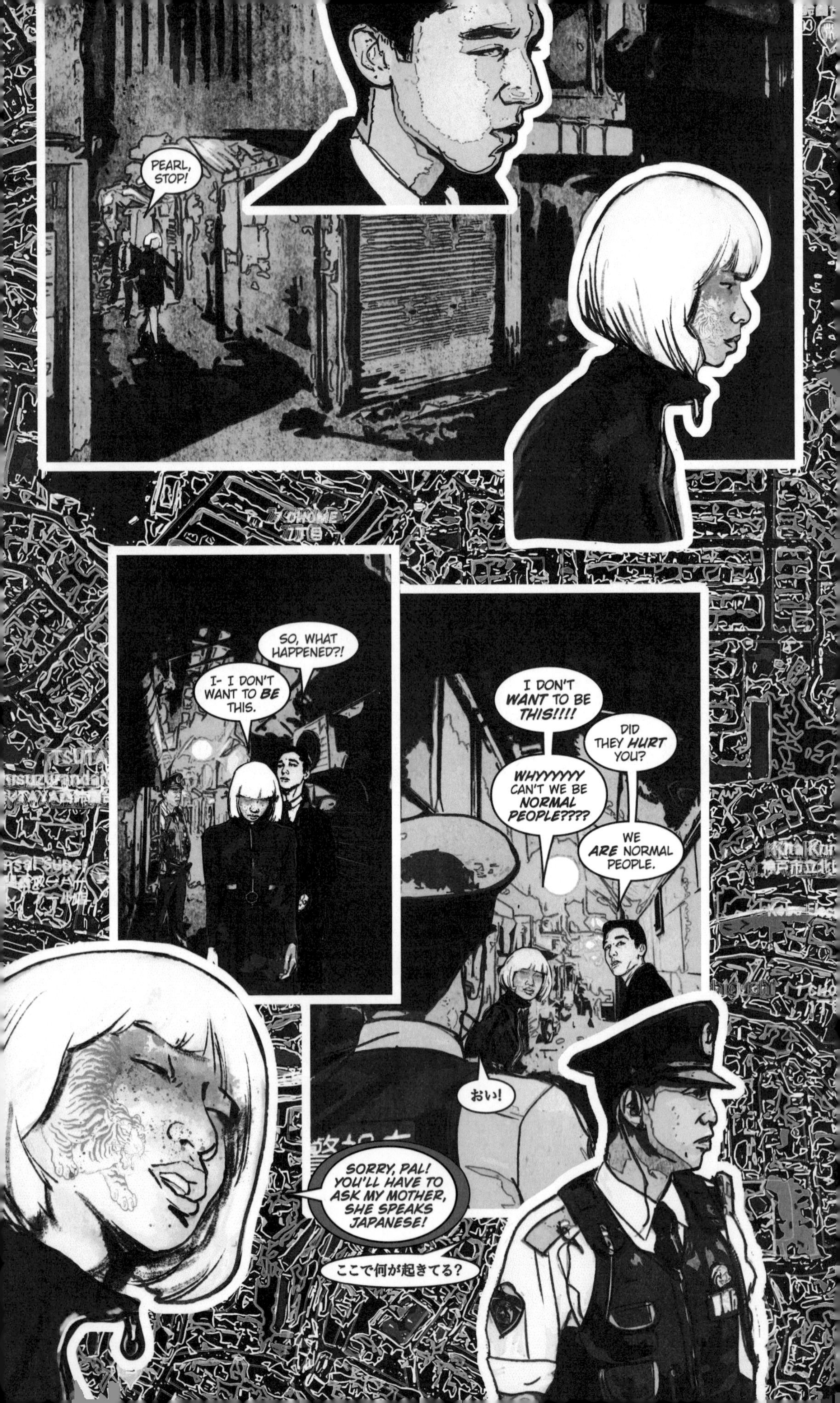
PEARL, STOP!
SO, WHAT HAPPENED?!
I- I DON'T WANT TO *BE* THIS.
I DON'T *WANT* TO BE *THIS!!!!*
DID THEY *HURT* YOU?
WHYYYYYY CAN'T WE BE *NORMAL PEOPLE????*
WE *ARE* NORMAL PEOPLE.
おい!
ここで何が起きてる?
SORRY, PAL! YOU'LL HAVE TO ASK MY MOTHER, SHE SPEAKS JAPANESE!

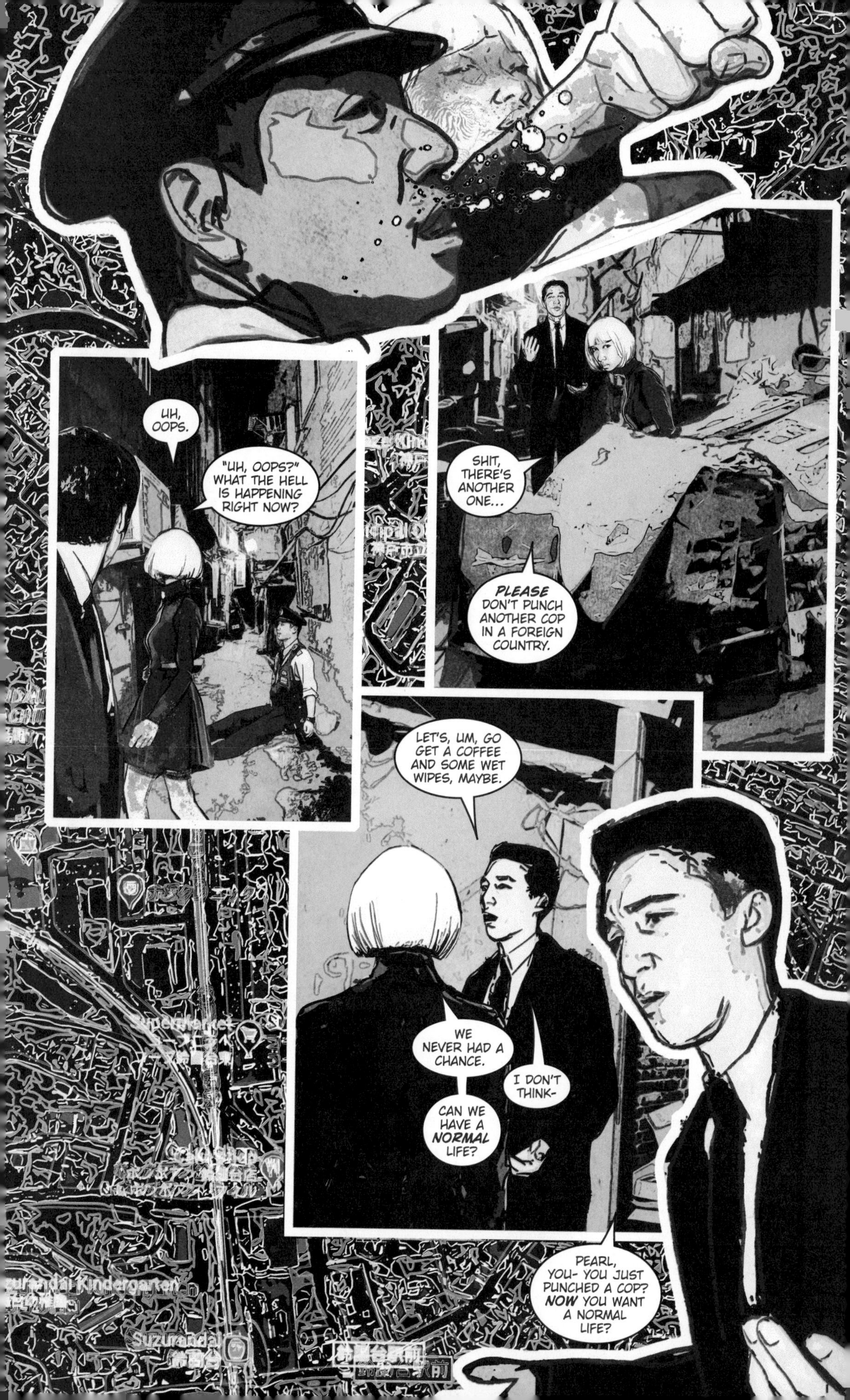
UH, OOPS.
"UH, OOPS?" WHAT THE HELL IS HAPPENING RIGHT NOW?
SHIT, THERE'S ANOTHER ONE...
PLEASE DON'T PUNCH ANOTHER COP IN A FOREIGN COUNTRY.
LET'S, UM, GO GET A COFFEE AND SOME WET WIPES, MAYBE.
WE NEVER HAD A CHANCE.
I DON'T THINK-
CAN WE HAVE A NORMAL LIFE?
PEARL, YOU- YOU JUST PUNCHED A COP? NOW YOU WANT A NORMAL LIFE?

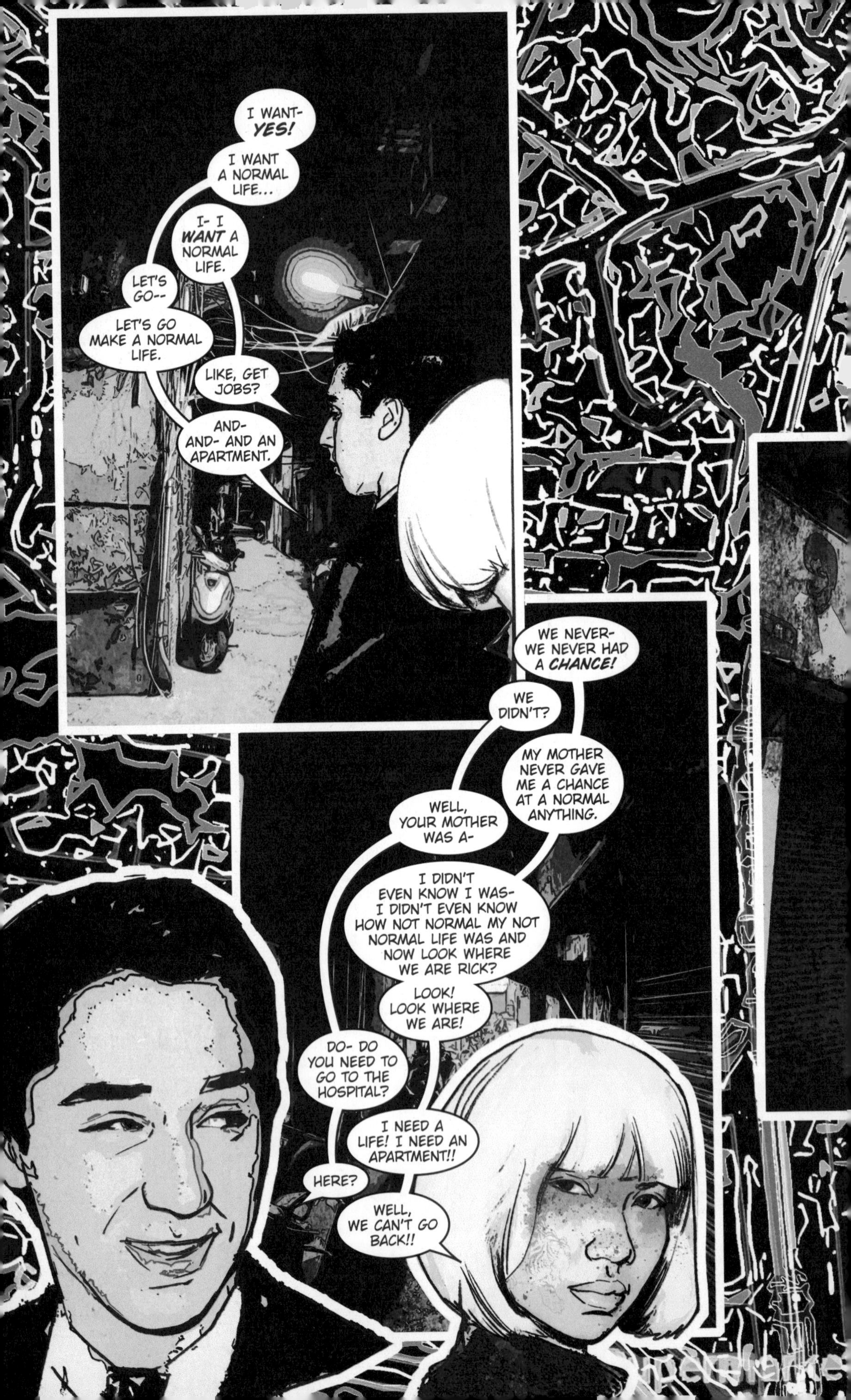
I WANT-
YES!
I WANT A NORMAL LIFE...
I- I WANT A NORMAL LIFE.
LET'S GO--
LET'S GO MAKE A NORMAL LIFE.
LIKE, GET JOBS?
AND- AND- AND AN APARTMENT.
WE NEVER- WE NEVER HAD A CHANCE!
WE DIDN'T?
MY MOTHER NEVER GAVE ME A CHANCE AT A NORMAL ANYTHING.
WELL, YOUR MOTHER WAS A-
I DIDN'T EVEN KNOW I WAS- I DIDN'T EVEN KNOW HOW NOT NORMAL MY NOT NORMAL LIFE WAS AND NOW LOOK WHERE WE ARE RICK?
LOOK! LOOK WHERE WE ARE!
DO- DO YOU NEED TO GO TO THE HOSPITAL?
I NEED A LIFE! I NEED AN APARTMENT!!
HERE?
WELL, WE CAN'T GO BACK!!

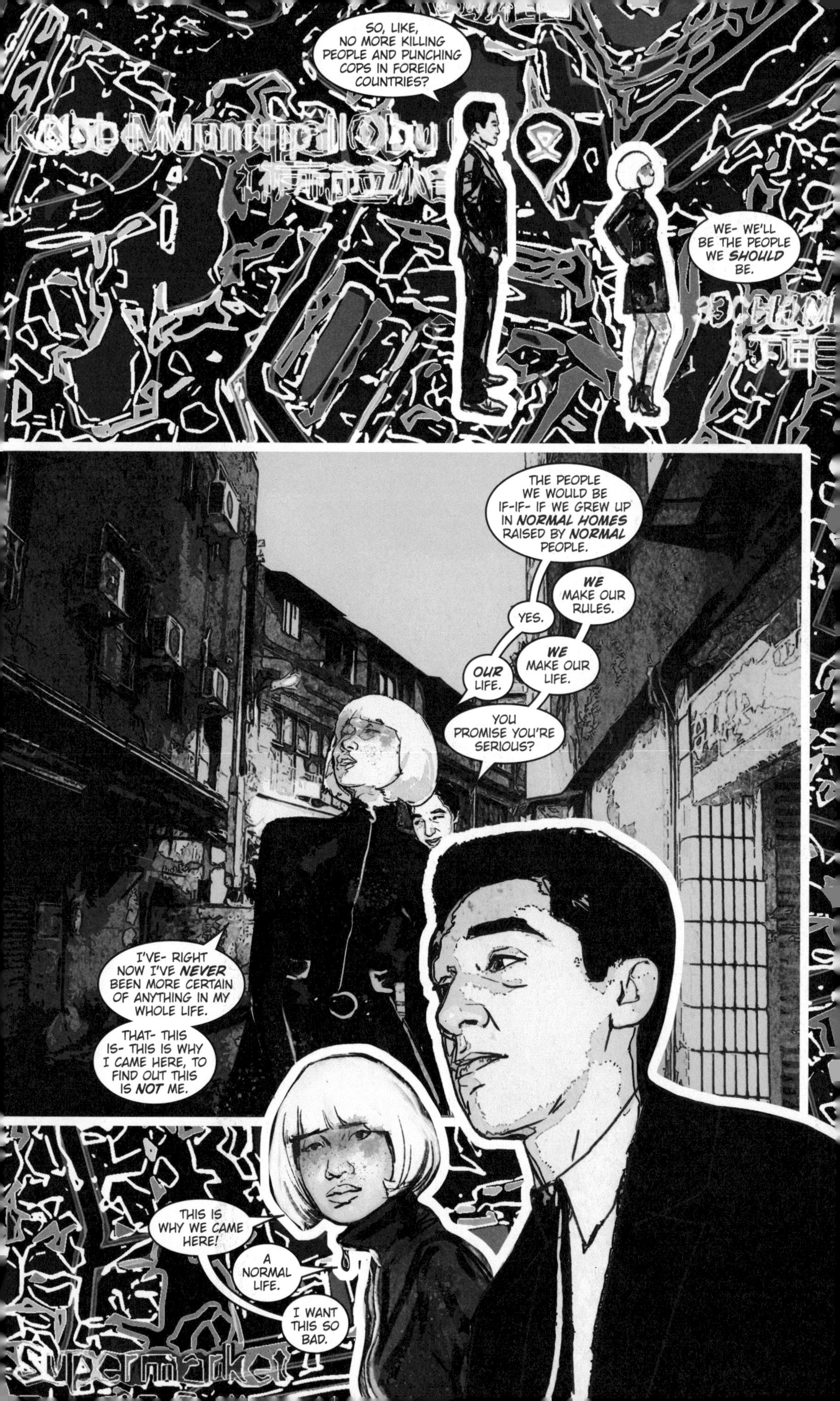

SO, LIKE, NO MORE KILLING PEOPLE AND PUNCHING COPS IN FOREIGN COUNTRIES?
WE- WE'LL BE THE PEOPLE WE SHOULD BE.
THE PEOPLE WE WOULD BE IF-IF- IF WE GREW UP IN NORMAL HOMES RAISED BY NORMAL PEOPLE.
YES.
WE MAKE OUR RULES.
OUR LIFE.
WE MAKE OUR LIFE.
YOU PROMISE YOU'RE SERIOUS?
I'VE- RIGHT NOW I'VE NEVER BEEN MORE CERTAIN OF ANYTHING IN MY WHOLE LIFE.
THAT- THIS IS- THIS IS WHY I CAME HERE, TO FIND OUT THIS IS NOT ME.
THIS IS WHY WE CAME HERE!
A NORMAL LIFE.
I WANT THIS SO BAD.
supermarket

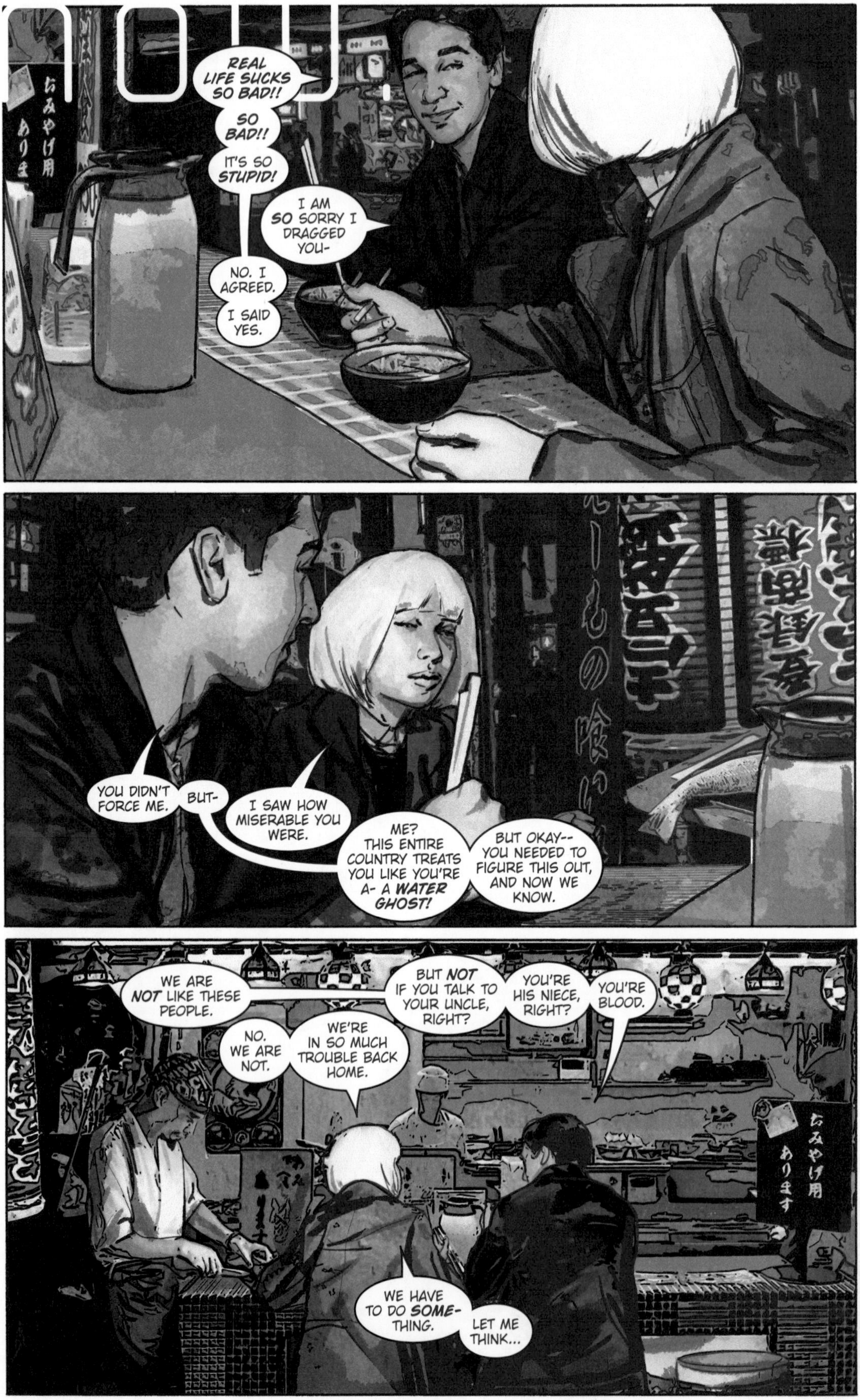
REAL LIFE SUCKS SO BAD!!
SO BAD!!
IT'S SO **STUPID!**
I AM **SO** SORRY I DRAGGED YOU-
NO. I AGREED.
I SAID YES.
YOU DIDN'T FORCE ME.
BUT-
I SAW HOW MISERABLE YOU WERE.
ME? THIS ENTIRE COUNTRY TREATS YOU LIKE YOU'RE A- A ***WATER GHOST!***
BUT OKAY-- YOU NEEDED TO FIGURE THIS OUT, AND NOW WE KNOW.
WE ARE ***NOT*** LIKE THESE PEOPLE.
NO. WE ARE NOT.
WE'RE IN SO MUCH TROUBLE BACK HOME.
BUT ***NOT*** IF YOU TALK TO YOUR UNCLE, RIGHT?
YOU'RE HIS NIECE, RIGHT?
YOU'RE BLOOD.
おみやげ用 あります
WE HAVE TO DO **SOME**-THING.
LET ME THINK...

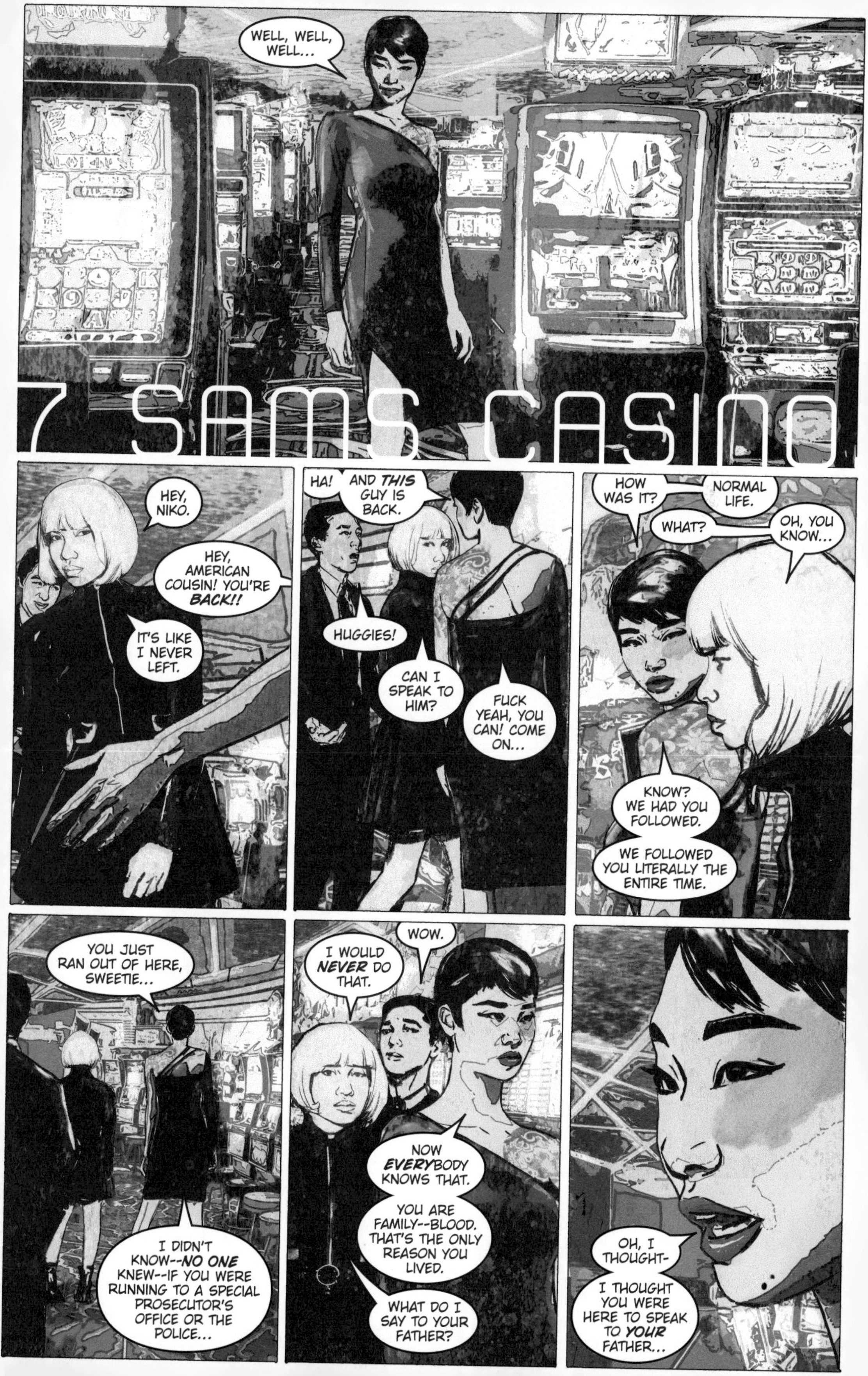
WELL, WELL, WELL...
7 SAMS CASINO
HEY, NIKO.
HEY, AMERICAN COUSIN! YOU'RE BACK!!
IT'S LIKE I NEVER LEFT.
HA!
AND THIS GUY IS BACK.
HUGGIES!
CAN I SPEAK TO HIM?
FUCK YEAH, YOU CAN! COME ON...
HOW WAS IT?
NORMAL LIFE.
WHAT?
OH, YOU KNOW...
KNOW? WE HAD YOU FOLLOWED.
WE FOLLOWED YOU LITERALLY THE ENTIRE TIME.
YOU JUST RAN OUT OF HERE, SWEETIE...
I DIDN'T KNOW--NO ONE KNEW--IF YOU WERE RUNNING TO A SPECIAL PROSECUTOR'S OFFICE OR THE POLICE...
I WOULD NEVER DO THAT.
WOW.
NOW EVERYBODY KNOWS THAT.
YOU ARE FAMILY--BLOOD. THAT'S THE ONLY REASON YOU LIVED.
WHAT DO I SAY TO YOUR FATHER?
OH, I THOUGHT-
I THOUGHT YOU WERE HERE TO SPEAK TO YOUR FATHER...

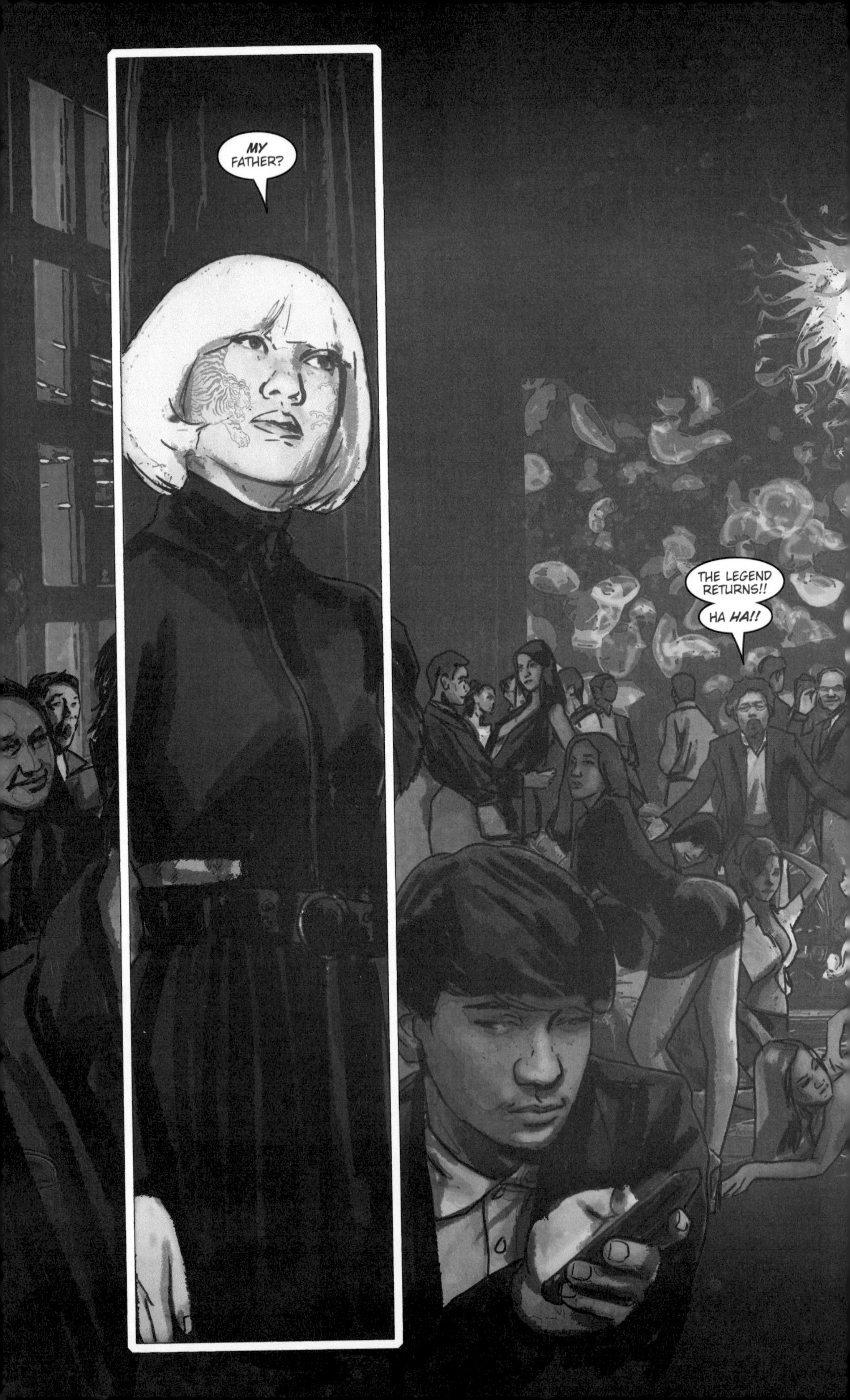
MY FATHER?
THE LEGEND RETURNS!!
HA HA!!

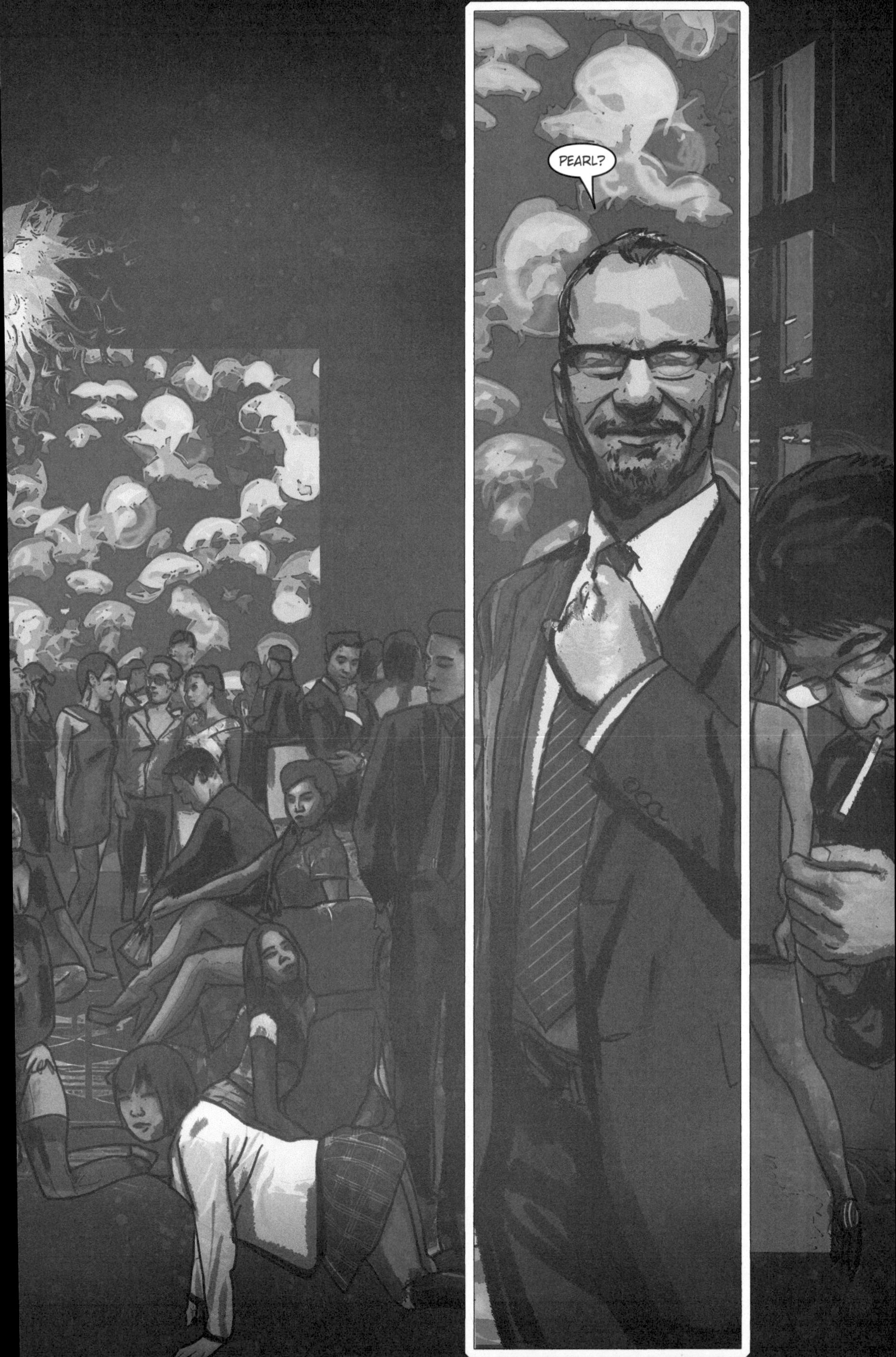
PEARL?

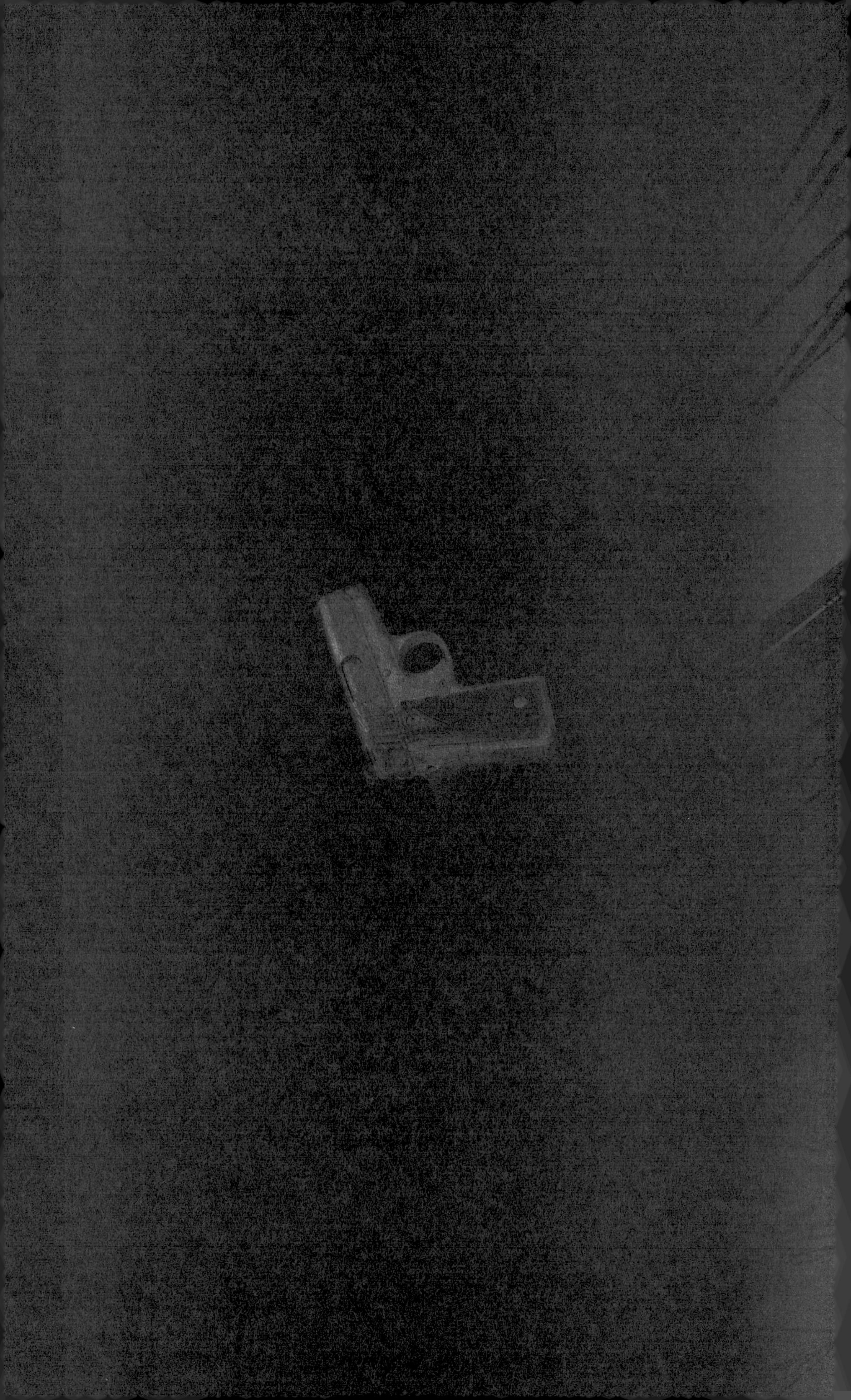

Variant cover art for issue #11
by TAKI SOMA

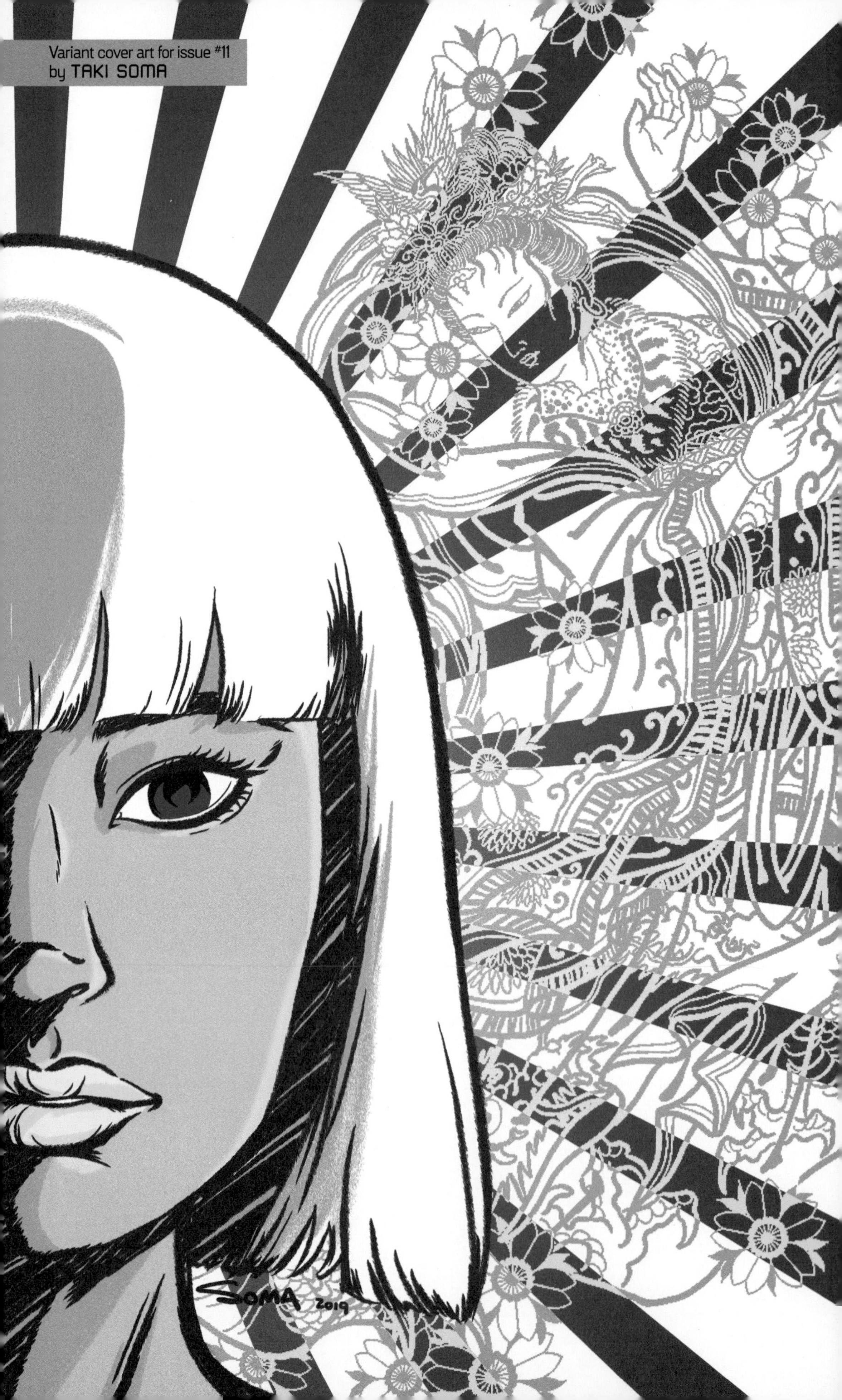
SOMA 2019

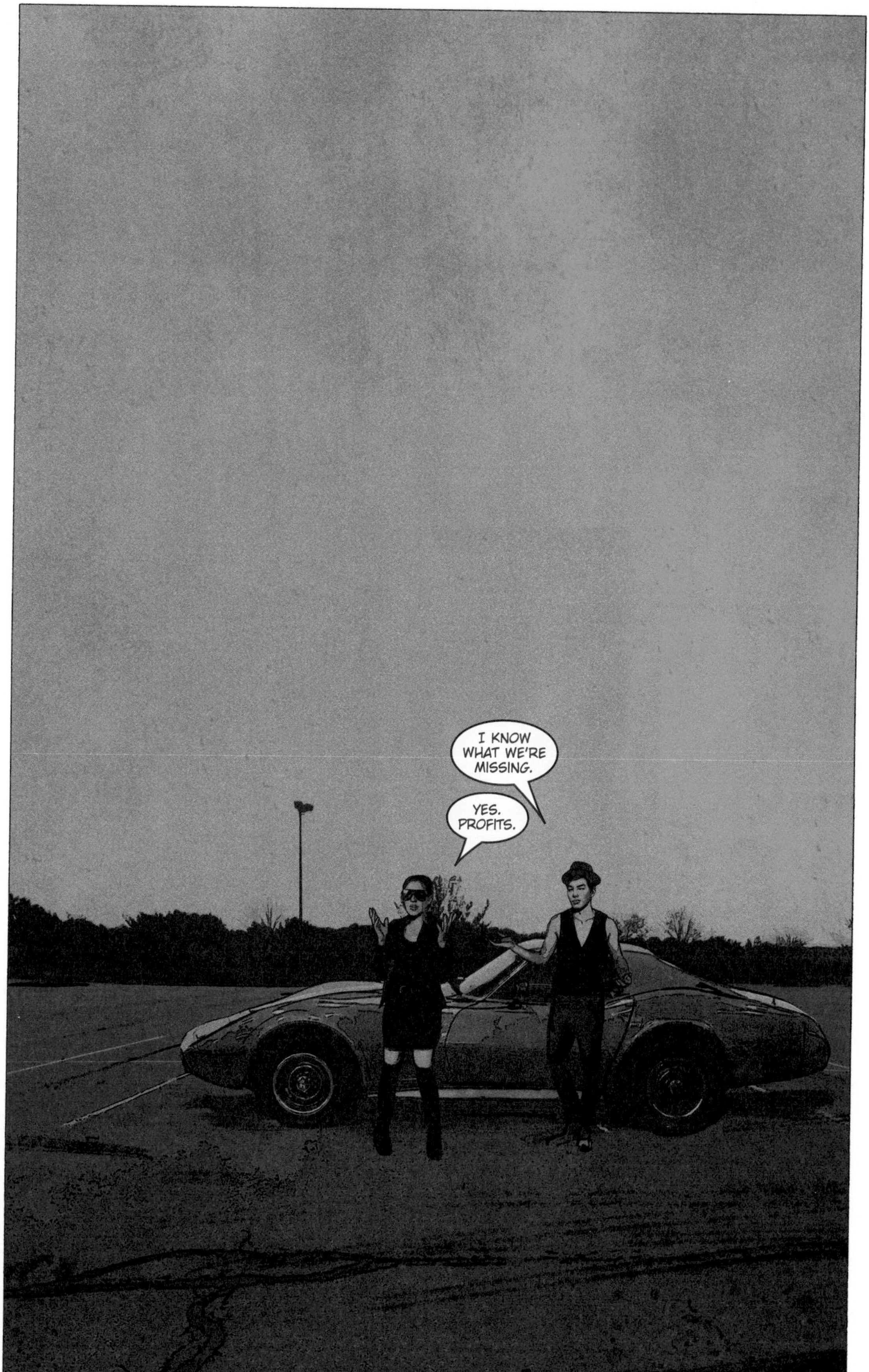
I KNOW WHAT WE'RE MISSING.
YES. PROFITS.

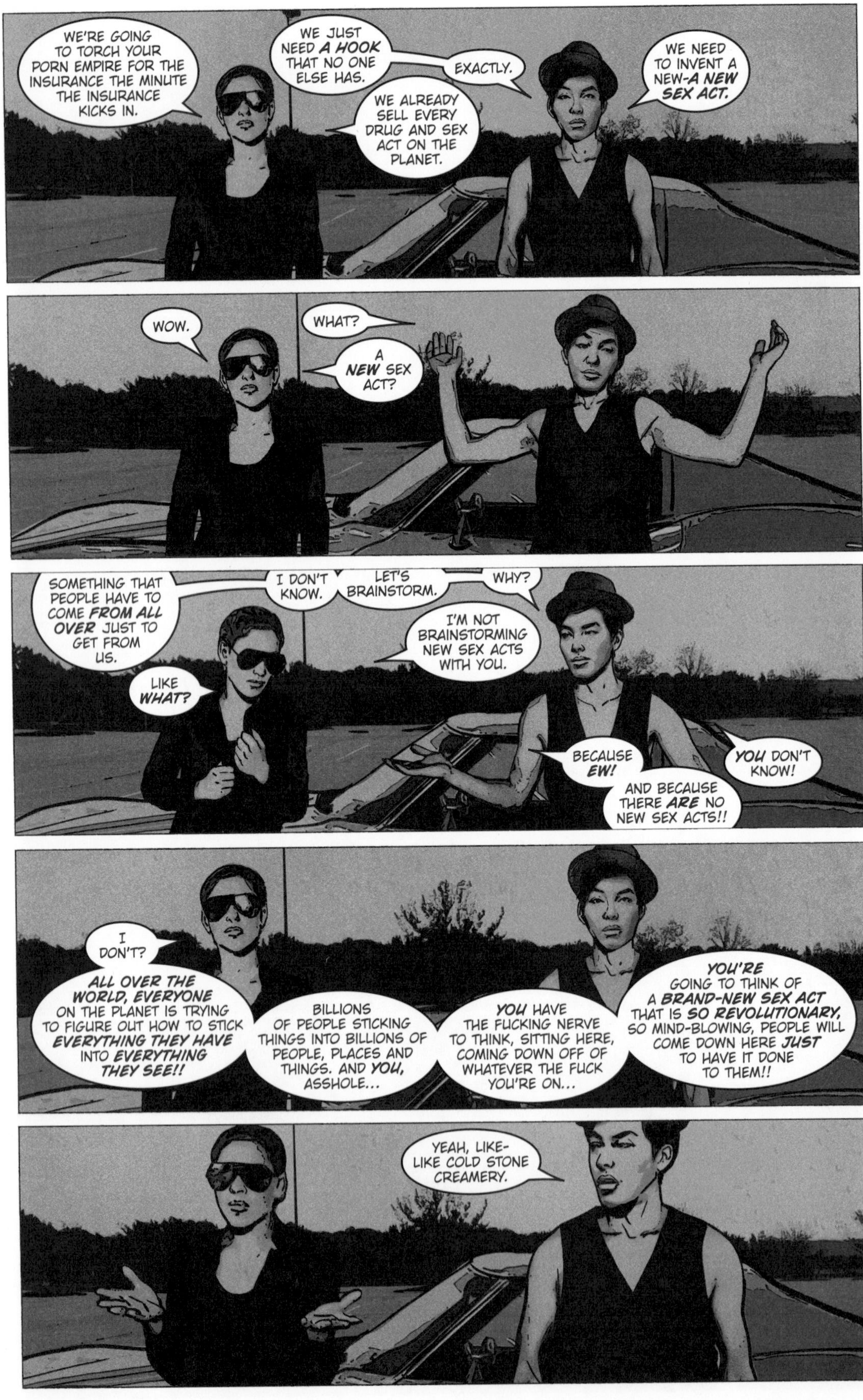
WE'RE GOING TO TORCH YOUR PORN EMPIRE FOR THE INSURANCE THE MINUTE THE INSURANCE KICKS IN.
WE JUST NEED ***A HOOK*** THAT NO ONE ELSE HAS.
EXACTLY.
WE ALREADY SELL EVERY DRUG AND SEX ACT ON THE PLANET.
WE NEED TO INVENT A NEW-***A NEW SEX ACT.***
WOW.
WHAT?
A ***NEW*** SEX ACT?
SOMETHING THAT PEOPLE HAVE TO COME ***FROM ALL OVER*** JUST TO GET FROM US.
I DON'T KNOW.
LET'S BRAINSTORM.
WHY?
I'M NOT BRAINSTORMING NEW SEX ACTS WITH YOU.
LIKE ***WHAT?***
BECAUSE ***EW!***
AND BECAUSE THERE ***ARE*** NO NEW SEX ACTS!!
YOU DON'T KNOW!
I DON'T?
ALL OVER THE WORLD, EVERYONE ON THE PLANET IS TRYING TO FIGURE OUT HOW TO STICK ***EVERYTHING THEY HAVE*** INTO ***EVERYTHING THEY SEE!!***
BILLIONS OF PEOPLE STICKING THINGS INTO BILLIONS OF PEOPLE, PLACES AND THINGS. AND ***YOU,*** ASSHOLE...
YOU HAVE THE FUCKING NERVE TO THINK, SITTING HERE, COMING DOWN OFF OF WHATEVER THE FUCK YOU'RE ON...
YOU'RE GOING TO THINK OF A ***BRAND-NEW SEX ACT*** THAT IS ***SO REVOLUTIONARY,*** SO MIND-BLOWING, PEOPLE WILL COME DOWN HERE ***JUST*** TO HAVE IT DONE TO THEM!!
YEAH, LIKE- LIKE COLD STONE CREAMERY.

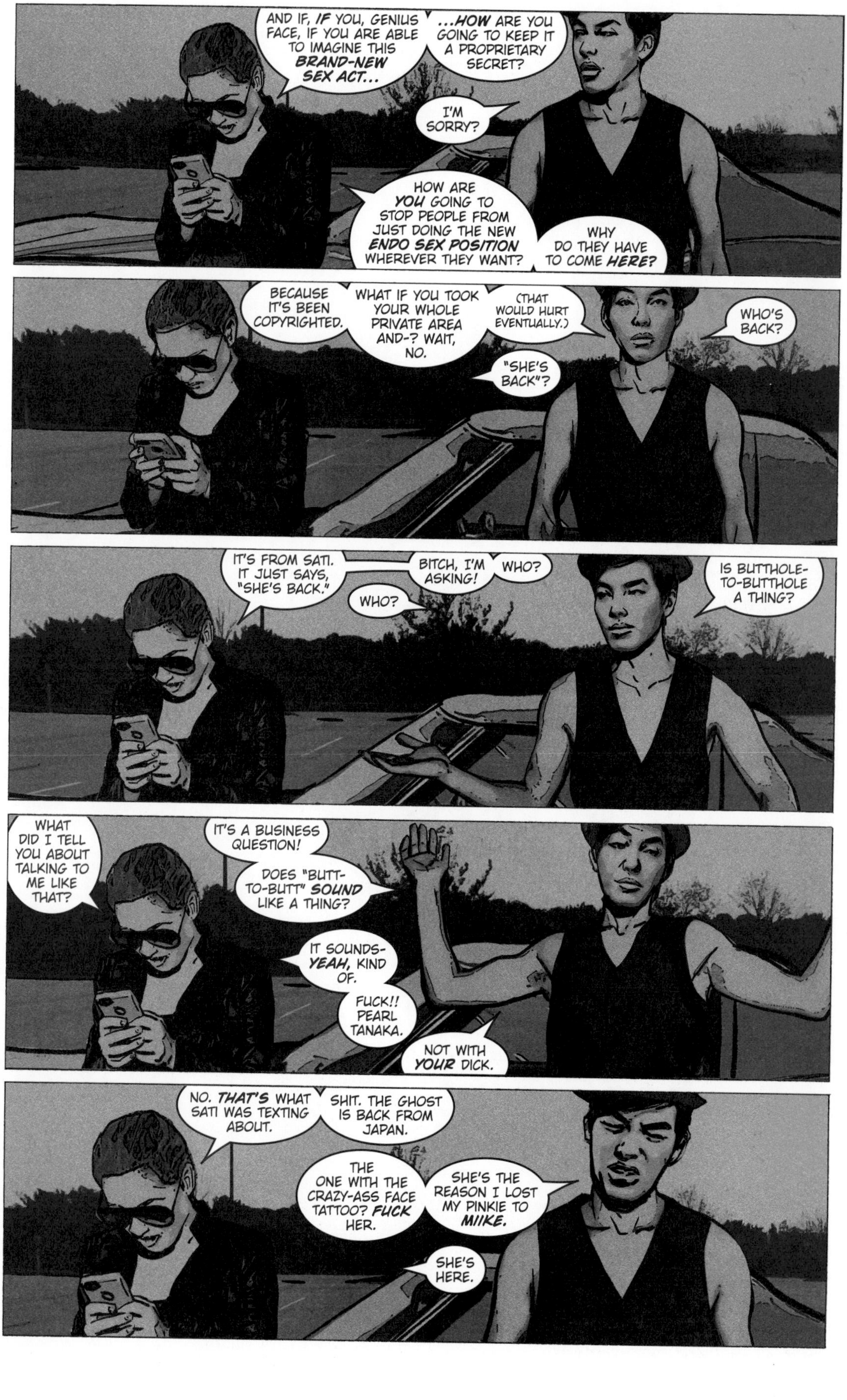
AND IF, *IF* YOU, GENIUS FACE, IF YOU ARE ABLE TO IMAGINE THIS *BRAND-NEW SEX ACT...*
...HOW ARE YOU GOING TO KEEP IT A PROPRIETARY SECRET?
I'M SORRY?
HOW ARE *YOU* GOING TO STOP PEOPLE FROM JUST DOING THE NEW *ENDO SEX POSITION* WHEREVER THEY WANT?
WHY DO THEY HAVE TO COME *HERE?*
BECAUSE IT'S BEEN COPYRIGHTED.
WHAT IF YOU TOOK YOUR WHOLE PRIVATE AREA AND-? WAIT, NO.
(THAT WOULD HURT EVENTUALLY.)
WHO'S BACK?
"SHE'S BACK"?
IT'S FROM SATI. IT JUST SAYS, "SHE'S BACK."
BITCH, I'M ASKING!
WHO?
WHO?
IS BUTTHOLE-TO-BUTTHOLE A THING?
WHAT DID I TELL YOU ABOUT TALKING TO ME LIKE THAT?
IT'S A BUSINESS QUESTION!
DOES "BUTT-TO-BUTT" *SOUND* LIKE A THING?
IT SOUNDS- *YEAH,* KIND OF.
FUCK!! PEARL TANAKA.
NOT WITH *YOUR* DICK.
NO. *THAT'S* WHAT SATI WAS TEXTING ABOUT.
SHIT. THE GHOST IS BACK FROM JAPAN.
THE ONE WITH THE CRAZY-ASS FACE TATTOO? *FUCK* HER.
SHE'S THE REASON I LOST MY PINKIE TO *MIIKE.*
SHE'S HERE.

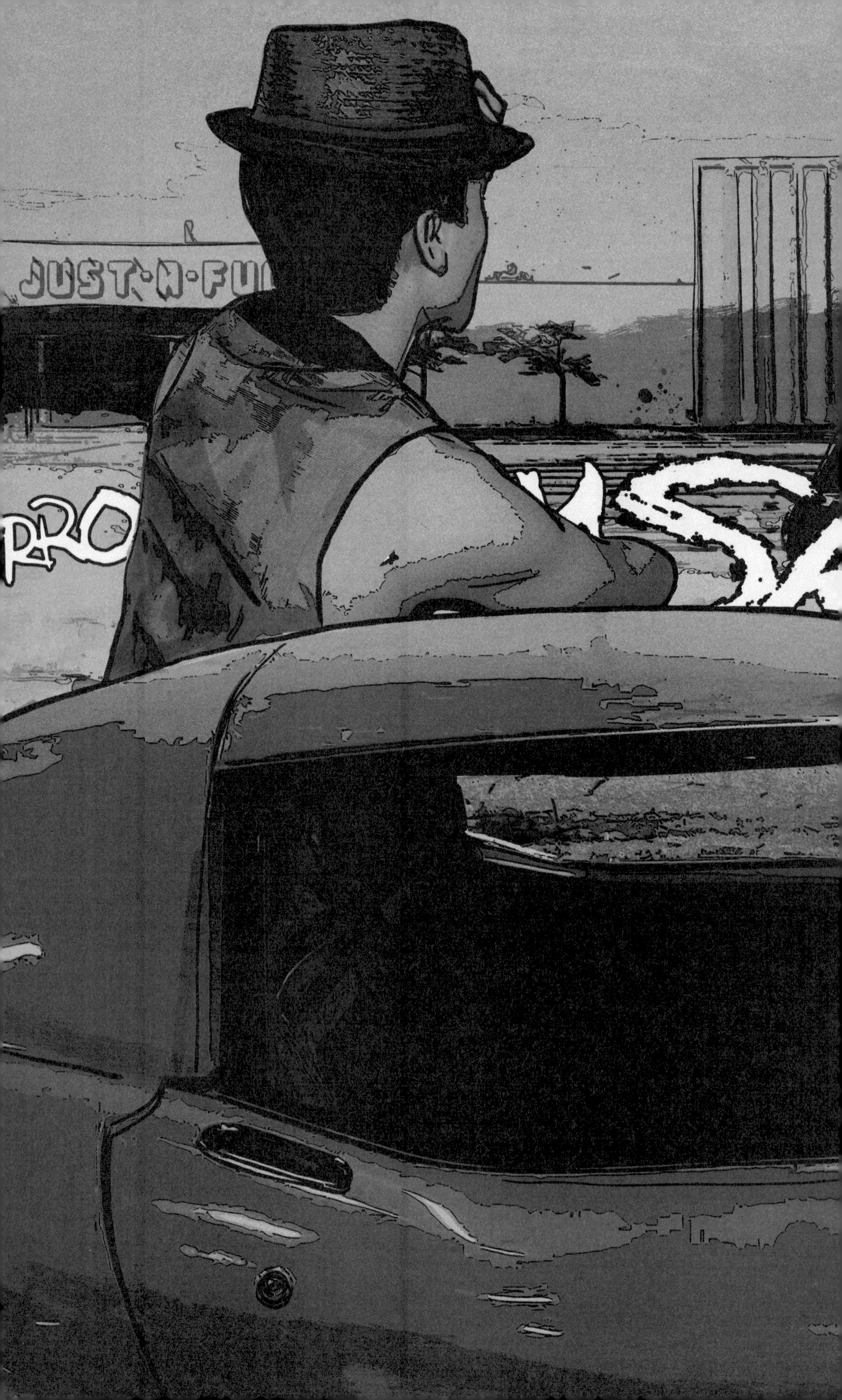

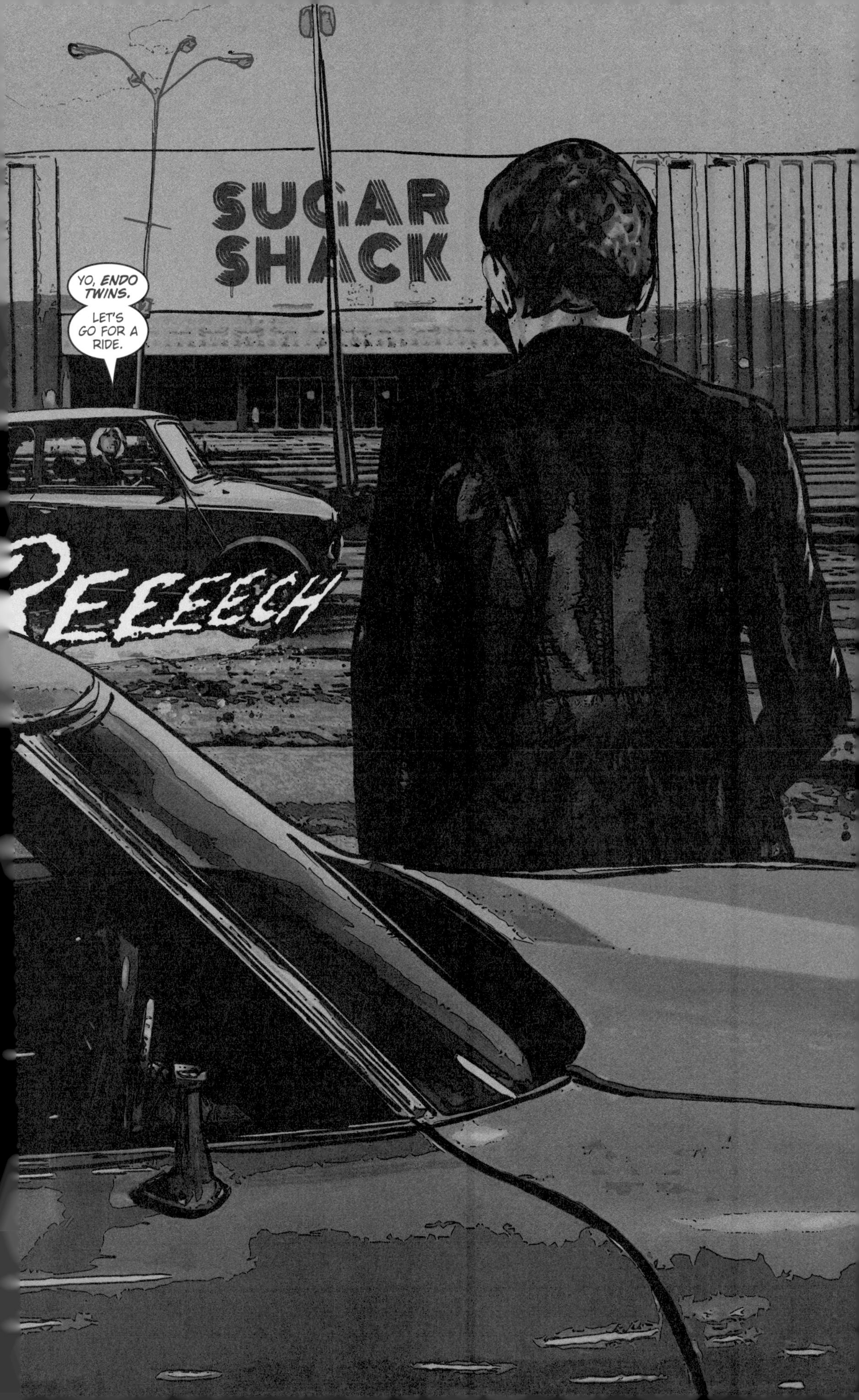
SUGAR SHACK
YO, ENDO TWINS.
LET'S GO FOR A RIDE.
REEEECH

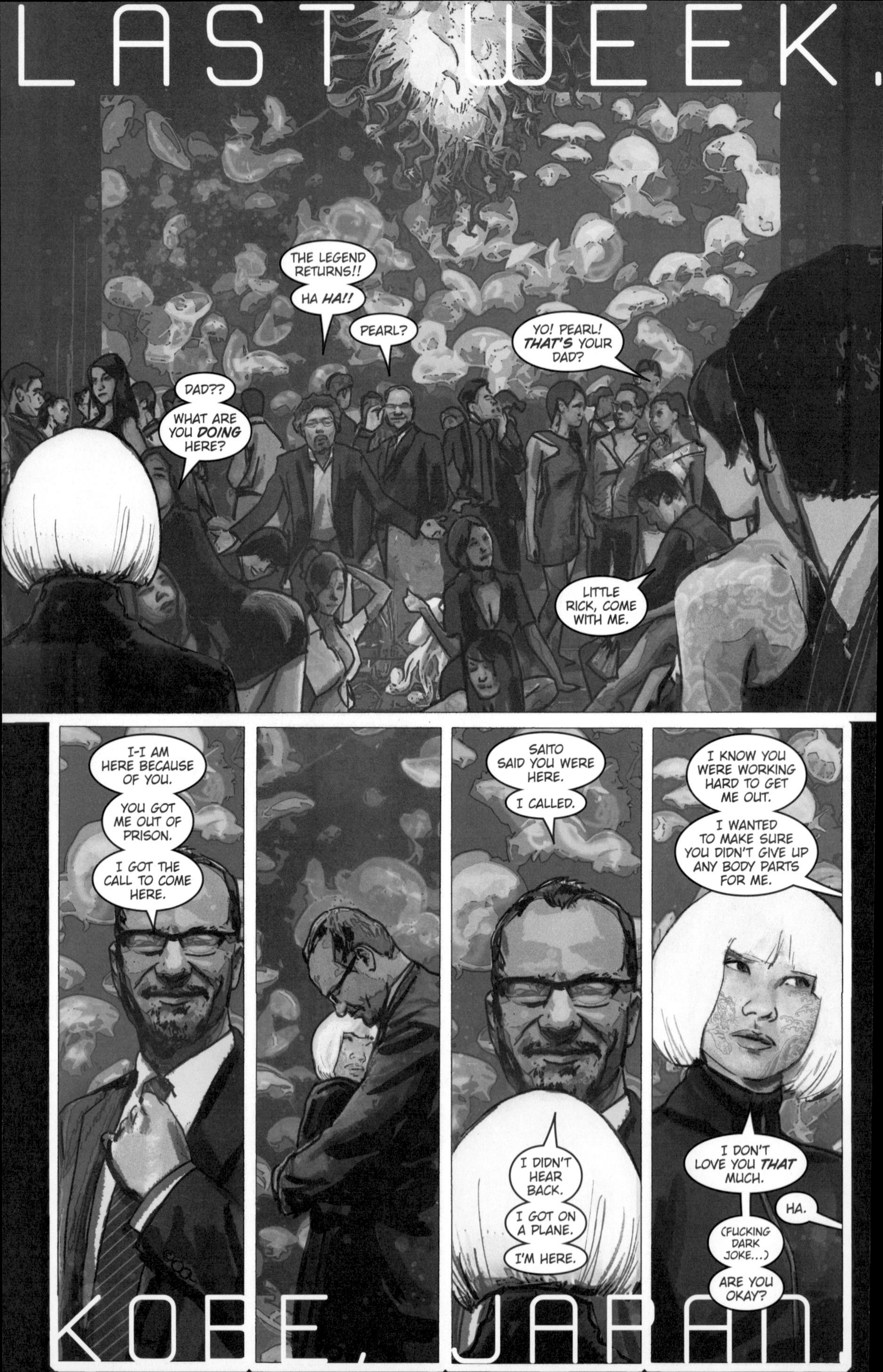
LAST WEEK.
THE LEGEND RETURNS!!
HA HA!!
PEARL?
YO! PEARL! THAT'S YOUR DAD?
DAD??
WHAT ARE YOU DOING HERE?
LITTLE RICK, COME WITH ME.
I-I AM HERE BECAUSE OF YOU.
YOU GOT ME OUT OF PRISON.
I GOT THE CALL TO COME HERE.
SAITO SAID YOU WERE HERE.
I CALLED.
I DIDN'T HEAR BACK.
I GOT ON A PLANE.
I'M HERE.
I KNOW YOU WERE WORKING HARD TO GET ME OUT.
I WANTED TO MAKE SURE YOU DIDN'T GIVE UP ANY BODY PARTS FOR ME.
I DON'T LOVE YOU THAT MUCH.
HA.
(FUCKING DARK JOKE...)
ARE YOU OKAY?
KOBE, JAPAN.

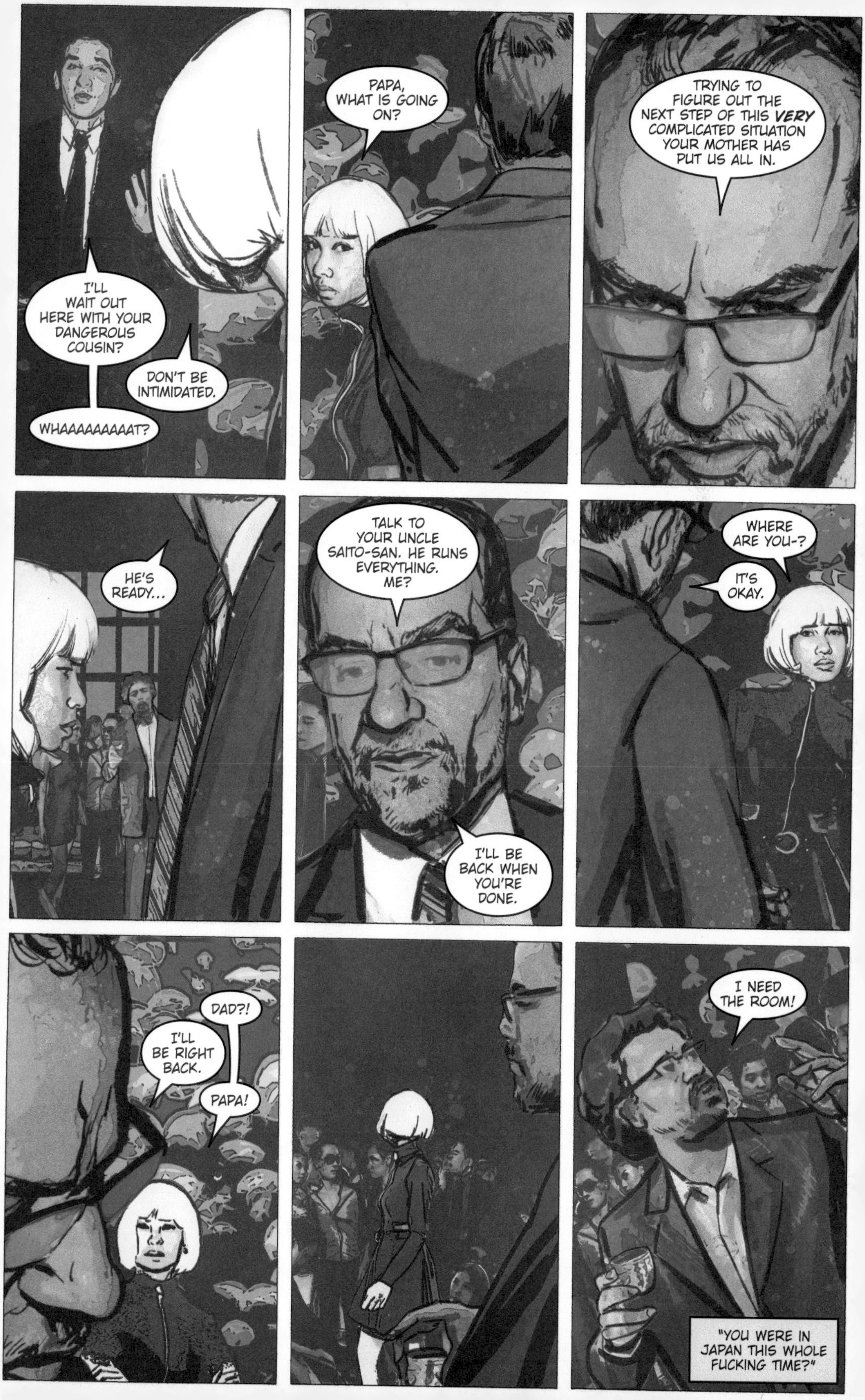
I'LL WAIT OUT HERE WITH YOUR DANGEROUS COUSIN?
DON'T BE INTIMIDATED.
WHAAAAAAAAAT?
PAPA, WHAT IS GOING ON?
TRYING TO FIGURE OUT THE NEXT STEP OF THIS VERY COMPLICATED SITUATION YOUR MOTHER HAS PUT US ALL IN.
HE'S READY...
TALK TO YOUR UNCLE SAITO-SAN. HE RUNS EVERYTHING. ME?
I'LL BE BACK WHEN YOU'RE DONE.
WHERE ARE YOU-?
IT'S OKAY.
I'LL BE RIGHT BACK.
DAD?!
PAPA!
I NEED THE ROOM!
"YOU WERE IN JAPAN THIS WHOLE FUCKING TIME?"

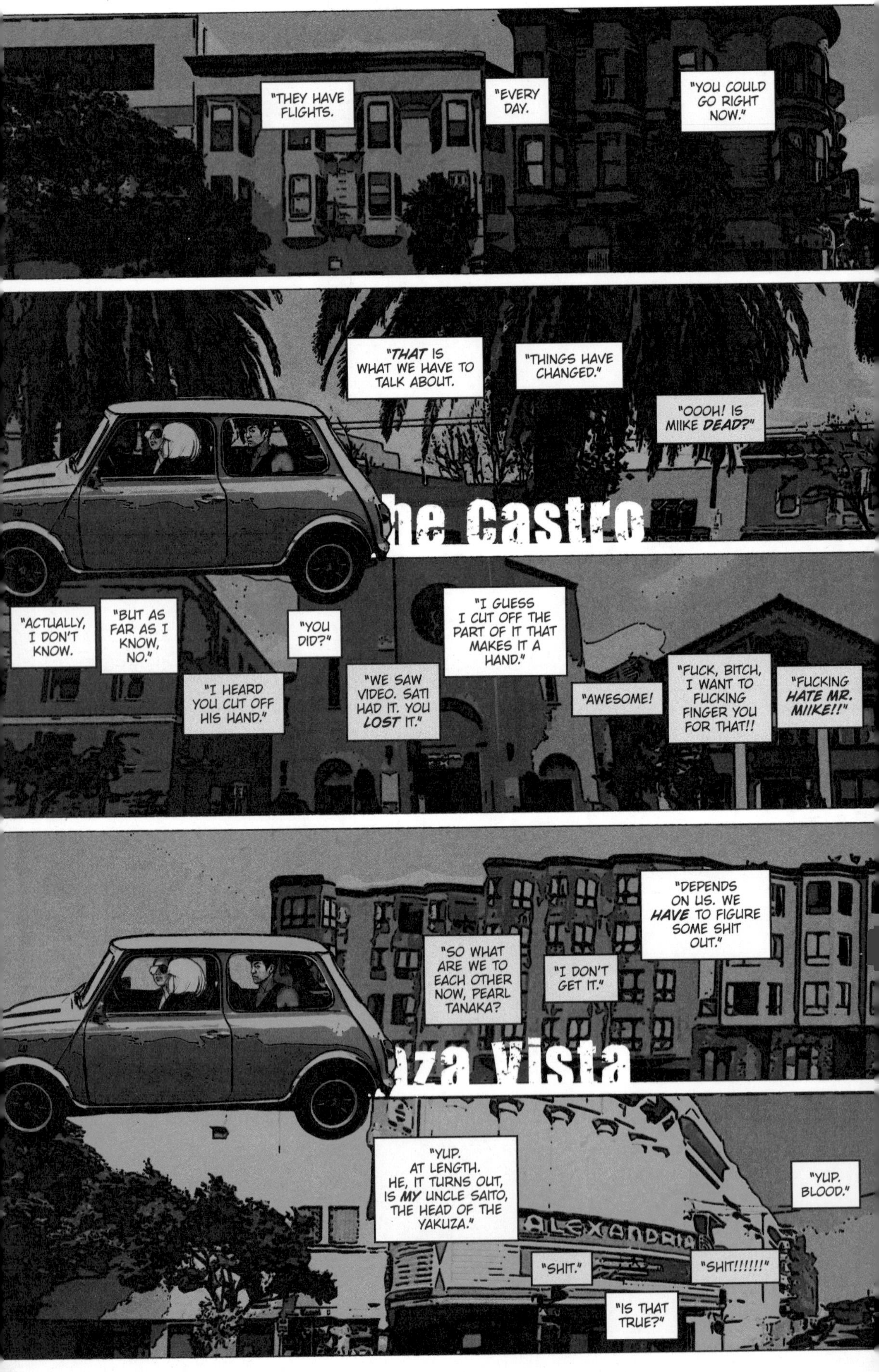
"THEY HAVE FLIGHTS.
"EVERY DAY.
"YOU COULD GO RIGHT NOW."
"THAT IS WHAT WE HAVE TO TALK ABOUT.
"THINGS HAVE CHANGED."
"OOOH! IS MIIKE DEAD?"
he Castro
"ACTUALLY, I DON'T KNOW.
"BUT AS FAR AS I KNOW, NO."
"I HEARD YOU CUT OFF HIS HAND."
"YOU DID?"
"WE SAW VIDEO. SATI HAD IT. YOU LOST IT."
"I GUESS I CUT OFF THE PART OF IT THAT MAKES IT A HAND."
"AWESOME!
"FUCK, BITCH, I WANT TO FUCKING FINGER YOU FOR THAT!!
"FUCKING HATE MR. MIIKE!!"
"SO WHAT ARE WE TO EACH OTHER NOW, PEARL TANAKA?
"I DON'T GET IT."
"DEPENDS ON US. WE HAVE TO FIGURE SOME SHIT OUT."
za Vista
"YUP. AT LENGTH. HE, IT TURNS OUT, IS MY UNCLE SAITO, THE HEAD OF THE YAKUZA."
"SHIT."
"IS THAT TRUE?"
"SHIT!!!!!!"
"YUP. BLOOD."
ALEXANDRIA

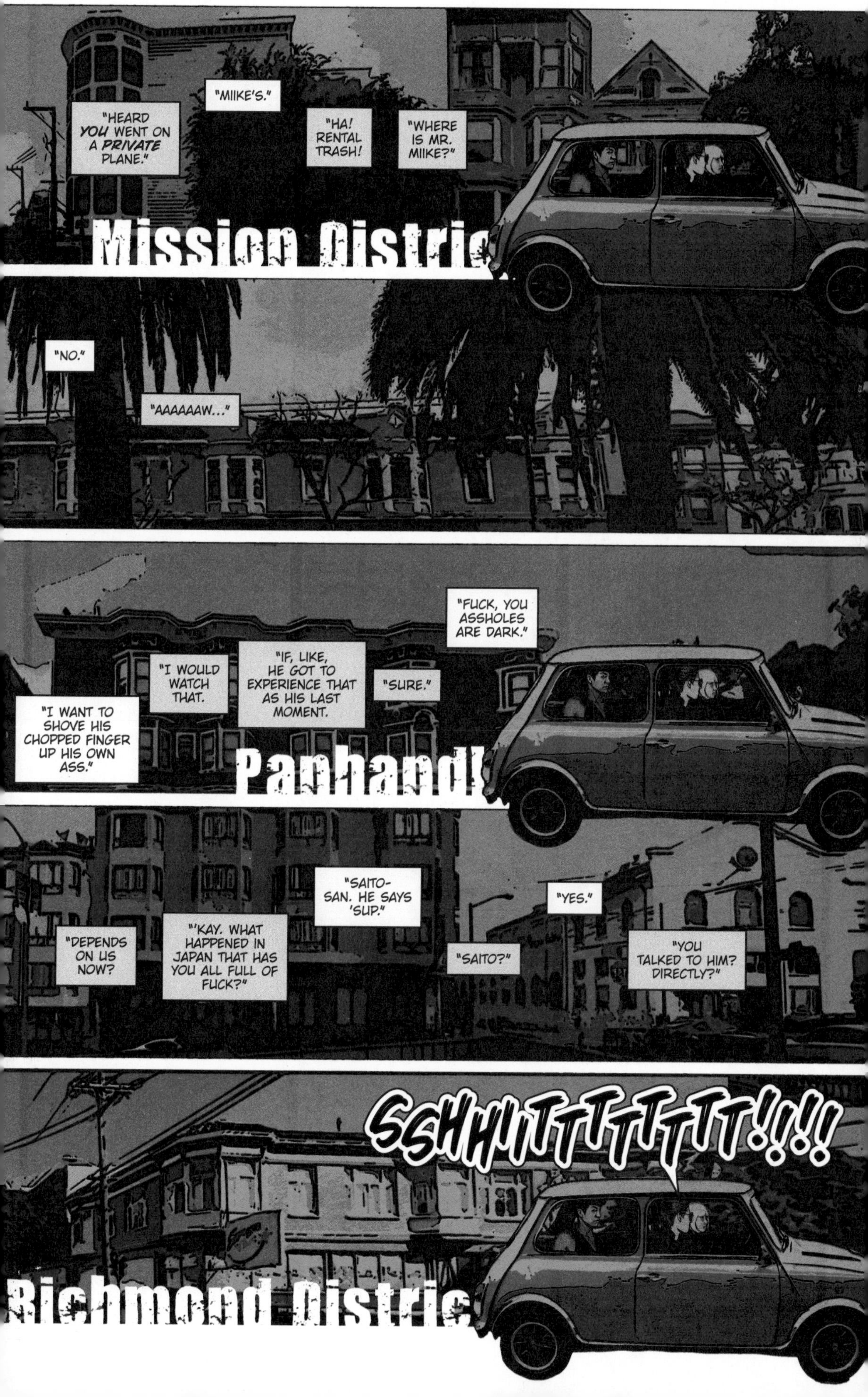
"HEARD YOU WENT ON A PRIVATE PLANE."
"MIIKE'S."
"HA! RENTAL TRASH!"
"WHERE IS MR. MIIKE?"
Mission Distric
"NO."
"AAAAAAW..."
"I WANT TO SHOVE HIS CHOPPED FINGER UP HIS OWN ASS."
"I WOULD WATCH THAT.
"IF, LIKE, HE GOT TO EXPERIENCE THAT AS HIS LAST MOMENT.
"SURE."
"FUCK, YOU ASSHOLES ARE DARK."
Panhandl
"DEPENDS ON US NOW?
"'KAY. WHAT HAPPENED IN JAPAN THAT HAS YOU ALL FULL OF FUCK?"
"SAITO-SAN. HE SAYS 'SUP."
"SAITO?"
"YES."
"YOU TALKED TO HIM? DIRECTLY?"
SSHHIITTTTTTTT!!!!
Richmond Distric

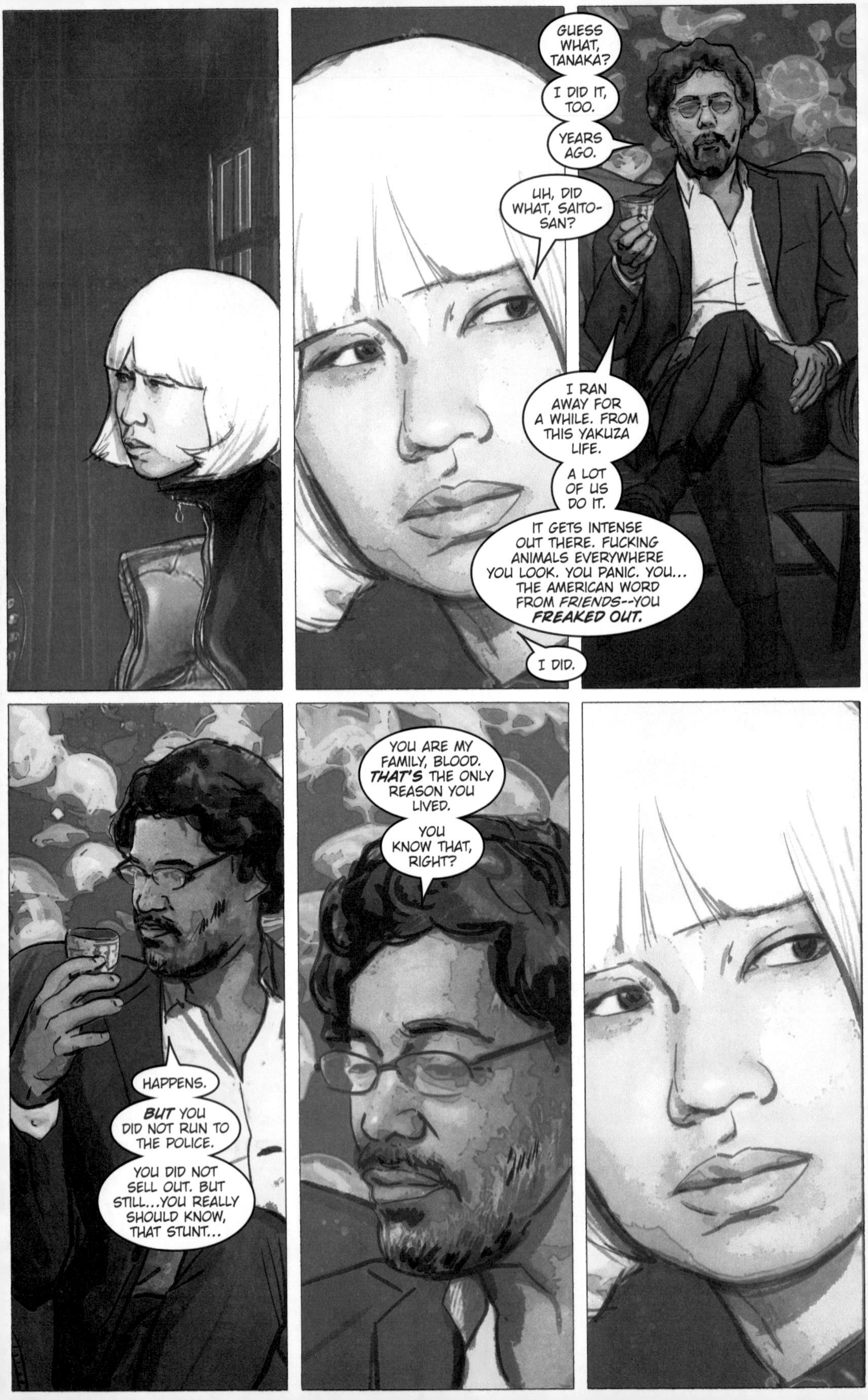
GUESS WHAT, TANAKA?
I DID IT, TOO.
YEARS AGO.
UH, DID WHAT, SAITO-SAN?
I RAN AWAY FOR A WHILE. FROM THIS YAKUZA LIFE.
A LOT OF US DO IT.
IT GETS INTENSE OUT THERE. FUCKING ANIMALS EVERYWHERE YOU LOOK. YOU PANIC. YOU... THE AMERICAN WORD FROM *FRIENDS*--YOU ***FREAKED OUT.***
I DID.
HAPPENS.
BUT YOU DID NOT RUN TO THE POLICE.
YOU DID NOT SELL OUT. BUT STILL...YOU REALLY SHOULD KNOW, THAT STUNT...
YOU ARE MY FAMILY, BLOOD. ***THAT'S*** THE ONLY REASON YOU LIVED.
YOU KNOW THAT, RIGHT?

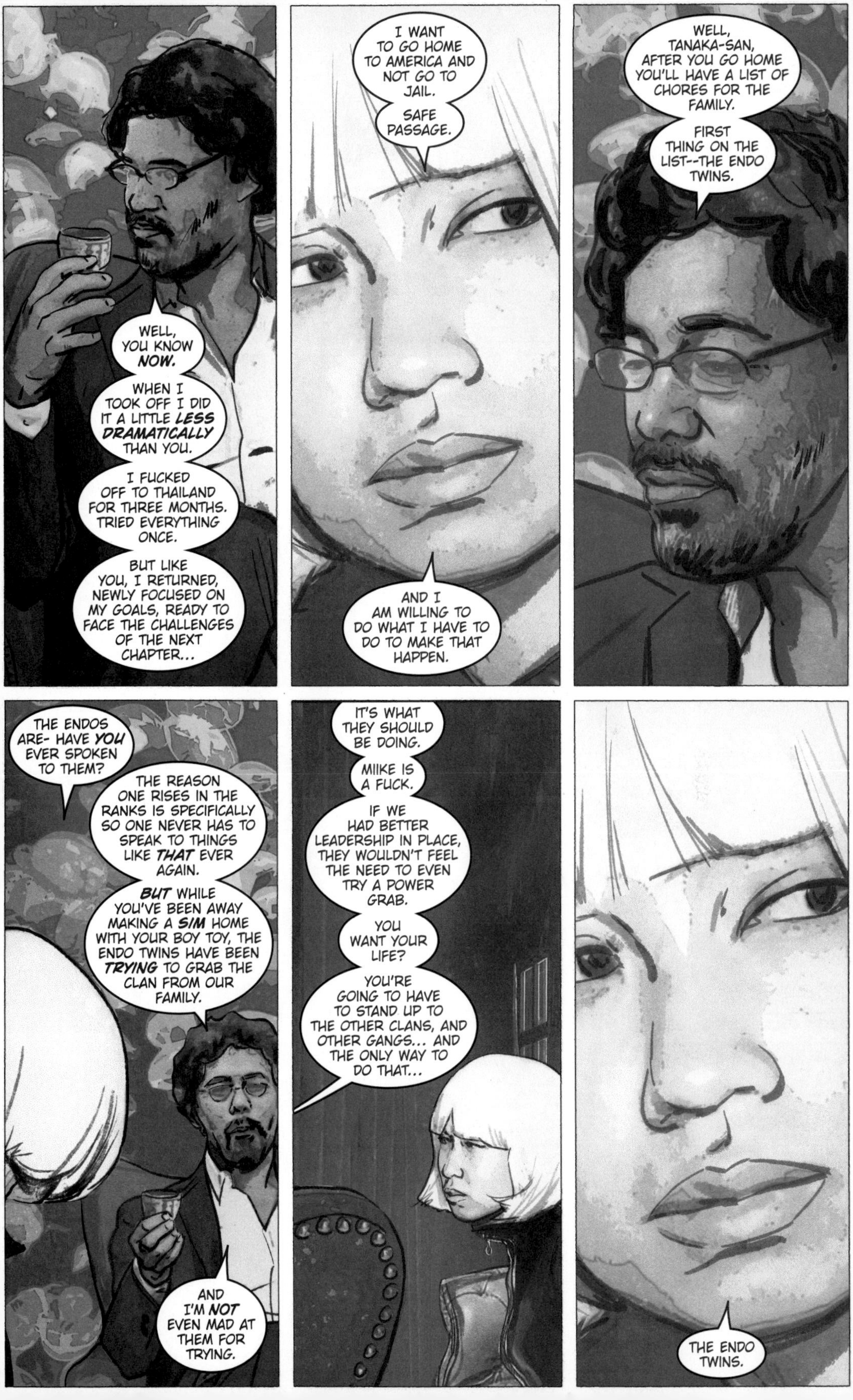
WELL, YOU KNOW NOW.
WHEN I TOOK OFF I DID IT A LITTLE LESS DRAMATICALLY THAN YOU.
I FUCKED OFF TO THAILAND FOR THREE MONTHS. TRIED EVERYTHING ONCE.
BUT LIKE YOU, I RETURNED, NEWLY FOCUSED ON MY GOALS, READY TO FACE THE CHALLENGES OF THE NEXT CHAPTER...
I WANT TO GO HOME TO AMERICA AND NOT GO TO JAIL.
SAFE PASSAGE.
AND I AM WILLING TO DO WHAT I HAVE TO DO TO MAKE THAT HAPPEN.
WELL, TANAKA-SAN, AFTER YOU GO HOME YOU'LL HAVE A LIST OF CHORES FOR THE FAMILY.
FIRST THING ON THE LIST--THE ENDO TWINS.
THE ENDOS ARE- HAVE YOU EVER SPOKEN TO THEM?
THE REASON ONE RISES IN THE RANKS IS SPECIFICALLY SO ONE NEVER HAS TO SPEAK TO THINGS LIKE THAT EVER AGAIN.
BUT WHILE YOU'VE BEEN AWAY MAKING A SIM HOME WITH YOUR BOY TOY, THE ENDO TWINS HAVE BEEN TRYING TO GRAB THE CLAN FROM OUR FAMILY.
AND I'M NOT EVEN MAD AT THEM FOR TRYING.
IT'S WHAT THEY SHOULD BE DOING.
MIIKE IS A FUCK.
IF WE HAD BETTER LEADERSHIP IN PLACE, THEY WOULDN'T FEEL THE NEED TO EVEN TRY A POWER GRAB.
YOU WANT YOUR LIFE?
YOU'RE GOING TO HAVE TO STAND UP TO THE OTHER CLANS, AND OTHER GANGS... AND THE ONLY WAY TO DO THAT...
THE ENDO TWINS.

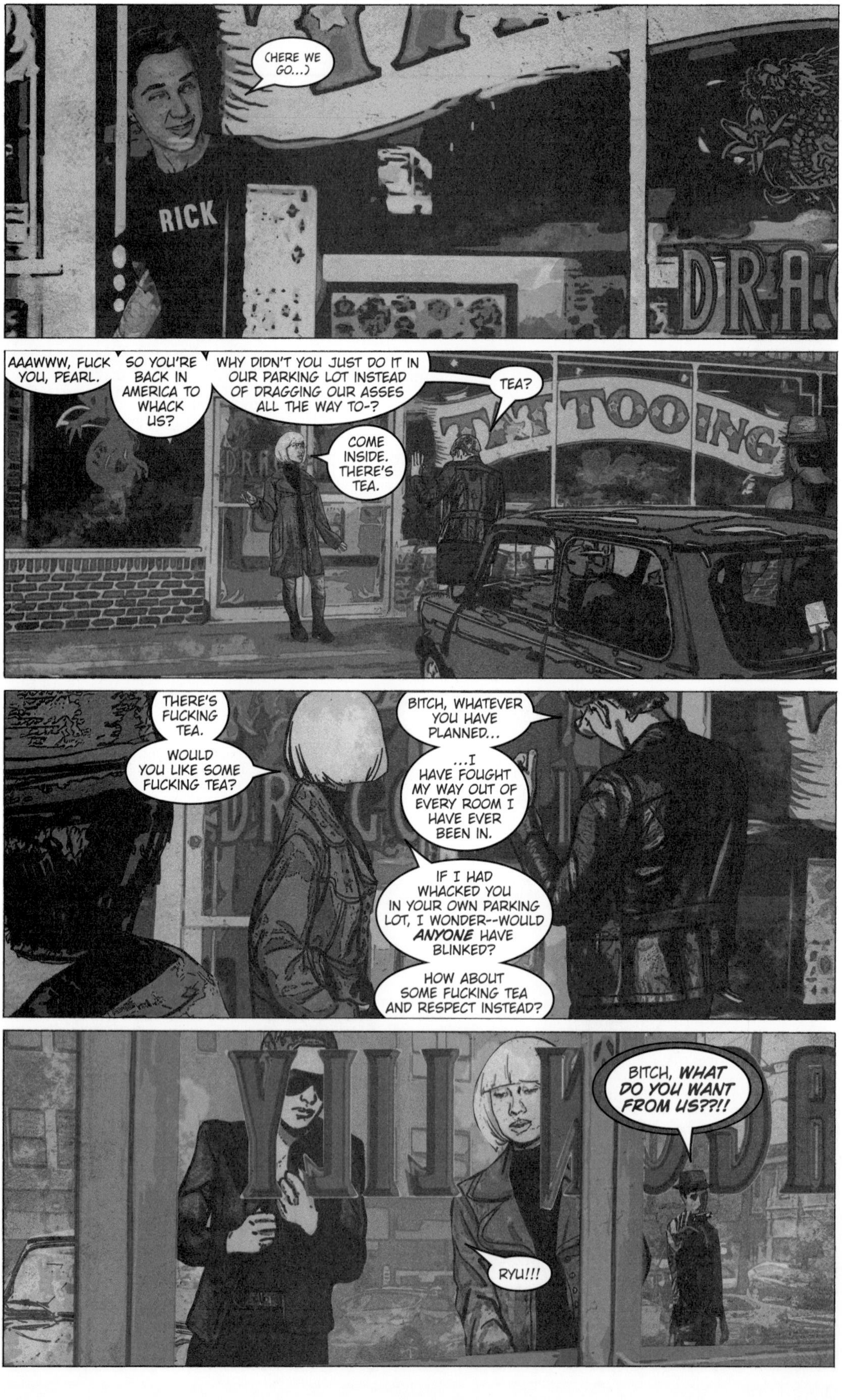
(HERE WE GO...)
RICK
DRAG
AAAWWW, FUCK YOU, PEARL.
SO YOU'RE BACK IN AMERICA TO WHACK US?
WHY DIDN'T YOU JUST DO IT IN OUR PARKING LOT INSTEAD OF DRAGGING OUR ASSES ALL THE WAY TO-?
TEA?
TATTOOING
COME INSIDE. THERE'S TEA.
THERE'S FUCKING TEA.
WOULD YOU LIKE SOME FUCKING TEA?
BITCH, WHATEVER YOU HAVE PLANNED...
...I HAVE FOUGHT MY WAY OUT OF EVERY ROOM I HAVE EVER BEEN IN.
IF I HAD WHACKED YOU IN YOUR OWN PARKING LOT, I WONDER--WOULD ***ANYONE*** HAVE BLINKED?
HOW ABOUT SOME FUCKING TEA AND RESPECT INSTEAD?
BITCH, ***WHAT DO YOU WANT FROM US??!!***
RYU!!!

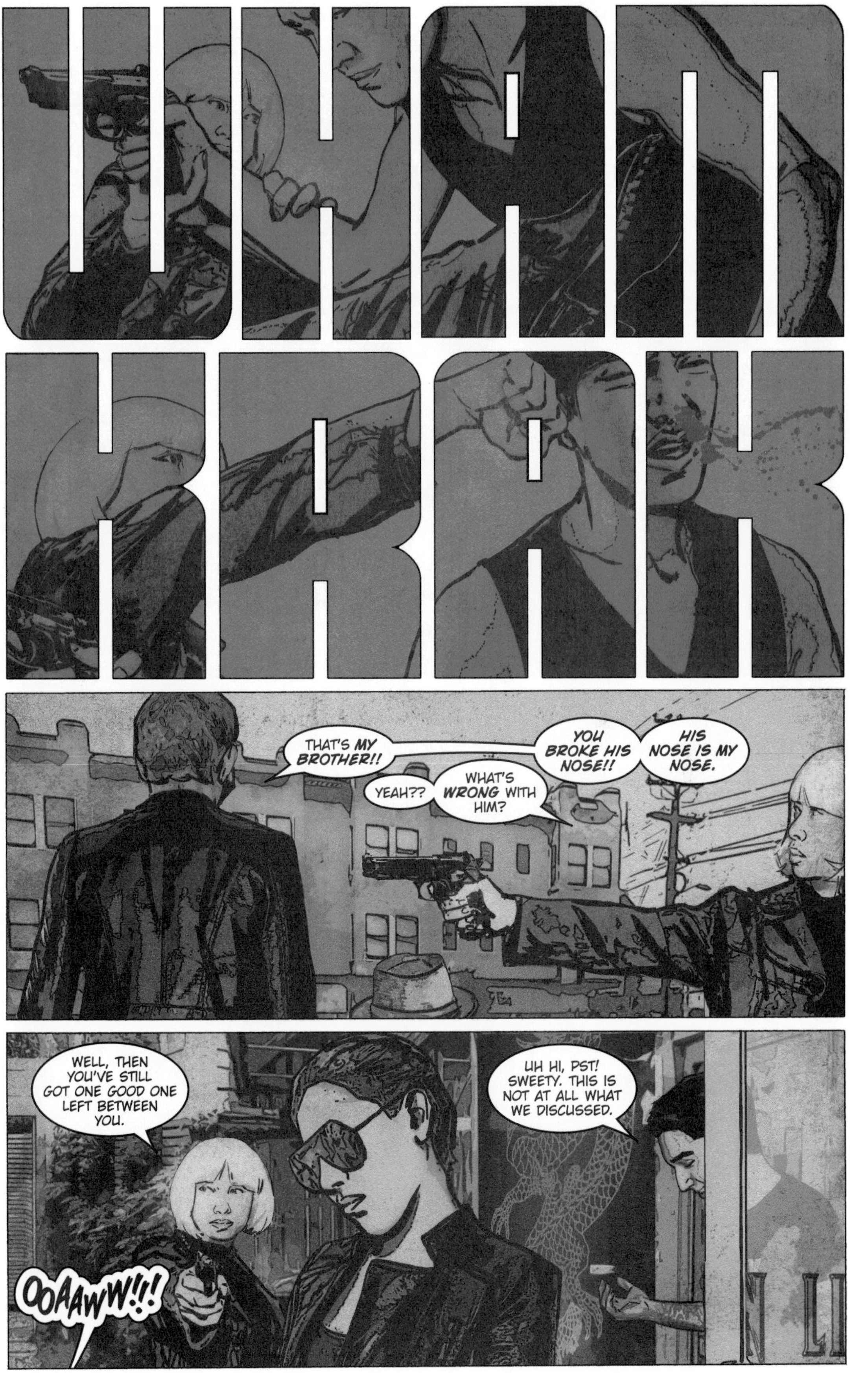
WHAM
KRAK
THAT'S MY BROTHER!!
YEAH??
WHAT'S WRONG WITH HIM?
YOU BROKE HIS NOSE!!
HIS NOSE IS MY NOSE.
WELL, THEN YOU'VE STILL GOT ONE GOOD ONE LEFT BETWEEN YOU.
UH HI, PST! SWEETY. THIS IS NOT AT ALL WHAT WE DISCUSSED.
OOAAWW!!!

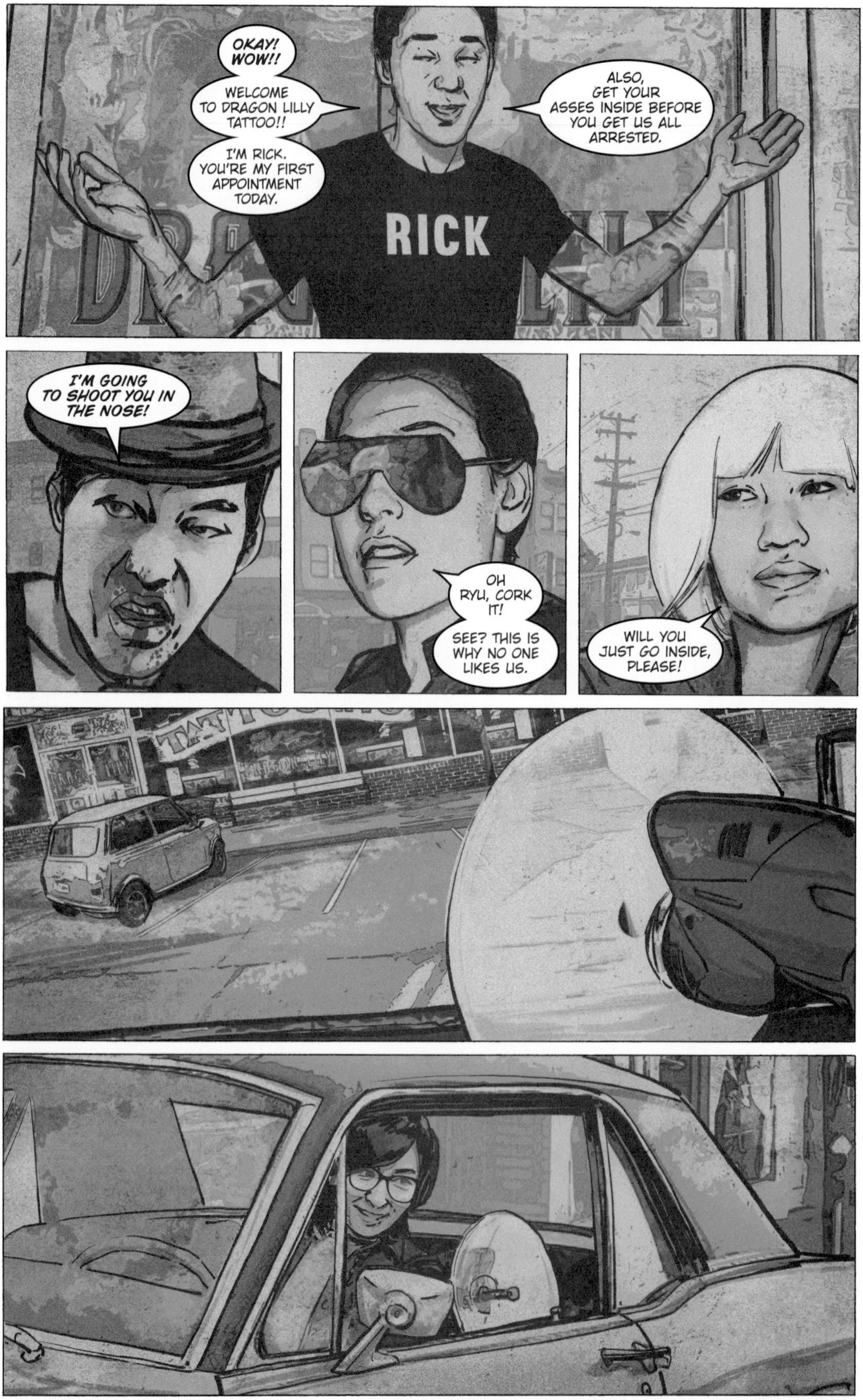
OKAY! WOW!!
WELCOME TO DRAGON LILLY TATTOO!!
I'M RICK. YOU'RE MY FIRST APPOINTMENT TODAY.
ALSO, GET YOUR ASSES INSIDE BEFORE YOU GET US ALL ARRESTED.
RICK
I'M GOING TO SHOOT YOU IN THE NOSE!
OH RYU, CORK IT!
SEE? THIS IS WHY NO ONE LIKES US.
WILL YOU JUST GO INSIDE, PLEASE!

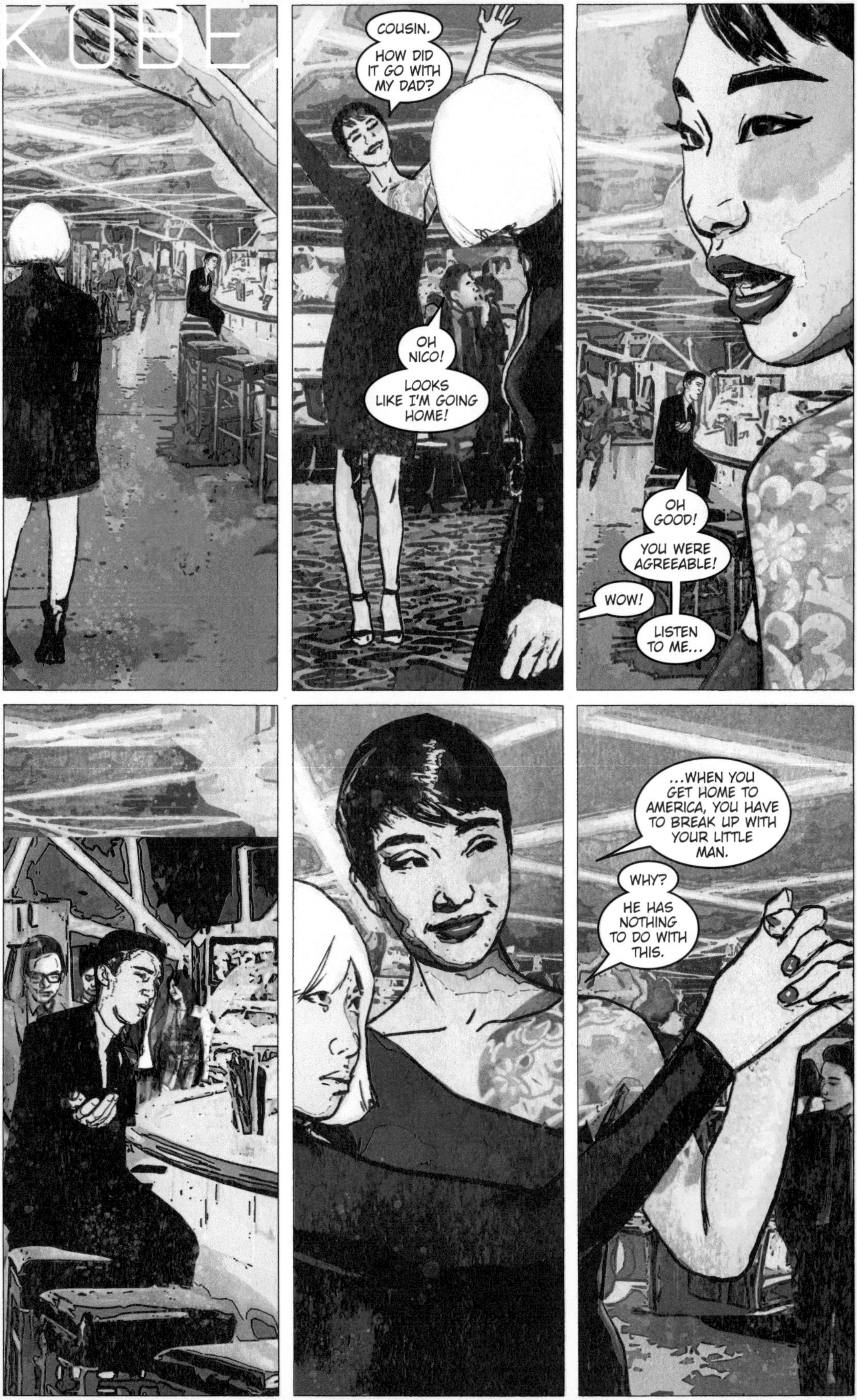
KOBE.
COUSIN.
HOW DID IT GO WITH MY DAD?
OH NICO!
LOOKS LIKE I'M GOING HOME!
OH GOOD!
YOU WERE AGREEABLE!
WOW!
LISTEN TO ME...
...WHEN YOU GET HOME TO AMERICA, YOU HAVE TO BREAK UP WITH YOUR LITTLE MAN.
WHY?
HE HAS NOTHING TO DO WITH THIS.

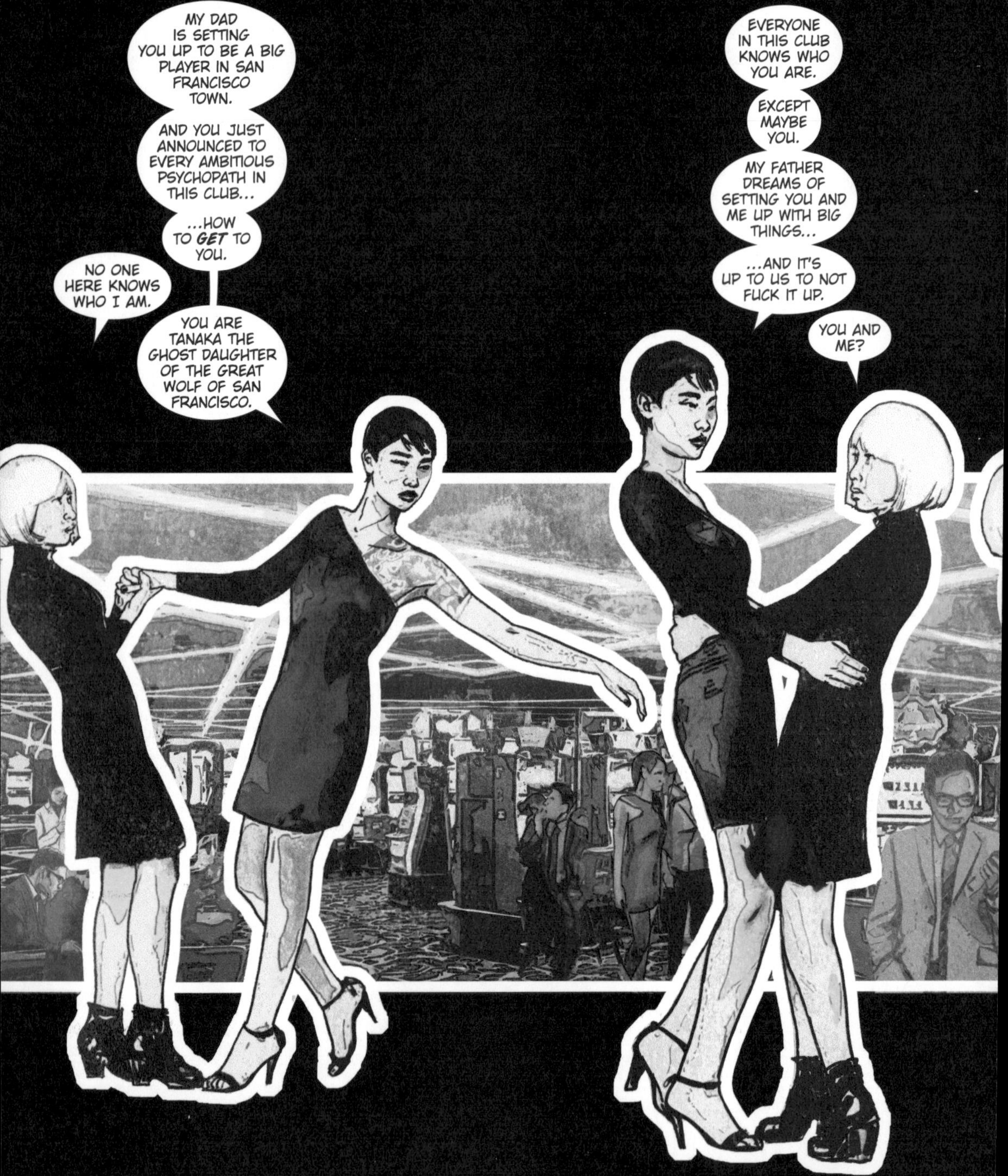
MY DAD IS SETTING YOU UP TO BE A BIG PLAYER IN SAN FRANCISCO TOWN.
AND YOU JUST ANNOUNCED TO EVERY AMBITIOUS PSYCHOPATH IN THIS CLUB...
...HOW TO *GET* TO YOU.
NO ONE HERE KNOWS WHO I AM.
YOU ARE TANAKA THE GHOST DAUGHTER OF THE GREAT WOLF OF SAN FRANCISCO.
EVERYONE IN THIS CLUB KNOWS WHO YOU ARE.
EXCEPT MAYBE YOU.
MY FATHER DREAMS OF SETTING YOU AND ME UP WITH BIG THINGS...
...AND IT'S UP TO US TO NOT FUCK IT UP.
YOU AND ME?

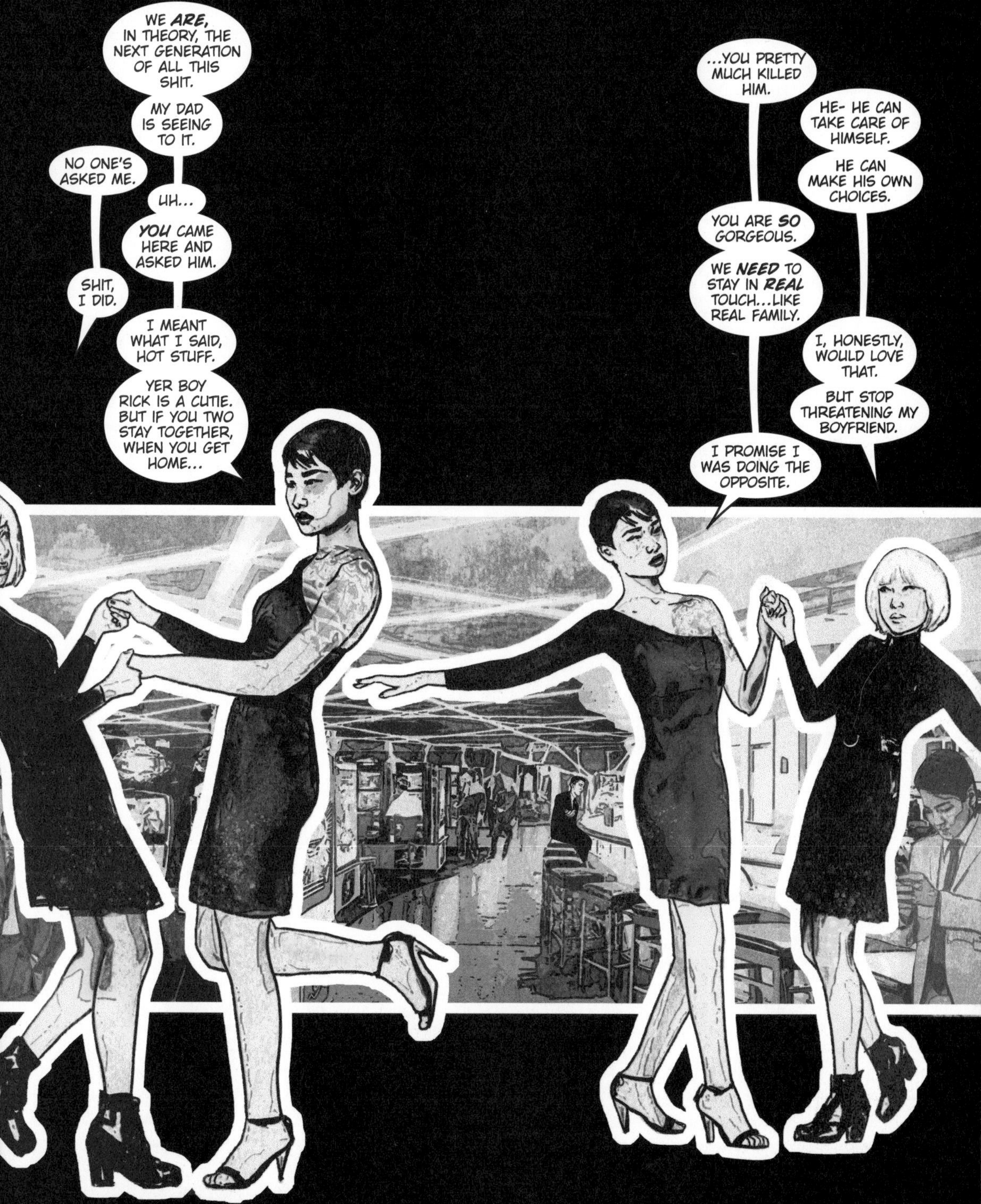

WE ARE, IN THEORY, THE NEXT GENERATION OF ALL THIS SHIT.
MY DAD IS SEEING TO IT.
NO ONE'S ASKED ME.
UH...
YOU CAME HERE AND ASKED HIM.
SHIT, I DID.
I MEANT WHAT I SAID, HOT STUFF.
YER BOY RICK IS A CUTIE. BUT IF YOU TWO STAY TOGETHER, WHEN YOU GET HOME...
...YOU PRETTY MUCH KILLED HIM.
HE- HE CAN TAKE CARE OF HIMSELF.
HE CAN MAKE HIS OWN CHOICES.
YOU ARE SO GORGEOUS.
WE NEED TO STAY IN REAL TOUCH...LIKE REAL FAMILY.
I, HONESTLY, WOULD LOVE THAT.
BUT STOP THREATENING MY BOYFRIEND.
I PROMISE I WAS DOING THE OPPOSITE.

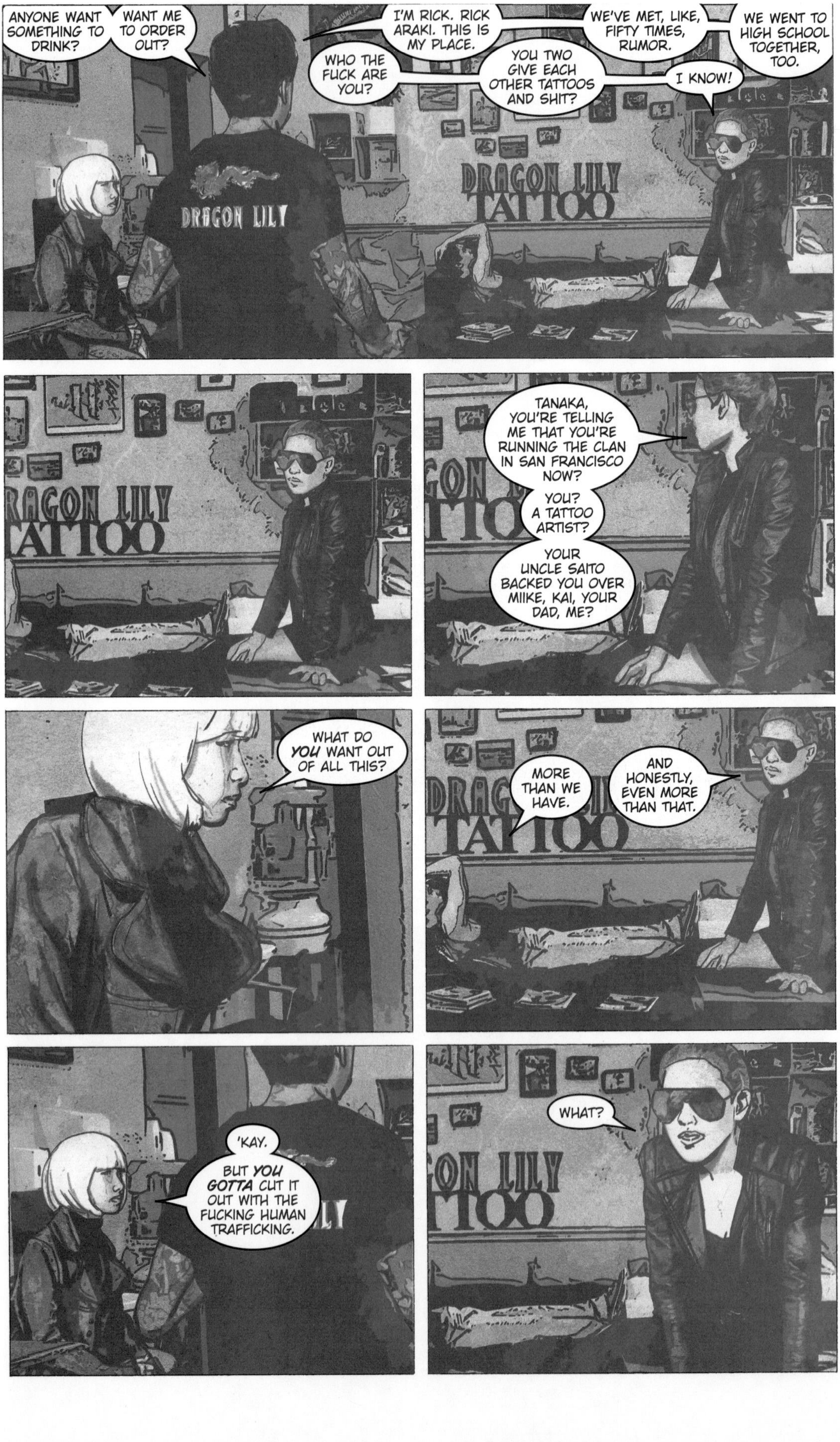
ANYONE WANT SOMETHING TO DRINK?
WANT ME TO ORDER OUT?
I'M RICK. RICK ARAKI. THIS IS MY PLACE.
WHO THE FUCK ARE YOU?
WE'VE MET, LIKE, FIFTY TIMES, RUMOR.
WE WENT TO HIGH SCHOOL TOGETHER, TOO.
YOU TWO GIVE EACH OTHER TATTOOS AND SHIT?
I KNOW!
DRAGON LILY
DRAGON LILY TATTOO
TANAKA, YOU'RE TELLING ME THAT YOU'RE RUNNING THE CLAN IN SAN FRANCISCO NOW?
YOU? A TATTOO ARTIST?
YOUR UNCLE SAITO BACKED YOU OVER MIIKE, KAI, YOUR DAD, ME?
WHAT DO *YOU* WANT OUT OF ALL THIS?
MORE THAN WE HAVE.
AND HONESTLY, EVEN MORE THAN THAT.
'KAY.
BUT *YOU GOTTA* CUT IT OUT WITH THE FUCKING HUMAN TRAFFICKING.
WHAT?

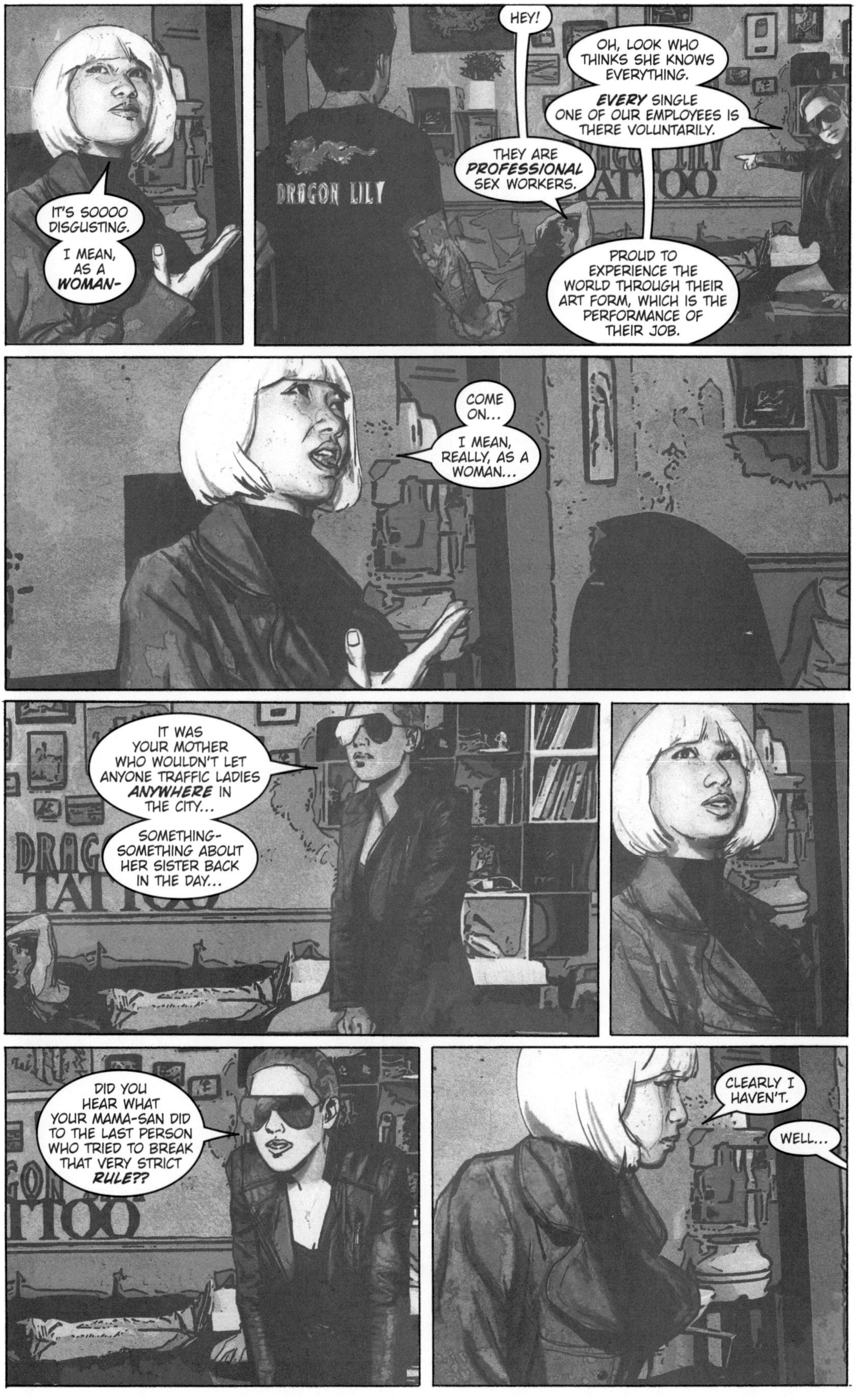
IT'S SOOOO DISGUSTING.
I MEAN, AS A WOMAN-
HEY!
THEY ARE PROFESSIONAL SEX WORKERS.
OH, LOOK WHO THINKS SHE KNOWS EVERYTHING.
EVERY SINGLE ONE OF OUR EMPLOYEES IS THERE VOLUNTARILY.
PROUD TO EXPERIENCE THE WORLD THROUGH THEIR ART FORM, WHICH IS THE PERFORMANCE OF THEIR JOB.
DRAGON LILY
TATTOO
COME ON...
I MEAN, REALLY, AS A WOMAN...
IT WAS YOUR MOTHER WHO WOULDN'T LET ANYONE TRAFFIC LADIES ANYWHERE IN THE CITY...
SOMETHING-SOMETHING ABOUT HER SISTER BACK IN THE DAY...
DID YOU HEAR WHAT YOUR MAMA-SAN DID TO THE LAST PERSON WHO TRIED TO BREAK THAT VERY STRICT RULE??
CLEARLY I HAVEN'T.
WELL...

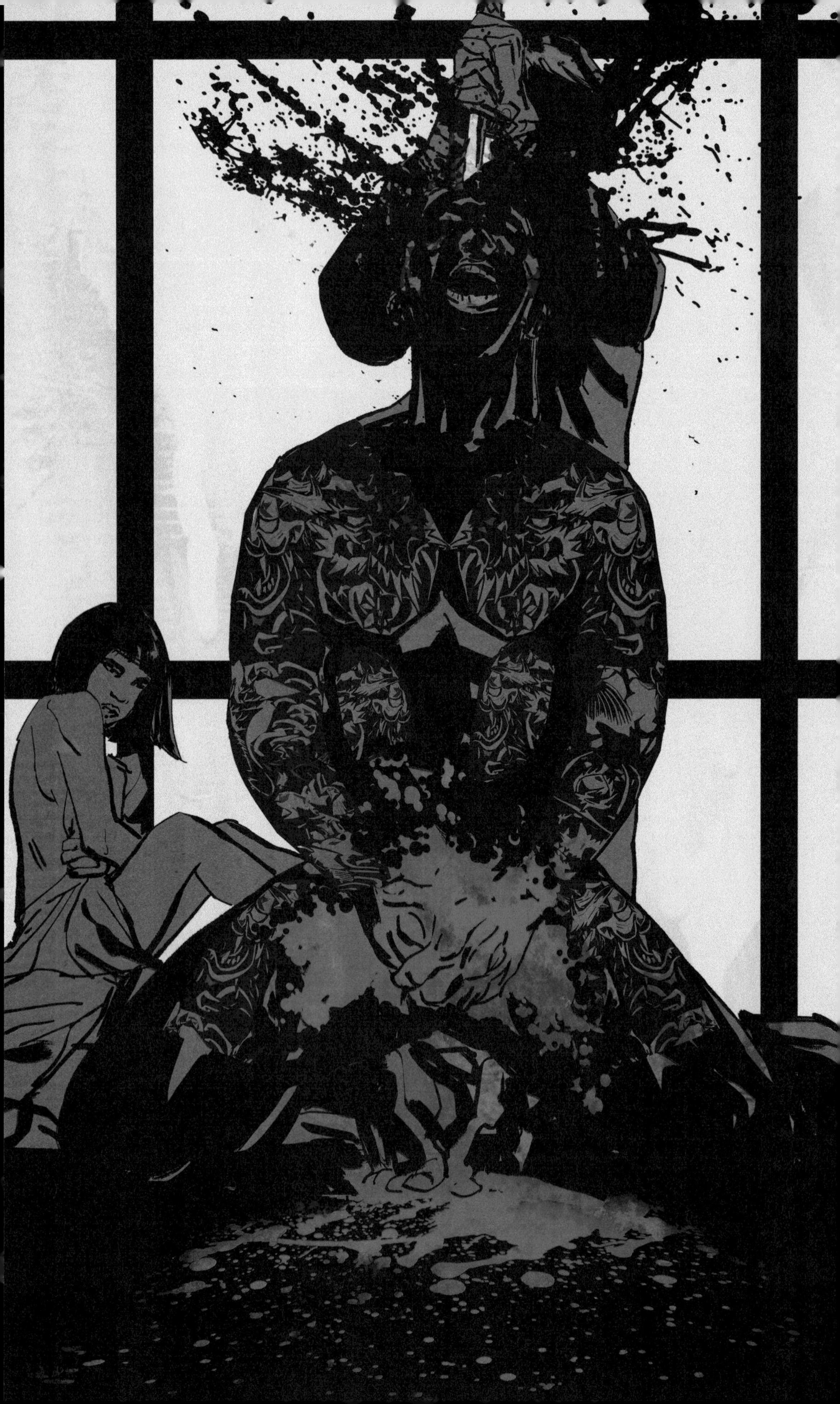

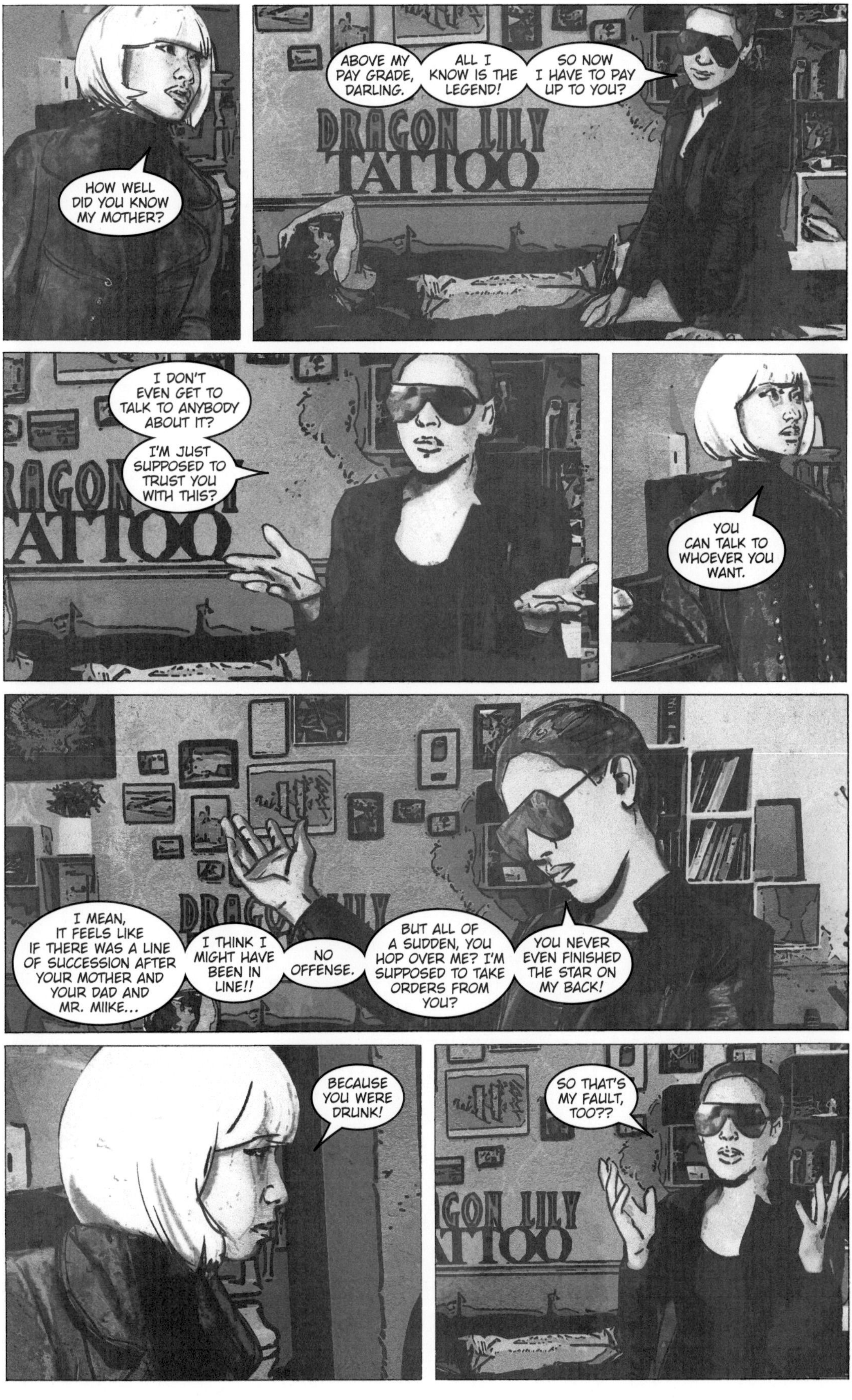
HOW WELL DID YOU KNOW MY MOTHER?
SO NOW I HAVE TO PAY UP TO YOU?
ALL I KNOW IS THE LEGEND!
ABOVE MY PAY GRADE, DARLING.
DRAGON LILY TATTOO
I DON'T EVEN GET TO TALK TO ANYBODY ABOUT IT?
I'M JUST SUPPOSED TO TRUST YOU WITH THIS?
YOU CAN TALK TO WHOEVER YOU WANT.
I MEAN, IT FEELS LIKE IF THERE WAS A LINE OF SUCCESSION AFTER YOUR MOTHER AND YOUR DAD AND MR. MIIKE...
I THINK I MIGHT HAVE BEEN IN LINE!!
NO OFFENSE.
BUT ALL OF A SUDDEN, YOU HOP OVER ME? I'M SUPPOSED TO TAKE ORDERS FROM YOU?
YOU NEVER EVEN FINISHED THE STAR ON MY BACK!
BECAUSE YOU WERE DRUNK!
SO THAT'S MY FAULT, TOO??

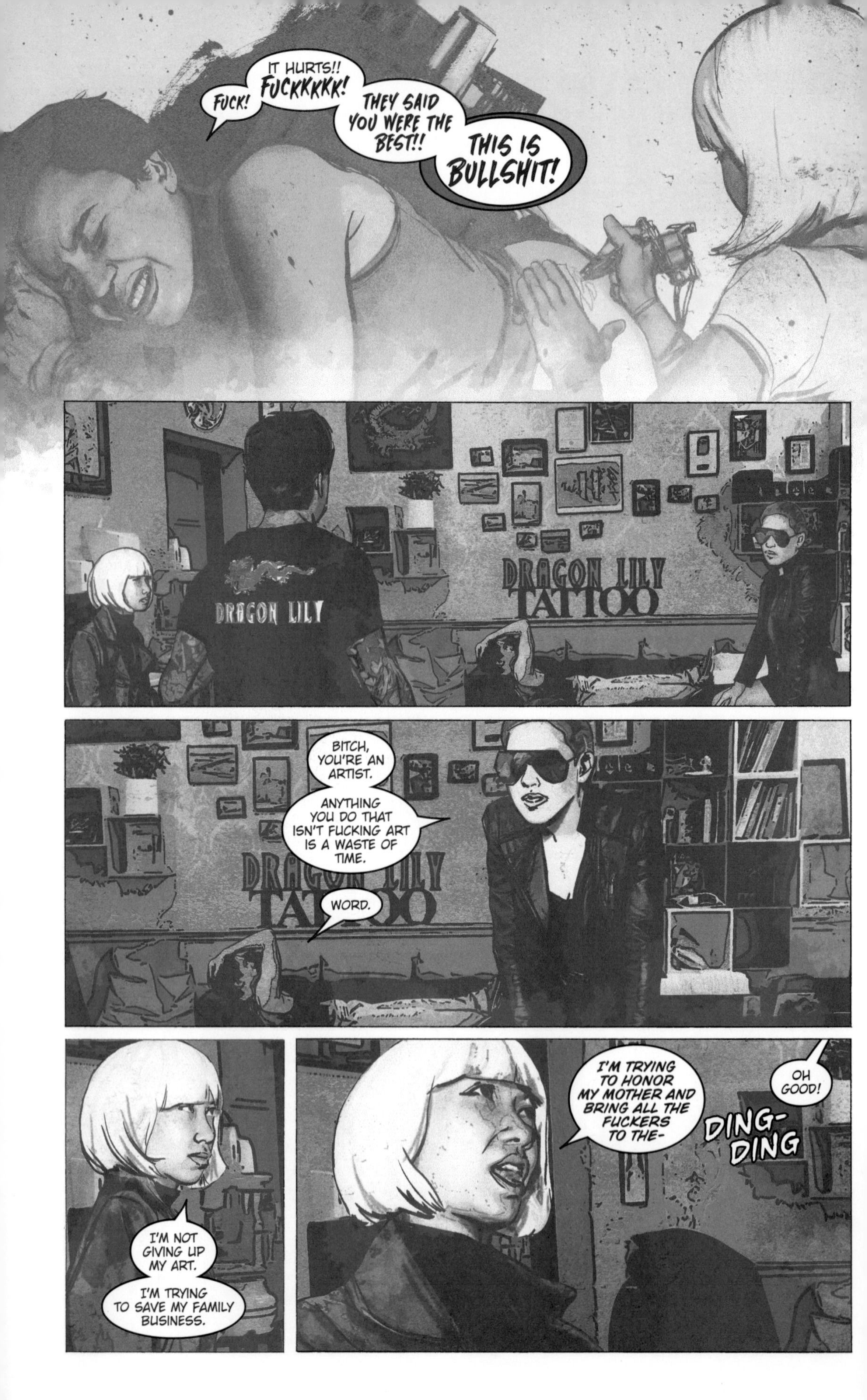
FUCK!
IT HURTS!! FUCKKKKK!
THEY SAID YOU WERE THE BEST!!
THIS IS BULLSHIT!
DRAGON LILY
DRAGON LILY TATTOO
BITCH, YOU'RE AN ARTIST.
ANYTHING YOU DO THAT ISN'T FUCKING ART IS A WASTE OF TIME.
WORD.
I'M NOT GIVING UP MY ART.
I'M TRYING TO SAVE MY FAMILY BUSINESS.
I'M TRYING TO HONOR MY MOTHER AND BRING ALL THE FUCKERS TO THE-
DING-DING
OH GOOD!

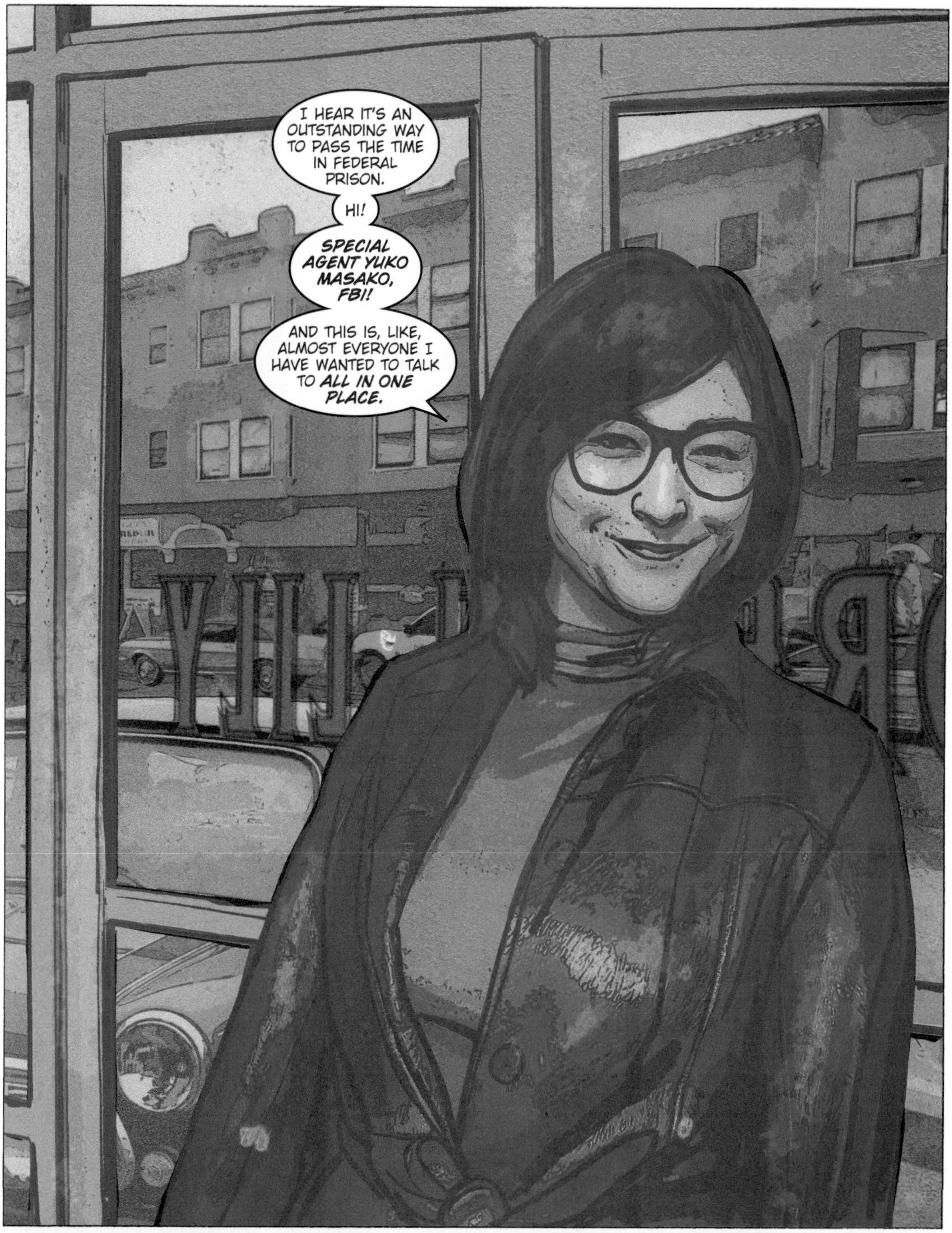
I HEAR IT'S AN OUTSTANDING WAY TO PASS THE TIME IN FEDERAL PRISON.
HI!
SPECIAL AGENT YUKO MASAKO, FBI!
AND THIS IS, LIKE, ALMOST EVERYONE I HAVE WANTED TO TALK TO ALL IN ONE PLACE.

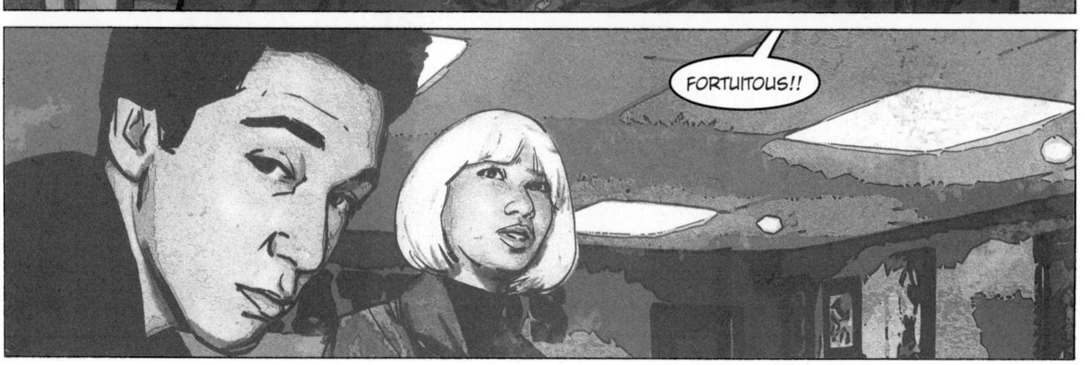
FORTUITOUS!!

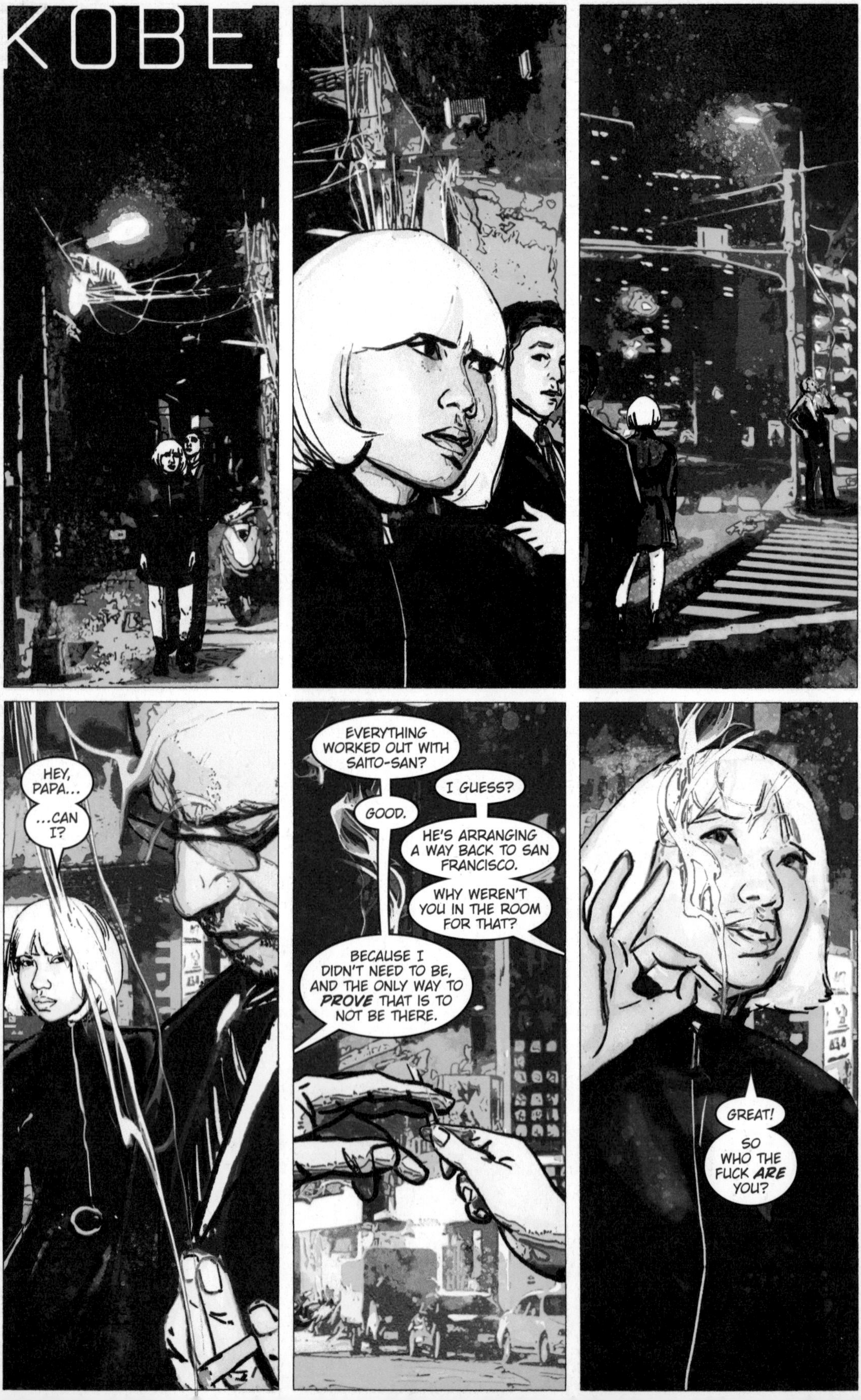
KOBE
HEY, PAPA...
...CAN I?
EVERYTHING WORKED OUT WITH SAITO-SAN?
I GUESS?
GOOD.
HE'S ARRANGING A WAY BACK TO SAN FRANCISCO.
WHY WEREN'T YOU IN THE ROOM FOR THAT?
BECAUSE I DIDN'T NEED TO BE, AND THE ONLY WAY TO *PROVE* THAT IS TO NOT BE THERE.
GREAT!
SO WHO THE FUCK *ARE* YOU?

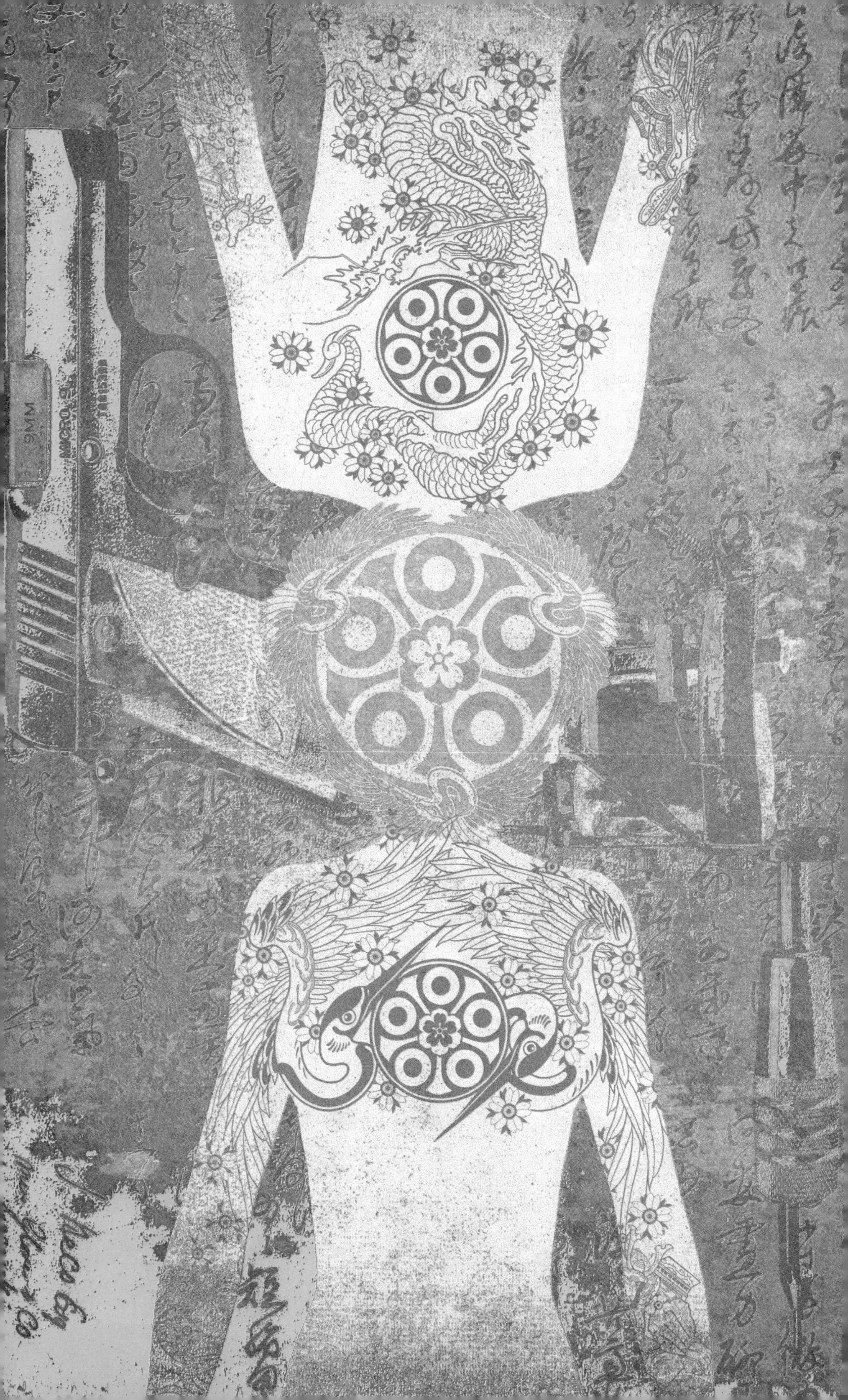
9MM

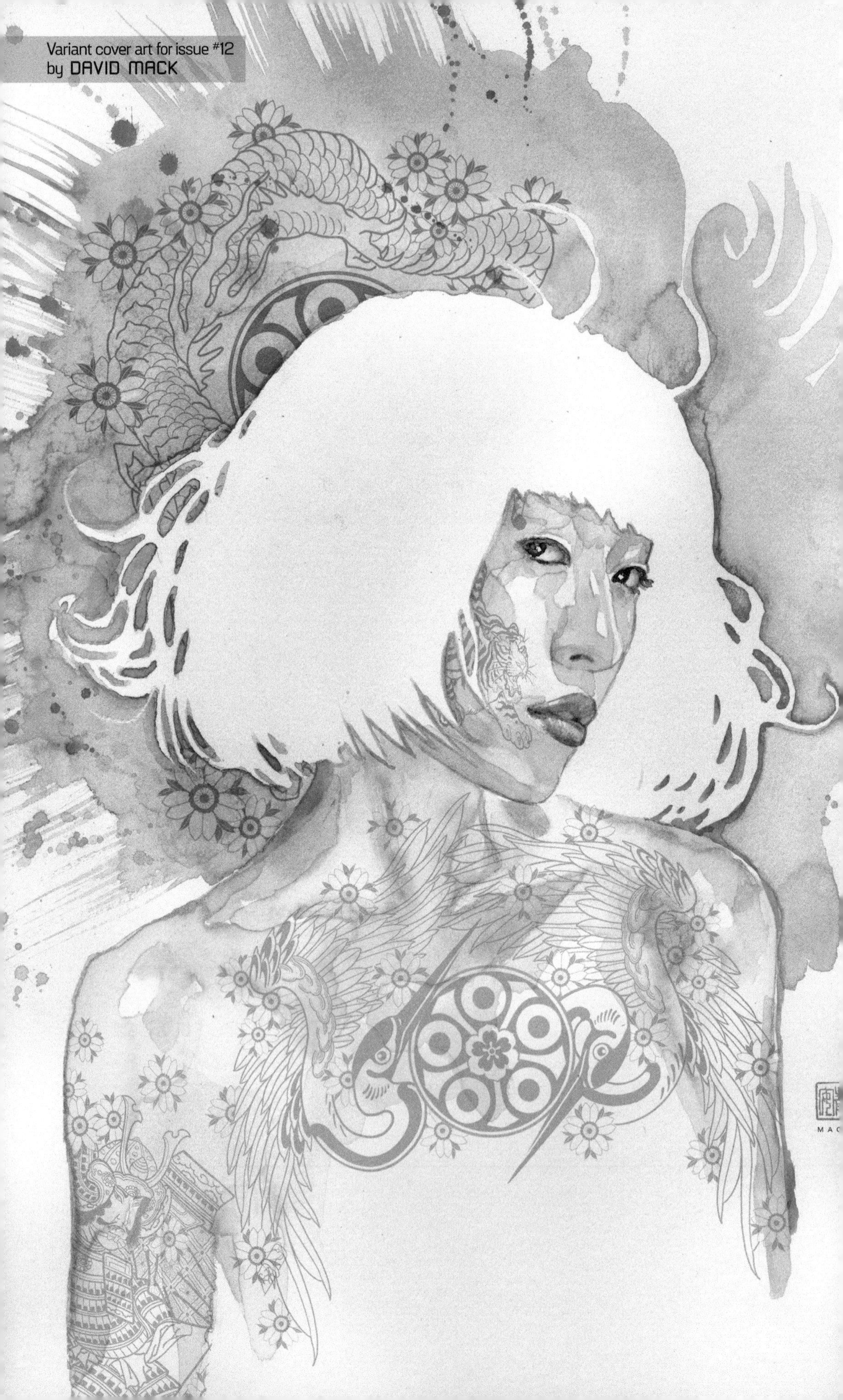

Variant cover art for issue #12
by DAVID MACK

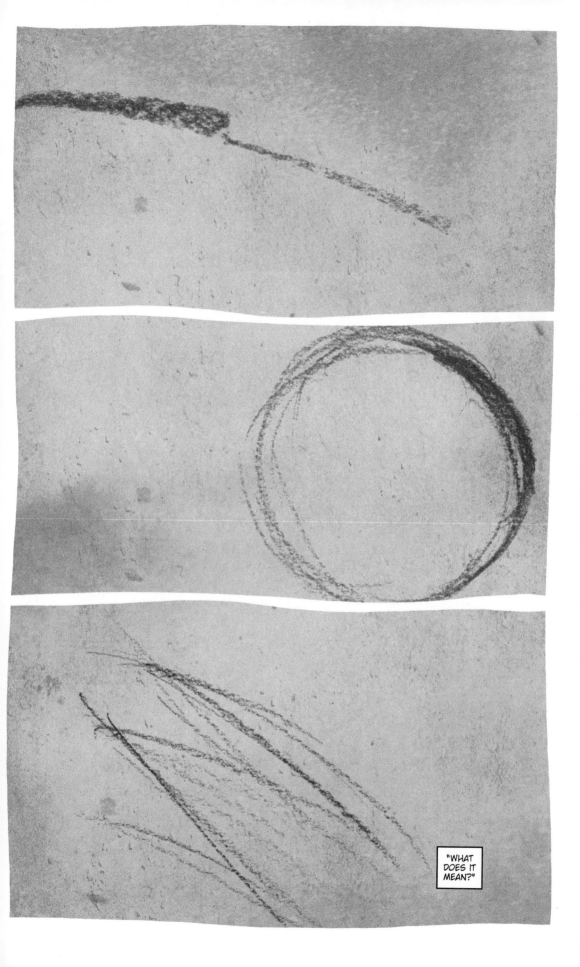

"WHAT
DOES IT
MEAN?"

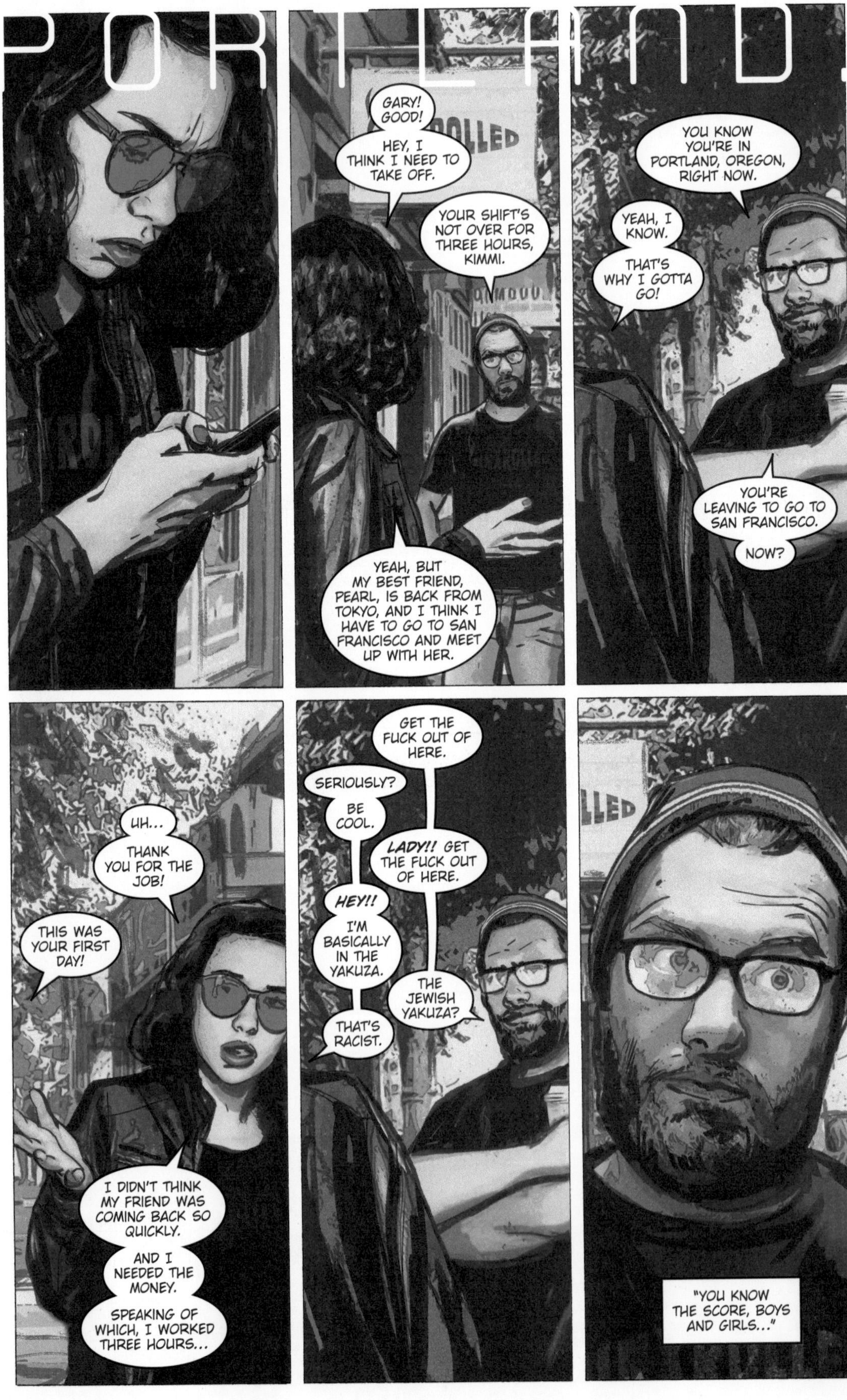
PORTLAND.
GARY! GOOD!
HEY, I THINK I NEED TO TAKE OFF.
YOUR SHIFT'S NOT OVER FOR THREE HOURS, KIMMI.
YEAH, BUT MY BEST FRIEND, PEARL, IS BACK FROM TOKYO, AND I THINK I HAVE TO GO TO SAN FRANCISCO AND MEET UP WITH HER.
YOU KNOW YOU'RE IN PORTLAND, OREGON, RIGHT NOW.
YEAH, I KNOW.
THAT'S WHY I GOTTA GO!
YOU'RE LEAVING TO GO TO SAN FRANCISCO.
NOW?
UH...
THANK YOU FOR THE JOB!
THIS WAS YOUR FIRST DAY!
I DIDN'T THINK MY FRIEND WAS COMING BACK SO QUICKLY.
AND I NEEDED THE MONEY.
SPEAKING OF WHICH, I WORKED THREE HOURS...
GET THE FUCK OUT OF HERE.
SERIOUSLY?
BE COOL.
LADY!! GET THE FUCK OUT OF HERE.
HEY!!
I'M BASICALLY IN THE YAKUZA.
THE JEWISH YAKUZA?
THAT'S RACIST.
"YOU KNOW THE SCORE, BOYS AND GIRLS..."

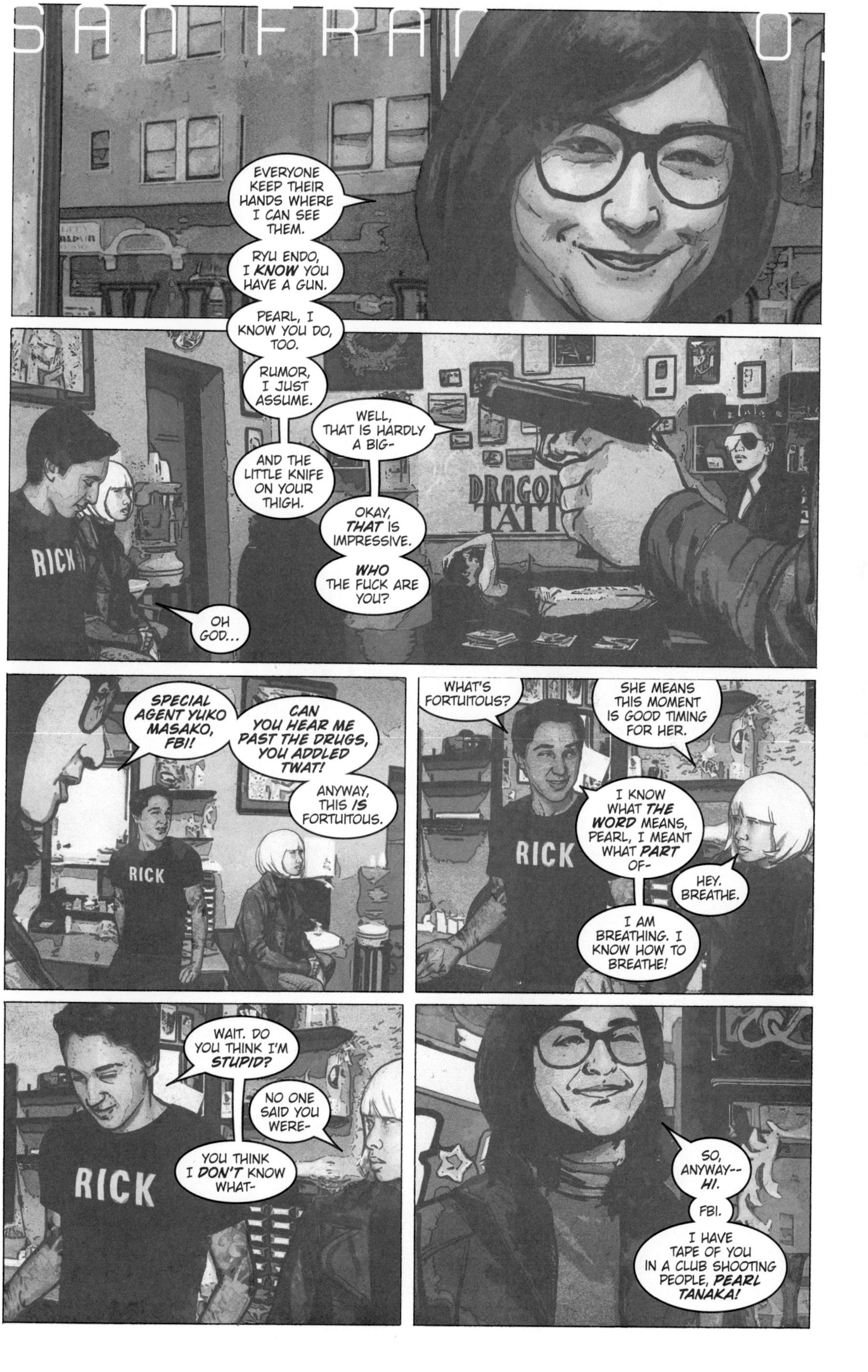
SAN FRAN O.
EVERYONE KEEP THEIR HANDS WHERE I CAN SEE THEM.
RYU ENDO, I **KNOW** YOU HAVE A GUN.
PEARL, I KNOW YOU DO, TOO.
RUMOR, I JUST ASSUME.
AND THE LITTLE KNIFE ON YOUR THIGH.
WELL, THAT IS HARDLY A BIG-
OKAY, ***THAT*** IS IMPRESSIVE.
WHO THE FUCK ARE YOU?
OH GOD...
DRAGON TATT
SPECIAL AGENT YUKO MASAKO, FBI!
CAN YOU HEAR ME PAST THE DRUGS, YOU ADDLED TWAT!
ANYWAY, THIS ***IS*** FORTUITOUS.
RICK
WHAT'S FORTUITOUS?
SHE MEANS THIS MOMENT IS GOOD TIMING FOR HER.
I KNOW WHAT ***THE WORD*** MEANS, PEARL, I MEANT WHAT ***PART*** OF-
HEY. BREATHE.
I AM BREATHING. I KNOW HOW TO BREATHE!
RICK
WAIT. DO YOU THINK I'M ***STUPID?***
NO ONE SAID YOU WERE-
YOU THINK I ***DON'T*** KNOW WHAT-
RICK
SO, ANYWAY-- ***HI.***
FBI.
I HAVE TAPE OF YOU IN A CLUB SHOOTING PEOPLE, ***PEARL TANAKA!***

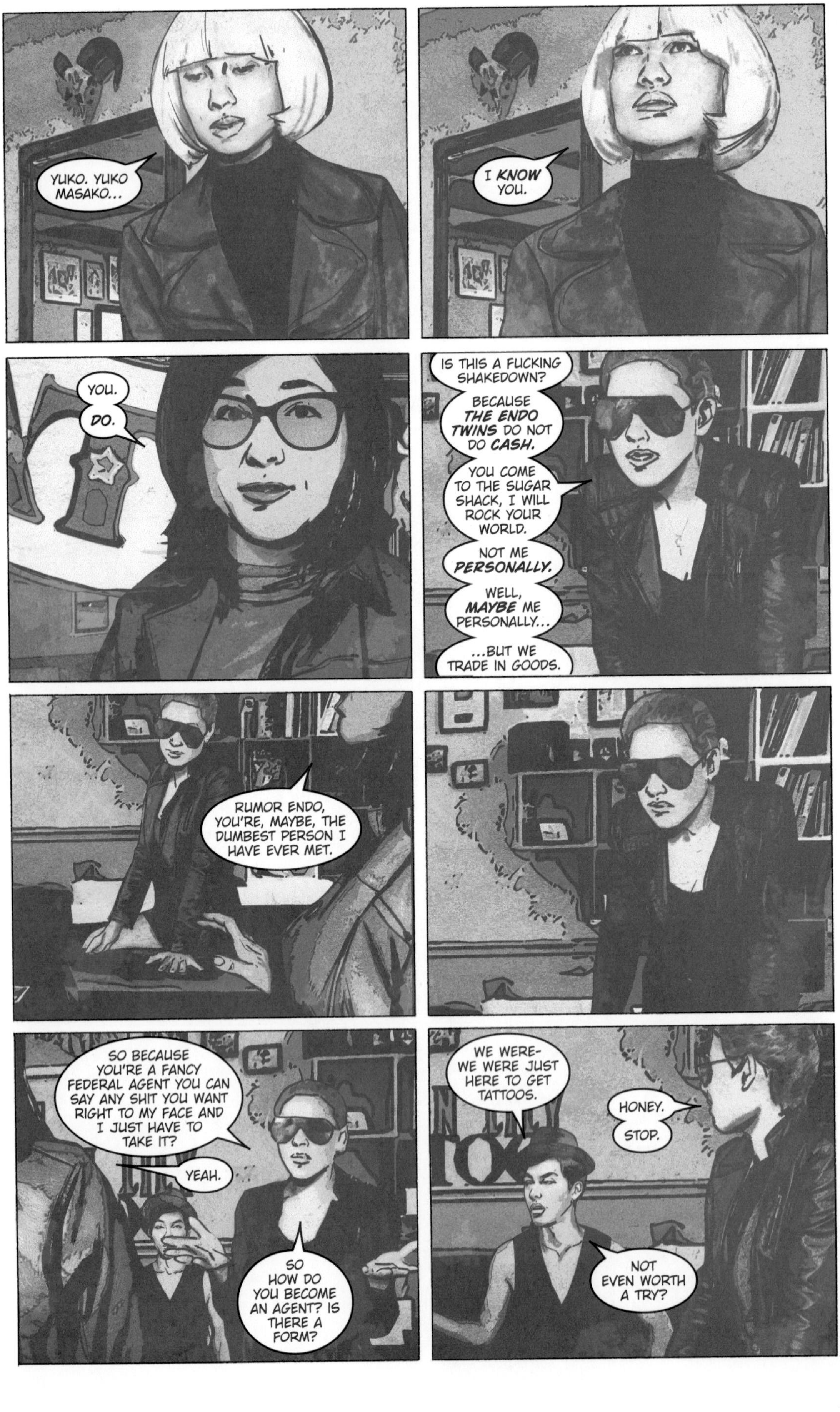
YUKO. YUKO MASAKO...
I **KNOW** YOU.
YOU.
DO.
IS THIS A FUCKING SHAKEDOWN?
BECAUSE **THE ENDO TWINS** DO NOT DO **CASH.**
YOU COME TO THE SUGAR SHACK, I WILL ROCK YOUR WORLD.
NOT ME **PERSONALLY.**
WELL, **MAYBE** ME PERSONALLY...
...BUT WE TRADE IN GOODS.
RUMOR ENDO, YOU'RE, MAYBE, THE DUMBEST PERSON I HAVE EVER MET.
SO BECAUSE YOU'RE A FANCY FEDERAL AGENT YOU CAN SAY ANY SHIT YOU WANT RIGHT TO MY FACE AND I JUST HAVE TO TAKE IT?
YEAH.
SO HOW DO YOU BECOME AN AGENT? IS THERE A FORM?
WE WERE- WE WERE JUST HERE TO GET TATTOOS.
HONEY.
STOP.
NOT EVEN WORTH A TRY?

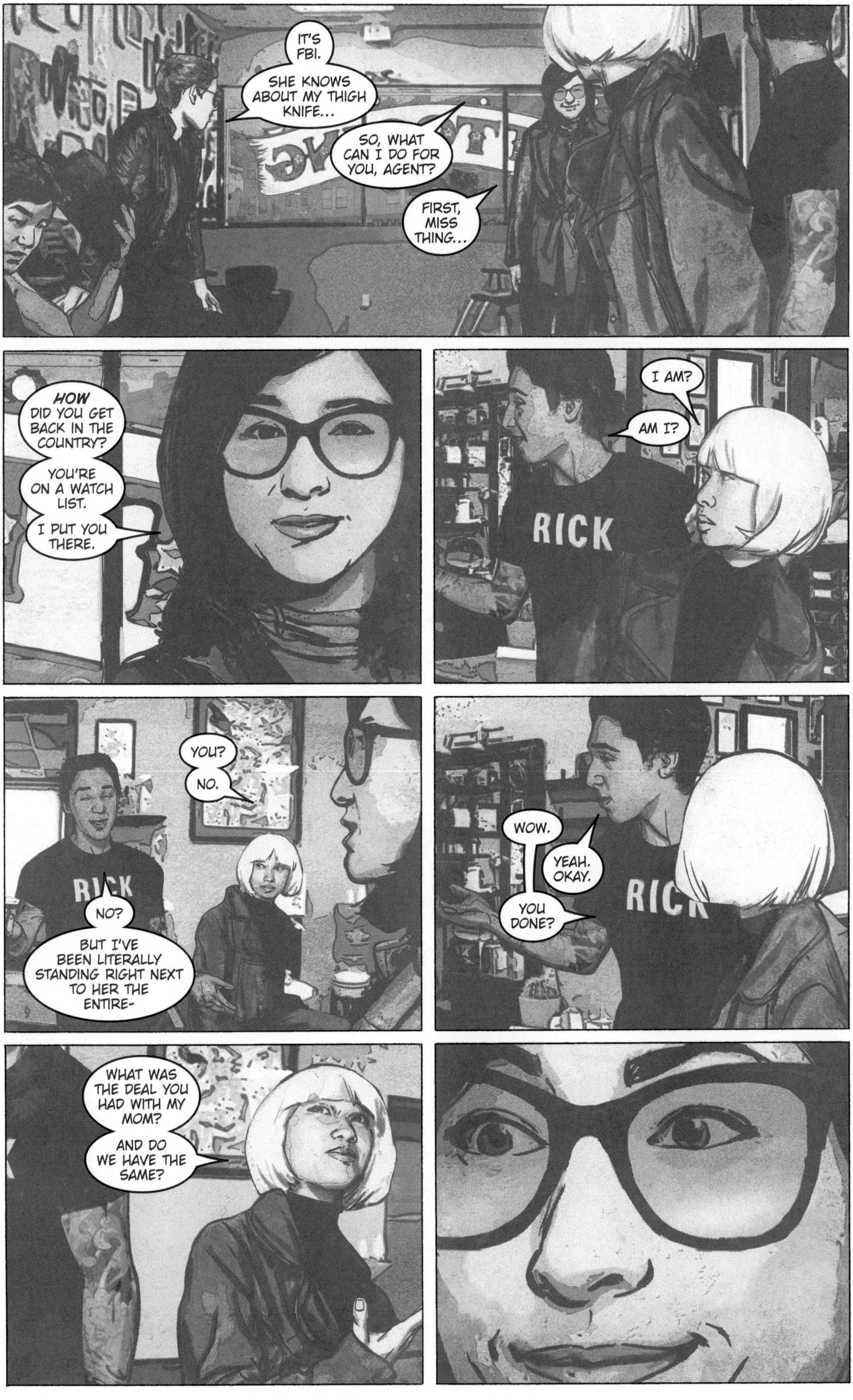
IT'S FBI.
SHE KNOWS ABOUT MY THIGH KNIFE...
SO, WHAT CAN I DO FOR YOU, AGENT?
FIRST, MISS THING...
HOW DID YOU GET BACK IN THE COUNTRY?
YOU'RE ON A WATCH LIST.
I PUT YOU THERE.
I AM?
AM I?
RICK
YOU?
NO.
RICK
NO?
BUT I'VE BEEN LITERALLY STANDING RIGHT NEXT TO HER THE ENTIRE-
WOW.
YEAH. OKAY.
YOU DONE?
RICK
WHAT WAS THE DEAL YOU HAD WITH MY MOM?
AND DO WE HAVE THE SAME?

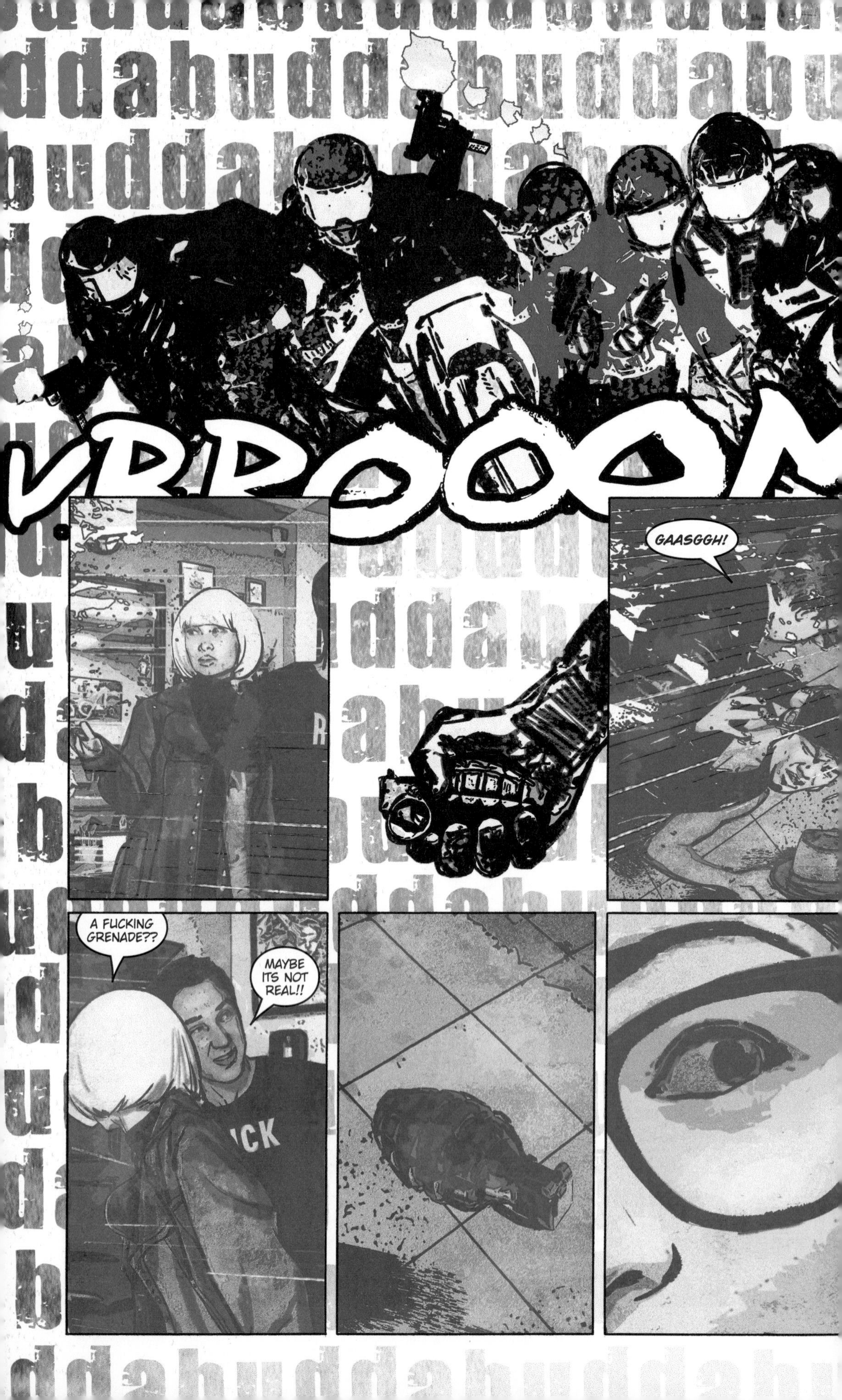
VRROOOM
GAASGGH!
A FUCKING GRENADE??
MAYBE ITS NOT REAL!!

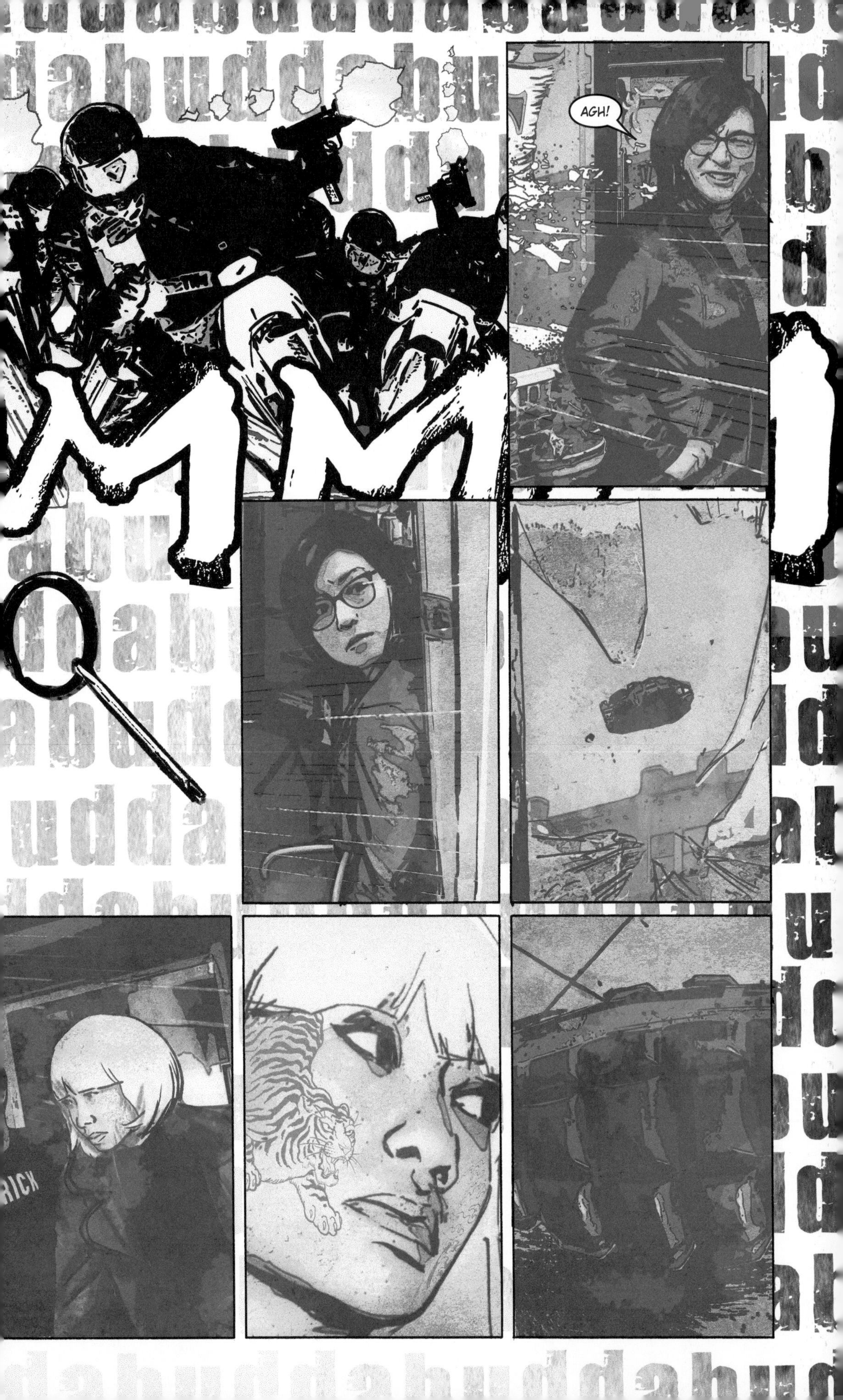
AGH!

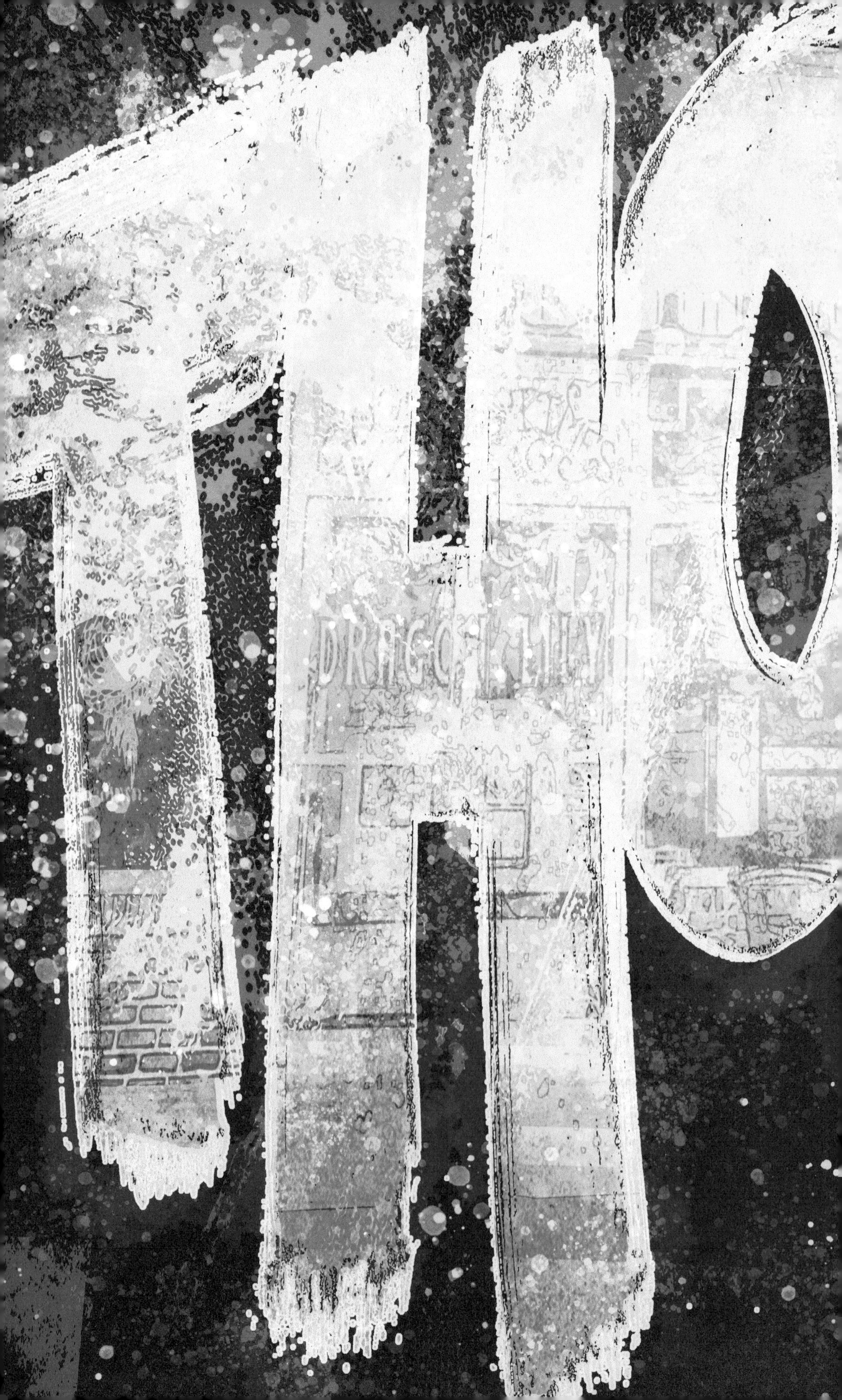
THO

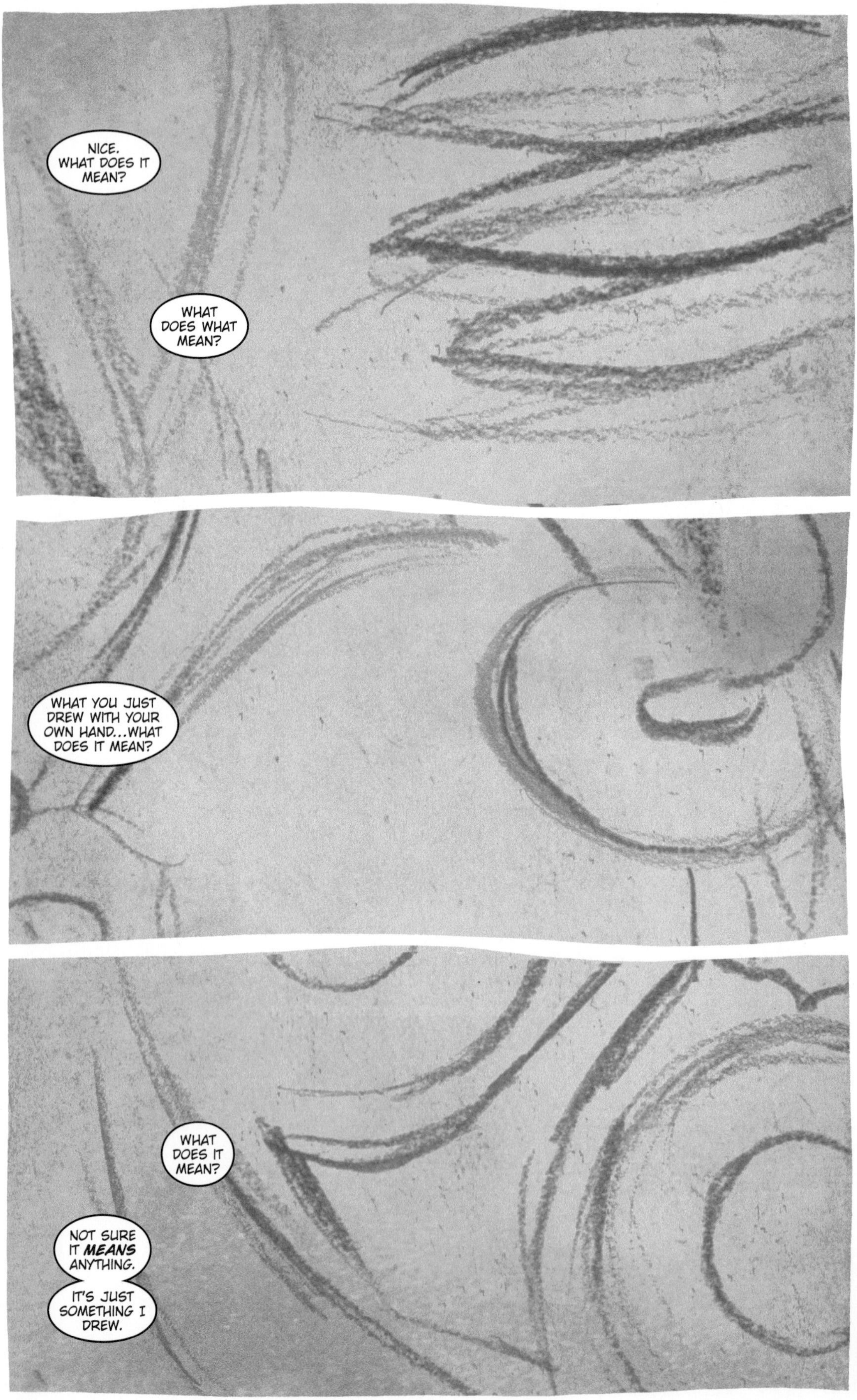
NICE. WHAT DOES IT MEAN?
WHAT DOES WHAT MEAN?
WHAT YOU JUST DREW WITH YOUR OWN HAND...WHAT DOES IT MEAN?
WHAT DOES IT MEAN?
NOT SURE IT **MEANS** ANYTHING.
IT'S JUST SOMETHING I DREW.

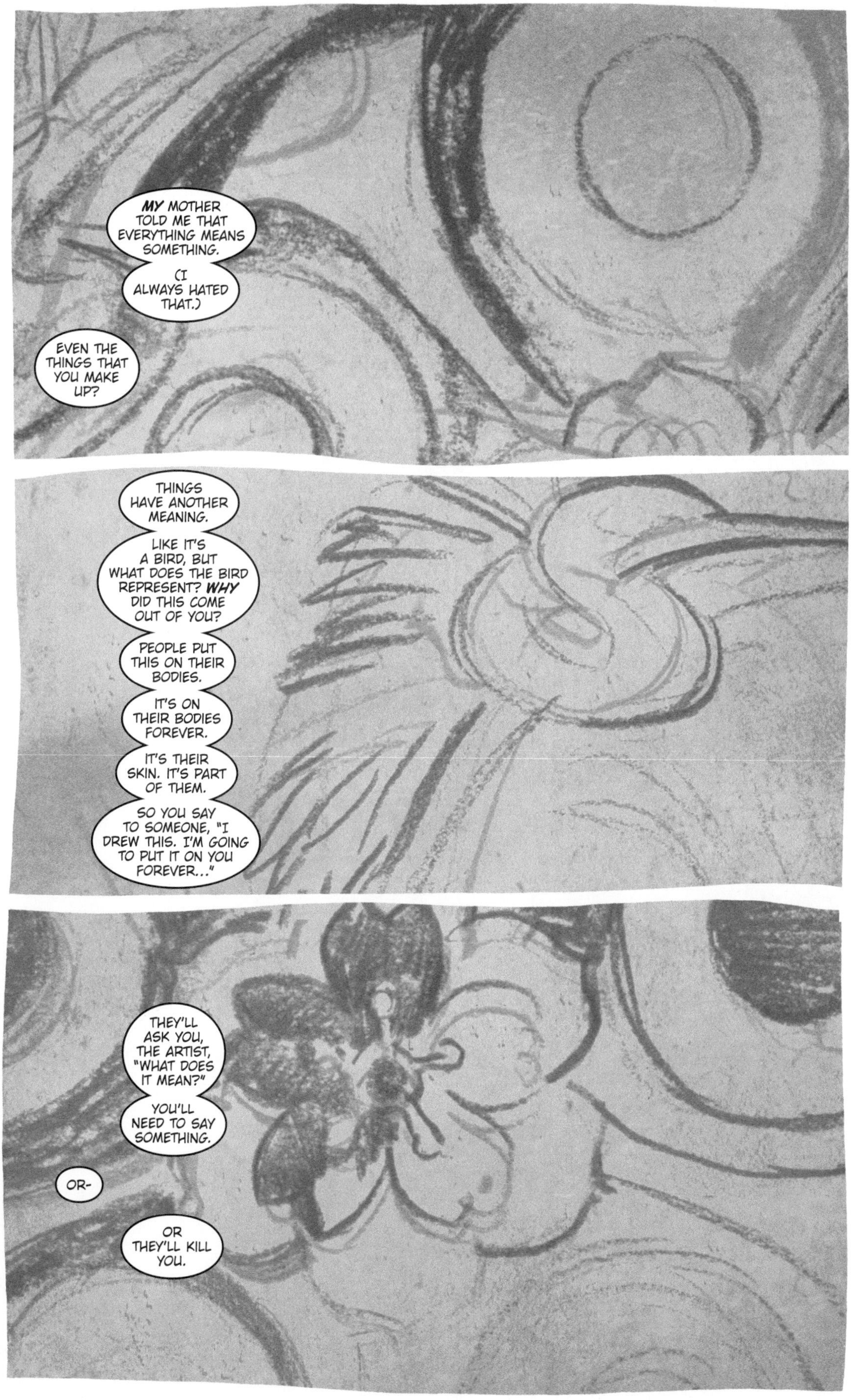
MY MOTHER TOLD ME THAT EVERYTHING MEANS SOMETHING.
(I ALWAYS HATED THAT.)
EVEN THE THINGS THAT YOU MAKE UP?
THINGS HAVE ANOTHER MEANING.
LIKE IT'S A BIRD, BUT WHAT DOES THE BIRD REPRESENT? WHY DID THIS COME OUT OF YOU?
PEOPLE PUT THIS ON THEIR BODIES.
IT'S ON THEIR BODIES FOREVER.
IT'S THEIR SKIN. IT'S PART OF THEM.
SO YOU SAY TO SOMEONE, "I DREW THIS. I'M GOING TO PUT IT ON YOU FOREVER..."
THEY'LL ASK YOU, THE ARTIST, "WHAT DOES IT MEAN?"
YOU'LL NEED TO SAY SOMETHING.
OR-
OR THEY'LL KILL YOU.

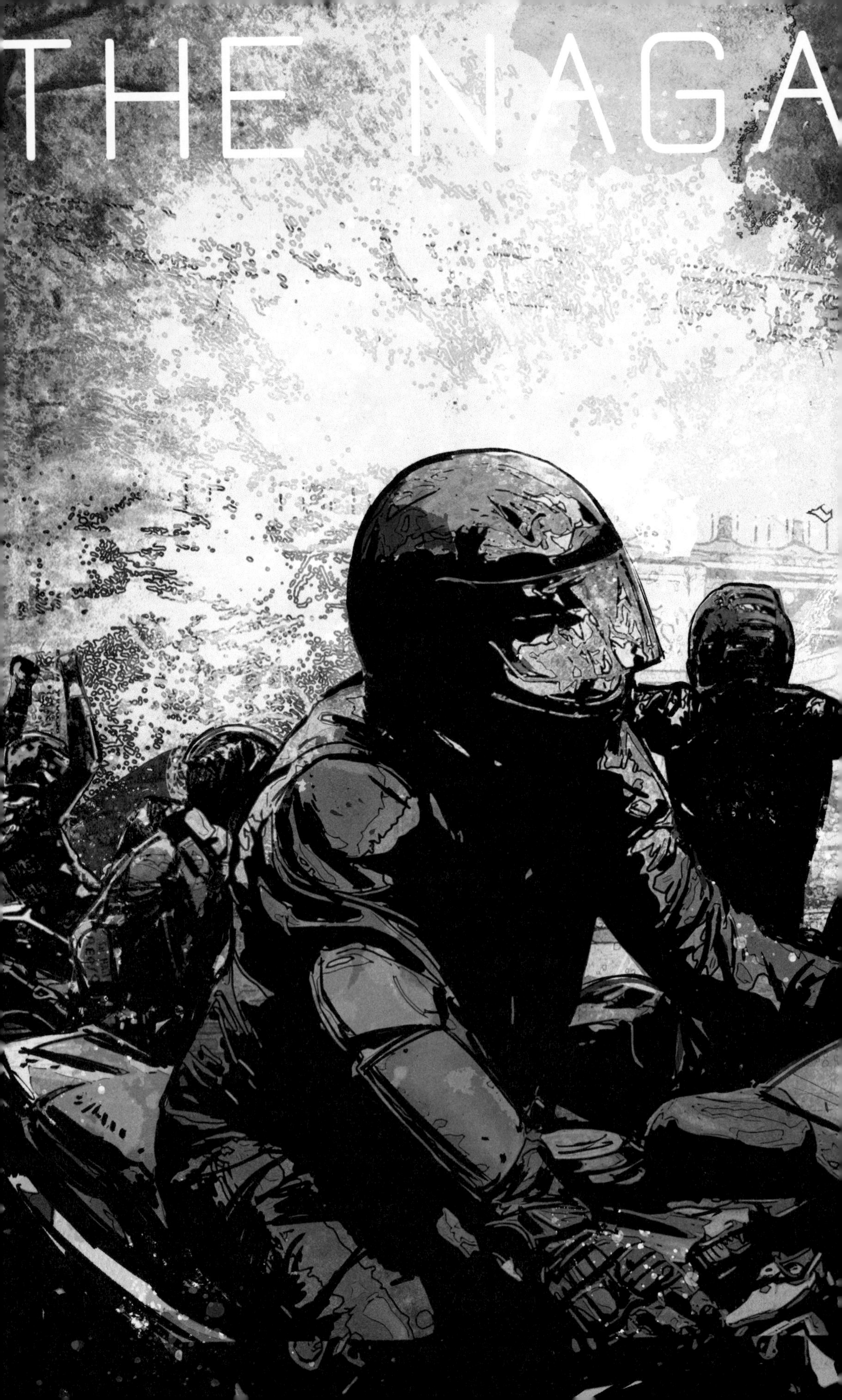
THE NAGA

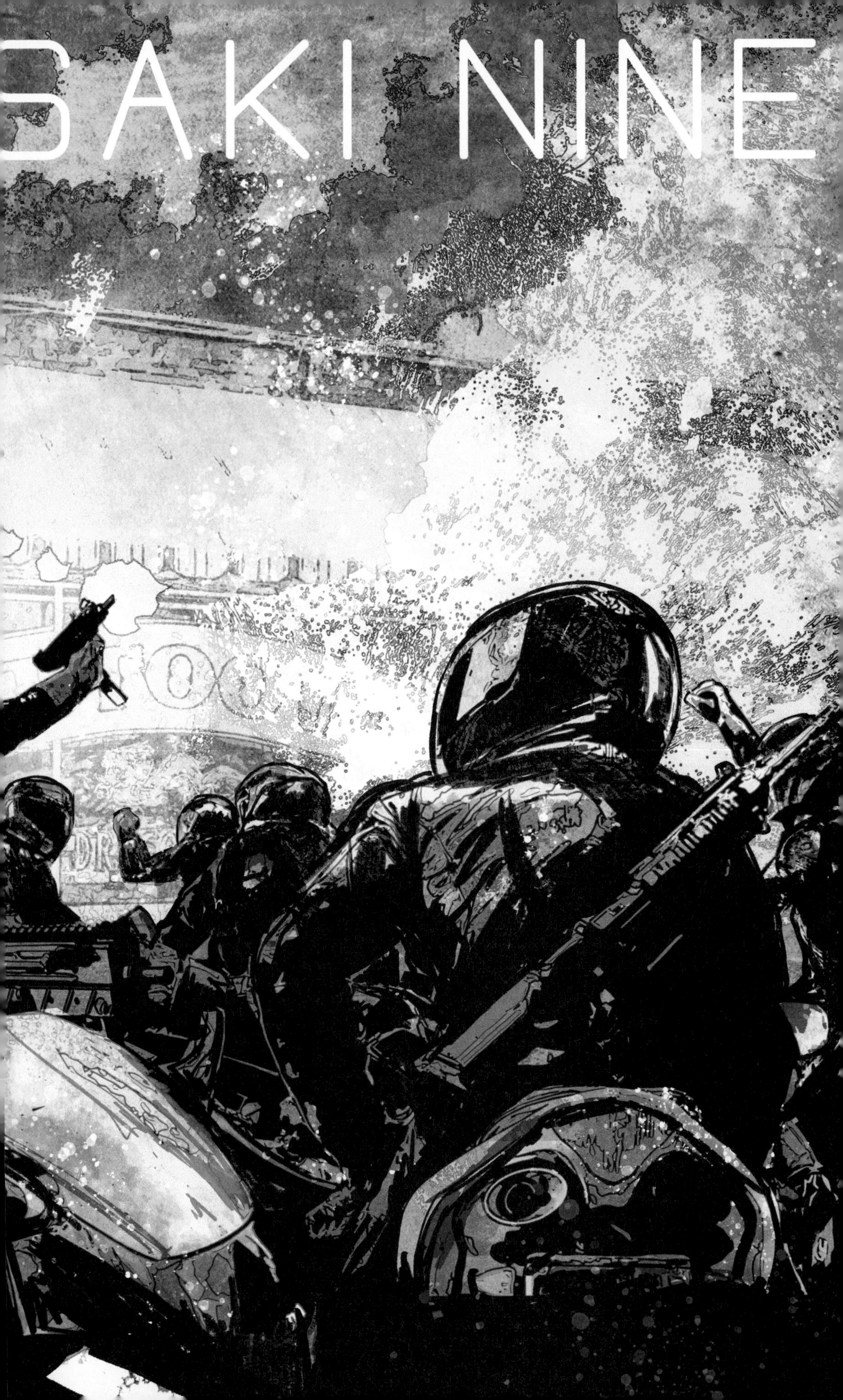
SAKI NINE

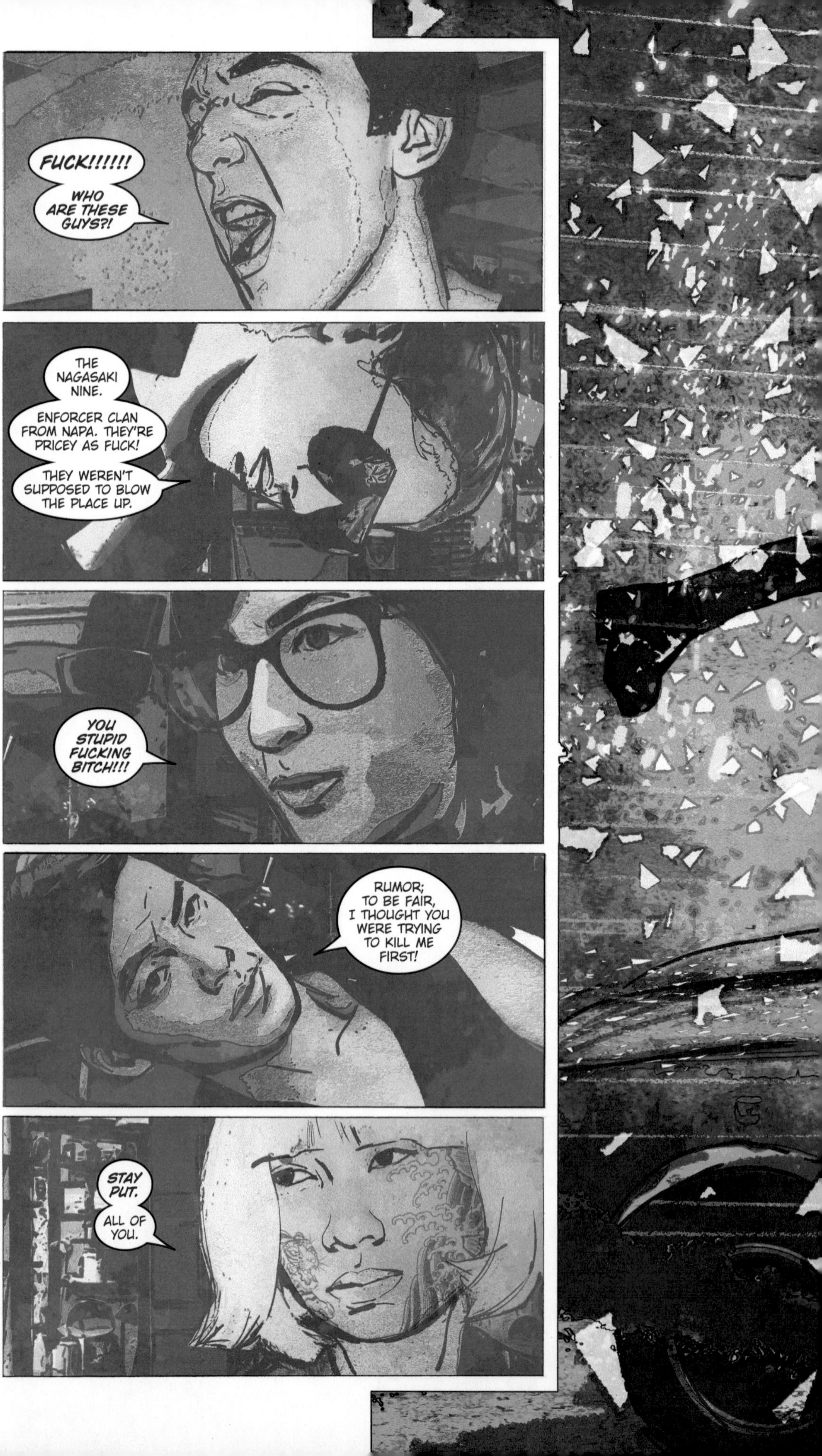
FUCK!!!!!!
WHO ARE THESE GUYS?!
THE NAGASAKI NINE.
ENFORCER CLAN FROM NAPA. THEY'RE PRICEY AS FUCK!
THEY WEREN'T SUPPOSED TO BLOW THE PLACE UP.
YOU STUPID FUCKING BITCH!!!
RUMOR; TO BE FAIR, I THOUGHT YOU WERE TRYING TO KILL ME FIRST!
STAY PUT.
ALL OF YOU.

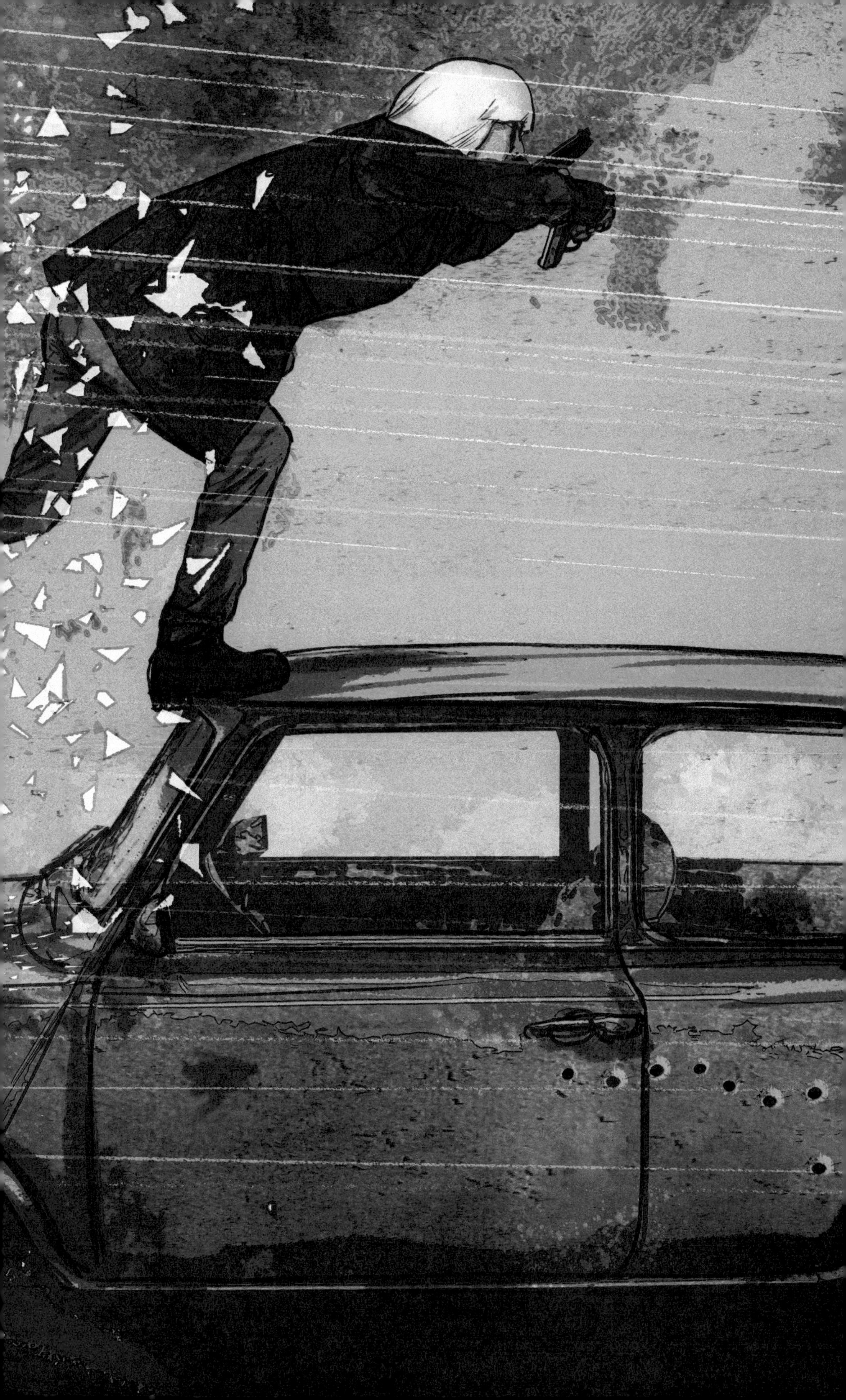

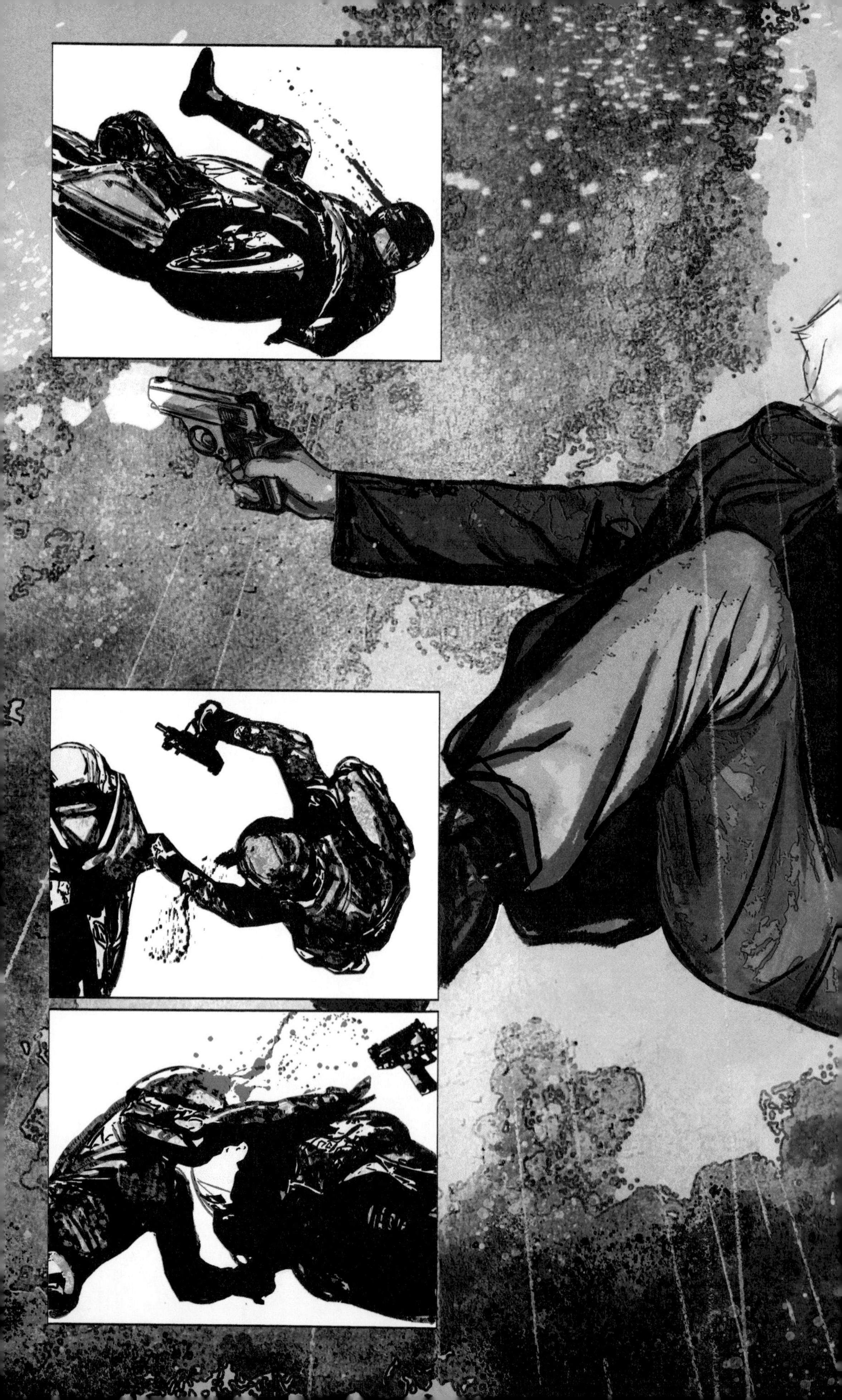

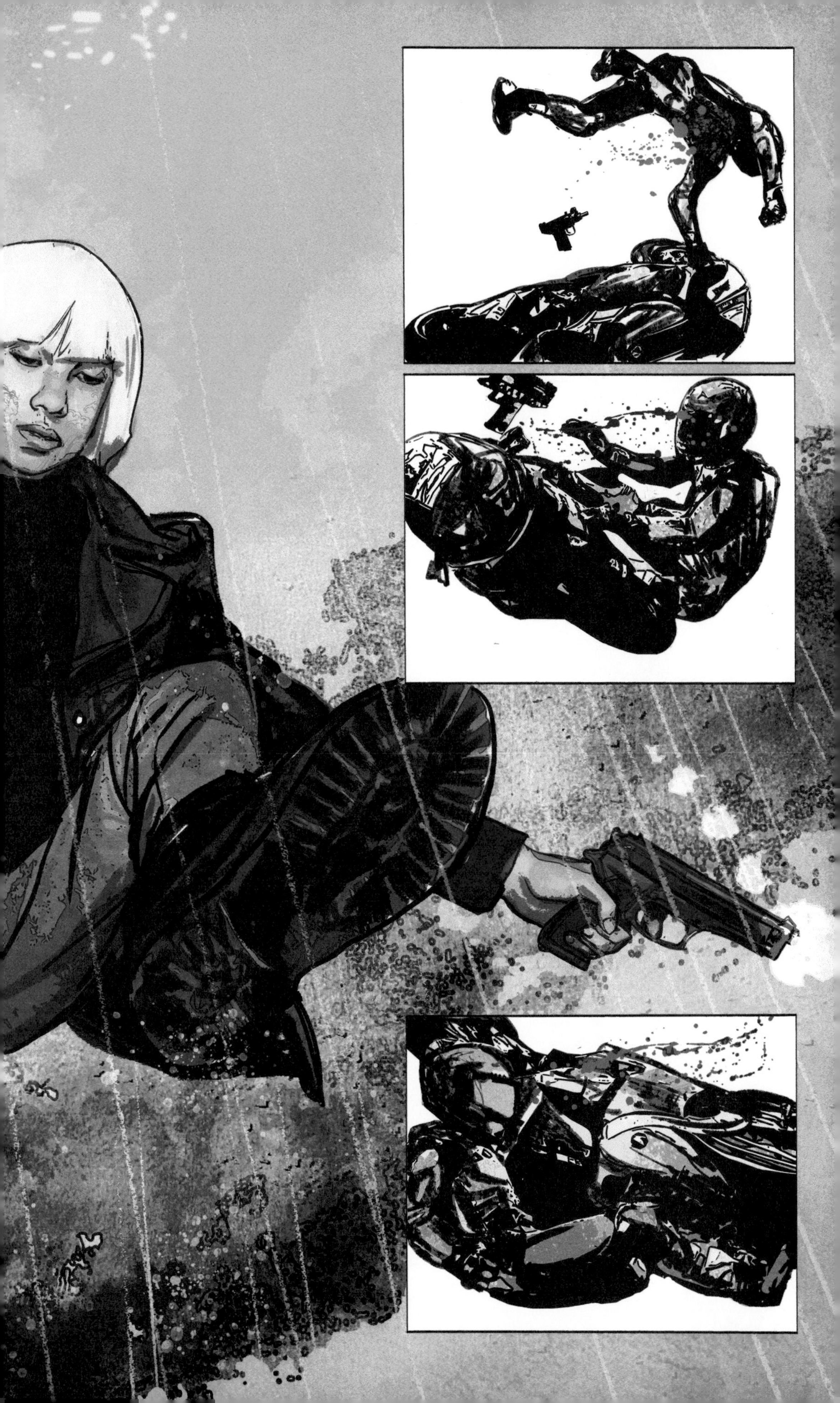

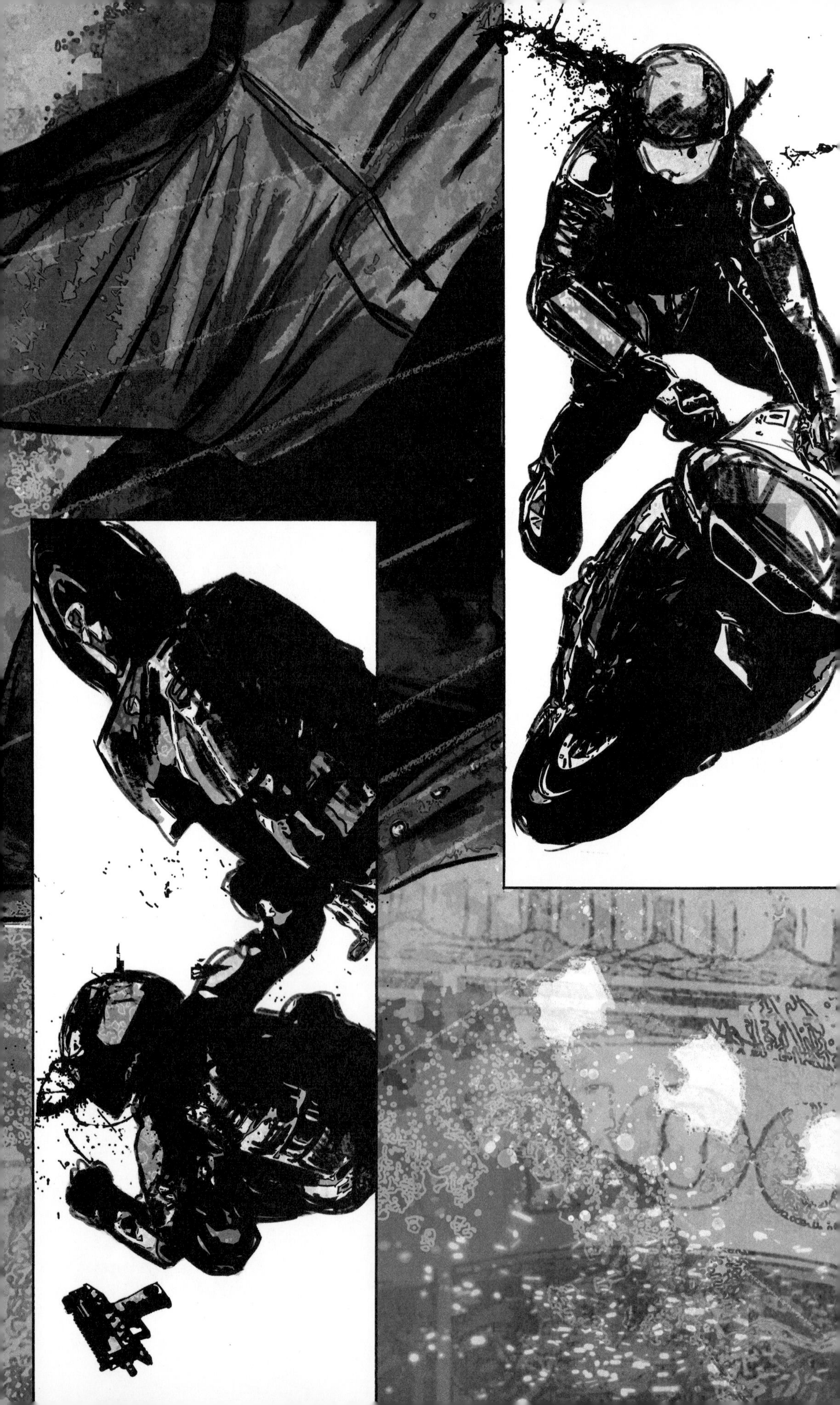

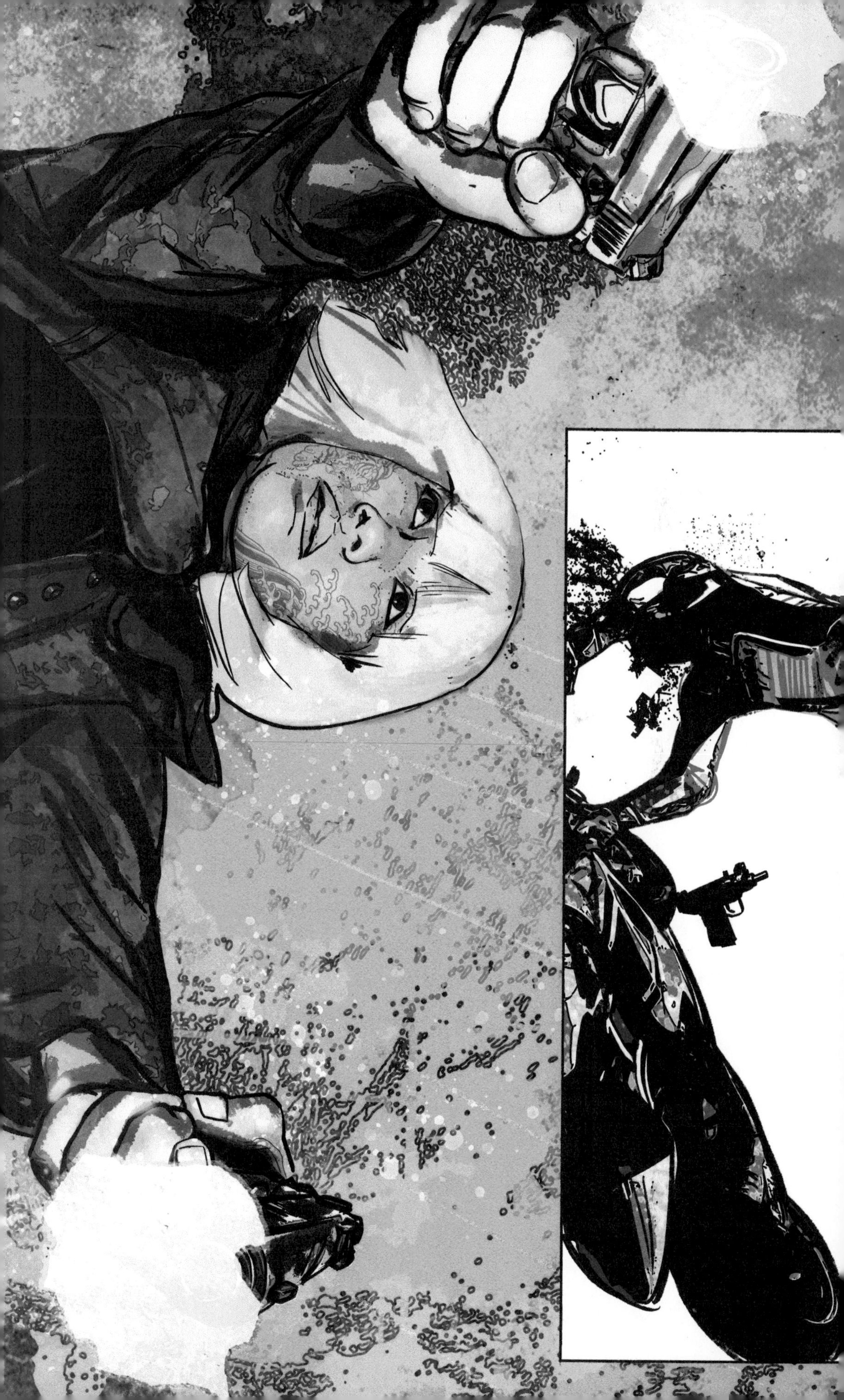

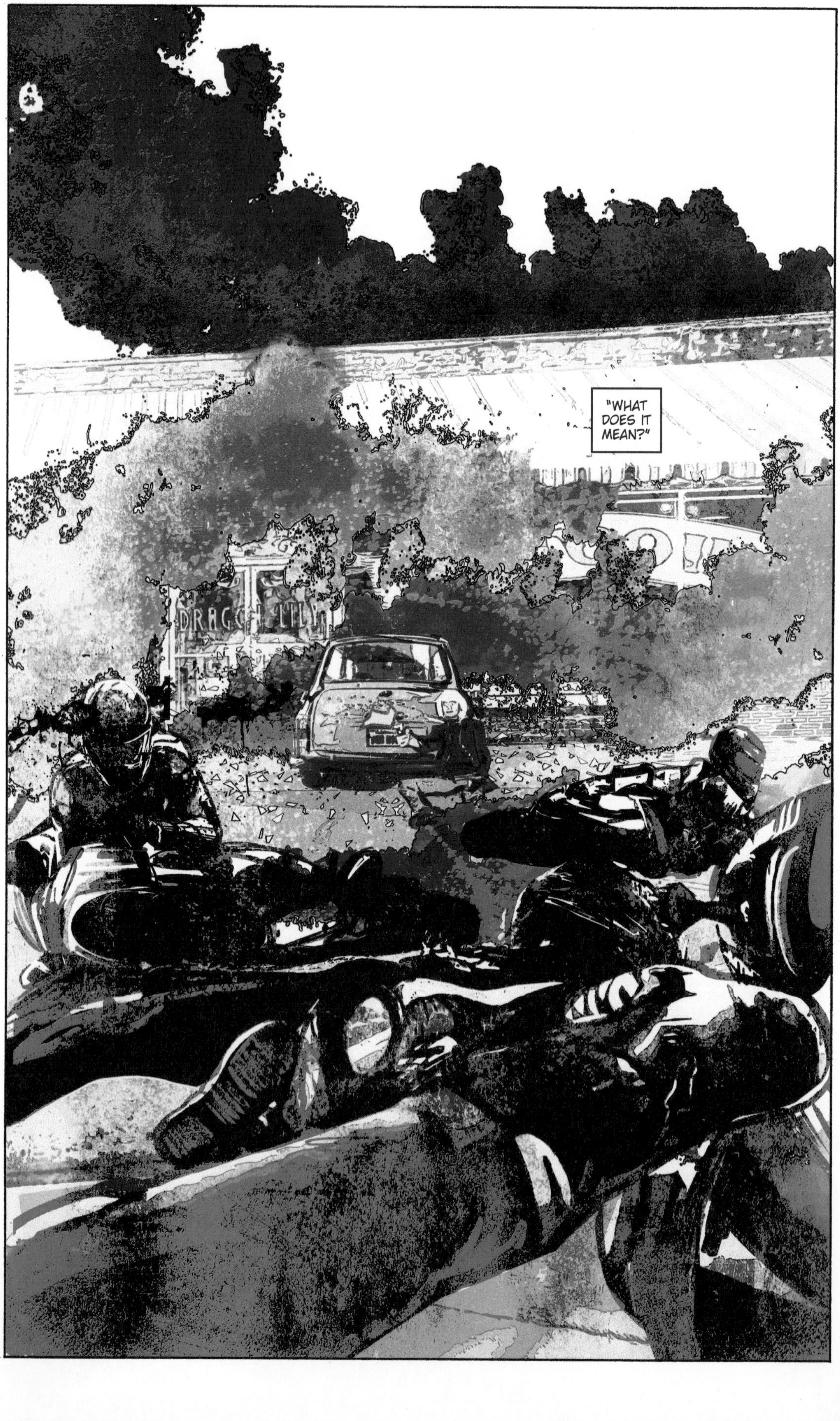
"WHAT DOES IT MEAN?"
DRAGONLILY

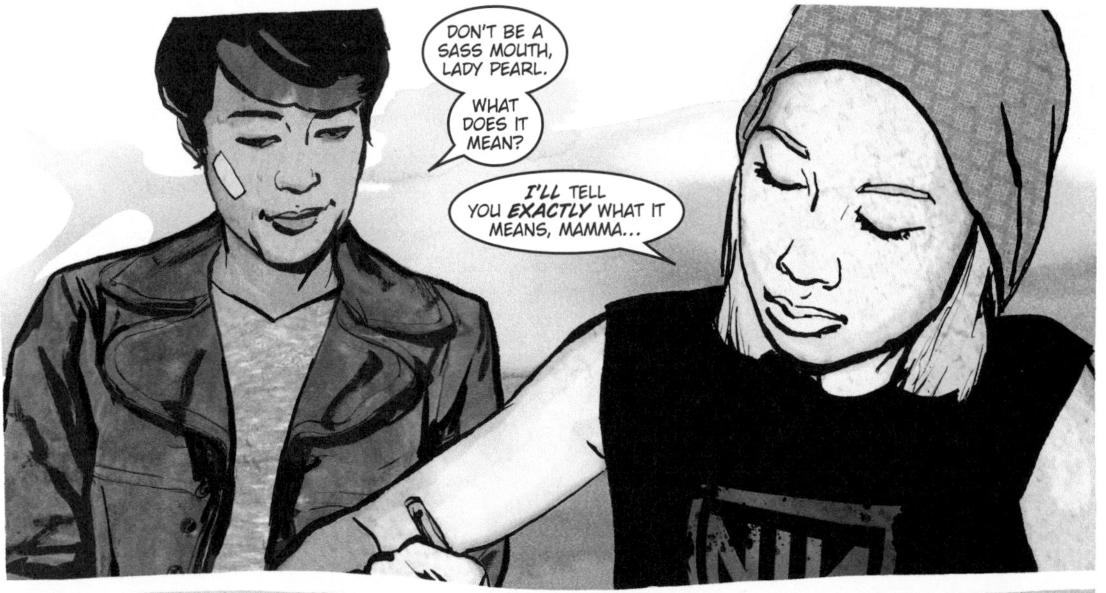
DON'T BE A SASS MOUTH, LADY PEARL.
WHAT DOES IT MEAN?
I'LL TELL YOU EXACTLY WHAT IT MEANS, MAMMA...
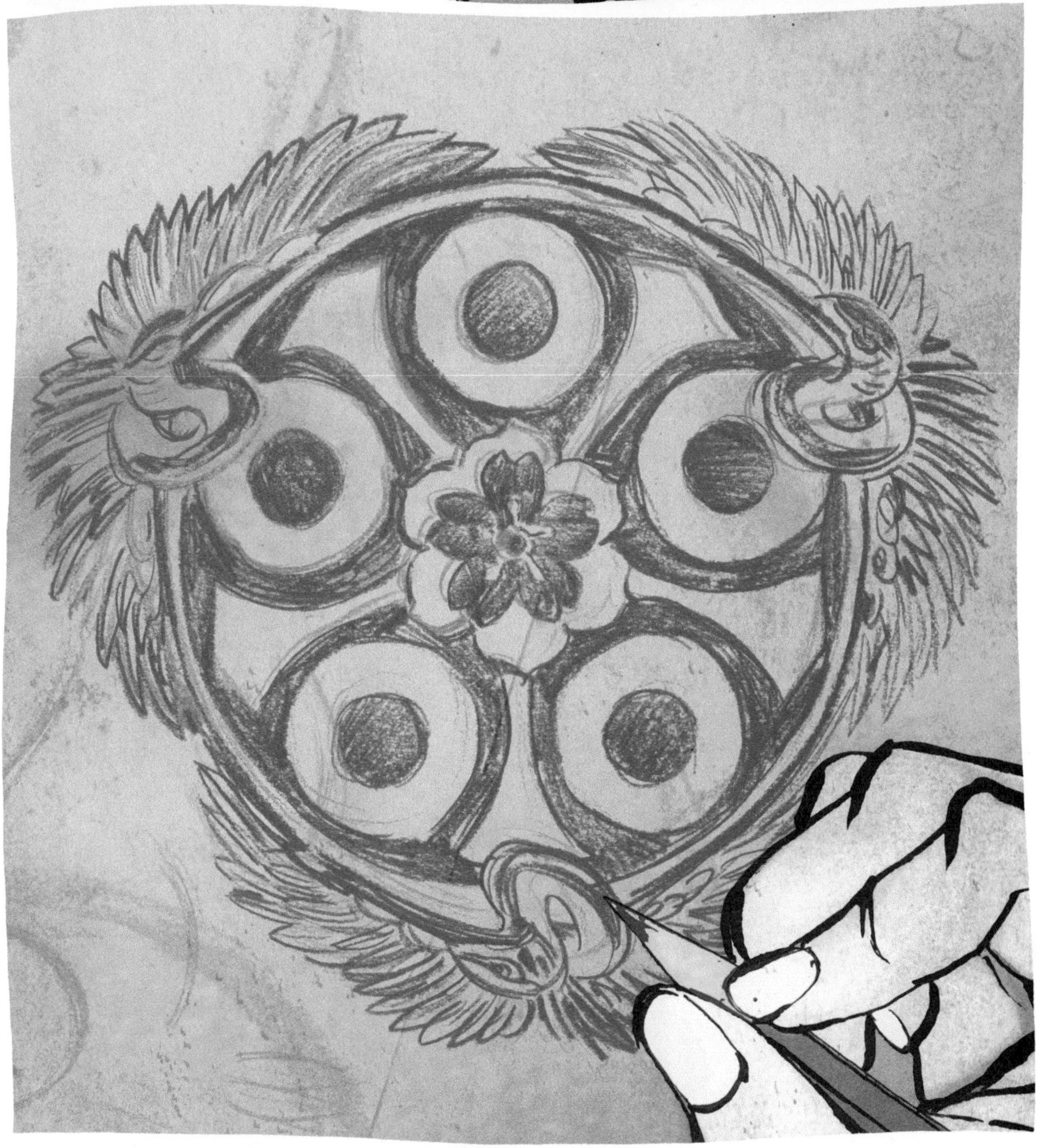

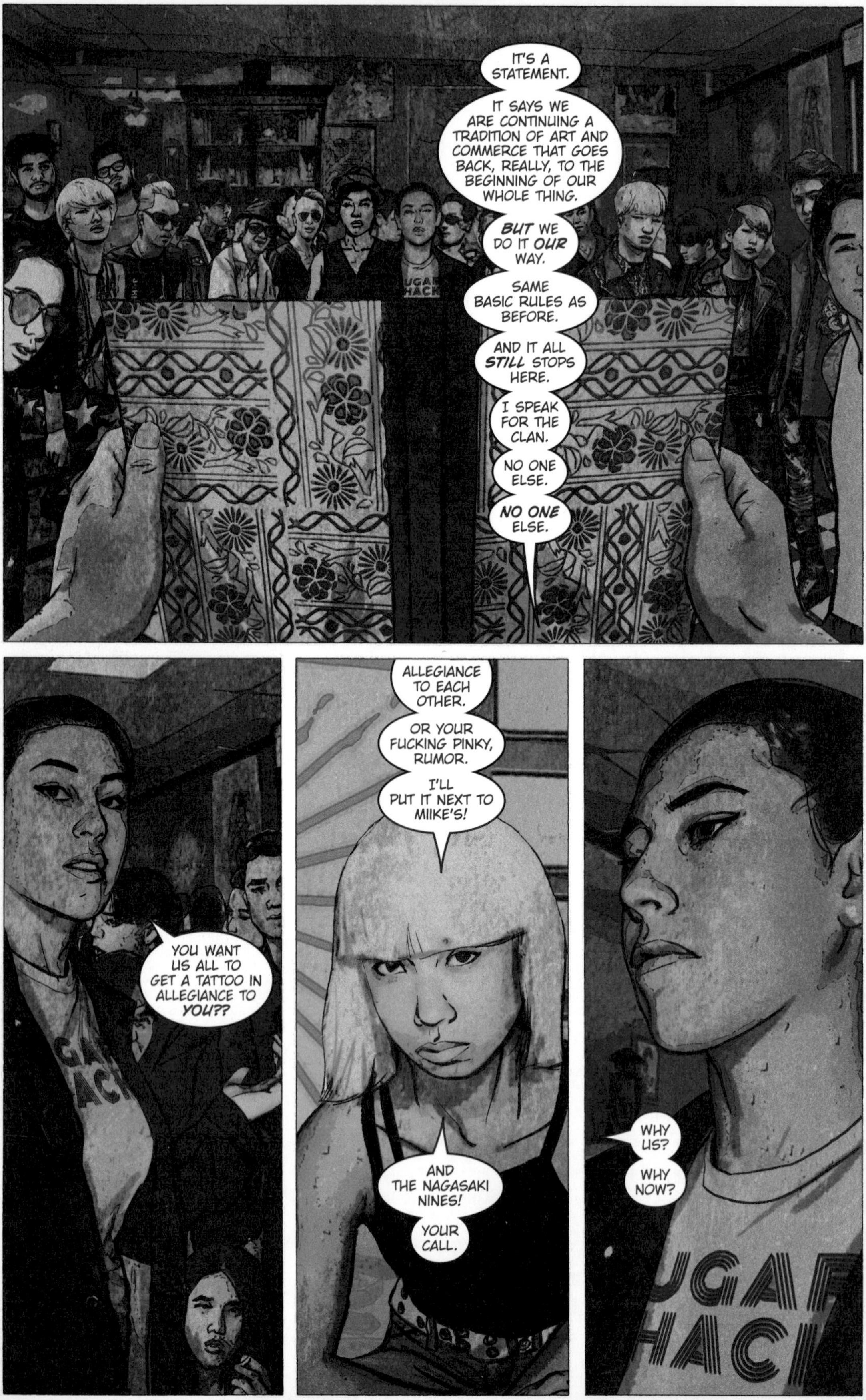
IT'S A STATEMENT.
IT SAYS WE ARE CONTINUING A TRADITION OF ART AND COMMERCE THAT GOES BACK, REALLY, TO THE BEGINNING OF OUR WHOLE THING.
BUT WE DO IT *OUR* WAY.
SAME BASIC RULES AS BEFORE.
AND IT ALL *STILL* STOPS HERE.
I SPEAK FOR THE CLAN.
NO ONE ELSE.
NO ONE ELSE.
YOU WANT US ALL TO GET A TATTOO IN ALLEGIANCE TO *YOU??*
ALLEGIANCE TO EACH OTHER.
OR YOUR FUCKING PINKY, RUMOR.
I'LL PUT IT NEXT TO MIIKE'S!
AND THE NAGASAKI NINES!
YOUR CALL.
WHY US?
WHY NOW?

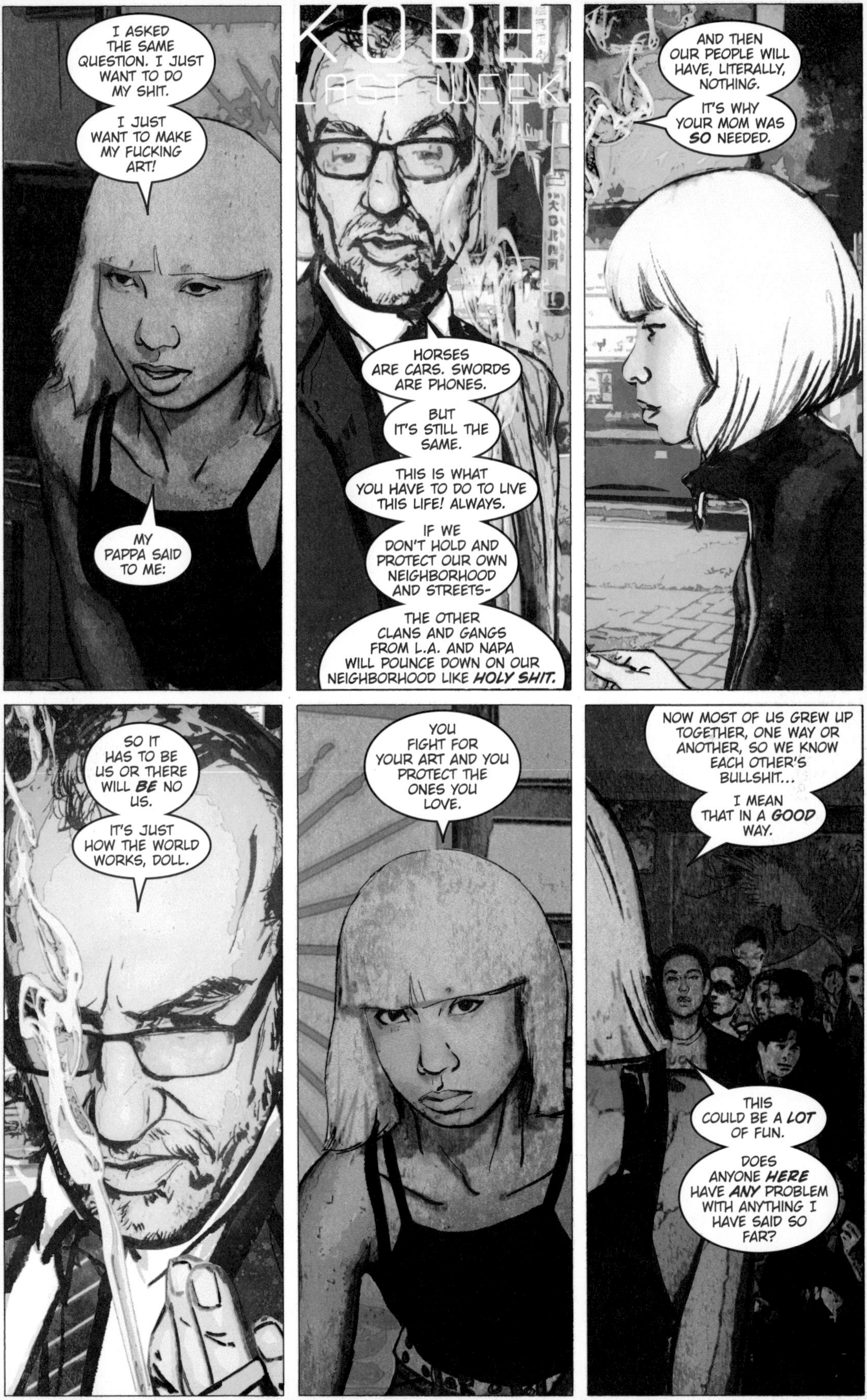
I ASKED THE SAME QUESTION. I JUST WANT TO DO MY SHIT.
I JUST WANT TO MAKE MY FUCKING ART!
MY PAPPA SAID TO ME:
KOBE LAST WEEK
HORSES ARE CARS. SWORDS ARE PHONES.
BUT IT'S STILL THE SAME.
THIS IS WHAT YOU HAVE TO DO TO LIVE THIS LIFE! ALWAYS.
IF WE DON'T HOLD AND PROTECT OUR OWN NEIGHBORHOOD AND STREETS-
THE OTHER CLANS AND GANGS FROM L.A. AND NAPA WILL POUNCE DOWN ON OUR NEIGHBORHOOD LIKE HOLY SHIT.
AND THEN OUR PEOPLE WILL HAVE, LITERALLY, NOTHING.
IT'S WHY YOUR MOM WAS SO NEEDED.
SO IT HAS TO BE US OR THERE WILL BE NO US.
IT'S JUST HOW THE WORLD WORKS, DOLL.
YOU FIGHT FOR YOUR ART AND YOU PROTECT THE ONES YOU LOVE.
NOW MOST OF US GREW UP TOGETHER, ONE WAY OR ANOTHER, SO WE KNOW EACH OTHER'S BULLSHIT...
I MEAN THAT IN A GOOD WAY.
THIS COULD BE A LOT OF FUN.
DOES ANYONE HERE HAVE ANY PROBLEM WITH ANYTHING I HAVE SAID SO FAR?

FUCK. I-I GOTTA SAY, PERSONALLY, I THINK I KIND OF LOVE THIS.

I *HATED* MIIKE.

FUCK THAT DICK!

I APPRECIATE THAT.

YEAH, KEEP GOING, GIRL.

NOW A LOT OF YOUR PARENTS ARE GOING TO HAVE A *BIIIG* PROBLEM WITH THIS NEW DEAL.

THEY LIKED IT THE WAY IT WAS, AND THEY LIKED MY MOM.

AND THEY *REALLY* LIKED MY DAD.

BUT *THEY'RE* JUST GOING TO HAVE TO GET USED TO IT BEING OUR TURN.

YOU HAVE MY-- AND MY UNCLE'S, AND MY PARTNER'S AT THE *FB*-YOU-KNOW-WHAT--PERMISSION NOT TO TAKE *ANY* SHIT FROM ANYBODY ABOUT *THAT*.

OH, AND *ALL* TATTOO WORK HERE IS ON THE HOUSE.

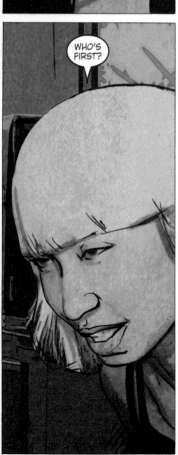

WHO'S FIRST?

OF COURSE IT'S *GOING TO BE ME*.

MOVE OVER, BITCHES!

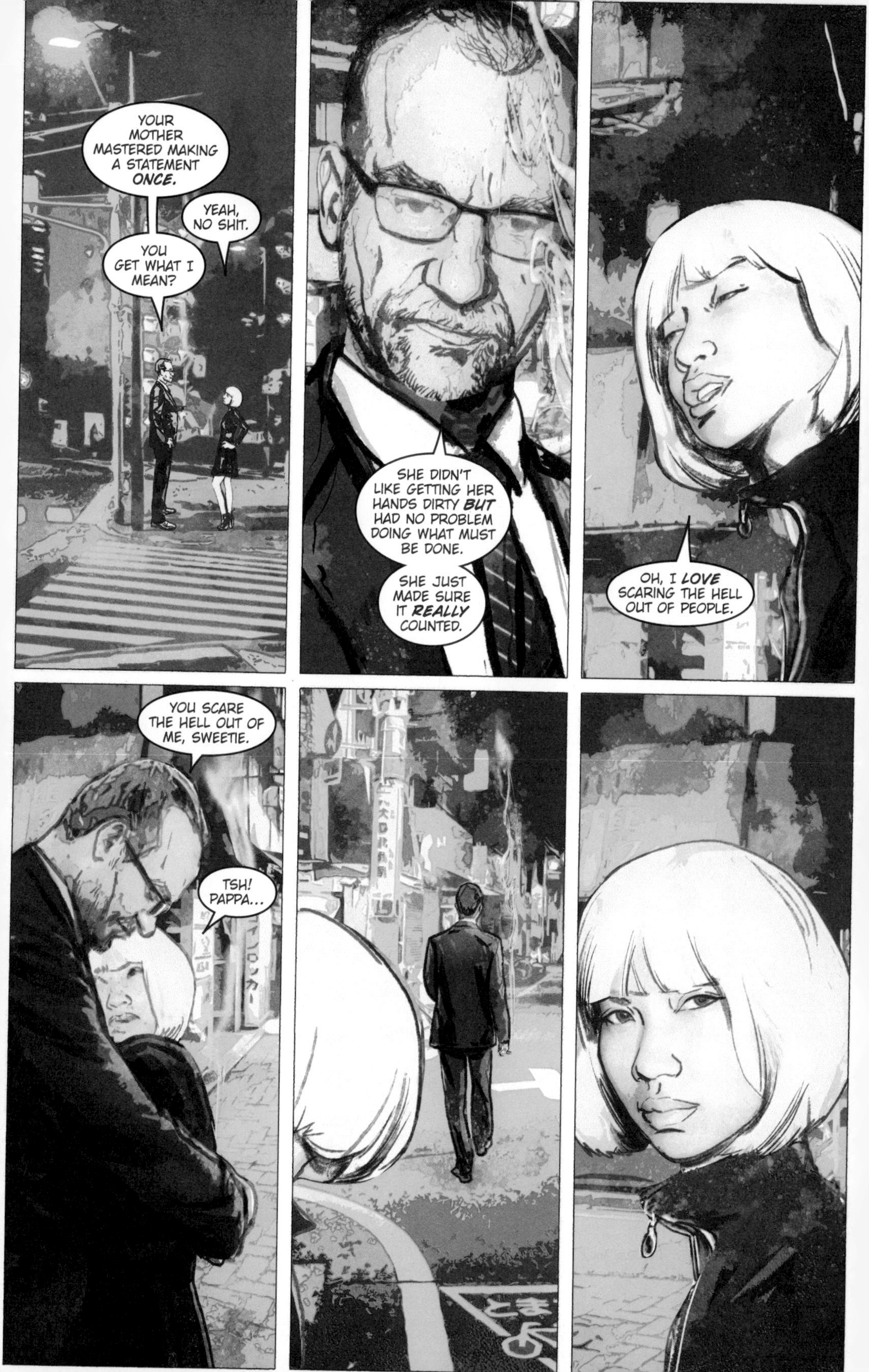
YOUR MOTHER MASTERED MAKING A STATEMENT ONCE.
YEAH, NO SHIT.
YOU GET WHAT I MEAN?
SHE DIDN'T LIKE GETTING HER HANDS DIRTY BUT HAD NO PROBLEM DOING WHAT MUST BE DONE.
SHE JUST MADE SURE IT REALLY COUNTED.
OH, I LOVE SCARING THE HELL OUT OF PEOPLE.
YOU SCARE THE HELL OUT OF ME, SWEETIE.
TSH! PAPPA...

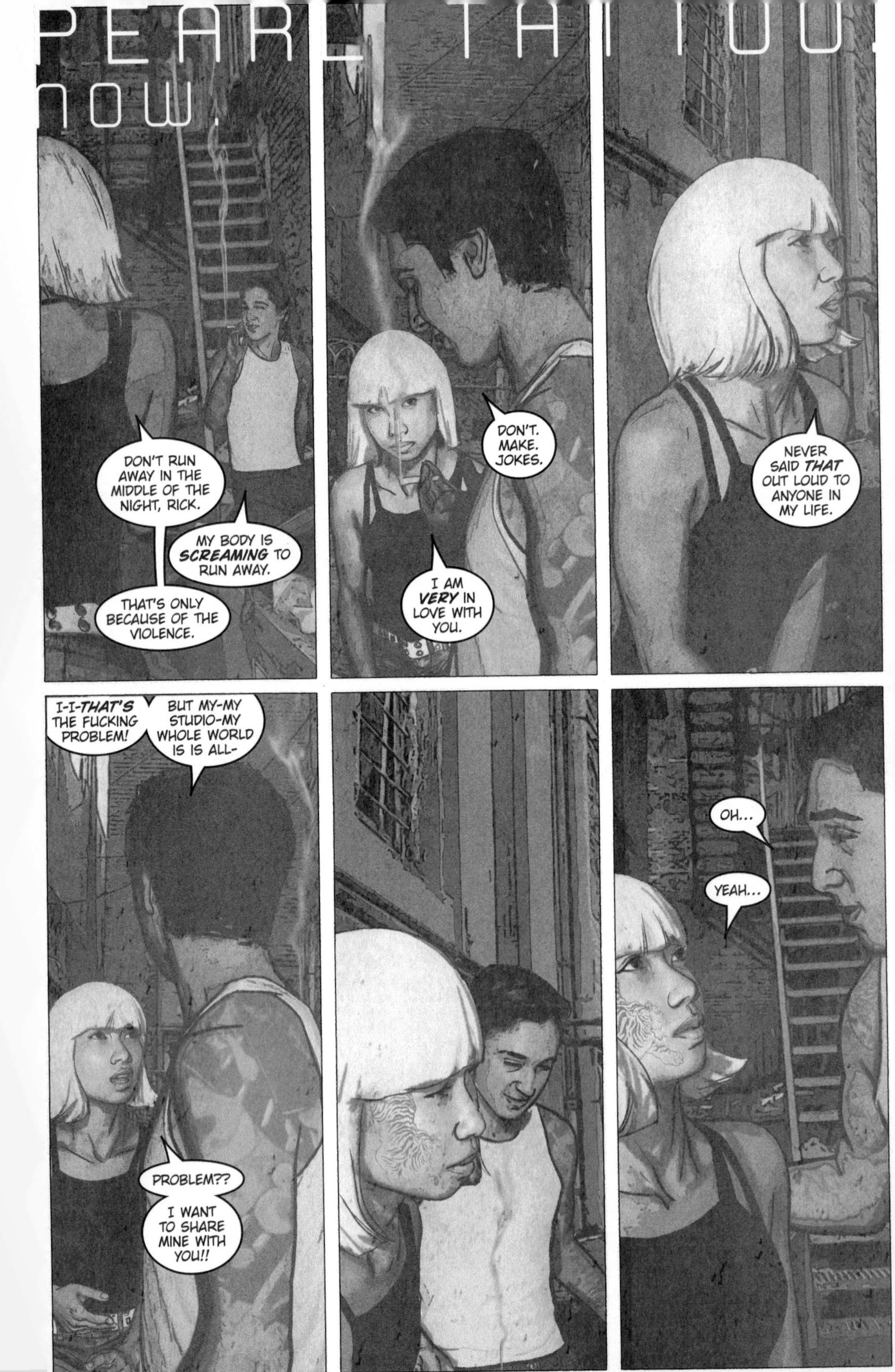
PEARL TATTOO!
now.
DON'T RUN AWAY IN THE MIDDLE OF THE NIGHT, RICK.
MY BODY IS SCREAMING TO RUN AWAY.
THAT'S ONLY BECAUSE OF THE VIOLENCE.
DON'T. MAKE. JOKES.
I AM VERY IN LOVE WITH YOU.
NEVER SAID THAT OUT LOUD TO ANYONE IN MY LIFE.
I-I-THAT'S THE FUCKING PROBLEM!
BUT MY-MY STUDIO-MY WHOLE WORLD IS IS ALL-
PROBLEM??
I WANT TO SHARE MINE WITH YOU!!
OH...
YEAH...

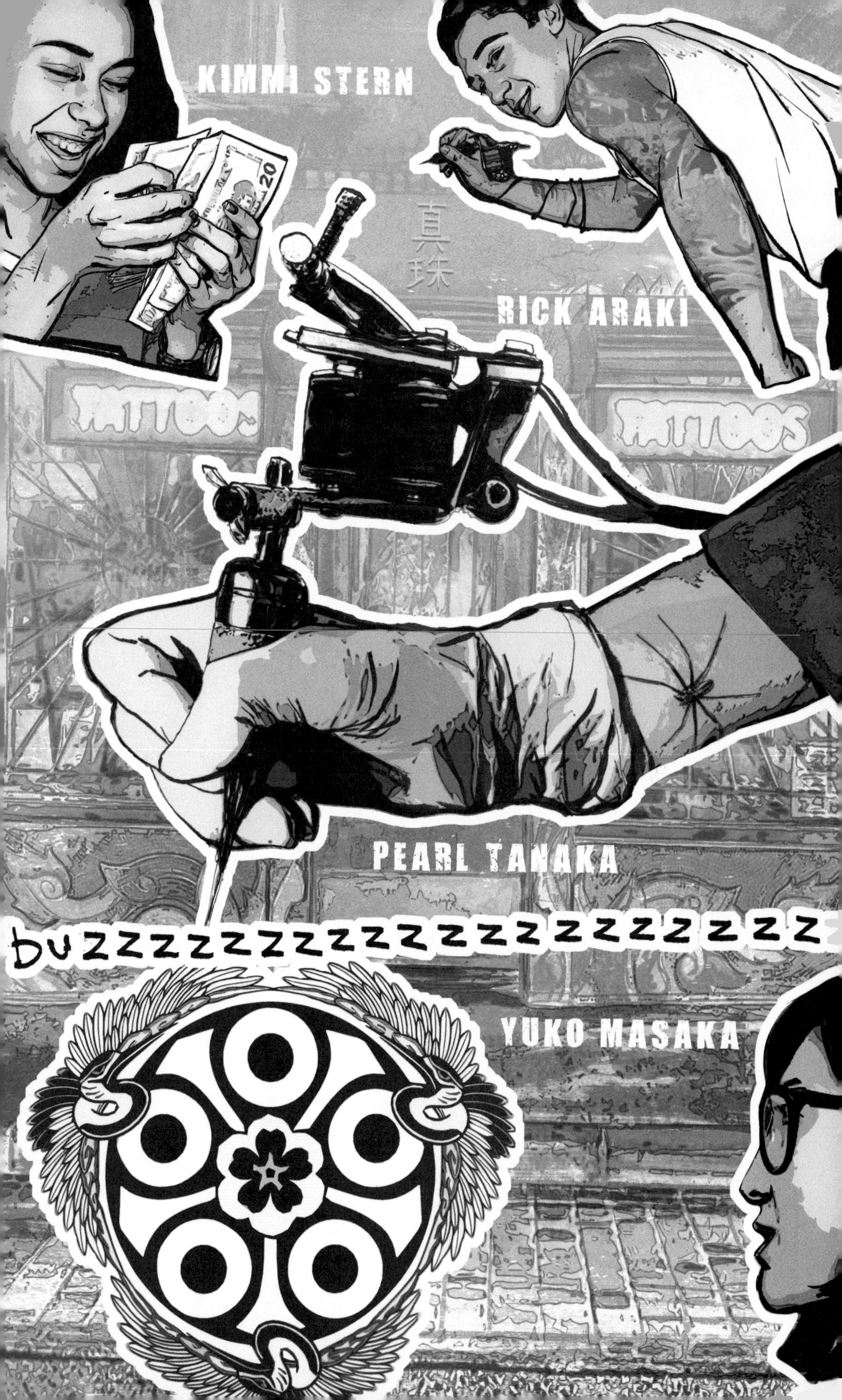

KIMMI STERN
RICK ARAKI
真珠
TATTOOS
TATTOOS
PEARL TANAKA
buzzzzzzzzzzzzzzzzzzz
YUKO MASAKA

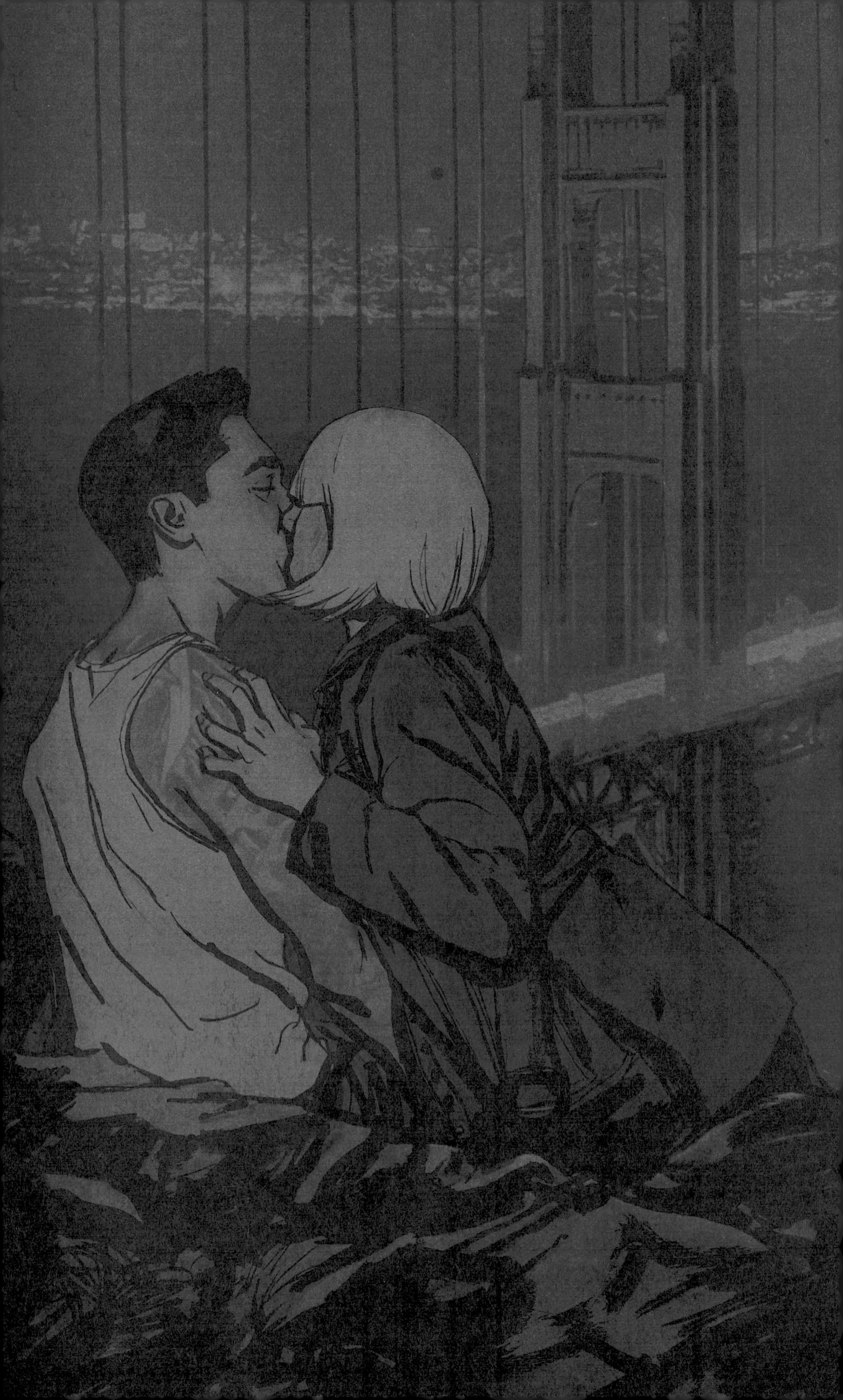

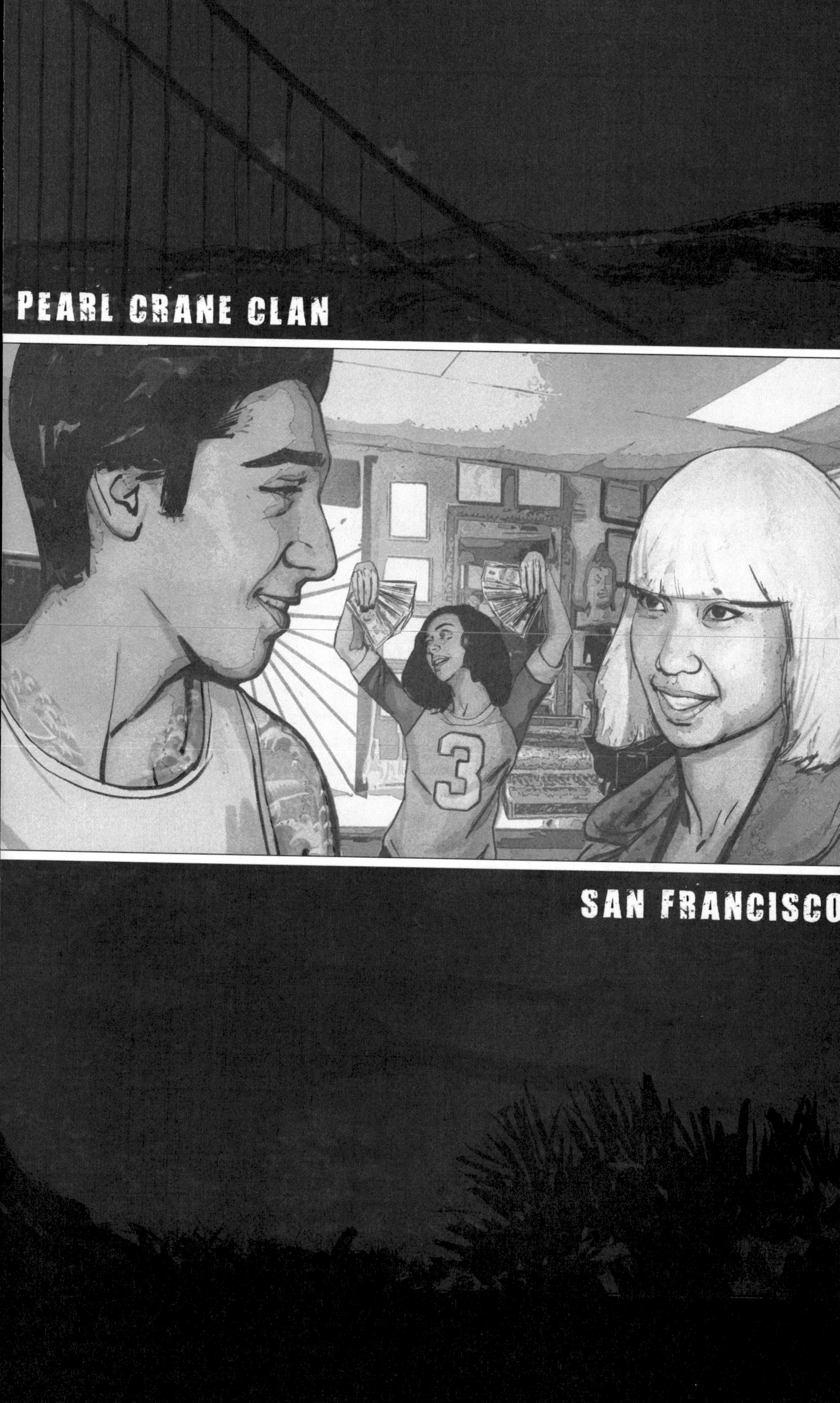
PEARL CRANE CLAN
3
SAN FRANCISCO

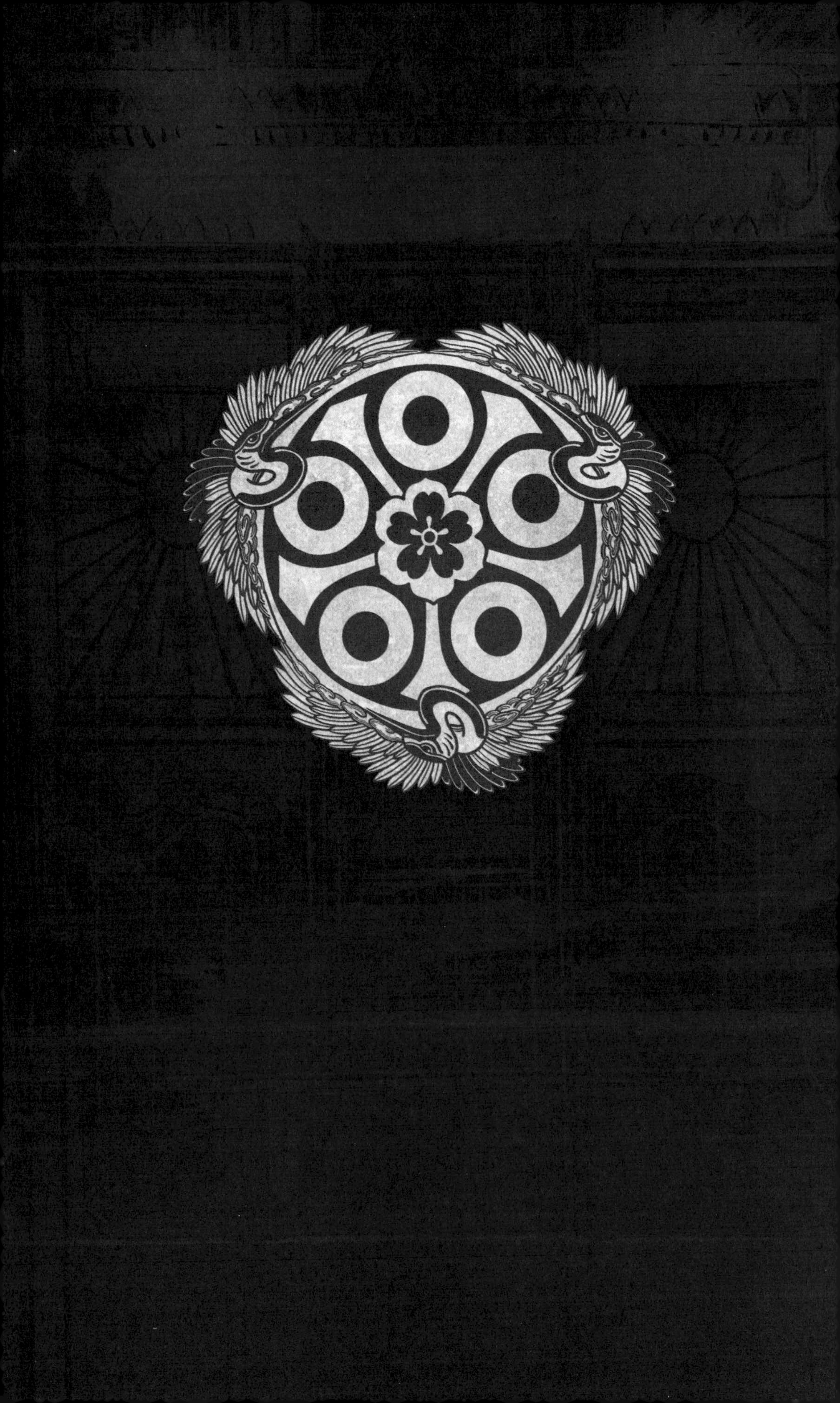